WOODSMITH CUSTOM WOODWORKING

The Complete Bedroom

WOODSMITH CUSTOM WOODWORKING

The Complete Bedroom

By the editors of Woodsmith magazine

The Complete Bedroom

Chest of Drawers

CONTEMPORARY SET   6

Frame and Panel Headboard..8

> *This headboard is easy to build thanks to simple joinery and an interesting method for mounting the panel. Its ageless styling looks great in any decor.*

Night Stand..14

> *Clean, simple lines and no visible hardware define this Night Stand. Machine-cut dovetails and web-frame construction ensure years of use.*

Chest of Drawers..20

> *A unique design makes this project a pleasure to build. The drawers have half-blind dovetails and a concealed cove on the bottom to open them.*

Wall Mirror..30

> *Complete the Contemporary Set with this mirror that "reflects" your craftsmanship. Sturdy construction allows you to hang it on a wall.*

BEDROOM ACCESSORIES 34

Under-Bed Storage Box

Quilt Rack 36

Display an heirloom quilt in style with our version of a colonial quilt rack. For an extra-special touch, try your hand at adding a decorative carving.

Cheval Mirror 41

The classic lines of another era are reflected in the rounded corners of this mirror. Special hardware allows the mirror to pivot in its frame.

Under-Bed Storage Box 50

Turn the unused space under your bed into a convenient storage area for clothes and such. It rolls back and forth on hidden wheels for quick access.

Jewelry Case 60

This beautiful case has a rich appearance that invites you to store your fine jewelry inside. An optional rose inlay in the lid adds a touch of elegance.

CLASSIC CHERRY SET 74

Night Stand 76

When you set out to build a classically-styled cabinet, it only seems natural to include details such as dovetailed drawers and frame and panel sides.

Lingerie Dresser 86

The second cabinet in this cherry set is tall and elegant. The drawers have raised-panel fronts and are all the same size so construction is quick.

Night Stand

Classic Cherry Bed 98

You won't lose any sleep figuring out how to make all the mortises for the slats in this bed. Our method makes it as easy as counting sheep.

Chest-on-Chest 112

With its cherry frame and panel construction and raised panel drawers, this Chest-on-Chest will be an elegant focal point in any bedroom.

Sources 126

Index 127

CONTEMPORARY SET

Design details tie a furniture set together. With that in mind, you might call this bedroom set a "two-in-one" package. That's because you can build it in one of two styles by simply changing a few details.

The primary design for these pieces is a simple, contemporary, straightforward look. It features wide bevels on the outside corners, and chamfered edges. And the clean appearance is enhanced by no visible hardware. But with just a few modifications, each piece can take on a more traditional feel, while maintaining the unified appearance of a set.

The frames for the headboard and wall mirror are constructed similarly, yet there are enough differences between them to make each one an interesting project. And the headboard can be customized easily to fit any size mattress.

The night stand and chest of drawers carry the same design details as the headboard and mirror. They also share an unusual drawer design. The drawers are joined with machine-cut, half-blind dovetails. The unusual part is that the drawer front is wider than the rest of the drawer. This allows for a built-in finger pull on the bottom edge.

Frame and Panel Headboard   8

Designer's Notebook: Alternate Sizes 9
Technique: Mortise and Tenon 10
Shop Tip: Long Piece Clamps 12
Designer's Notebook: Traditional Headboard 13

Night Stand   14

Designer's Notebook: Traditional Night Stand 18

Chest of Drawers   20

Designer's Notebook: Traditional Chest. 27
Technique: Building Drawers 28

Wall Mirror   30

Designer's Notebook: Traditional Mirror 33

Frame & Panel Headboard

Building this contemporary headboard will be easy, thanks to the simple mortise and tenon joinery used to connect the pieces. Adjust the length of a few pieces and you can build it to fit your mattress.

Contemporary furniture is seen as current or modern (which limits its broad appeal somewhat). But I look at it a little differently. To me, contemporary furniture looks great in just about any decor, since it isn't overly ornamental.

That's definitely the case with this Frame and Panel Headboard (and all the other projects in this section). I designed it with simple, straightforward lines to give it a clean, streamlined appearance.

This headboard is a good place to start if you'd like to build your own set of contemporary furniture. Once it's complete, you can tackle another fun project like the Night Stand (pages 14-19), or any other project in this book's first section.

QUEEN-SIZE. The headboard is designed to fit a queen-size bed. But it's very easy to alter the dimensions to fit any mattress size. The Designer's Notebook on the next page explains how to make a twin, full, or king-size headboard simply by altering a few dimensions.

MORTISE AND TENONS. I used mortise and tenon joinery on this project. It's a strong joint that's easy to cut. When you get started cutting the headboard workpieces, you'll quickly notice one thing that's a little different. Typically, when you build a frame for a large panel using mortise and tenon joints, the tenons are cut on the rails (the horizontal pieces) and the mortises are cut in the uprights (the vertical pieces).

But with the headboard, I broke with tradition somewhat and cut a tenon on the top end of each upright. Then I mortised the bottom edge of the top rail to accept these tenons. I liked the look even better after I had mitered the corners of the top rail to ease the transition between the upright and the rail.

Regardless of where you locate the joints, cutting them is the same. You can learn more about how to do this in the Technique article on page 10.

DESIGN OPTIONS. After I completed the headboard, I wondered how it would look with a few simple changes. For example, how would a cap look above the top rail? And instead of one large panel, how about smaller raised panels (or at least the illusion of them)? Take a minute to look at the Designer's Notebook on page 13 to see how these changes give the headboard an entirely different feel. If you like this look, I've provided similar design options for the other pieces in the bedroom set (see pages 18, 27, and 33).

EXPLODED VIEW

OVERALL DIMENSIONS:
60W x 1¾D x 42H

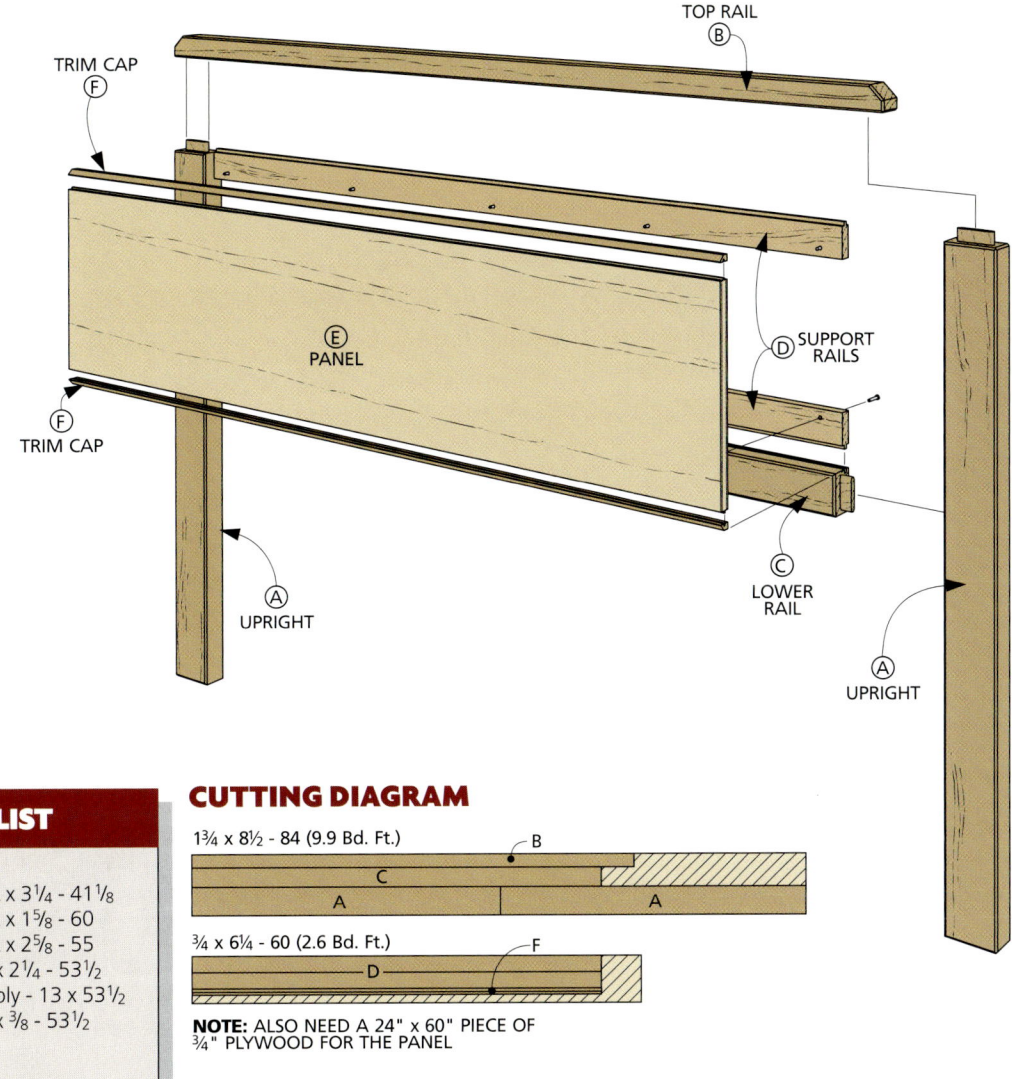

TOP RAIL
(B)

TRIM CAP
(F)

(E)
PANEL

(D) SUPPORT
RAILS

(F)
TRIM CAP

(A)
UPRIGHT

(C)
LOWER
RAIL

(A)
UPRIGHT

MATERIALS LIST

WOOD

A	Uprights (2)	1¾ x 3¼ - 41⅛
B	Top Rail (1)	1¾ x 1⅝ - 60
C	Lower Rail (1)	1¾ x 2⅝ - 55
D	Support Rails (2)	¾ x 2¼ - 53½
E	Panel (1)	¾ ply - 13 x 53½
F	Trim Caps (2)	¾ x ⅜ - 53½

HARDWARE SUPPLIES
(10) No. 8 x 1¼" woodscrews

CUTTING DIAGRAM

1¾ x 8½ - 84 (9.9 Bd. Ft.)

B

C

A

A

¾ x 6¼ - 60 (2.6 Bd. Ft.)

F

D

NOTE: ALSO NEED A 24" x 60" PIECE OF
¾" PLYWOOD FOR THE PANEL

DESIGNER'S NOTEBOOK

This contemporary headboard can be resized to fit your mattress by altering just a few dimensions.

ALTERNATE SIZES

■ You can take the Frame and Panel Headboard and easily stretch it to make a larger version for a king-sized mattress. And it's just as easy to reduce the width of the headboard to fit full or twin-size mattresses (see drawing).

■ You also may need to alter the length of the uprights as explained on page 10.

■ All you need to do is change the length of the top rail (B) to one of the dimensions shown at right. Once the length of the top rail has been changed, simply build the uprights (A) and adjust the lengths of the lower rail (C), support rails (D), panel (E), and trim caps (F).

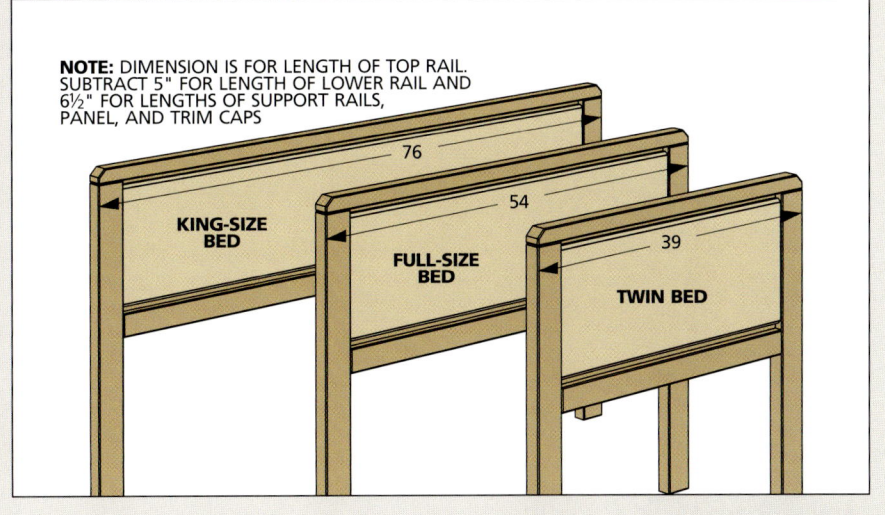

NOTE: DIMENSION IS FOR LENGTH OF TOP RAIL. SUBTRACT 5" FOR LENGTH OF LOWER RAIL AND 6½" FOR LENGTHS OF SUPPORT RAILS, PANEL, AND TRIM CAPS

76

KING-SIZE
BED

54

FULL-SIZE
BED

39

TWIN BED

Building this headboard is really just a matter of building a very large frame that's joined with mortise and tenon joints. To start construction, I cut the uprights (A), top rail (B), and lower rail (C) to size from $1^3/_4$"-thick stock.

UPRIGHTS. Start by cutting the uprights (A) to size ($3^1/_4$" x $41^1/_8$") *(Fig. 1)*. The length of the uprights actually determines the overall height of the headboard in relation to the mattress. If the headboard is built with $41^1/_8$"-long uprights, the bottom edge of the lower rail (C) will be 23" off the floor.

This is the right height for a mattress that's 24" off the floor — that is, so the top of the mattress is 1" above the bottom edge of the headboard.

Note: The 24" mattress height is to the top of a standard mattress and box spring combination on a metal frame with casters. If the height of the mattress is more or less than 24", alter the length of the uprights accordingly.

TOP RAIL. The next step is to cut the top rail (B) to size. First, rip the rail $1^5/_8$" wide from $1^3/_4$"-thick stock. As for the length of the rail, it depends on the width of the steel frame that supports your mattress and box springs.

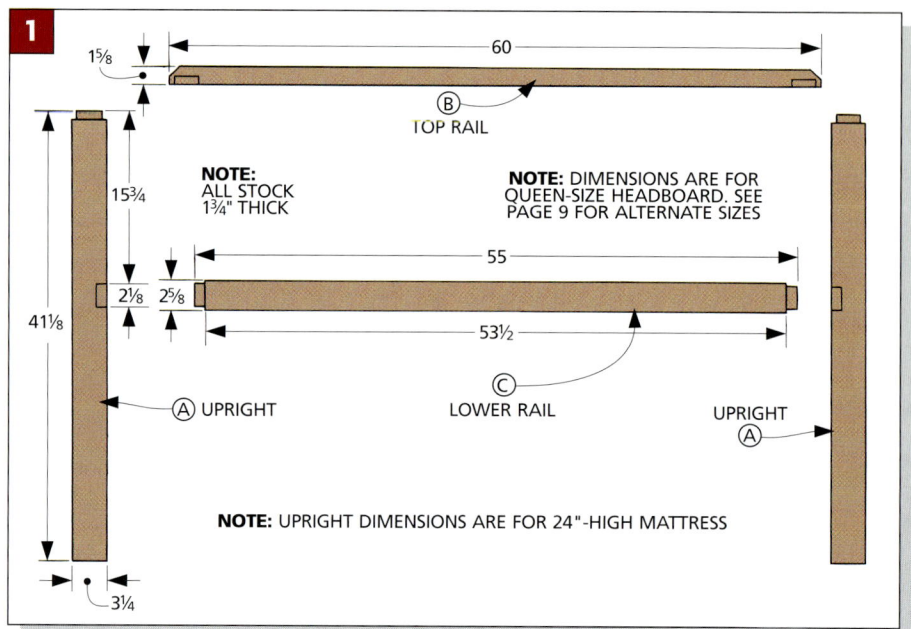

Check the mounting holes in the bed frame to determine exactly where you want the legs positioned. Then cut the top rail to the length necessary to put the uprights in the right position on the bed frame. To do this, first attach the uprights to the frame. Make sure the uprights are straight and parallel and measure from outside edge to outside edge of the uprights. (In my case, that was 60".)

LOWER RAIL. At this point, you can rip the lower rail (C) to width ($2^5/_8$"). Then to determine the length of this rail, take the final length of the top rail (B), subtract the width of both uprights (a total of $6^1/_2$"), and add $1^1/_2$" for the two tenons on the ends of the lower rail *(Fig. 1)*.

JOINERY. After the uprights and rails are cut to size, they're joined with mortises and tenons. But unlike a typical

---

TECHNIQUE . . . . *Mortise & Tenon*

Mortises and tenons can easily be cut using just two power tools and a file. For the Headboard, all this involves is boring a series of centered holes on the width of the stock *(Fig. 1)*. Then clean up the cheeks of the mortise with a chisel, leaving the ends in the half-round shape (refer to *Figs. 2 and 3* on page 11).

TENONS. After the mortises are cut, tenons are cut on the uprights and the middle rail. To cut the tenons, set the fence of the table saw $3/_4$" from the *outside* of the blade *(Figs. 2 and 2a)*.

Then use a piece of scrap to set the height of the blade. Make passes over both faces of the workpiece, and gradu-

ally raise the blade until the thickness of the tenon fits snugly in the mortise.

Follow the same procedure to cut the shoulders of the tenon *(Figs. 3 and 3a)*, carefully paring away the shoulders until it fits the length of the mortise. Then I use a file to round over the corners to fit the rounded ends of the mortises.

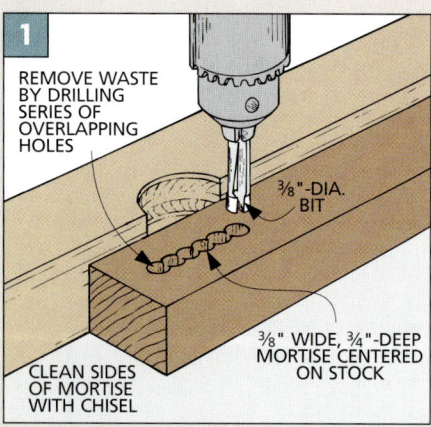

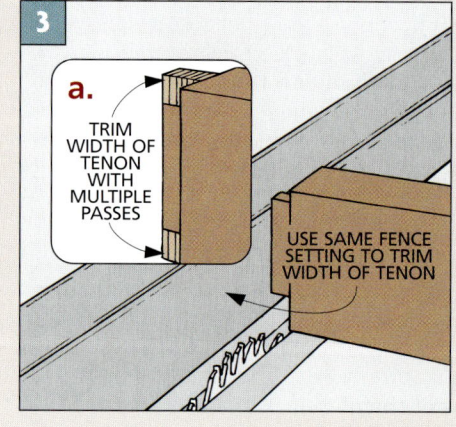

mortise and tenon joint, where an upright (or leg) will have a pair of mortises and the rails have tenons on each end, I've changed things a little. First I cut tenons on the *top* end of the uprights and cut a mortise in the *bottom* edge of the top rail *(Fig. 2)*. Then the lower rail has a tenon cut on each end, with a mortise cut in the uprights *(Fig. 3)*. (See the Technique box on the previous page for more on cutting these joints.)

SUPPORT RAILS

Once the mortises and tenons are cut, you can move on to building the support rails (D). The support rails are made from ³⁄₄"-thick stock. They'll support the large plywood panel that will be added to the headboard frame later (refer to *Fig. 7 on page 12*).

GROOVES. To accept the panel support rails, a groove is routed on the inside edge of the top and lower rails *(Fig. 4)*.

The groove on the top rail stops 3" from each end so it doesn't show. I cut this stopped groove on the router table.

Set the router table fence and install a ¹⁄₄" straight bit. Then mark the start and stop points on the edge of the rail and the fence *(Fig. 4)*. Now, plunge the rail on the bit to start the cut, and lift it off to stop it.

The groove on the lower rail is cut with the same setup, but this time, the groove isn't stopped *(Fig. 4)*.

After the grooves are routed, the support rails (D) are ripped 2¹⁄₄" wide and cut to rough length. (They're trimmed to final length later.)

TONGUES. Then a tongue is cut on one edge of each support rail *(Fig. 4)*. To make the tongues, rout rabbets on both faces of the rails leaving a tongue that fits snugly in the groove *(Fig. 4a)*.

CHAMFER THE EDGES

With the support rails finished, you can go back to work on the top rail.

To complete the top rail, cut a 45° miter on both ends *(Fig. 4b)*. Then before assembling the pieces, the edges of the top rail, lower rail, and uprights are chamfered. I did this on the router table, setting the height of a 45° chamfer bit to cut a ¹⁄₈"-wide chamfer.

There are three edges that don't receive chamfers. The inside top corner of the uprights *(Fig. 5)* and both the top and bottom corners of the lower rail are not chamfered *(Fig. 6)*.

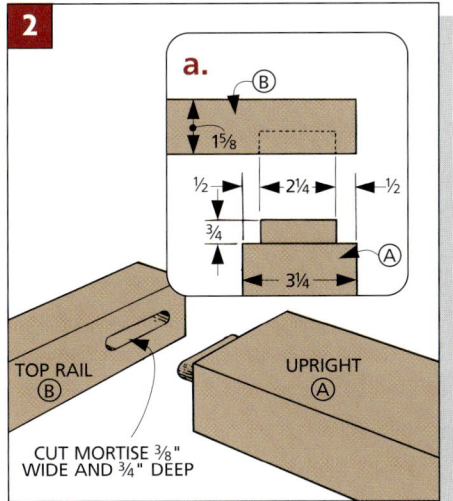

2

a.

CUT MORTISE ³⁄₈" WIDE AND ³⁄₄" DEEP

TOP RAIL Ⓑ

UPRIGHT Ⓐ

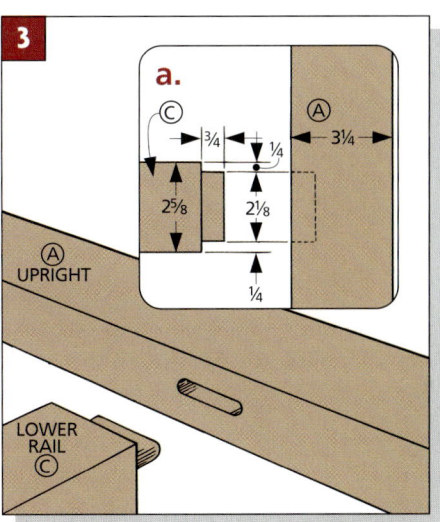

3

a.

UPRIGHT Ⓐ

LOWER RAIL Ⓒ

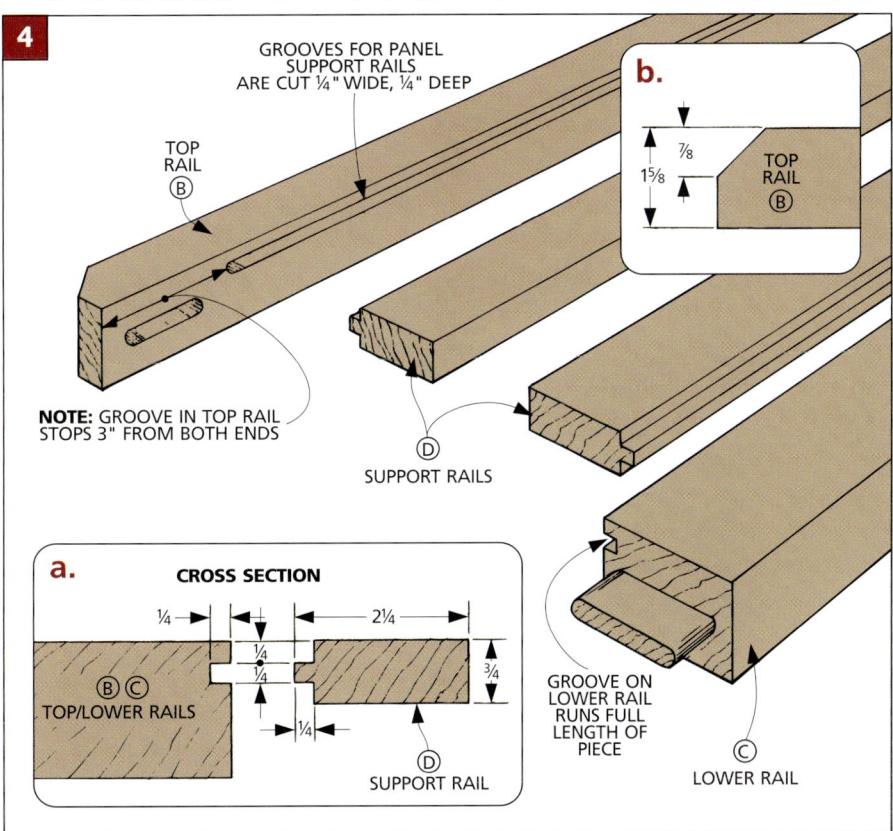

4

GROOVES FOR PANEL SUPPORT RAILS ARE CUT ¹⁄₄" WIDE, ¹⁄₄" DEEP

TOP RAIL Ⓑ

b.

TOP RAIL Ⓑ

NOTE: GROOVE IN TOP RAIL STOPS 3" FROM BOTH ENDS

SUPPORT RAILS Ⓓ

GROOVE ON LOWER RAIL RUNS FULL LENGTH OF PIECE

LOWER RAIL Ⓒ

a.

CROSS SECTION

TOP/LOWER RAILS Ⓑ Ⓒ

SUPPORT RAIL Ⓓ

5

TOP RAIL Ⓑ

DO NOT CHAMFER

¹⁄₈" CHAMFER

UPRIGHT Ⓐ

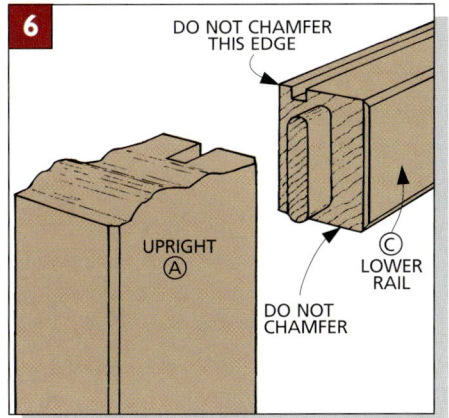

6

DO NOT CHAMFER THIS EDGE

UPRIGHT Ⓐ

DO NOT CHAMFER

LOWER RAIL Ⓒ

ASSEMBLE THE FRAME

After the edges are chamfered, the uprights can be glued and clamped to the top rail and the lower rail. This will form the basic headboard frame. (See the Shop Tip below.)

CUT SUPPORT RAILS. When the frame assembly has dried completely, measure the opening between the uprights and cut the support rails to final length. (You want them to fit snugly between the uprights.) Then they can be glued and clamped into the grooves in the top and lower rails *(Fig. 7)*.

PANEL

Now the ¾" plywood panel (E) can be cut to size. This panel is ripped to a width of 13" and cut to length so it fits tight between the uprights. (Mine was 53½".)

TRIM CAPS. To cover the exposed edges of the plywood panel, I added solid-wood trim caps (F). To mount these caps, first rout rabbets on both faces of the panel to produce centered ⅛"-square tongues on the top and bottom edges of the panel *(Fig. 8a)*.

Rip the trim caps to a width of ⅜", and to length to match the panel. Then cut a groove down the center of the trim cap to fit the tongue on the panel.

CHAMFER TRIM CAP. Now the trim caps can be glued and clamped to the edges of the panel. Then use the chamfer bit to rout a 45° chamfer on the inside edges of the trim caps *(Fig. 9)*.

This chamfer should be positioned so it leaves a 1/32"-wide shoulder next to the joint line between the cap and the panel. (It's best here to sneak up on this cut to make sure you don't cut too deep and expose the plywood's inner core.)

FINAL STEPS

With the panel complete, mount it to the support rails by drilling pilot holes through the back of the rails, and screwing it in place *(Fig. 7a)*.

MOUNTING HOLES. Before applying the finish to the headboard, locate and drill shank holes for the bolts used to mount the uprights to the bed frame.

FINISHING. Finally, I finish-sanded all surfaces of the headboard, being careful to not round over the crisp edges of the chamfers. Then I applied three coats of interior finish, sanding between coats with 320-grit wet/dry sandpaper. ■

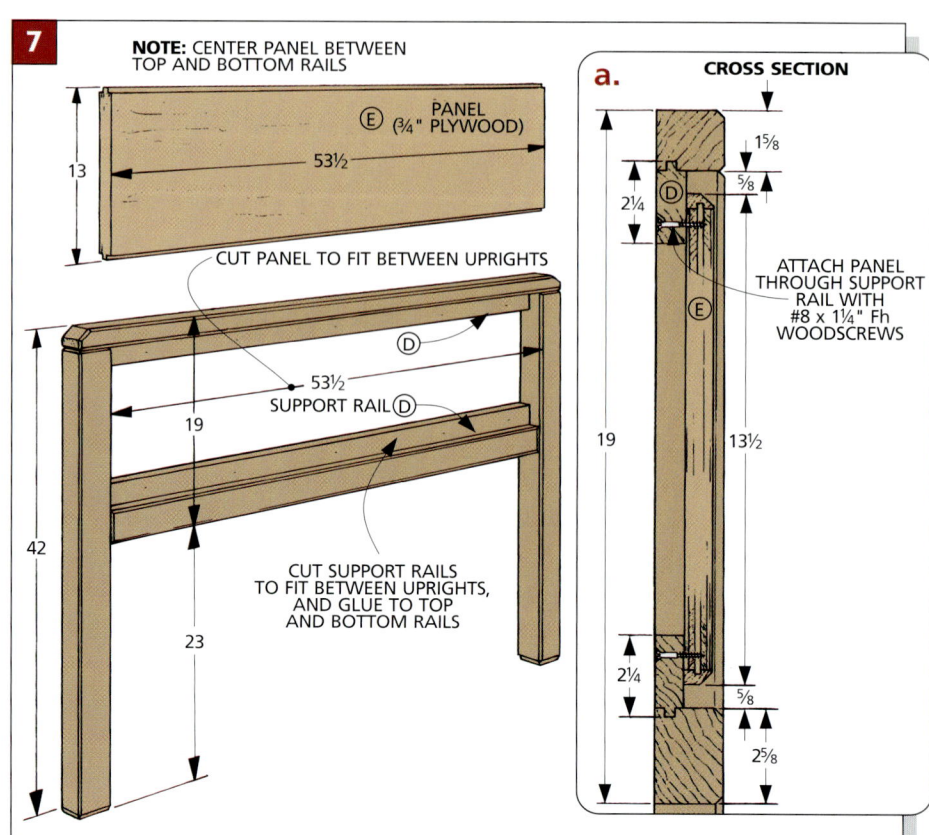

7 NOTE: CENTER PANEL BETWEEN TOP AND BOTTOM RAILS

PANEL (¾" PLYWOOD) E
13 — 53½
CUT PANEL TO FIT BETWEEN UPRIGHTS

42 — 19 — 23

53½ SUPPORT RAIL D

CUT SUPPORT RAILS TO FIT BETWEEN UPRIGHTS, AND GLUE TO TOP AND BOTTOM RAILS

a. CROSS SECTION

ATTACH PANEL THROUGH SUPPORT RAIL WITH #8 x 1¼" Fh WOODSCREWS

1⅝ — ⅝ — 2¼ — 19 — 13½ — 2¼ — ⅝ — 2⅝

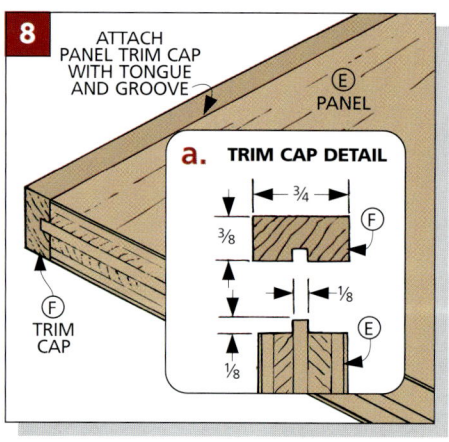

8 ATTACH PANEL TRIM CAP WITH TONGUE AND GROOVE

PANEL E
TRIM CAP F

a. TRIM CAP DETAIL
¾ — ⅜ — ⅛ — ⅛ F — E

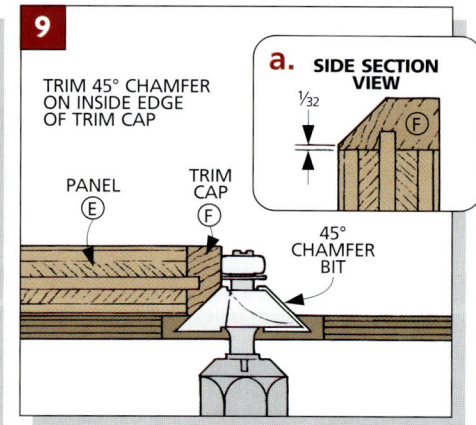

9 TRIM 45° CHAMFER ON INSIDE EDGE OF TRIM CAP

PANEL E — TRIM CAP F

a. SIDE SECTION VIEW
1/32 — F

45° CHAMFER BIT

SHOP TIP .... Long Piece Clamps

Construction of the headboard went together without a lot of problems. One problem I did have, though, came during the gluing and clamping stage. In order to clamp the lower rail to the two uprights, you need a very long clamp. Lacking a clamp long enough, I used two shorter clamps, interlocking them to get the length necessary (see drawing).

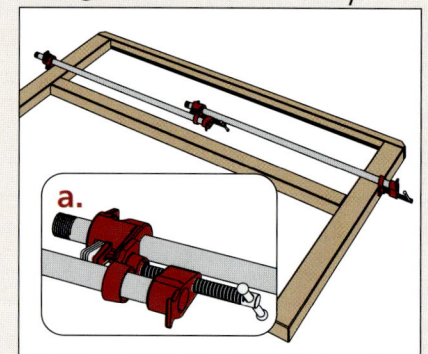

a.

DESIGNER'S NOTEBOOK

From contemporary to classic — the modifications on this version of the headboard make it a good example of how a dramatically different look can be achieved with just a few simple changes.

CONSTRUCTION NOTES:

■ There are two changes in this version of the headboard. The most noticeable is the large panel. Instead of using a plywood panel edged with hardwood, I glued up three pieces of hardwood stock to make a solid-wood panel that has the appearance of four raised panels. The other change is to the top rail, where I added a top cap to give the headboard a more tradional look.

Begin by building the uprights (A), the top rail (B), lower rail (C), and support rails (D) the same as before. Cut the mortise and tenon joints, and add the grooves to the top and lower rails. (The groove in the top rail needs to be stopped.) But this time don't chamfer any of the edges or miter the corners of the top rail. That's because on this headboard, you'll be adding a hardwood top cap.

■ I cut the top cap (G) to size from a piece of $1\frac{1}{16}$"-thick stock. It's sized to overhang the front and sides by $\frac{1}{2}$". Then I routed a $\frac{3}{8}$"-wide chamfer on the bottom edge of the front and ends of the cap rail (see drawing and detail 'b').

■ After you've assembled the headboard, go ahead and glue the top cap in place (see drawing). (It's positioned flush with the back edge of the top rail.)

■ Now you can begin working on the solid panel (H). It's glued up from three pieces of $\frac{3}{4}$"-thick hardwood stock.

■ Once the glue has dried, you can cut the panel to size (see drawing). It's cut to fit snug between the two uprights and, since you won't be needing the trim caps, its final width is $13\frac{1}{2}$".

■ The solid panel has a chamfer on each end and on the top and bottom inside edges, but this time it's only $\frac{3}{8}$" wide (half the thickness of the panel) (detail 'a').

■ Finally, to complete the solid panel, cut a series of V-grooves to make it look like

there are four small raised panels lined up in a row. To cut these grooves, mount a V-groove bit in a hand-held router. Then cut a centered groove on the length of the panel. To do this, I like to clamp a straightedge to the workpiece for the router base to ride against and then I rout the groove

in three passes, lowering the bit $\frac{1}{8}$" at a time to avoid burning the wood.

■ Complete the headboard by resetting the straightedge to rout the two outside grooves. These grooves are spaced to give the large solid-wood panel the look of four smaller, equal-size panels.

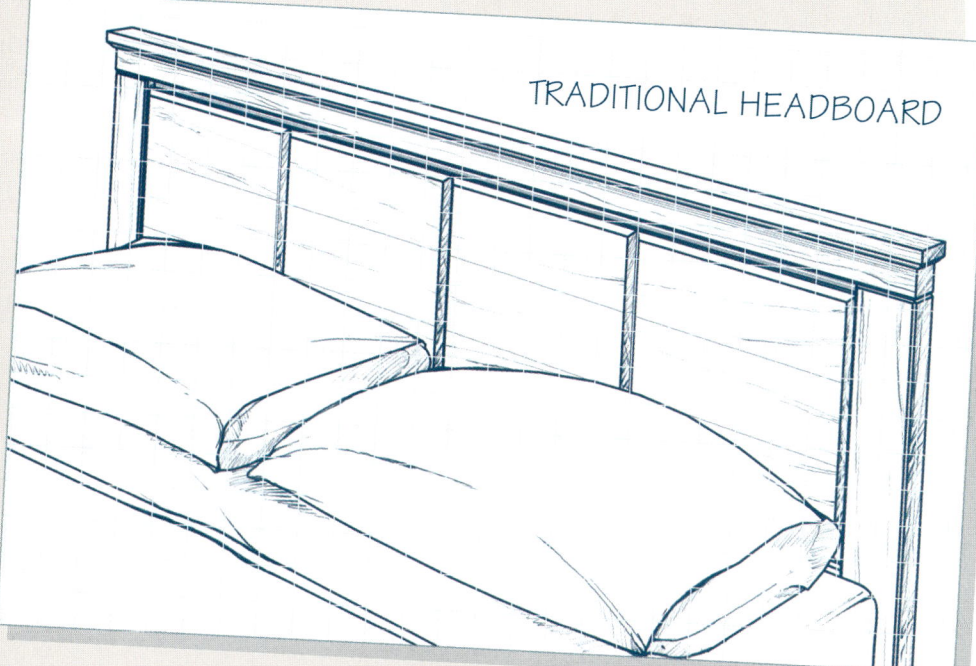

TRADITIONAL HEADBOARD

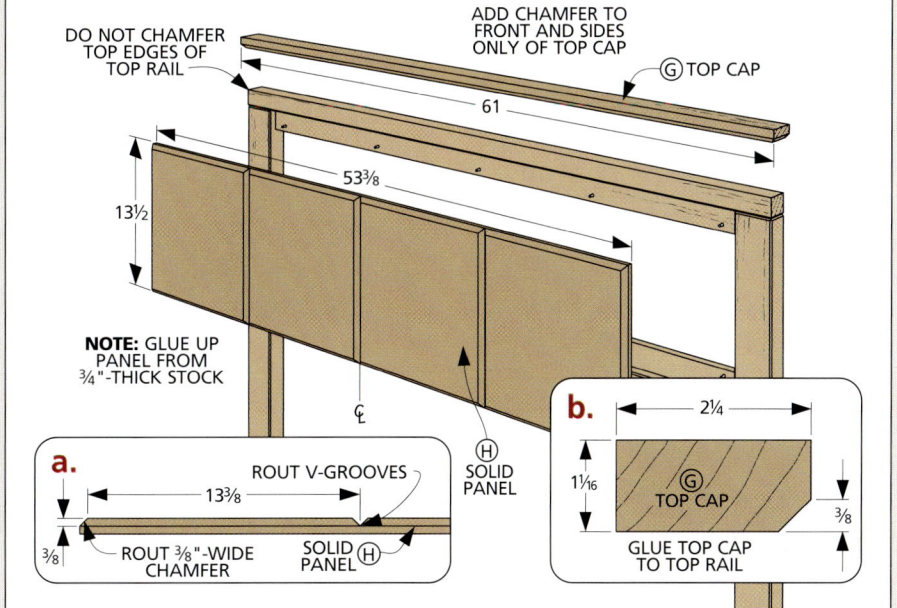

DO NOT CHAMFER TOP EDGES OF TOP RAIL

ADD CHAMFER TO FRONT AND SIDES ONLY OF TOP CAP

G TOP CAP

61

53⅜

13½

NOTE: GLUE UP PANEL FROM ¾"-THICK STOCK

H SOLID PANEL

a.

ROUT V-GROOVES

13⅜

⅜

ROUT ⅜"-WIDE CHAMFER

SOLID PANEL H

b.

2¼

1¹⁄₁₆

G TOP CAP

⅜

GLUE TOP CAP TO TOP RAIL

MATERIALS LIST

NEW PARTS

G Top Cap (1)		$1\frac{1}{16}$ x $2\frac{1}{4}$ - 61
H Solid Panel (1)		$\frac{3}{4}$ x $13\frac{1}{2}$ - $53\frac{1}{2}$

Note: Do not need parts E and F.

Night Stand

Clean, simple lines and no visible hardware define the contemporary look of this Night Stand. Machine-cut dovetails, plus tongue and groove web-frame construction, ensure it will last for years.

One nice thing about building a matching set of furniture is that you can start small and work your way up. For example, this Night Stand makes an excellent "warm-up" project before tackling the Chest of Drawers on pages 20-29. That's because they share a lot of the same design features, but they're on a smaller scale here.

The basic cabinet for the Night Stand is built exactly the same way as the chest, except it has only two web frames (one above and one below the drawers). And of course, there's only one drawer to build, which makes things a lot easier.

DESIGN DETAILS. The drawer features half-blind dovetail construction. And to make them even more interesting, I used clean drawer fronts with no drawer pulls. Instead, the lower edge of the drawer front has a concealed cove which is used to open the drawer. Take a look at the Technique article on page 28 for more on how I built the drawer.

The corner detail on the top of the Night Stand is similar in style to the miter on the corner of the headboard (see the photo on page 8). This time, though, instead of cutting a 45° miter, I cut a $5/8$"-wide bevel along the front of the cabinet.

MATERIALS. I used $3/4$" plywood for all the panels in the Night Stand. The top is edged by hardwood stiles and rails (I used mahogany), but the sides are edged with hardwood stiles on the front and back only. This way, when the top is glued in place, the stiles on the top assembly create the appearance of a rail on the upper edge of each side panel.

TRADITIONAL APPEARANCE. To change the look of the Contemporary Set featured in this section, I decided it would be nice to make things look a little more traditional. For the Night Stand, that meant adding a mitered frame and panel top, plus a knob intead of the coved pull on the drawer. See the Designer's Notebook on page 18 for more.

EXPLODED VIEW

OVERALL DIMENSIONS:
20W x 16D x 24H

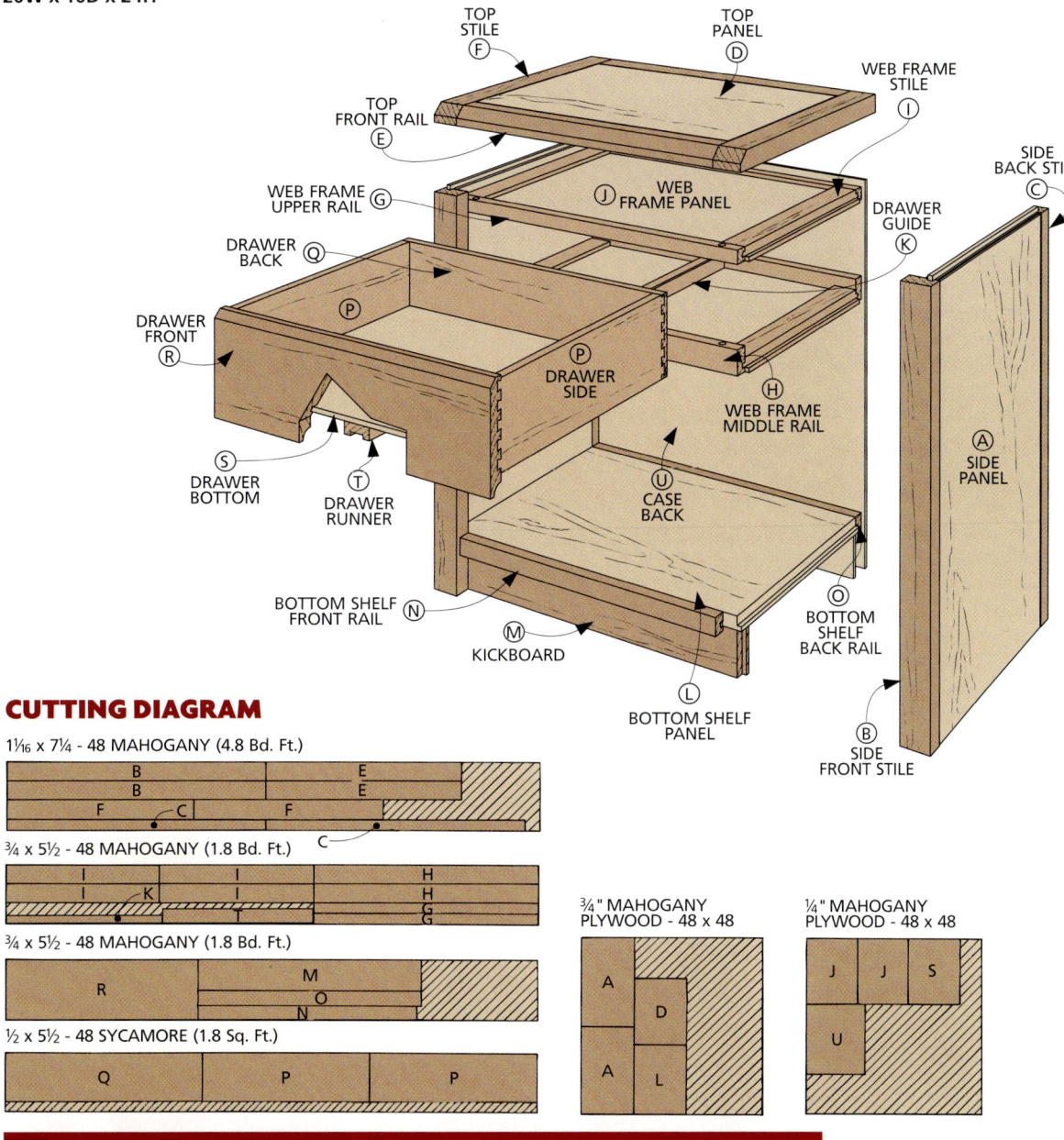

TOP STILE ⒡
TOP PANEL ⒟
TOP FRONT RAIL ⒠
WEB FRAME STILE ⒤
WEB FRAME UPPER RAIL ⒢
WEB FRAME PANEL ⒥
SIDE BACK STILE ⒞
DRAWER GUIDE ⒦
DRAWER BACK ⒬
DRAWER FRONT ⒭
⒫
DRAWER SIDE ⒫
WEB FRAME MIDDLE RAIL ⒣
SIDE PANEL ⒜
DRAWER BOTTOM ⒮
DRAWER RUNNER ⒯
CASE BACK ⒰
BOTTOM SHELF FRONT RAIL ⒩
KICKBOARD Ⓜ
BOTTOM SHELF BACK RAIL ⓄⓄ
BOTTOM SHELF PANEL ⒧
SIDE FRONT STILE ⒝

CUTTING DIAGRAM

1 1/16 x 7 1/4 - 48 MAHOGANY (4.8 Bd. Ft.)

3/4 x 5 1/2 - 48 MAHOGANY (1.8 Bd. Ft.)

3/4 x 5 1/2 - 48 MAHOGANY (1.8 Bd. Ft.)

1/2 x 5 1/2 - 48 SYCAMORE (1.8 Sq. Ft.)

3/4 " MAHOGANY PLYWOOD - 48 x 48

1/4 " MAHOGANY PLYWOOD - 48 x 48

MATERIALS LIST

SIDES
A Panels (2)   3/4 ply - 14 3/8 x 23 3/16
B Front Stiles (2)   1 1/16 x 1 5/8 - 22 15/16
C Back Stiles (2)   1 1/16 x 3/4 - 22 15/16

TOP
D Panel (1)   3/4 ply - 13 1/4 x 17 1/4
E Front/Back Rails (2) 1 1/16 x 1 5/8 - 16 3/4
F Stiles (2)   1 1/16 x 1 5/8 - 16

WEB FRAMES
G Upper Rails (2)   3/4 x 3/4 - 18 7/16
H Middle Rails (2)   3/4 x 1 3/8 - 18 7/16
I Stiles (4)   3/4 x 1 5/8 - 13 11/16
J Panels (2)   1/4 ply - 13 11/16 x 16 1/4
K Drawer Guide (1)   3/4 x 15/16 - 13 7/8

BOTTOM SHELF
L Panel (1)   3/4 ply - 14 3/8 x 19
M Kickboard (1)   3/4 x 2 1/2 - 19
N Front Rail (1)   3/4 x 1 - 16 3/4
O Back Rail (1)   3/4 x 1 - 18 7/16

DRAWER & BACK
P Sides (2)   1/2 x 4 3/8 - 13 3/4
Q Back (1)   1/2 x 4 3/8 - 16 5/8
R Front (1)   3/4 x 5 1/4 - 16 5/8
S Bottom (1)   1/4 ply - 16 1/8 x 13 3/4
T Runner (1)   3/4 x 1 1/2 - 13 1/4
U Case Back (1)   1/4 ply - 18 15/16 x 22 15/16

HARDWARE SUPPLIES
(2) Nylon glides

SIDES

To build this Night Stand, I started with the side frames, which consist of a plywood panel with hardwood stiles on the front and back edges.

PANEL. First, cut two $3/4$" plywood panels (A) to size. Then to hold the web frames and the bottom shelf later, three dadoes are cut across the inside face of each plywood panel.

ROUT DADOES. To cut the dadoes, I set up a $1/4$" straight bit in the router table and raised it $1/4$" above the table.

The top dado is positioned $3/4$" down from the top edge of the plywood panel to allow for the thickness of the stock used on the web frame (*Fig. 1*). The next dado should be located so its top edge is exactly $5^7/8$" down from the top edge of the top dado. This allows the proper spacing between the dadoes so that the drawer will fit in place.

The top of the third dado (the one used for the shelf) is located $2^3/4$" up from the bottom edge of the panel. After routing this dado, you also need a short vertical groove for the kickboard. To cut this groove, I clamped a fence to the plywood and used a hand-held router.

TONGUES. After the dadoes are cut, long tongues are cut on the front, back, and top edges of the side panels. Since these tongues will fit in grooves routed later in the stiles, I first routed a $1/4$"-wide groove in a test piece to use as a gauge.

Then to cut the tongues, I switched to a $3/8$" straight bit in the router table (*Steps 1 and 2 in Fig. 1a*). Rout a $1/4$"-wide rabbet on both faces of the plywood, adjusting the depth until the tongue fits the groove in the test piece.

SHOULDER RELIEF. To set the plywood side panels off in their frames, I routed a narrow shoulder next to the tongue (*Step 3 in Fig. 1a*). This shoulder produces a small gap between the edging and the plywood, making a nice shadowline around the panel.

STILES. Next, the hardwood stiles are made for the front and back edges of the plywood side panels.

Start by cutting the stiles to size. The front stiles (B) are ripped to width ($1^5/8$"), then cut to length (*Fig. 1*). To find the length of this stile, you need to measure the distance from the bottom of the cabinet side panel to the shoulder of the tongue cut on the top edge.

Now the back stiles (C) can be ripped to width ($1^1/16$"). Then they can be cut to the same length as the front stiles ($22^{15}/16$") (*Figs. 1 and 1b*).

GROOVES IN STILES. All four of the stiles are joined to the side panels by routing grooves for the tongues cut in the panels earlier. On the front stiles (B), the grooves are cut in the wide face, and positioned so the outside edge is flush with the surface of the panel (*Fig. 1b*).

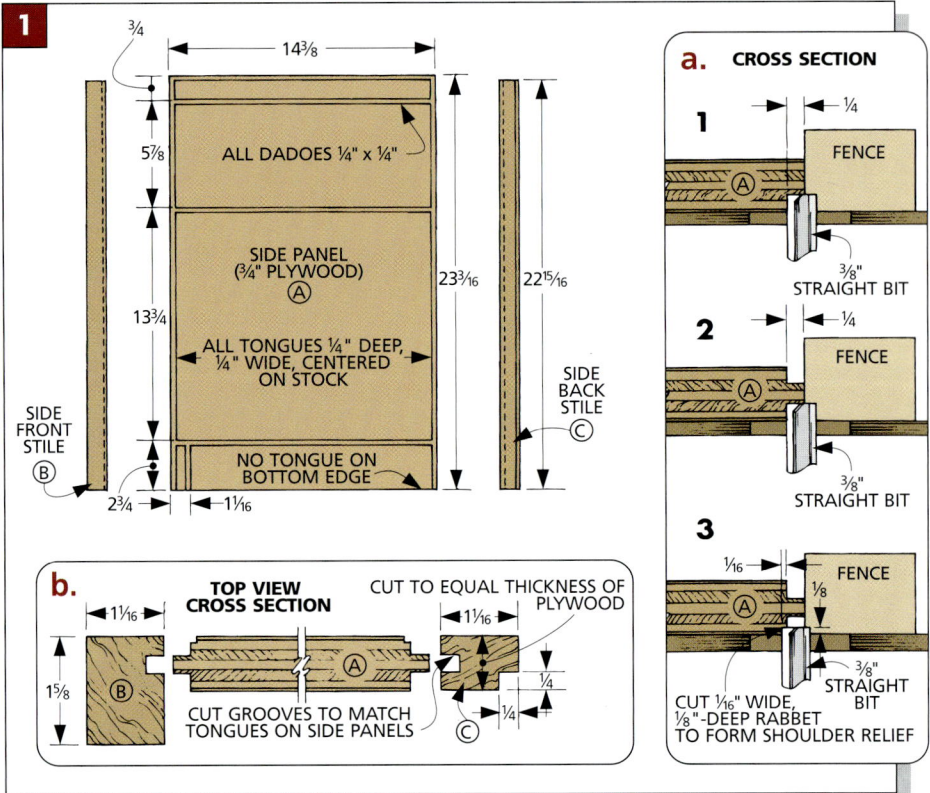

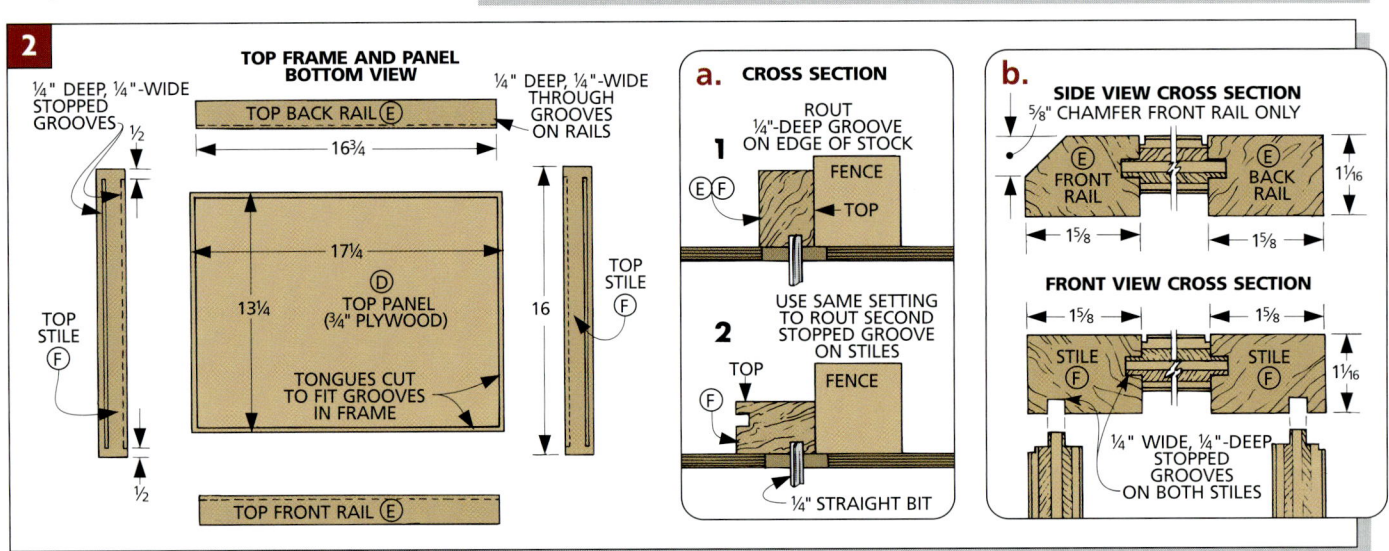

The back stile has a groove centered on one edge for the side panel. And a $\frac{1}{4}$"-deep rabbet cut on the inside back edge of the stiles is for a plywood case back.

With the grooves cut, glue the front and back stiles to the panels, making sure they're flush with the shoulder of the tongue on the top edge of the panel.

TOP FRAME & PANEL

The frame and panel for the top of the cabinet consists of a plywood panel with a hardwood rail and stile frame.

PANEL. The first step is to cut the $\frac{3}{4}$" plywood top panel (D) to size.

Then, as on the side panels, rout $\frac{1}{4}$"-long tongues — only this time on all four edges. Also, cut the relief shoulder around the panel (Fig. 2b).

RAILS. To make the frame, rip the top front and back rails (E) from $1\frac{1}{16}$"-thick stock so they're $1\frac{5}{8}$" wide.

Note: This width may have to be altered to make sure the top assembly is the same width (depth) as the side frame.

Then trim the rails to length to match the shoulder to shoulder length of the plywood panel (Fig. 2).

STILES. The top stiles (F) are also ripped $1\frac{5}{8}$" wide from $1\frac{1}{16}$"-thick stock. Then they're cut to length to equal the width of the cabinet sides.

GROOVES. To attach the top rails to the plywood panel, rout a $\frac{1}{4}$"-square groove on the inside edge of each piece (Step 1 in Fig. 2a). Position these grooves so the faces of the rails are flush with the face of the plywood panel (Fig. 2b).

The grooves routed in the top frame assembly's stiles will have to be stopped $\frac{1}{2}$" from both ends of the stile so they don't show through (Fig. 2).

Before gluing the stiles to the panel, I routed a second $\frac{1}{4}$" x $\frac{1}{4}$" stopped groove on the bottom face of the stile. This groove is used to hold the top frame to the side frame (Fig. 2b).

ASSEMBLY. Finally, the top front and back rails and top stiles can be glued to the plywood panel. Then, after the frame is assembled, cut a $\frac{5}{8}$"-wide bevel on the front of the frame (Fig. 2b).

WEB FRAMES

After the side frames and the top frame are complete, the two web frames and the bottom shelf can be built.

WEB FRAMES. The two web frames are almost identical. The overall dimensions

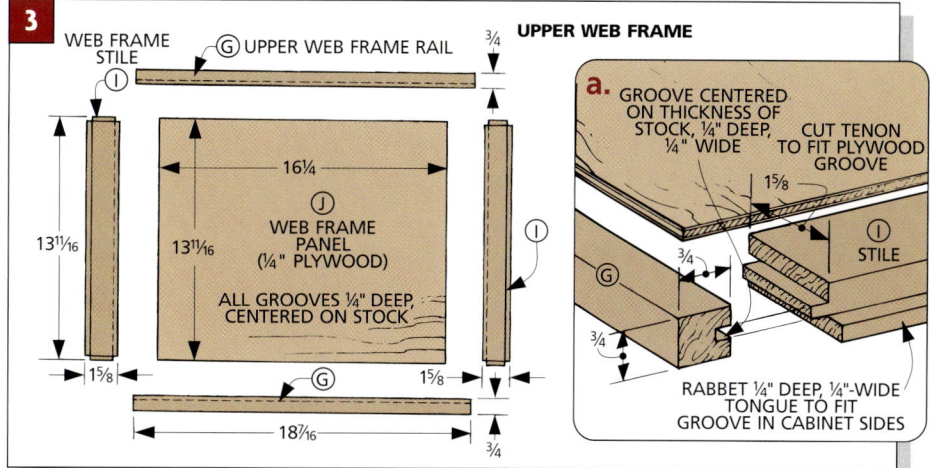

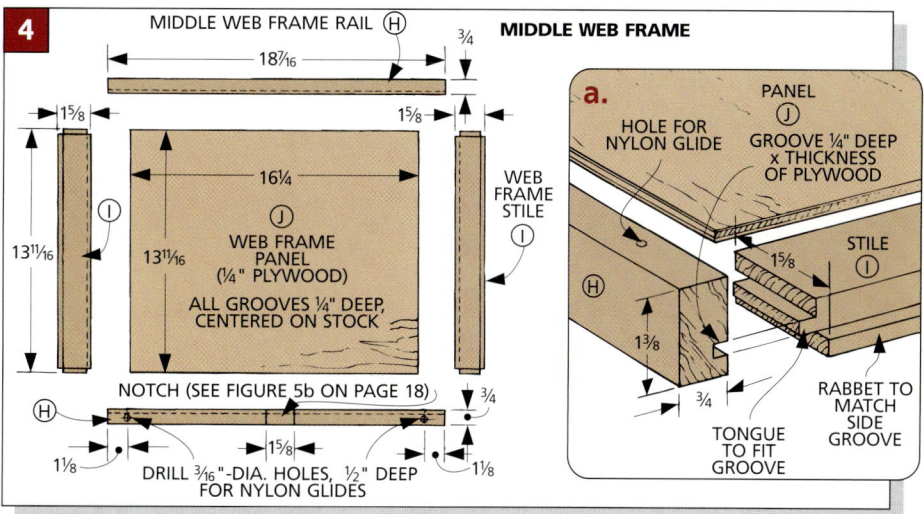

and the length of the individual pieces are the same. The only difference is the width of the rails on the web frames.

UPPER AND MIDDLE RAILS. To get the length of the rails for the web frames, dry-clamp the top frame to the cabinet sides. Then measure the distance between the side frames to get the length of the rails ($18\frac{7}{16}$") (Figs. 3 and 4).

Although the length of the rails on both frames is the same, the width is different. The upper frame rails (G) are ripped $\frac{3}{4}$" wide (Fig. 3a), and the middle frame rails (H) are $1\frac{3}{8}$" wide (Fig. 4a).

STILES. The stiles (I) on both web frames are the same size. To find their length, first measure from the back face of the front stile on the cabinet side to the rabbet in the back stile. Then subtract the combined thickness of the front and back rails ($1\frac{1}{2}$"), and add $\frac{1}{2}$" for the $\frac{1}{4}$"-long stub tenons on the ends of the stiles. (My stiles were all $13\frac{11}{16}$".) As for the width, the stiles are all $1\frac{5}{8}$" wide.

GROOVES. To join the web frame rails and stiles, first cut a groove on the inside

edge of each piece to match the thickness of the plywood panel (Figs. 3a and 4a). Then cut stub tenons on the ends of the stiles to match the groove in the rails. Also cut a rabbet on the outside edge of each stile to form a $\frac{1}{4}$" tongue to fit the grooves in the cabinet sides (Fig. 4a).

NOTCH. Before the middle frame is assembled, cut a $1\frac{5}{8}$" wide, $\frac{1}{4}$"-deep notch centered on the front rail for the drawer guide (Fig. 3). Then drill a $\frac{3}{16}$"-dia. hole in each end of the front rail for the nylon glides (Fig. 4).

ASSEMBLY. Now dry-assemble the web frames and take measurements for the plywood web frame panels (J). Finally, cut the panels to fit, and glue the web frames together around the panels.

DRAWER GUIDE. With the web frames assembled, rip a drawer guide (K) so it's $\frac{1}{16}$" higher than the front rail on the middle web frame (refer to Figs. 5 and 5a on page 18). Rabbet the front end of the drawer guide to fit over the notch in the front rail. Then glue it in place so it's centered on the width of the frame.

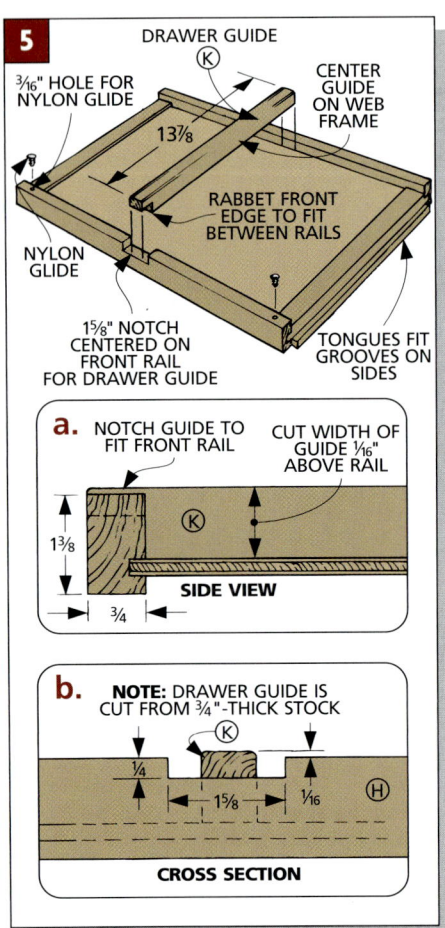

5

DRAWER GUIDE (K)

³⁄₁₆" HOLE FOR NYLON GLIDE

CENTER GUIDE ON WEB FRAME

13⅞

RABBET FRONT EDGE TO FIT BETWEEN RAILS

NYLON GLIDE

1⅝" NOTCH CENTERED ON FRONT RAIL FOR DRAWER GUIDE

TONGUES FIT GROOVES ON SIDES

a. NOTCH GUIDE TO FIT FRONT RAIL

CUT WIDTH OF GUIDE ¹⁄₁₆" ABOVE RAIL

(K)

13⅜

¾

SIDE VIEW

b. NOTE: DRAWER GUIDE IS CUT FROM ¾"-THICK STOCK

(K)

¼   1⅝   ¹⁄₁₆   (H)

CROSS SECTION

BOTTOM SHELF

The bottom shelf consists of a plywood panel with hardwood rails on the front and back edges.

CUT PANEL TO SIZE. To build this shelf, first cut the plywood bottom shelf panel (L) to length so it's ½" longer than the inside width of the cabinet.

Note: The extra ½" is for the ¼" tongues on both ends of the shelf.

Then cut the bottom shelf to width so it's ½" wider than the distance between the front and back stiles on the cabinet sides (Fig. 6b). (Again, the extra ½" is for the tongues on the front and back edges.)

TONGUES. After the plywood is cut, rout rabbets on all four edges to form ¼" tongues to fit the grooves in the cabinet sides (Fig. 6). Next, trim the tongues on the front and rear corners so they fit around the stiles on the sides (Fig. 6).

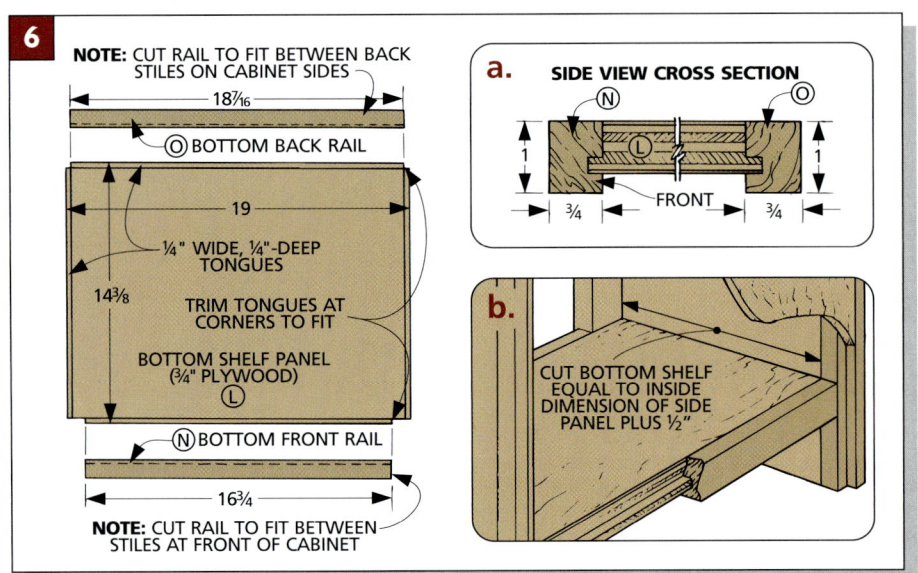

6

NOTE: CUT RAIL TO FIT BETWEEN BACK STILES ON CABINET SIDES

18⁷⁄₁₆

(O) BOTTOM BACK RAIL

19

¼" WIDE, ¼"-DEEP TONGUES

14⅜

TRIM TONGUES AT CORNERS TO FIT

BOTTOM SHELF PANEL (¾" PLYWOOD) (L)

(N) BOTTOM FRONT RAIL

16¾

NOTE: CUT RAIL TO FIT BETWEEN STILES AT FRONT OF CABINET

a. SIDE VIEW CROSS SECTION

(N)   (O)

1   (L)   1

¾   FRONT   ¾

b. CUT BOTTOM SHELF EQUAL TO INSIDE DIMENSION OF SIDE PANEL PLUS ½"

DESIGNER'S NOTEBOOK

Two changes transform the stand from contemporary to traditional.

CONSTRUCTION NOTES:

■ To give the top a more traditional look, I mitered the front edges of the top frame.
■ I also changed the chamfer. Instead of a deep chamfer across the front of the stand, I've routed a ⅜" chamfer along the bottom of the front rail (V) and stiles (F) (see drawing and detail 'a').

Note: Except for dimensions of the rails and stiles, these changes are the same as those in the Designer's

Notebook on page 27. The procedure is explained in more detail there.
■ Then, build the drawer front as before, but this time leave off the cove and rout a chamfer all the way around the outside edge of the front. Finally, add a wooden knob centered on the drawer front.

TRADITIONAL NIGHT STAND

MATERIALS LIST

CHANGED PARTS

E	Back Rail (1)	1¹⁄₁₆ x 1⅝ - 16¾
F	Top Stiles (2)	1¹⁄₁₆ x 2⅛ - 16½

NEW PART

V	Top Front Rail (1)	1¹⁄₁₆ x 2⅛ - 21

HARDWARE SUPPLIES

(1) 1½" knob

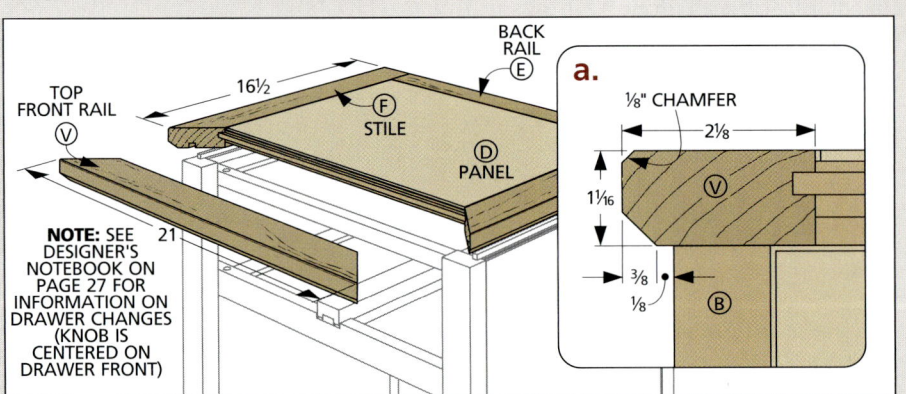

TOP FRONT RAIL (V)

16½

BACK RAIL (E)

(F) STILE

(D) PANEL

NOTE: SEE DESIGNER'S NOTEBOOK ON PAGE 27 FOR INFORMATION ON DRAWER CHANGES (KNOB IS CENTERED ON DRAWER FRONT)

21

a. ⅛" CHAMFER

2⅛

1¹⁄₁₆

(V)

⅜   ⅛   (B)

KICKBOARD. The last step before the cabinet can be assembled is to add a kickboard (M) *(Fig. 7)*. The kickboard is cut to width, but it must be cut $\frac{1}{2}$" longer than the inside width of the cabinet. Then you can cut a rabbet on each end of the kickboard to form the tongues that fit the grooves in the cabinet sides *(Fig. 7a)*.

ASSEMBLY. To assemble the cabinet, glue the side frames, both web frames, the bottom shelf, and the kickboard together *(Fig. 7)*. When the glue is dry, attach the top frame.

BOTTOM SHELF RAILS. Finally, to complete construction of the cabinet, cut the bottom shelf rails (N, O). They're used to cover the plywood edges of the bottom shelf. Rip both pieces to width and long enough to fit between the cabinet sides. Then cut $\frac{1}{4}$" deep, $\frac{1}{4}$"-wide grooves in the strips to position them so the top edge of the edging will be flush with the face of the panel *(Fig. 6a)*.

DRAWER

The drawer for the Night Stand is built with half-blind dovetails on the front and back. Plus, the drawer front has a concealed cove on the bottom edge.

CUT PIECES. The first step in building the drawer is to cut the drawer sides (P) and back (Q) to width ($\frac{1}{8}$" narrower than the opening), and to length *(Fig. 8)*. Then cut the drawer front (R) $\frac{3}{4}$" wider than the height of the drawer opening.

To join the pieces for the drawer, I used a dovetail jig to rout the half-blind dovetails on the front and back corners. (For a more detailed description of cutting the drawers, see the Technique article on page 28.)

When the corner joinery is completed, cut a 45° bevel on the top edge of the drawer front. Then rout a $\frac{1}{2}$" cove on the bottom inside edge to provide a finger pull for the drawer *(Fig. 8a)*. The last step is to cut the drawer bottom (S) to fit, and to glue the drawer together.

RUNNER. To complete the drawer guide system, cut a drawer runner (T) with a groove down the center that fits over the drawer guide (K) on the middle web frame *(Fig. 9)*. Then glue the runner centered on the drawer bottom.

FINISHING STEPS. To complete the stand, I routed a $\frac{1}{8}$" chamfer on all the outside edges of the cabinet and drawer front. Finally, I cut the case back (U) to size from $\frac{1}{4}$" plywood and glued it in place between the cabinet sides. ∎

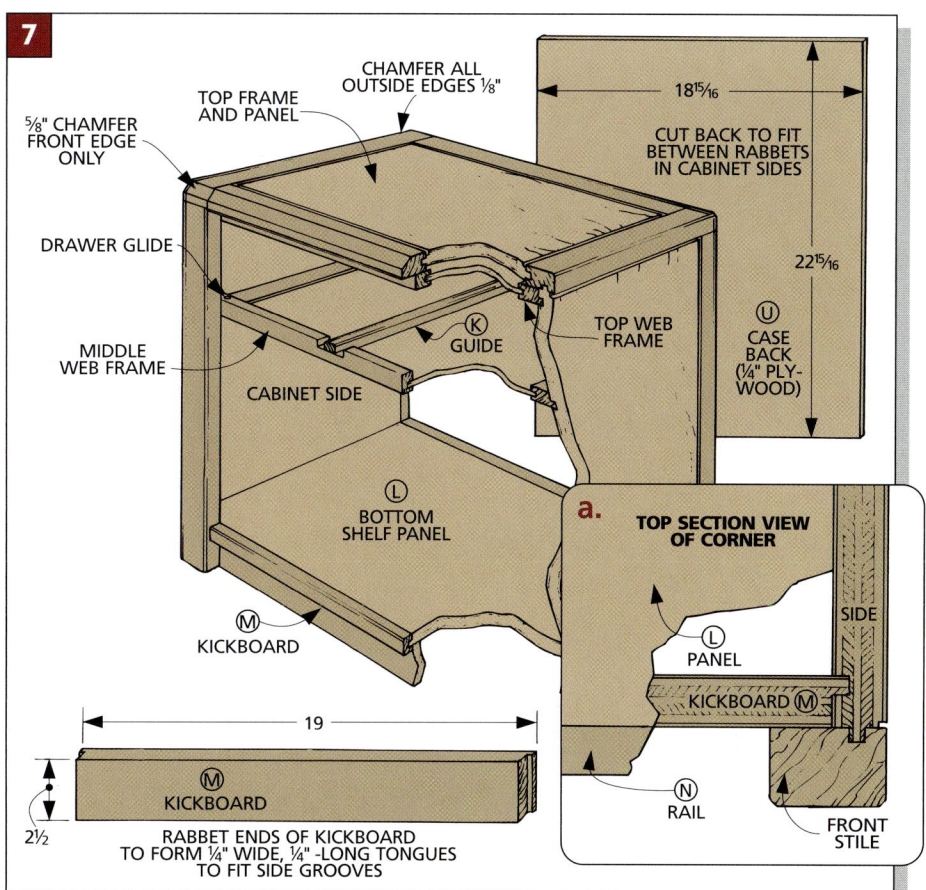

7

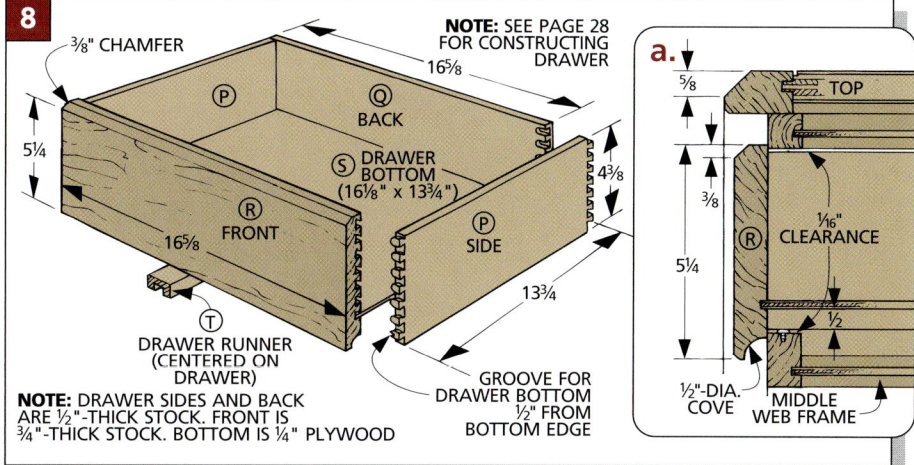

8

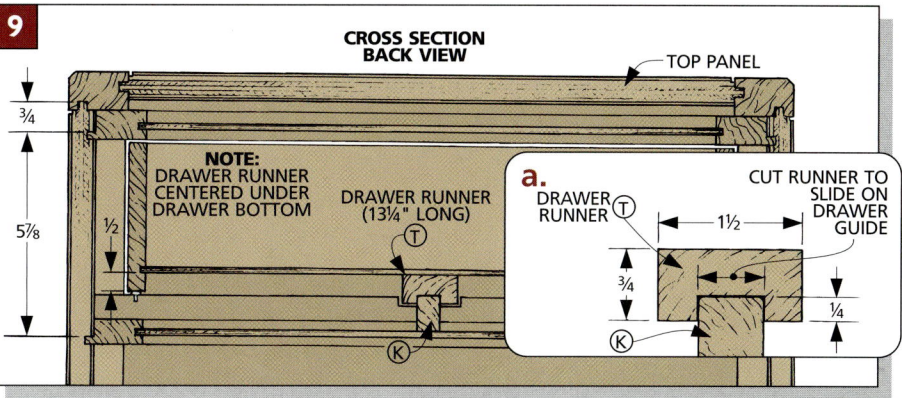

9

Chest of Drawers

The front of this chest is uncluttered by hardware because the drawer fronts have a hidden finger pull built in. This adds a slightly different twist to the routine of routing machine-cut dovetails.

This Chest of Drawers is built exactly the opposite of the way it was designed. That may not make much sense, but that's one of the problems you face when you set out to build a Chest of Drawers — to get everything to fit, you have to design the drawers first and then design the cabinet around them.

This is especially true of this chest, because I wanted to build it with drawers that were a little out of the ordinary. There's no hardware in sight — no pulls, plus no metal drawer guides. Instead, the drawers are designed with a concealed cove as a finger pull, and a guide system that's made completely of wood.

In order to make all of this work, the cabinet has to take into account the coved lip on the drawer fronts, the method used to mount the drawers in the cabinet, and the final size of the drawers. Plus, the drawers are joined with dovetails cut in a jig. This dictates specific heights for the drawers. These design considerations are discussed in more detail in the Technique article on building drawers that begins on page 28.

HALF-BLIND DOVETAILS. I used half-blind dovetails to join the drawer parts. They're not only attractive, but they're also functional, since there will be stress placed directly on the joints when the drawers are opened and closed. And I used a half-blind dovetail jig to make routing these dovetails easier. (See the Joinery article starting on page 56 for more on machine-cut dovetails.)

MATERIALS. I used mahogany for all visible parts on this project. On the parts that aren't visible, like the drawer sides and backs, I used a less expensive wood. Poplar or sycamore are two good choices. But for the panels, drawer bottoms, and back, I used hardwood plywood.

OPTIONS. Add a frame and panel top with miters on the front of the frame to change the chest's look. See the Designer's Notebook on page 27.

EXPLODED VIEW

OVERALL DIMENSIONS:
32W x 17¾D x 33¾H

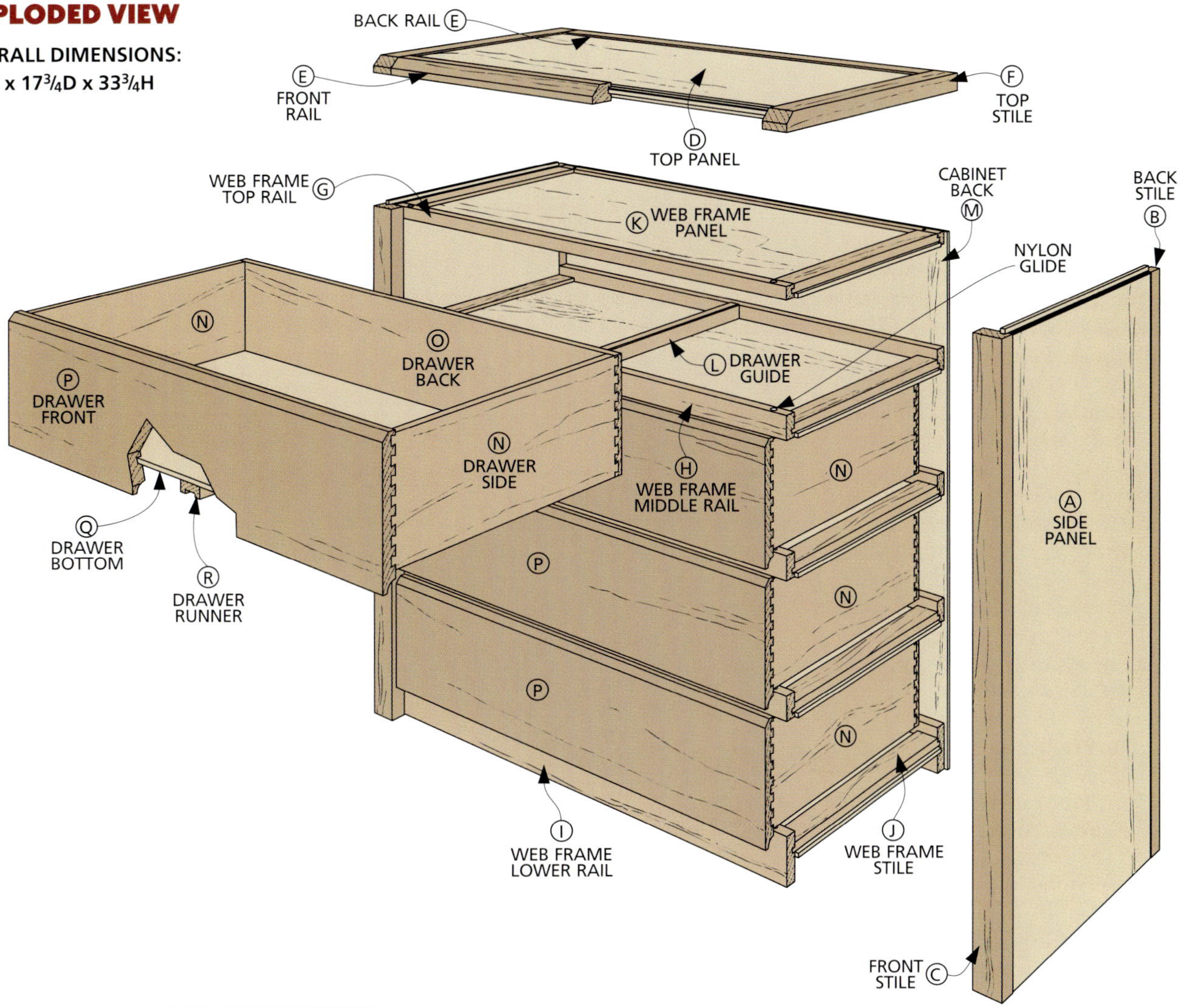

BACK RAIL (E)

(E)
FRONT
RAIL

(F)
TOP
STILE

(D) TOP PANEL

WEB FRAME
TOP RAIL (G)

(K) WEB FRAME
PANEL

CABINET
BACK
(M)

BACK
STILE
(B)

NYLON
GLIDE

(N)

(O)
DRAWER
BACK

(L) DRAWER
GUIDE

(P)
DRAWER
FRONT

(N)
DRAWER
SIDE

(H)
WEB FRAME
MIDDLE RAIL

(N)

(A)
SIDE
PANEL

(Q)
DRAWER
BOTTOM

(R)
DRAWER
RUNNER

(P)

(P)

(N)

(I)
WEB FRAME
LOWER RAIL

(P)

(N)

(J)
WEB FRAME
STILE

FRONT (C)
STILE

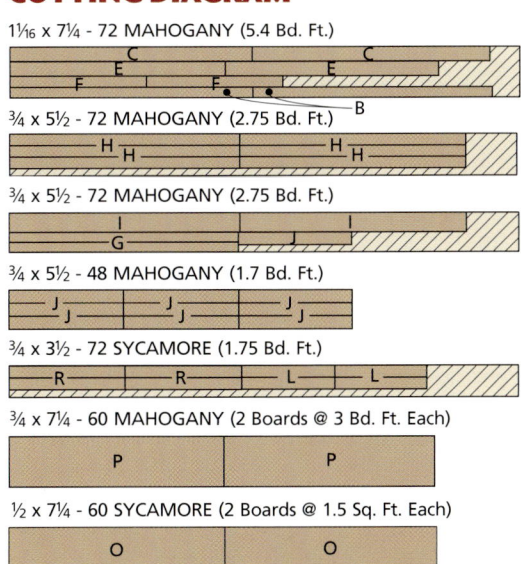

MATERIALS LIST

SIDES
A Panels (2)		¾ ply - 16⅛ x 32⅞
B Back Stiles (2)		1¹⁄₁₆ x ¾ - 32⅝
C Front Stiles (2)		1¹⁄₁₆ x 1⅝ - 32⅝

TOP
D Panel (1)		¾ ply - 15 x 29¼
E Front/Back Rails (2)		1¹⁄₁₆ x 1⅝ - 28¾
F Stiles (2)		1¹⁄₁₆ x 1⅝ - 17¾

WEB FRAMES
G Top Rails (2)		¾ x ¾ - 30⁷⁄₁₆
H Middle Rails (6)		¾ x 1⅜ - 30⁷⁄₁₆
I Lower Rails (2)		¾ x 2¾ - 30⁷⁄₁₆
J Stiles (10)		¾ x 1⅝ - 15⅜
K Panels (5)		¼ ply - 15⅜ x 28¼
L Drawer Guides (4)		¾ x ¹⁵⁄₁₆ - 15⅝
M Cabinet Back (1)		¼ ply - 30¹⁵⁄₁₆ x 32⅝

DRAWERS
N Sides (8)		½ x 6⅛ - 15
O Backs (4)		½ x 6⅛ - 28⅝
P Fronts (4)		¾ x 7 - 28⅝
Q Bottoms (4)		¼ ply - 15 x 28⅛
R Runners (4)		¾ x 1½ - 14½

HARDWARE SUPPLIES
(8) Nylon glides

CUTTING DIAGRAM

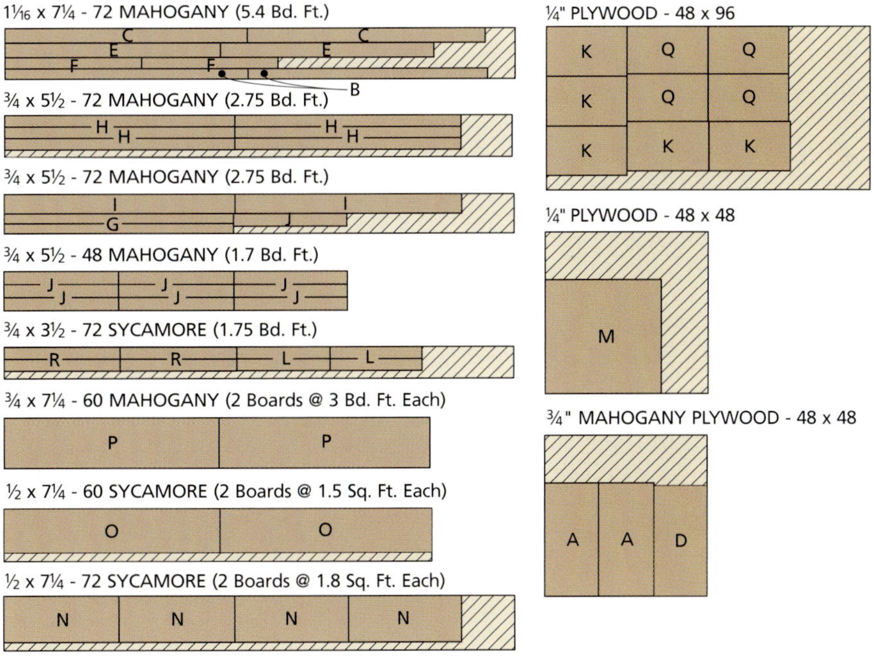

1¹⁄₁₆ x 7¼ - 72 MAHOGANY (5.4 Bd. Ft.)
C — C
E — E
F — F
B

¾ x 5½ - 72 MAHOGANY (2.75 Bd. Ft.)
H — H — H — H

¾ x 5½ - 72 MAHOGANY (2.75 Bd. Ft.)
I — I
G

¾ x 5½ - 48 MAHOGANY (1.7 Bd. Ft.)
J — J — J — J

¾ x 3½ - 72 SYCAMORE (1.75 Bd. Ft.)
R — R — L — L

¾ x 7¼ - 60 MAHOGANY (2 Boards @ 3 Bd. Ft. Each)
P — P

½ x 7¼ - 60 SYCAMORE (2 Boards @ 1.5 Sq. Ft. Each)
O — O

½ x 7¼ - 72 SYCAMORE (2 Boards @ 1.8 Sq. Ft. Each)
N — N — N — N

¼" PLYWOOD - 48 x 96
K	Q	Q
K	Q	Q
K	K	K

¼" PLYWOOD - 48 x 48
M

¾" MAHOGANY PLYWOOD - 48 x 48
| A | A | D |

The sides of the chest consist of plywood panels with hardwood stiles on the front and back edges *(Fig. 1)*. The plywood panels also have a series of $1/4$" dadoes routed on the inside face for web frames that are added to the cabinet later. (These frames are used to connect the cabinet sides, and they also support the drawers.)

CUT SIDES. Start by cutting the $3/4$"-plywood side panels (A) to size *(Fig. 1)*. The length (height) of these panels was determined by the spacing needed for the drawers and web frames. (This is explained in detail in the Technique article on page 28.)

The plywood panels will be $16 1/8$" wide. But rather than cutting the plywood to this width, I cut it a little more than double-wide ($32 1/2$") so I could rout the dadoes for the web frames in one pass *(Fig. 2)*. This assures the dadoes are routed in the same position on both sides.

ROUT DADOES. To rout the dadoes, clamp an auxiliary fence to the plywood and use a hand-held router with a $1/4$" straight bit *(Fig. 2)*.

I started with the top dado. This dado should be $3/4$" down from the top edge of the plywood *(Fig. 2a)*. (This measurement matches the thickness of the stock for the web frame.)

The position of the next four dadoes is important because they will determine the sizes of the openings for the drawers.

To produce the correct height for the drawer openings, rout these four dadoes so they're exactly $7 5/8$" apart, measuring from the top of each dado *(Fig. 1)*.

After the dadoes are routed, rip the double-wide panel in half and trim it to form two panels, each $16 1/8$" wide.

ROUT TONGUES. Now the tongues can be routed on the front, back, and top edges of each side panel. The tongues on the front and back edges are used to hold a pair of stiles *(Figs. 5 and 6)*. The tongue on the top edge is used to hold a top frame and panel built later.

These tongues fit into the grooves routed in the stiles. To gauge their thickness, I first routed a groove in a test piece with a $1/4$" straight bit. Then I routed the tongues on a router table to fit this groove.

To cut these tongues, I used a $3/8$" straight bit in a router table to rout a $1/4$"-wide rabbet on each face of the plywood panels *(Fig. 3)*. Make adjustments to the depth of cut until the tongue fits the groove in the test piece.

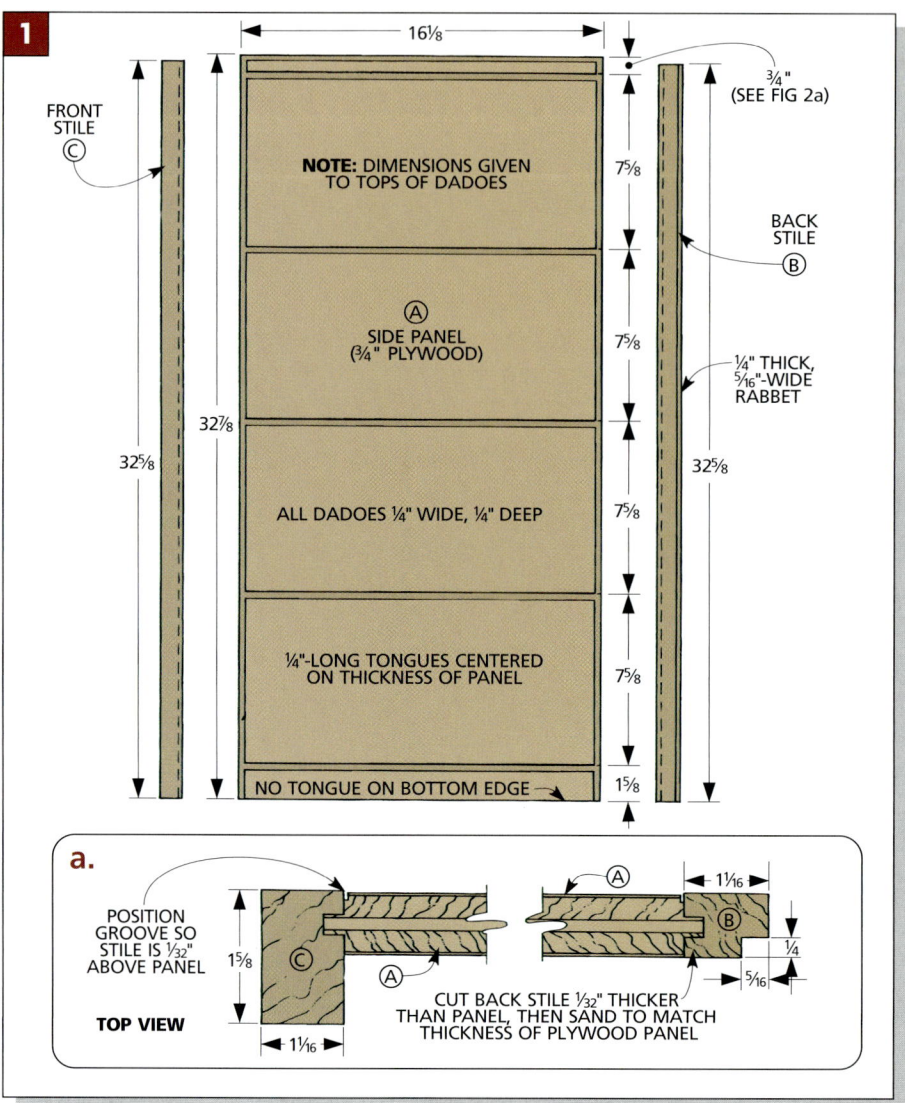

1

16⅛

FRONT STILE C

¾" (SEE FIG 2a)

BACK STILE B

NOTE: DIMENSIONS GIVEN TO TOPS OF DADOES

7⅝

A SIDE PANEL (¾" PLYWOOD)

7⅝

¼" THICK, 5/16"-WIDE RABBET

32⅞

32⅝

ALL DADOES ¼" WIDE, ¼" DEEP

7⅝

32⅝

¼"-LONG TONGUES CENTERED ON THICKNESS OF PANEL

7⅝

NO TONGUE ON BOTTOM EDGE

1⅝

a.

POSITION GROOVE SO STILE IS 1/32" ABOVE PANEL

1⅝

C

A

TOP VIEW

1 1/16

A

1 1/16

B

¼

5/16

CUT BACK STILE 1/32" THICKER THAN PANEL, THEN SAND TO MATCH THICKNESS OF PLYWOOD PANEL

DECORATIVE SHADOW LINE. After the tongues were cut, I added a $1/16$"-wide shadow line on the front, back, and top edges of the panel to set it off in the frame *(Figs. 5 and 6)*. To do this, rout a $1/16$" wide and $1/8$"-deep rabbet on the outside face of the plywood panels *(Fig. 4)*.

STILES

Now the stiles can be added to the front and back edges of the side panels. These pieces are cut from $1 1/16$"-thick stock.

BACK STILE. First, the back stiles (B) are ripped to width so they're just slightly ($1/32$") wider than the thickness of the plywood sides *(Fig. 1a)*. Then the stile can be sanded down flush with the plywood side panels.

Then the back stiles are cut to length so they are equal to the distance from the bottom of the plywood panel to the shoulder of the tongue on the top edge.

JOINERY. After the back stiles are cut to size, rout a $1/4$"-square groove on the edge of the stile to match the tongue on the back edge of the panel *(Fig. 1a)*. Rout this groove on the router table. Save this router table setup. (You'll need it when cutting a groove later on the front stile.)

Also, cut a $5/16$"-wide rabbet on the back edge of the edging strip for the $1/4$" plywood back *(Figs. 1a and 5)*.

Note: I used a table saw to cut this rabbet because it produces a clean edge along the shoulder of the rabbet.

FRONT STILE. Next, the front stiles (C) are ripped $1 5/8$" wide and cut to length *(Fig. 1a)*. Then a $1/4$"-square groove is routed on the inside face to fit a tongue on the front edge of the side panel *(Fig. 1a)*.

This groove is positioned exactly the same distance from the outside edge as the groove on the back stile. (That is, so the edge lines up exactly with the surface of the plywood panel.)

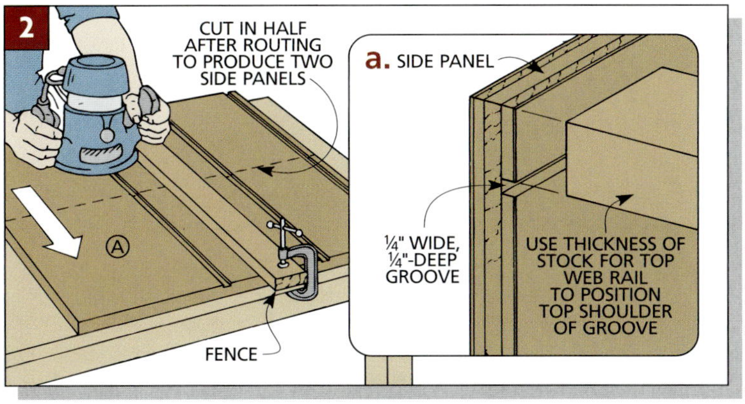
2
CUT IN HALF AFTER ROUTING TO PRODUCE TWO SIDE PANELS
A
FENCE
a. SIDE PANEL
¼" WIDE, ¼"-DEEP GROOVE
USE THICKNESS OF STOCK FOR TOP WEB RAIL TO POSITION TOP SHOULDER OF GROOVE

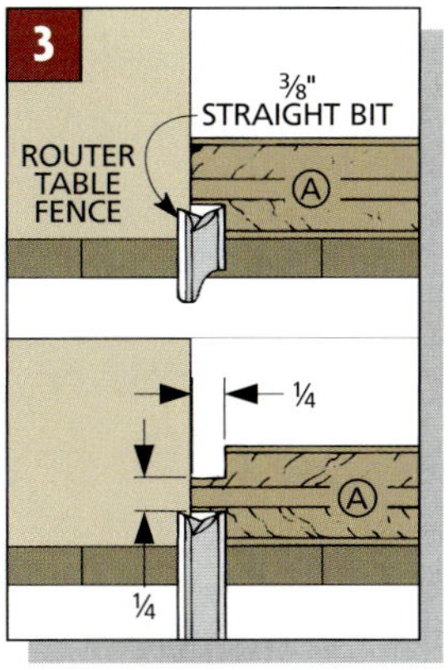
3
ROUTER TABLE FENCE
⅜" STRAIGHT BIT
A
¼
A
¼

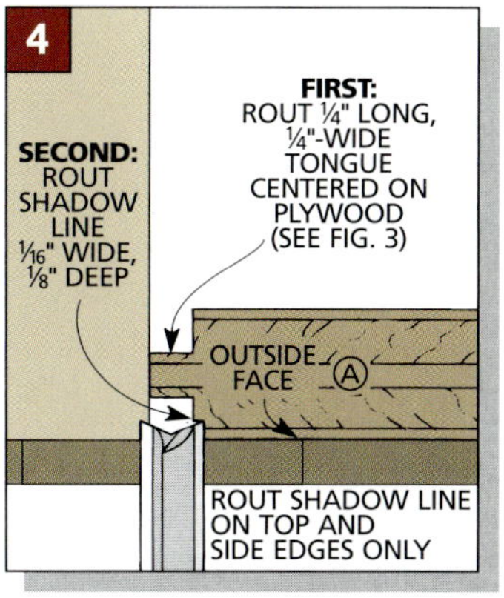
4
SECOND: ROUT SHADOW LINE 1⁄16" WIDE, ⅛" DEEP
FIRST: ROUT ¼" LONG, ¼"-WIDE TONGUE CENTERED ON PLYWOOD (SEE FIG. 3)
OUTSIDE FACE
A
ROUT SHADOW LINE ON TOP AND SIDE EDGES ONLY

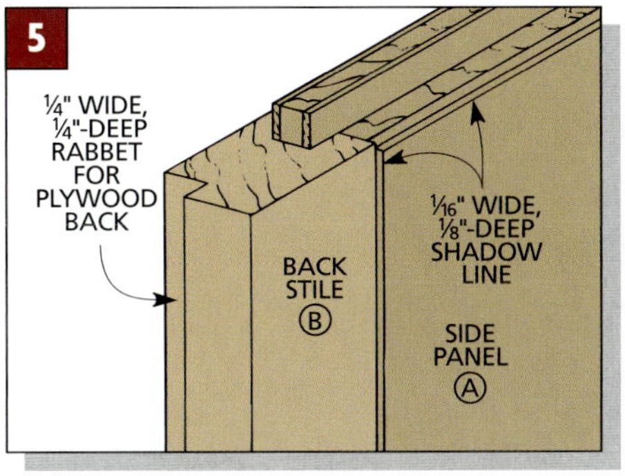
5
¼" WIDE, ¼"-DEEP RABBET FOR PLYWOOD BACK
BACK STILE
B
1⁄16" WIDE, ⅛"-DEEP SHADOW LINE
SIDE PANEL
A

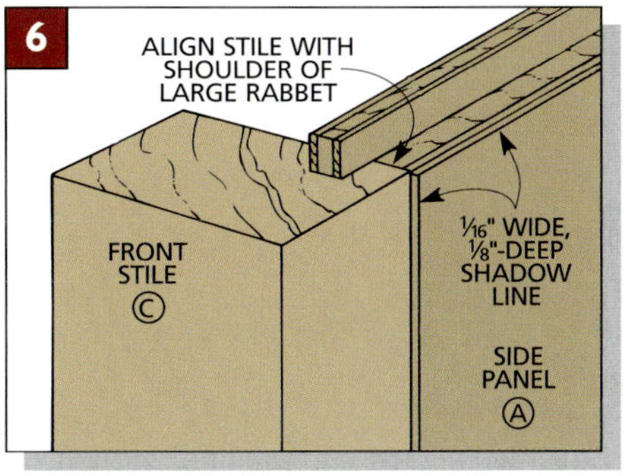
6
ALIGN STILE WITH SHOULDER OF LARGE RABBET
FRONT STILE
C
1⁄16" WIDE, ⅛"-DEEP SHADOW LINE
SIDE PANEL
A

ASSEMBLY. Finally, glue the stiles onto the side panels. Be sure the top of each stile is flush with the shoulder on the top of the side panel *(Figs. 5 and 6)*.

TOP FRAME & PANEL

To complete the basic cabinet, the sides are joined together with a top frame and panel and five web frames.

TOP PANEL. The first step in building the top frame is to cut the $^3/_4$" plywood panel (D) to size *(Fig. 7)*. Then cut rabbets on both faces to form $^1/_4$"-long tongues on all four edges. Also rout a $^1/_{16}$" wide, $^1/_8$"-deep shoulder on the outside face of the plywood *(Fig. 7c)*.

FRAME. After the panel is cut, the frame pieces can be cut to size. Start by cutting the front and back rails (E) to length so they're equal to the shoulder to shoulder length of the panel *(Fig. 7)*.

The width of the rails should be $1^5/_8$". However, this width may have to be adjusted because you want to be sure that when these rails are attached to the panel, the total width of this top assembly is equal to the width of the cabinet sides.

As for the top stiles (F), they're cut $1^5/_8$" wide and as long as the cabinet sides are wide ($17^3/_4$").

GROOVES. Next, grooves are cut in the frame pieces to accept the tongues already cut on the top panel. On the front and back rails, I routed a groove on the edge of both pieces so the face of each rail is slightly above ($^1/_{32}$") the surface of the panel *(Figs. 7a and 7c)*.

But on the top stiles (F), the groove has to be stopped at least $^1/_2$" from each end to prevent it from showing *(Fig. 7)*. I routed this stopped groove with a straight bit in the router table, making a plunge cut to start the groove and lifting the stile off the bit to end the cut.

Then I routed an identical stopped groove on the bottom edge of the stiles *(Fig. 7a)*. This groove is for attaching the top frame to the cabinet sides.

BEVEL EDGE. After the grooves are cut, glue all four frame members to the top panel. When the glue has had time to set up, rip a $^5/_8$" wide, 45° bevel on the front edge of the top frame *(Fig. 7b)*.

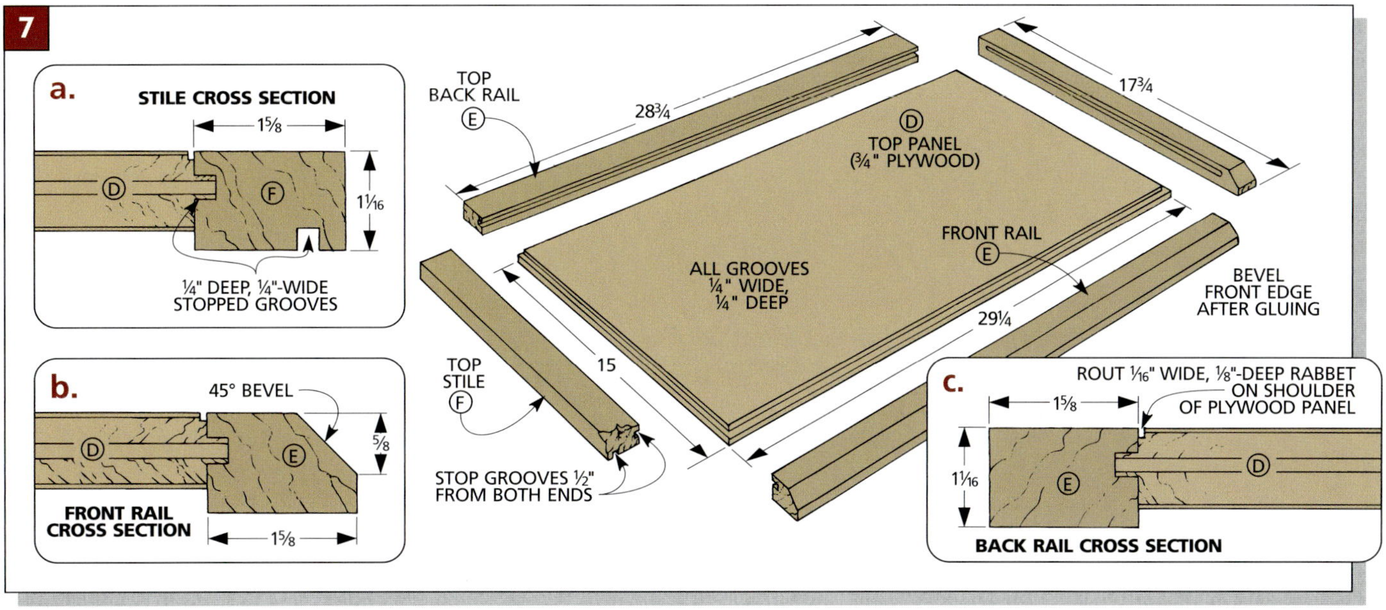
7
a. STILE CROSS SECTION
1⅝
D
F
1 1⁄16
¼" DEEP, ¼"-WIDE STOPPED GROOVES
b. 45° BEVEL
D
E
⅝
FRONT RAIL CROSS SECTION
1⅝
TOP BACK RAIL
E
28¾
D
TOP PANEL (¾" PLYWOOD)
17¾
FRONT RAIL
E
ALL GROOVES ¼" WIDE, ¼" DEEP
29¼
BEVEL FRONT EDGE AFTER GLUING
TOP STILE
F
15
STOP GROOVES ½" FROM BOTH ENDS
c. ROUT 1⁄16" WIDE, ⅛"-DEEP RABBET ON SHOULDER OF PLYWOOD PANEL
1⅝
1 1⁄16
E
D
BACK RAIL CROSS SECTION

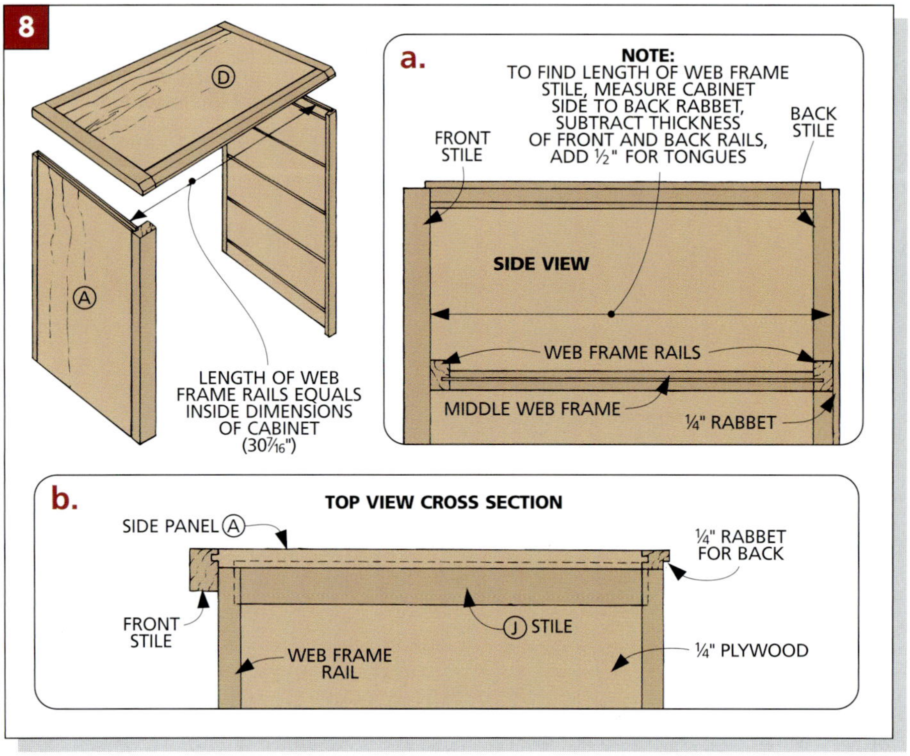
8
D
A
LENGTH OF WEB FRAME RAILS EQUALS INSIDE DIMENSIONS OF CABINET ($30\frac{7}{16}$")
a.
NOTE:
TO FIND LENGTH OF WEB FRAME STILE, MEASURE CABINET SIDE TO BACK RABBET, SUBTRACT THICKNESS OF FRONT AND BACK RAILS, ADD ½" FOR TONGUES
FRONT STILE
BACK STILE
SIDE VIEW
WEB FRAME RAILS
MIDDLE WEB FRAME
¼" RABBET
b.
TOP VIEW CROSS SECTION
SIDE PANEL A
¼" RABBET FOR BACK
FRONT STILE
J STILE
WEB FRAME RAIL
¼" PLYWOOD

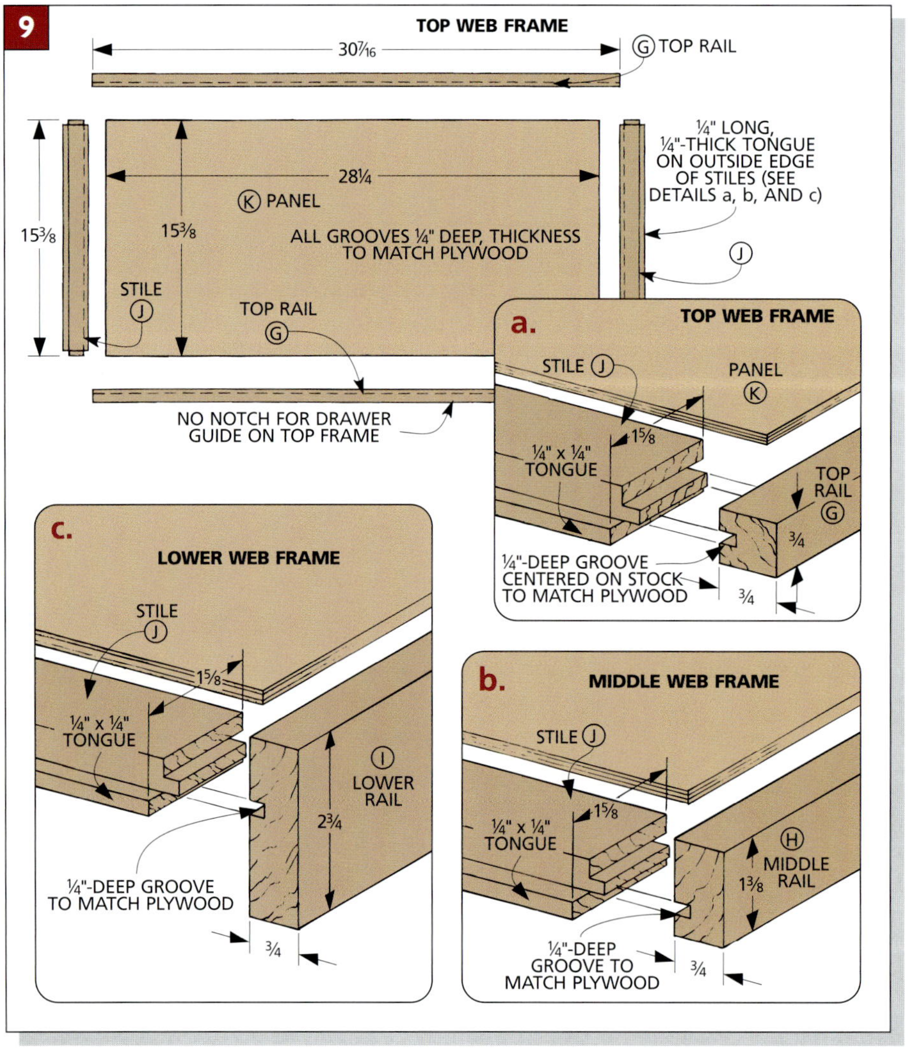
9
TOP WEB FRAME
$30\frac{7}{16}$
G TOP RAIL
¼" LONG, ¼"-THICK TONGUE ON OUTSIDE EDGE OF STILES (SEE DETAILS a, b, AND c)
$28\frac{1}{4}$
K PANEL
$15\frac{3}{8}$
$15\frac{3}{8}$
ALL GROOVES ¼" DEEP, THICKNESS TO MATCH PLYWOOD
STILE J
TOP RAIL G
J
NO NOTCH FOR DRAWER GUIDE ON TOP FRAME
a.
TOP WEB FRAME
STILE J
PANEL K
$1\frac{5}{8}$
¼" x ¼" TONGUE
TOP RAIL G
¾
¼"-DEEP GROOVE CENTERED ON STOCK TO MATCH PLYWOOD
¾
c.
LOWER WEB FRAME
STILE J
$1\frac{5}{8}$
¼" x ¼" TONGUE
I LOWER RAIL
$2\frac{3}{4}$
¼"-DEEP GROOVE TO MATCH PLYWOOD
¾
b.
MIDDLE WEB FRAME
STILE J
$1\frac{5}{8}$
¼" x ¼" TONGUE
H MIDDLE RAIL
$1\frac{3}{8}$
¼"-DEEP GROOVE TO MATCH PLYWOOD
¾

WEB FRAMES

Now that the cabinet sides and the top frame are complete, the five web frames can be built. These frames connect the cabinet sides and make openings for four identically-sized drawers.

RAILS. In order to find the size of each web frame, first dry-assemble the completed top frame to the cabinet sides. Now, measure the distance between the sides to find the exact length of the top, middle, and lower web frame rails (G, H, I) *(Figs. 8 and 9)*. (In my case, this was $30\frac{7}{16}$".) But the width of these rails will vary with each frame: the top rails (G) are $\frac{3}{4}$" wide, the middle rails (H) are $1\frac{3}{8}$" wide, and the lower rails (I) are $2\frac{3}{4}$" wide *(Figs. 9a, 9b, and 9c)*.

STILES. To find the length for the web frame stiles (J), you have to do a little math: first, measure the distance between the back face of the side front stile and the rabbet on the back stile ($16\frac{3}{8}$" for me) *(Fig. 8a)*. Then subtract the thickness of the top rails ($1\frac{1}{2}$"), and add $\frac{1}{2}$" for the two $\frac{1}{4}$"-long stub tenons that will be cut on the ends of the web frame stiles (J). This should produce a final length of $15\frac{3}{8}$" for the web frame stiles. The width of all the stiles is $1\frac{5}{8}$".

GROOVES FOR PANEL. After the web frame rails and stiles are cut to size, a groove is cut on the inside edge of each piece for a web frame panel. The groove in each web frame stile is centered on the edge of the piece. They should match the thickness of the plywood that will be used for the web frame panels.

TOP WEB FRAME. The groove in the top rails (G) is also centered on the thickness of the rail — the same as the stiles.

However, the procedure for cutting the grooves on the other rails varies because of their width.

MIDDLE WEB FRAMES. The three middle web frame rails (H) are $1\frac{3}{8}$" wide *(Fig. 9b)*. This extra width means the groove for the stile can't be centered. Instead, it's positioned the same distance from the bottom edge as the groove on the stiles *(Fig. 9b)*.

To cut these grooves, set the saw fence using the groove in a stile as a guide. Make the first pass, and then adjust the fence to widen the groove to match the thickness of the $\frac{1}{4}$" plywood, and make a second pass to finish the groove.

LOWER WEB FRAME. On the lower web frame, the extra-wide lower rails (I) also serve as a kickboard for the cabinet. The

¼"-deep groove in these web frame rails is a little bit tricky to cut.

To locate the position of the groove, I used a rail from one of the middle frames as a guide *(Fig. 10)*. Line up the top edges of both pieces, and mark the location of the groove on the lower rail (I). Then cut the groove using the mark as a guide.

JOINERY. After all the grooves are cut, stub tenons are cut on the ends of the web frame stiles (J) to fit the grooves in the rails. This is simply a matter of cutting two rabbets on the ends of the stiles to produce the stub tenon *(Figs. 9a, 9b, and 9c)*.

Next, cut a rabbet on the outside top edge of all the web frame stiles to produce a tongue that fits the grooves in the sides of the cabinet *(Fig. 9)*.

Finally, cut a notch on the front rail of the three middle frames and the bottom frame *(Fig. 11)*. This notch is used to attach the drawer guides.

ASSEMBLY. When all the work has been completed on the frame members, dry-assemble them and measure the inside opening to determine the size of the web frame panels (K). Finally, glue and clamp the web frames together with the plywood panels in place.

DRAWER GUIDE & BACK

When the web frames are complete, the next step is to attach drawer guides (L) to the tops of the web frames *(Fig. 14)*. Cut each drawer guide wide enough so the top edge of the guide is ¹⁄₁₆" above the front rail *(Fig. 12)*. (This keeps the drawer from dragging against the rail.) Then trim the guides to length so they butt against the back rail and extend to the front edge of the front rail *(Fig. 14)*.

Next, cut a rabbet on the front end of each guide so it overlaps the notch in the front rail *(Figs. 12 and 14)*. Also, chamfer the top edges of the guides slightly to reduce binding. Then glue the guides to the plywood panel of the web frame so they're centered on the length of the rails.

DRAWER GLIDES. The last step before gluing the cabinet together is to drill holes for the nylon drawer glides on the lower four web frames *(Fig. 14)*.

ASSEMBLY. At this point, glue the cabinet sides together with all five web frames in place, making sure to keep each of the web frames tight against the front moldings on the cabinet sides. Next, cut the cabinet back to size from ¼" plywood *(Fig. 14)*. Then glue the cabinet back and the top frame and panel assembly in place.

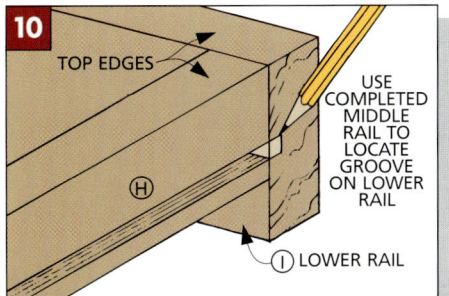

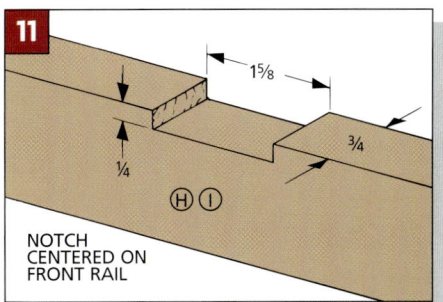

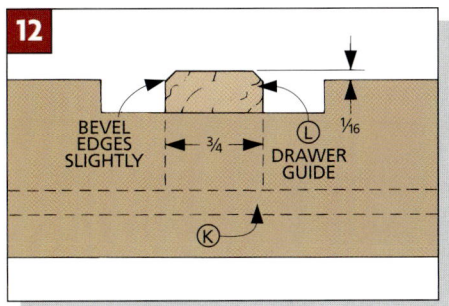

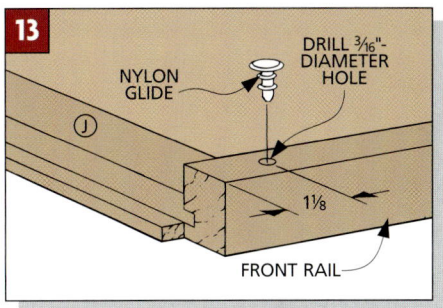

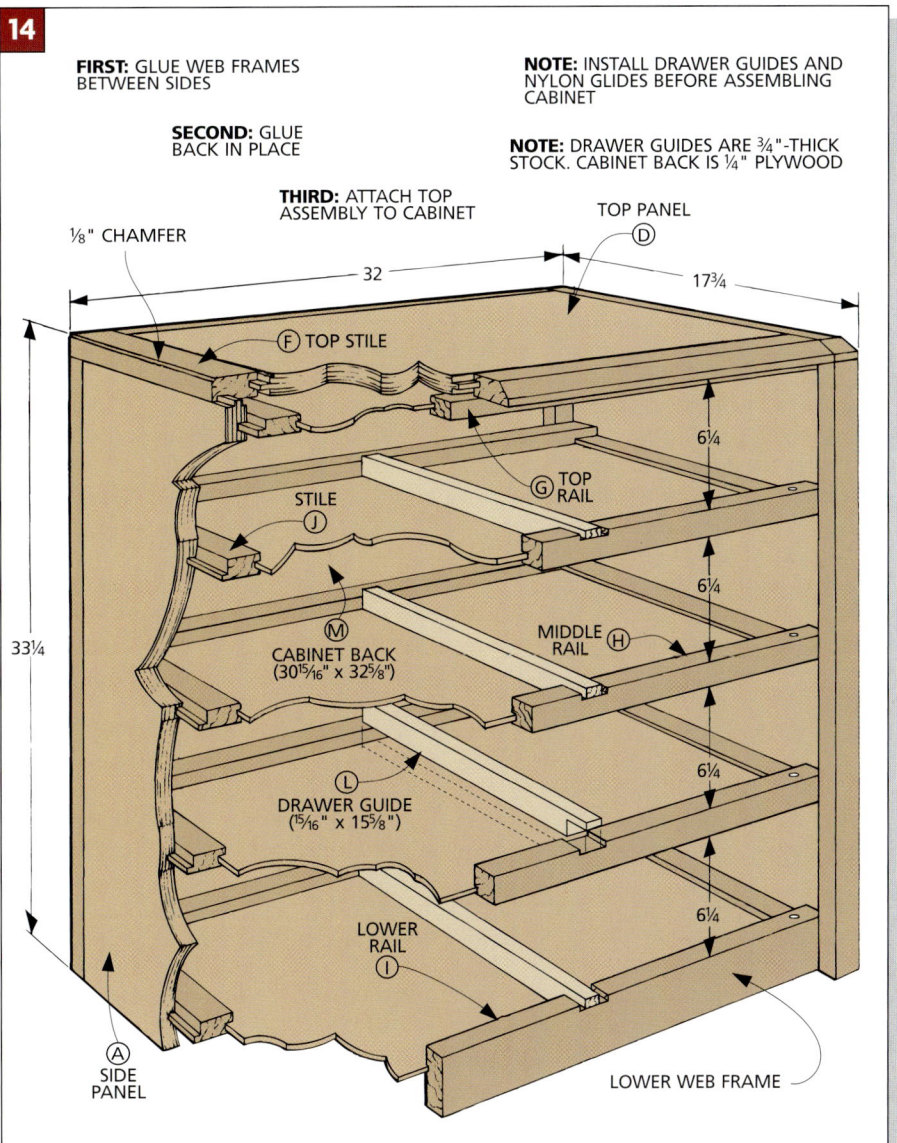

The drawer fronts are wider than the drawer sides to provide an overlap with the web frames. The Technique article on page 28 takes you through routing this variation of a dovetail joint.

DRAWERS

At last, we arrive at the whole point of building this chest: the drawers. The drawers are designed with a concealed cove on the bottom edge of each drawer front *(Fig. 16)*. Although this makes the drawer fronts interesting from a design and construction standpoint, it also makes the drawers slightly more complicated to build. But don't worry. I'll walk you through the process.

SIDES AND BACK. The first step is to cut ¹⁄₂"-thick drawer sides (N) and backs (O) to width so they're ¹⁄₈" narrower than the height of the opening between the web frames *(Figs. 15 and 16)*.

DRAWER FRONTS. The drawer fronts (P) are cut ³⁄₄" wider than the height of the drawer opening to allow for the overlap on the web frames, and for the ¹⁄₂" cove on the bottom edge *(Fig. 16)*.

JOINERY. To join these drawers, I wanted to use half-blind dovetails. When making several drawers like this, it's easier, and certainly faster, to use a router and dovetail jig to cut these joints.

Normally, joining the sides of a drawer using a dovetail jig is relatively easy. But when the drawer front extends both above and below the drawer sides, routing the dovetails requires some special techniques. Luckily, the overlap of the drawer fronts can be produced easily by simply cutting the drawer front wider than normal and using a small shim to position the drawer side in the dovetail jig.

Note: To construct these drawers, see the Technique article on page 28. For general information on routing machine-cut dovetails, turn to page 56.

COVE. Once the corner joinery is complete, a ¹⁄₂" cove is cut on the bottom

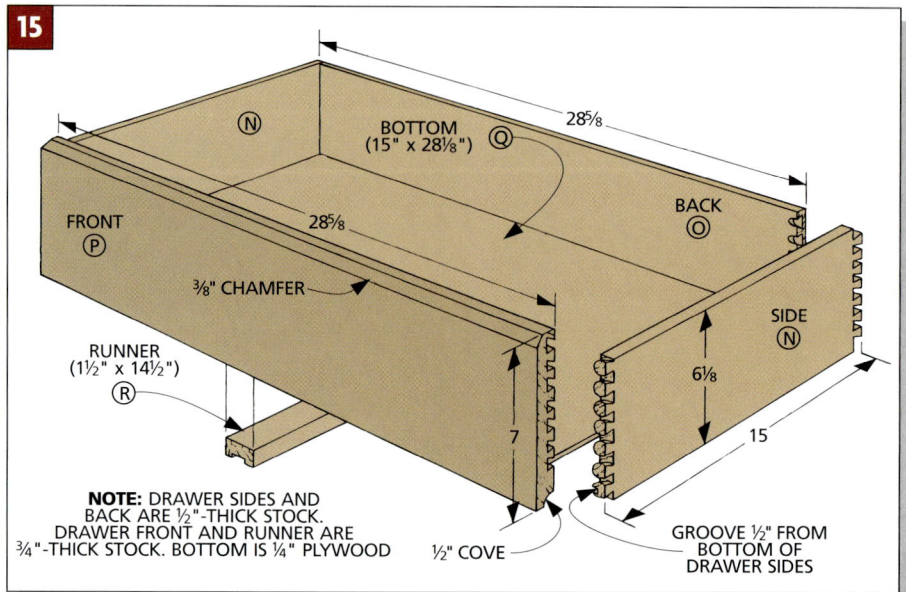

NOTE: DRAWER SIDES AND BACK ARE ¹⁄₂"-THICK STOCK. DRAWER FRONT AND RUNNER ARE ³⁄₄"-THICK STOCK. BOTTOM IS ¹⁄₄" PLYWOOD

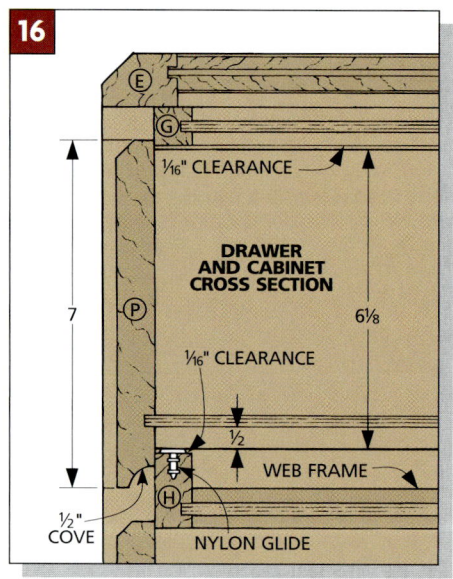

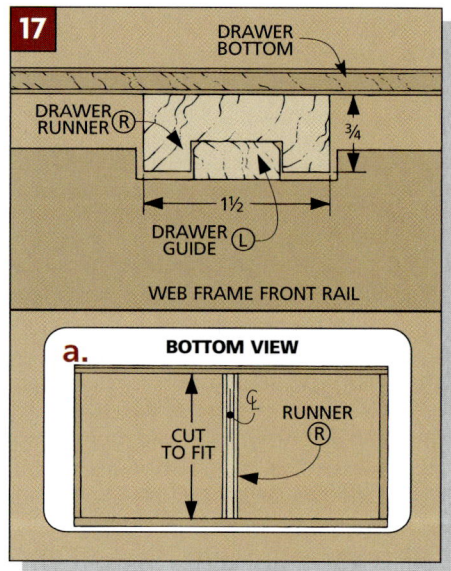

inside edge of the drawer fronts to provide a finger pull for opening the drawers *(Fig. 16)*. Then a ³⁄₈" chamfer is cut on the top edge of each drawer front to provide enough room for easy access to the finger pull on the drawer above it *(Fig. 15)*.

DRAWER BOTTOMS. Next, a groove is cut for the plywood drawer bottoms (Q). Position this groove ¹⁄₂" from the bottom edge of the drawer sides *(Fig. 16)*.

ASSEMBLY. After the grooves are cut, dry-assemble a drawer and take measurements for the bottom. Then cut the bottoms to size and glue the drawers together with the bottom in place.

DRAWER GUIDES. To complete the drawer guide system, cut the drawer runners (R) to size *(Fig. 15)*. Then rout a groove down the center of the runner so it's just slightly wider than the width of the

drawer guide (L). Finally, you'll need to glue a runner to each of the drawer bottoms, centered on the width of the drawer *(Fig. 17)*. To do this, first fasten a runner to a bottom, checking its operation to ensure that it's centered. Then glue each runner in place, waxing the runner and guide to help them slide smoothly.

FINISHING TOUCHES

One of the last steps to completing the Chest of Drawers is to soften any sharp edges by routing an ¹⁄₈" chamfer on all of the exposed edges, except the back edge of the cabinet sides.

I finished the chest with three coats of interior polyurethane finish, lightly sanding between each coat with 400 grit wet-or-dry sandpaper. ∎

DESIGNER'S NOTEBOOK

A couple of changes give the Chest of Drawers a traditional appearance. Start by wrapping the top panel with rails and stiles that are mitered at the front. Chamfers and knobs complete the drawer fronts.

CONSTRUCTION NOTES:

■ To give the chest a more traditional appeal, I modified the top frame and panel and drawers. In the process of changing the drawers, I left off the cove at the bottom and I decided to use a basic wooden drawer knob instead.

To get started, build the cabinet sides and the web frames as before.

■ Now start construction of the top frame by ripping a new front rail blank (S) and two blanks for stiles (F) to width from $1^1/_{16}$"-thick stock. Cut them slightly longer than needed so you can miter these pieces to exact length later *(Fig. 1)*. (My front rail blank was 34" long and the stile blanks were each 19" long.)

■ Next, use the router table to cut $1/_4$"-deep grooves in the bottom and one edge of the stiles. The grooves are sized to hold the $1/_4$" plywood panel. But this time, since the stiles will be mitered on the front end, these grooves are stopped at the back end only.

■ To size the top stiles (and front rail), you'll need to dry-assemble the side assemblies along with the top and lower web frames. Then add the top stiles to the assembly, making sure they're flush with the back edges of the side assemblies and that the grooves on the edges are facing in *(Fig. 1)*. Now, mark the miter so you will end up with a $1/_2$" reveal at the front end of the cabinet *(Fig. 1a)*.

■ Cut the miters on the top stiles and replace them onto the cabinet assembly. Now you can measure the exact length of the top front rail (S) *(Fig. 1)*. (Mine was 33".) Once the top front rail is mitered to length, and dry-assembled in place, you can measure for the top panel (D) and back rail (E). Then cut each of

them to size and install them as you did before (refer to *Fig. 6* on page 23).

■ All that's left is to make the drawers. Each of them are exactly the same size as before, except this time instead of routing

a cove in the bottom edge of the drawer, I routed a $3/_8$" chamfer on all four edges of the drawer fronts (P) *(Figs. 2 and 2a)*.

■ Finally, add two wooden knobs to each drawer front *(Fig. 2)*.

MATERIALS LIST

CHANGED PARTS

E	Top Back Rail (1)	$1^1/_{16}$ x $1^5/_8$ - $28^3/_4$
F	Top Stiles (2)	$1^1/_{16}$ x $2^1/_8$ - $18^1/_4$

NEW PART

S	Top Front Rail (1)	$1^1/_{16}$ x $2^1/_8$ - 33

HARDWARE SUPPLIES

(8) $1^1/_2$" wooden knobs

TRADITIONAL CHEST

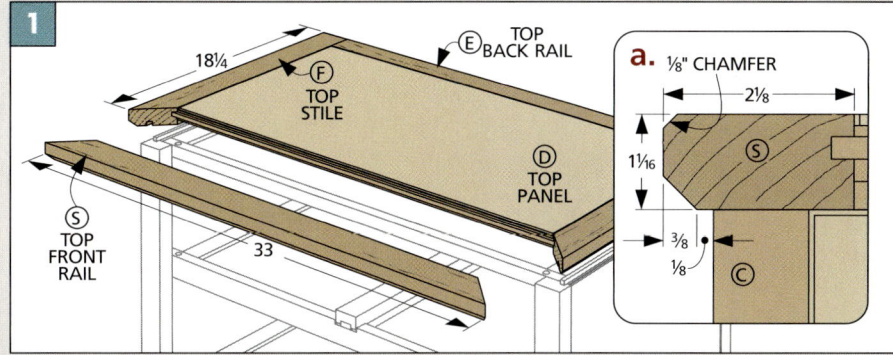

TECHNIQUE .... *Building Drawers*

The drawers used in the chest and the Night Stand (pages 14-19) are interesting from a woodworking standpoint. But not just because they feature half-blind dovetail construction.

To make them even more interesting, I decided to have clean drawer fronts with no drawer pulls. Instead, the lower edge of the drawer front has a concealed cove which is used to open the drawer.

This feature had to be taken into consideration when designing the cabinet, as well as the drawer. That's because the front has to have room for the cove, and the cabinet needs to provide enough clearance for your fingers to reach the cove lip to open the drawer.

DESIGN CONSIDERATIONS

I mentioned on the first page of this project that I had to design the drawers first, then design the cabinet around the drawers. Now I'll explain why.

The chest has openings that are $6\frac{1}{4}$" high, which accounts for drawer sides that are $6\frac{1}{8}$" high, plus $\frac{1}{8}$" for clearance. These are not arbitrary dimensions.

DOVETAIL SPACING. The $6\frac{1}{8}$" height produces the proper spacing for a dovetail joint that's cut in a dovetail jig. This means that the dovetails are evenly spaced on the drawer side with a half pin on the top and bottom edge (*Fig. 1*).

Note: Most commercial dovetail jigs allow you to cut half-blind dovetails in increments of $\frac{7}{8}$", with the smallest drawer width possible being $1\frac{3}{4}$". The chest uses one of these increments ($6\frac{1}{8}$"), and the Night Stand another ($4\frac{3}{8}$").

CLEARANCE. Also figured in the height of the drawer opening is a clearance of $\frac{1}{8}$". This allows $\frac{1}{16}$" for clearance between the top edge of the drawer and the web frame above it, plus $\frac{1}{16}$" for the head of the nylon glide that the bottom edge of the drawer side rides on (*Fig. 1*).

These two allowances demonstrate the importance of planning ahead — you have to know how the drawer is going to be built and how it's to be mounted. By using a nylon glide, you have to plan ahead for the $\frac{1}{16}$" space that it requires. So, we're dealing with rather small tolerances for the cabinet openings.

Note: If there's much more than $\frac{1}{16}$" clearance above the drawer, it will tend to tip down too much when it's opened.

CUT DRAWER PIECES

To build the drawers for the cabinets in the Contemporary Set, I started with the sides and back. The first step is to rip $\frac{1}{2}$"-thick stock to width ($4\frac{3}{8}$" for the Night Stand, $6\frac{1}{8}$" for the Chest of Drawers).

Then these pieces are cut to length. When cutting the sides to length, they must fit the opening with a little room to spare between the back of the drawer and the back of the cabinet.

CUT SIDES TO LENGTH. To do this, first measure the depth of the cabinet. Then subtract the thickness of the drawer front ($\frac{3}{4}$") and the back ($\frac{1}{2}$"), add on the length of the dovetails (they overlap on the front and back a total of $\frac{5}{8}$") and finally subtract the amount of clearance needed at the back (usually $\frac{1}{2}$" is enough). Then cut the drawer sides to length (15" for the Chest of Drawers, $13\frac{3}{4}$" for the Night Stand).

CUT BACK TO LENGTH. Next, the drawer backs can be cut to length. To determine their length measure the width of the cabinet opening and subtract $\frac{1}{8}$" for clearance ($\frac{1}{16}$" on each side).

WIDTH OF FRONT. The only thing left is to cut the fronts to size. My drawer fronts overlap the web frames at both the top and bottom (*Fig. 1*).

But remember, the chest and Night Stand have a drawer pull incorporated in the front, so the overlap is not equal at the top and bottom. I wanted $\frac{1}{8}$" overlap at the top, but a total of $\frac{5}{8}$" overlap was needed at the bottom ($\frac{1}{8}$" for the overlap and $\frac{1}{2}$" for the cove) (*Fig. 1*).

MARK FOR ASSEMBLY. When all the pieces for the drawers are cut to final size, it helps to mark them to keep things straight — especially when the joints are going to be routed on a dovetail jig.

Basically, you have to mark both ends of each drawer piece to indicate which drawer it's for (I use a number for this)

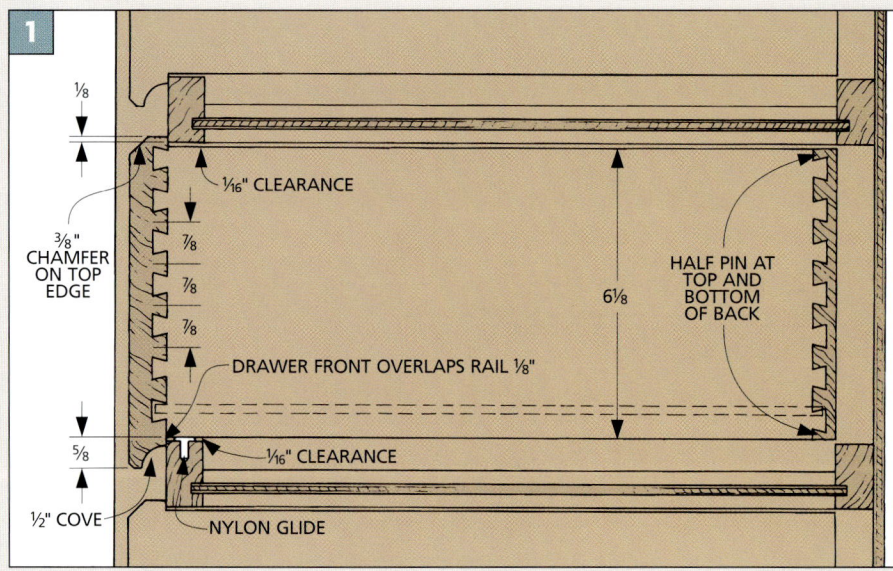

1

$\frac{1}{8}$

$\frac{1}{16}$" CLEARANCE

$\frac{3}{8}$" CHAMFER ON TOP EDGE

$\frac{1}{8}$

$\frac{1}{8}$

$\frac{1}{8}$

HALF PIN AT TOP AND BOTTOM OF BACK

$6\frac{1}{8}$

DRAWER FRONT OVERLAPS RAIL $\frac{1}{8}$"

$\frac{5}{8}$

$\frac{1}{16}$" CLEARANCE

$\frac{1}{2}$" COVE

NYLON GLIDE

and which joint on that drawer it is (a letter) *(Fig. 2)*. The marks should be on the inside face of the drawer, because this is the face that will be visible when the piece is placed on the dovetail jig.

CUT JOINTS

When all the pieces are cut to size and marked, the next step is to cut the joints.

SIDES AND BACK. Start by routing the dovetails to join the back to the two sides. This is the easiest joint to cut because there are no special setups *(Fig. 4)*. (For more on routing machine-cut, half-blind dovetails with a jig, see the Joinery article starting on page 56.)

FRONT JOINTS. Normally, the joint for the drawer front and the sides is no big deal. But for these drawers, the side has to be offset to allow for the lip on the top edge of the drawer front *(Fig. 3)*. And the dovetails have to stop before getting to the bottom of the drawer front to allow for clearance and the cove.

TWO STEPS. Setting up the jig to cut this offset joint presents some challenges. I wound up cutting the joint in two steps.

The first step is to clamp the front on the top side of the jig in the normal manner (with the inside face up and the top edge of the drawer against the stop).

However, to create the $^3/_{16}$" lip on the top edge of the drawer front, the drawer side is jogged over with a $^3/_{16}$" shim *(Fig. 5)*.

Now the dovetails can be routed. But you have to stop before "rounding the corner" to complete the last pin so you don't rout the last socket in the drawer *front*. This leaves room for the cove on the bottom of the drawer front.

The only problem is that the pins have to be completed. To do this, replace the drawer front with a piece of scrap, and continue routing *(Fig. 6)*. (The scrap will help to prevent chipout on the drawer side as the last pin is routed.)

ROUT COVE. Next, rout the cove on the bottom edge of the drawer fronts using a $^1/_2$" cove bit on a router table.

Then I chamfered the top edge at 45°. This allows a little extra space to get your fingers into the cove to open the drawer.

Before assembling the drawer, I also rounded over the top edges of the drawer sides with a $^1/_8$" roundover bit. This is not a necessary step, but it just looks nicer when you open the drawer.

MOUNT THE BOTTOM

The last step in making the drawer is to cut the grooves to mount the drawer bottom. Again, this requires just a little

planning ahead. The grooves should be positioned so they don't create a gap that's visible on the outside of the drawer. You also want to cut them so the drawer bottom is high enough to leave room for the runner that's part of the guide system (refer to *Fig. 16* on page 26).

For these drawers, I positioned the groove so it's $^1/_2$" from the bottom edge of the drawer side *(Fig. 7)*. This, unfortunately, creates a small gap on the back joint. If you don't want to have a gap, you could rout stopped grooves on the back piece, or fill the gap with a plug.

DRAWER BOTTOMS. The drawer bottoms are made out of $^1/_4$" plywood. Since $^1/_4$" plywood is actually more like $^7/_{32}$" thick, I custom-cut the grooves on a table saw, sneaking up on the width.

CUT DRAWER BOTTOM. After the grooves are cut, the drawer bottom itself can be cut to size. To get the final dimensions of the bottom, dry-assemble the drawer and measure the inside width and depth. Then add the depth of the grooves to both dimensions.

I usually cut the drawer bottom so it has a good tight fit in the grooves. This way the bottom will help square up the drawer as the pieces are clamped together. Finally, I assembled all the drawer pieces with glue.

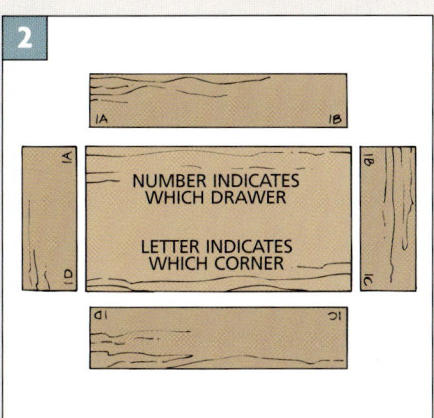

2 NUMBER INDICATES WHICH DRAWER / LETTER INDICATES WHICH CORNER

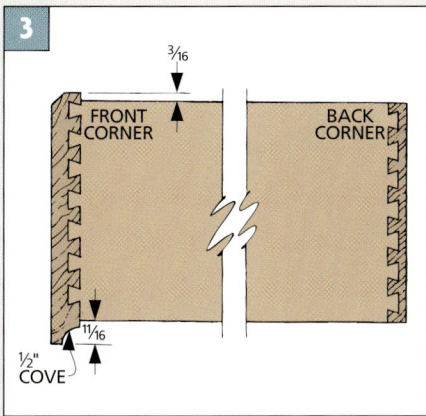

3 3/16 — FRONT CORNER / BACK CORNER — 11/16 — 1/2" COVE

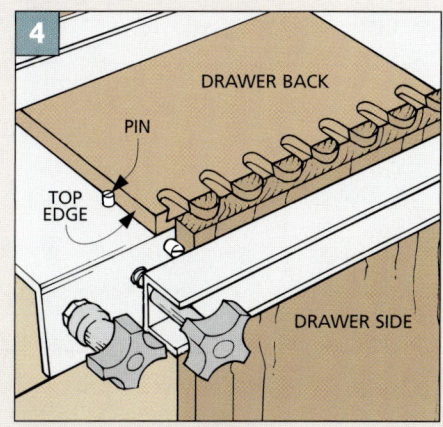

4 DRAWER BACK / PIN / TOP EDGE / DRAWER SIDE

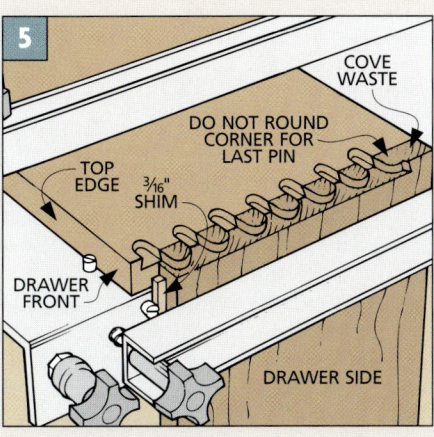

5 COVE WASTE / DO NOT ROUND CORNER FOR LAST PIN / TOP EDGE / 3/16" SHIM / DRAWER FRONT / DRAWER SIDE

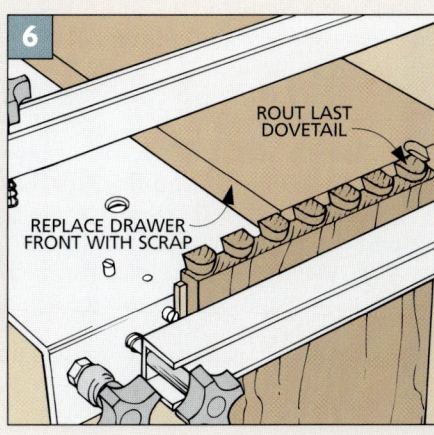

6 ROUT LAST DOVETAIL / REPLACE DRAWER FRONT WITH SCRAP

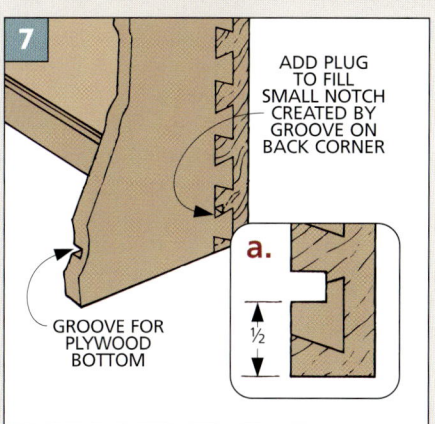

7 ADD PLUG TO FILL SMALL NOTCH CREATED BY GROOVE ON BACK CORNER / GROOVE FOR PLYWOOD BOTTOM / a. 1/2

Wall Mirror

This mirror's simple design complements the Chest of Drawers. With easy-to-cut mortise and tenon joinery for the frame, its sturdy construction will allow you to safely hang it on a wall.

After building the Chest of Drawers (page 20), I decided I should build a mirror to go with it. Usually that would simply mean building a frame and then having the mirror cut to size. But that wasn't the case with my Wall Mirror.

With the design of this mirror, I approached things a little bit differently. Instead of building the frame first, the mirror is cut to size and then the frame is built to fit around it.

Since I designed the project with such close tolerances between the frame and the mirror, this reverse procedure elim-inates any chance of the mirror not fitting the frame perfectly.

WALL-MOUNTED. The frame for this mirror matches the chest design. And that brings up another difference between my mirror and mirrors that you'll find used with most chests of drawers — mine is wall-mounted.

CONTEMPORARY SET. I liked that each piece in this set is slightly different, but they share the same common elements.

For instance, all the frames and panels are easy to build and modify in size. The top rail of the headboard (page 8) is repeated on the mirror, with an identical bottom rail that's flipped upside-down to make a frame. I also wanted each piece to last, so I used solid joinery. A mitered joint for the frame just might not be strong enough to hold a heavy mirror. Finally, I used chamfers and beveled edges on all four pieces in the set. These stylish details tie the Contemporary Set together.

TRADITIONAL MIRROR. Like the other pieces in the Contemporary Set, the mirror can be given a more traditional look. The Designer's Notebook on page 33 shows you how.

EXPLODED VIEW

OVERALL DIMENSIONS:
25¼"W x 1¹⁄₁₆"D x 32"H

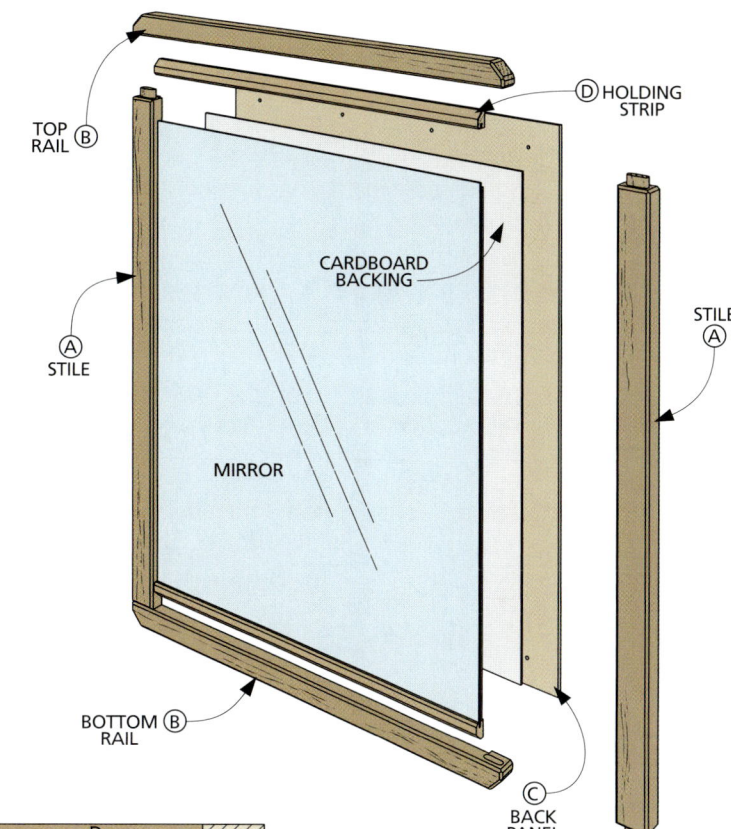

TOP RAIL Ⓑ

Ⓓ HOLDING STRIP

STILE Ⓐ

Ⓐ STILE

CARDBOARD BACKING

MIRROR

BOTTOM Ⓑ RAIL

Ⓒ BACK PANEL

MATERIALS LIST

WOOD

A	Stiles (2)	1¹⁄₁₆ x 1⅝ - 30½
B	Top/Bottom Rails (2)	1¹⁄₁₆ x 1¼ - 25¼
C	Back Panel (1)	¼ ply - 22¾ x 30¼
D	Holding Strips (2)	⅝ x ⅞ - 22

HARDWARE SUPPLIES
(8) No. 6 x ½" Fh woodscrews
(1) ⅛" mirror (22" x 26¹⁵⁄₁₆")
(2 pcs.) ⅛"-thick cardboard backing (22" x 26⁷⁄₁₆")
(2) Keyhole hangers w/ screws
(2) No. 8 x 1¼" Rh woodscrews

CUTTING DIAGRAM

1¹⁄₁₆ x 4 - 84 (3.5 Bd. Ft.)

A   B   D

NOTE: ALSO NEED ONE 24" x 48" PIECE OF ¼" PLYWOOD FOR PART C

FRAME

To make sure the frame is sized correctly, I had the mirror cut to size first (22" x 26¹⁵⁄₁₆") at a local glass store. After it was cut and the edges were burnished, I started construction on the frame. It's simply four pieces of ¾"-thick hardwood joined with mortise and tenon joints.

CUT PIECES. The first step is to cut the frame pieces to size *(Fig. 1)*. The stiles (A) are ripped to width (1⅝"), and 3⁹⁄₁₆" longer than the length of the mirror (mine were 30½"). Then the top and bottom rails (B) are ripped to width (1¼"). The rails need to be cut 3⁵⁄₁₆" longer than the width of the mirror. (In my case, this was 25¼".)

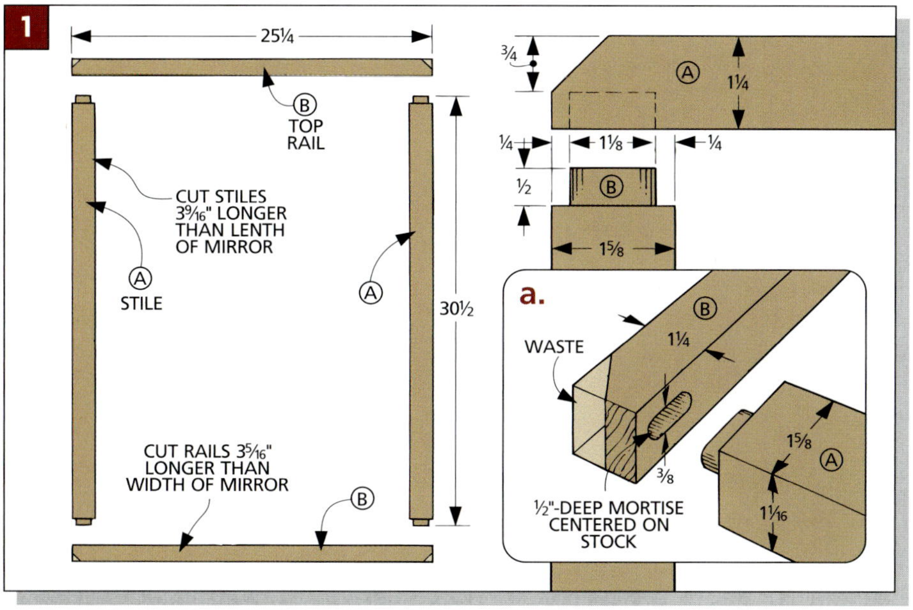

This 3⁵⁄₁₆" of extra length accounts for the width of the two stiles (1⅝" each) plus ¹⁄₁₆" for expansion space between the edges of the mirror and the stiles.

MORTISES. After the pieces are cut to size, the next step is to cut the mortises in the rails. These mortises are ⅜" wide, 1⅛" long and are centered on the edge of the rails *(Fig. 1a)*. Also, they're only ½" deep to allow for the miter on the ends of the rails *(Fig. 1)*.

To cut the mortises, I used a ⅜" bit in a drill press, drilling overlapping holes to remove the waste (see the Technique box on page 10).

Note: Since the ends of the tenons will be rounded over, there's no need to chisel the edges of the mortises square.

TENONS. Next, tenons are cut on the ends of the stiles to fit the mortises. Cut them on a table saw, using the rip fence to set the length, and raising the blade to center the tenon on the thickness of the stock. Then, to fit the routed mortises, round the ends with a file.

MITER CORNERS. After the mortise and tenon joints are cut on all the pieces, both ends of each rail are mitered at 45°. To do this, cut a ¾"-wide miter on the outside corners of both rails *(Figs. 1 and 1a)*.

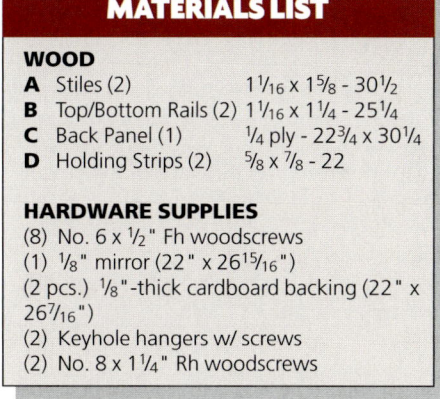

1

25¼

Ⓑ TOP RAIL

CUT STILES 3⁹⁄₁₆" LONGER THAN LENTH OF MIRROR

Ⓐ STILE

Ⓐ

30½

CUT RAILS 3⁵⁄₁₆" LONGER THAN WIDTH OF MIRROR

Ⓑ

Ⓐ

¾

Ⓐ 1¼

¼   1⅛   ¼

½   Ⓑ

1⅝

a.

WASTE

Ⓑ 1¼

⅜

½"-DEEP MORTISE CENTERED ON STOCK

1⅝

Ⓐ

1¹⁄₁₆

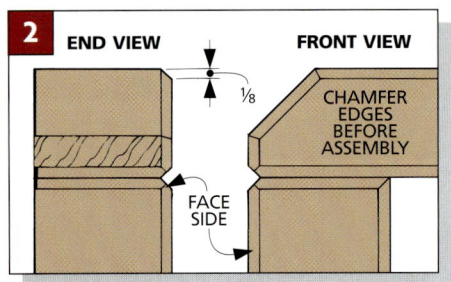

2 END VIEW | FRONT VIEW

1/8

CHAMFER EDGES BEFORE ASSEMBLY

FACE SIDE

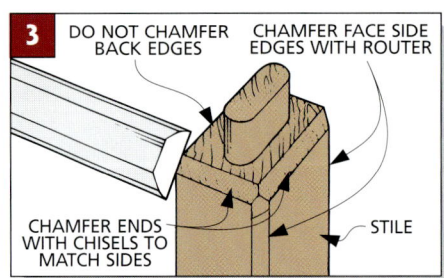

3 DO NOT CHAMFER BACK EDGES | CHAMFER FACE SIDE EDGES WITH ROUTER

CHAMFER ENDS WITH CHISELS TO MATCH SIDES

STILE

CHAMFER EDGES. To soften the edges on the frame, the front edges of the rails and stiles are chamfered. (I did this on a router table with a 45° chamfer bit.) On the rails, rout the front edges and the corner under the mitered end *(Fig. 2)*.

On the stiles, rout all the front edges. Then I also wanted to chamfer the outside corner *(Fig. 3)*. The problem is that the tenon on the end of the stile is right in the way of the pilot on the chamfer bit. So a little different procedure has to be used to chamfer the ends of the stiles.

I used a sharp chisel to shave off the corners to match the chamfered edges cut with the router bit *(Fig. 3)*.

After the edges of the frame have been chamfered, the frame can be glued together and checked for square.

RABBET. When the frame is assembled, a 3/8"-wide rabbet is routed on the inside back edge for a 1/4" plywood back. To rout it, I used a 3/8" rabbet bit in a hand-held router *(Fig. 5a)*.

The rabbet for the frame's back has to be stopped on both ends of the rails. Using a hand-held router and a 3/8" rabbet bit with a pilot bearing makes this job easy. But, there is one problem with using a router to cut the rabbet — you may end up with chipout at the bottom of the shoulder where it's likely to show on the front of the frame.

So to get a clean cut while routing, I set the depth of cut equal to the thickness of the plywood back. Then make a light

scoring pass on the inside edge moving the router in a counter-clockwise direction, which is the opposite direction you would normally rout it *(Fig. 4)*.

Note: If you're routing a rabbet deeper than 1/4", it's best to use several passes.

When backrouting, the rotation of the bit tends to push the bit away from the piece. So you really have to concentrate to keep the bit in contact with the edge. This method produces a very smooth cut on the bottom shoulder.

After the initial scoring pass, move the router in the normal clockwise direction to complete the rabbet *(Fig. 5)*. Then use a sharp chisel to square up the round corners of the rabbet.

BACK. Now the 1/4" plywood back panel (C) can be cut to fit in the rabbet on the back of the frame. Then glue it in place.

KEYHOLE HANGERS. I used surface-mounted keyhole hangers to hang the mirror. Simply drill a pair of overlapping 3/8"-dia. holes in each stile to create clearance for roundhead screws that get screwed in a wall stud *(Fig. 6)*. Then use a couple of screws to secure the keyhole hangers in place on the back of each stile.

HOLDING STRIPS

Once the hangers have been installed, you can mount the mirror to the frame. All you'll need are two holding strips to do this. The strips are used to grip the top and bottom edges of the mirror. Then these strips are in turn held to the plywood back with screws *(Fig. 8)*.

HOLDING STRIPS. To make them, first cut the holding strips (D) to size. Rip the strips to width from a piece of 5/8"-thick stock (7/8") *(Step 1 in Fig. 7)*. Then cut

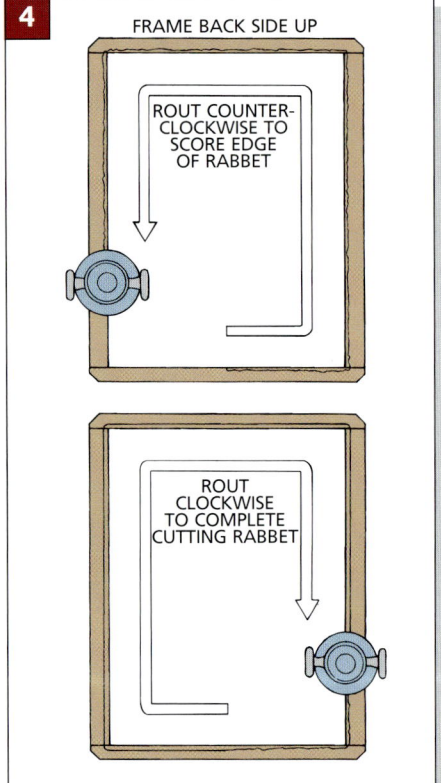

4 FRAME BACK SIDE UP

ROUT COUNTER-CLOCKWISE TO SCORE EDGE OF RABBET

ROUT CLOCKWISE TO COMPLETE CUTTING RABBET

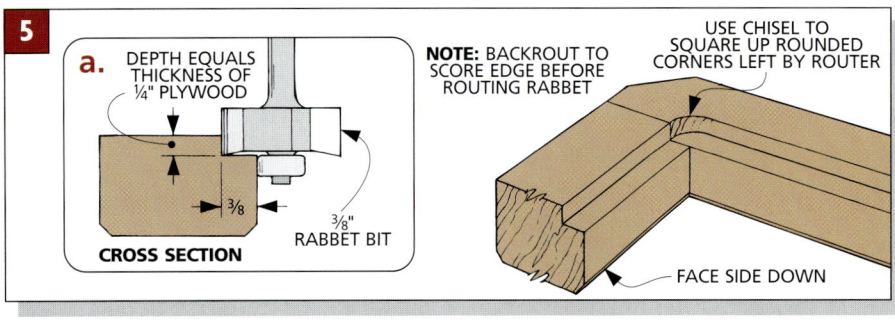

5 **a.** DEPTH EQUALS THICKNESS OF 1/4" PLYWOOD

3/8

3/8" RABBET BIT

CROSS SECTION

NOTE: BACKROUT TO SCORE EDGE BEFORE ROUTING RABBET

USE CHISEL TO SQUARE UP ROUNDED CORNERS LEFT BY ROUTER

FACE SIDE DOWN

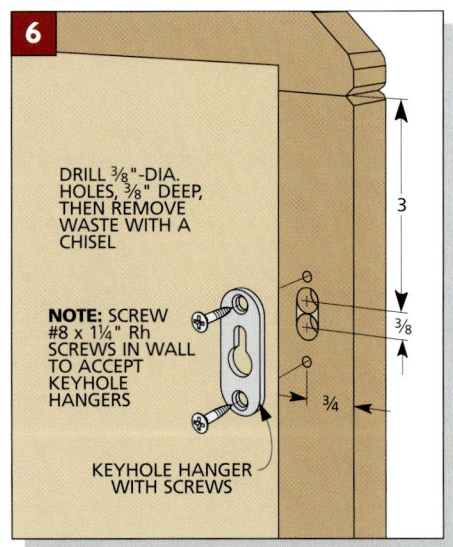

6 DRILL 3/8"-DIA. HOLES, 3/8" DEEP, THEN REMOVE WASTE WITH A CHISEL

NOTE: SCREW #8 x 1 1/4" Rh SCREWS IN WALL TO ACCEPT KEYHOLE HANGERS

KEYHOLE HANGER WITH SCREWS

3

3/8

3/4

7 CUT 1/8" GROOVE FOR MIRROR CENTERED ON STOCK | WASTE | CHAMFER BOTTOM EDGE

1 5/8 | 7/8 | CUT STRIP TO SIZE | (D) HOLDING STRIP

2 (D) | 1/4

3 3/8 | (D) | ROUT 3/8" CHAMFER

4 1/8 | (D)

them about 1" longer than the inside dimensions of the frame. (They're trimmed to final length later.)

CUT GROOVE. To attach the strips to the mirror, you'll need to cut a groove the same thickness as the mirror ($1/8$") down the edge of the strips. Cut this kerf $1/4$" deep and centered on the edge of the strip *(Step 2 in Fig. 7).*

CHAMFER EDGES. After the groove is cut, the front edges of the strips are chamfered. I routed a $3/8$"-wide chamfer on the top edge of the strip *(Step 3).* Then I routed a small $1/8$"-wide chamfer on the bottom edge *(Step 4).*

ASSEMBLY. Now, to mount the mirror and the strips in the frame, cut the holding strips to length to fit snugly between the stiles on the mirror frame.

Then slide each holding strip over the edges of the mirror and position the mirror in the frame so there's equal

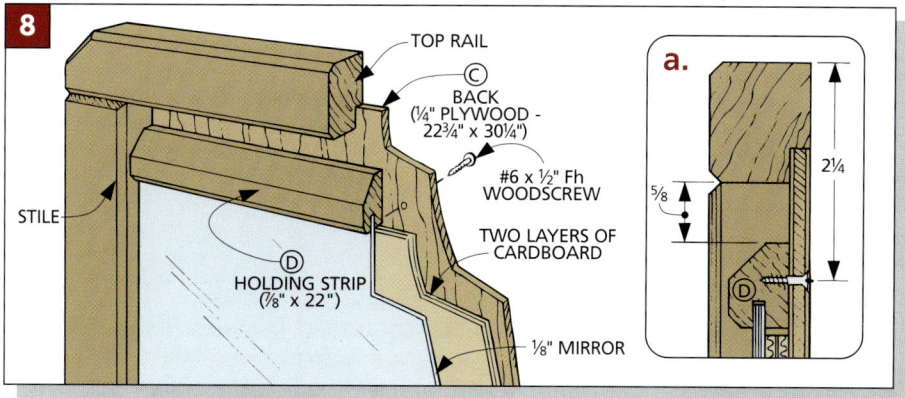

spacing between the holding strips and the top and bottom rails *(Fig. 8a).*

Mark this position and remove the strips from the mirror. Then clamp them to the plywood, and drill pilot holes through the back for the screws *(Fig. 8).*

FINISH. Before mounting the mirror to the frame, I applied three coats of interior

polyurethane finish to the frame, the back, and the holding strips.

Now the mirror can be installed. I placed a couple of pieces of cardboard in between the mirror and the plywood back for added support in the center. Then the holding strips can be screwed in place to hold the mirror in the frame. ∎

DESIGNER'S NOTEBOOK
Two caps and mitered strips around the mirror add a traditional look.

CONSTRUCTION NOTES:

■ Build the stiles (A) and rails (B) as before. But don't cut the decorative miters on the ends. You'll be adding a cap piece to the top and bottom of the frame instead.
■ After the joinery is cut, chamfer each rail and stile as before, except for the top edge of the top rail and the bottom edge of the bottom rail. Instead, leave them square where they meet the caps.
■ Now assemble the frame and rout the rabbet for a plywood back. Then cut the back (C) to size and glue it in place.
■ Next cut two caps (E) to size *(Fig. 1).* Then rout a $1/8$"-wide chamfer on the top edge of the cap and one that's $3/8$" wide on the bottom edge *(Fig. 1a).*
■ On this version, the holding strips (D) are mitered to wrap around all four sides

of the mirror *(Fig. 2).* Start by cutting four holding strips to rough length (two at 22" and two more at 30"). Then cut a groove and chamfer each piece as before (refer to *Fig. 7* on the facing page).
■ Now, before mounting the mirror in the frame, apply the finish and add the keyhole hardware for mounting the mirror on the wall.
■ Once that's complete, the holding strips can be mitered to length and the mirror, cardboard backing, and holding strips can be mounted. (I centered the mirror in the frame and allowed a $5/8$" gap at the top and bottom as before.)

TRADITIONAL MIRROR

■ Finally, glue the caps in place to complete the frame. I aligned the back edge flush with the backs of the rails to provide a $1/2$" reveal at the front *(Fig. 1a).*

MATERIALS LIST

CHANGED PART
D Holding Strip	$5/8$ x $7/8$ - 106 ln. in.	

NEW PART
E Caps (2)	$1^{1}/_{16}$ x $1^{9}/_{16}$ - $26^{1}/_{4}$	

HARDWARE SUPPLIES
(2 pcs.) $1/8$"-thick cardboard backing ($19^{7}/_{16}$" x $26^{7}/_{16}$")
(1) $1/8$" mirror ($19^{15}/_{16}$" x $26^{15}/_{16}$")

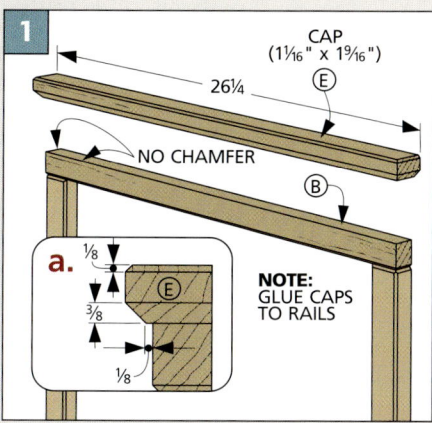

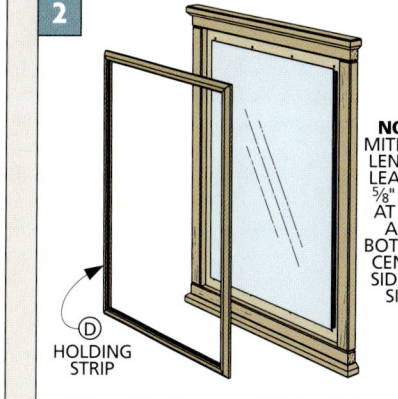

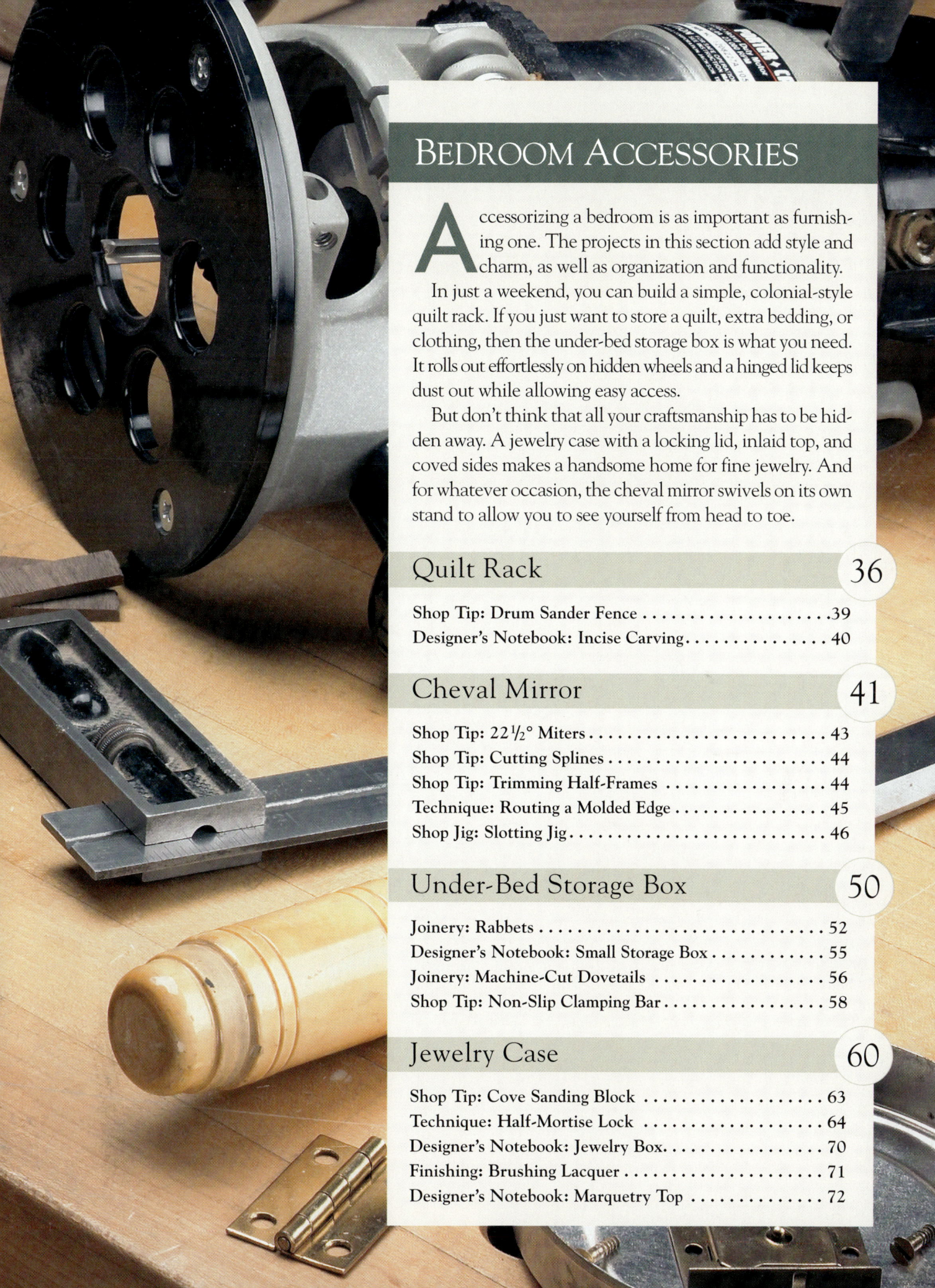

BEDROOM ACCESSORIES

Accessorizing a bedroom is as important as furnishing one. The projects in this section add style and charm, as well as organization and functionality. In just a weekend, you can build a simple, colonial-style quilt rack. If you just want to store a quilt, extra bedding, or clothing, then the under-bed storage box is what you need. It rolls out effortlessly on hidden wheels and a hinged lid keeps dust out while allowing easy access.

But don't think that all your craftsmanship has to be hidden away. A jewelry case with a locking lid, inlaid top, and coved sides makes a handsome home for fine jewelry. And for whatever occasion, the cheval mirror swivels on its own stand to allow you to see yourself from head to toe.

Quilt Rack   36

Shop Tip: Drum Sander Fence .39
Designer's Notebook: Incise Carving 40

Cheval Mirror   41

Shop Tip: $22\frac{1}{2}°$ Miters 43
Shop Tip: Cutting Splines 44
Shop Tip: Trimming Half-Frames 44
Technique: Routing a Molded Edge 45
Shop Jig: Slotting Jig 46

Under-Bed Storage Box   50

Joinery: Rabbets 52
Designer's Notebook: Small Storage Box 55
Joinery: Machine-Cut Dovetails 56
Shop Tip: Non-Slip Clamping Bar 58

Jewelry Case   60

Shop Tip: Cove Sanding Block 63
Technique: Half-Mortise Lock 64
Designer's Notebook: Jewelry Box 70
Finishing: Brushing Lacquer 71
Designer's Notebook: Marquetry Top 72

Quilt Rack

This project provides the perfect place to display your heirloom quilts in style. Build it with cherry hardwood or from a softer wood like pine and try your hand at incise carving for a special touch.

For the past few years, my grandmother has spent at least a couple of afternoons each week with a group of her friends keeping the art of quilt-making alive. (In fact, I think it's helped keep her healthy and happy, considering she's nearing 90 years old.)

When I received one of her quilts as a gift, I wanted to find a way to complement her handiwork with some of my own. The Quilt Rack is styled along simple colonial lines with curved profiles cut along all four edges of the uprights and on one edge of the bottom stretcher. It looks great, but it won't compete for attention with the quilt.

MATERIALS. Since the Quilt Rack has a simple colonial design with lines reminiscent of fine furniture, I decided to build it out of cherry hardwood. You could stain the cherry to give it an aged look, but I let it age naturally, finishing it with a sealer and three coats of tung oil. And there's no hardware. Just mortise and tenon joints.

Or if you'd like to build a rack that fits in more of a country decor, you could use No. 2 common pine. It has knots that give it some character and a rustic look.

DESIGN OPTIONS. Since grandmas like to add some special touches to their quilts (grandmothers call it love), you could

also add some special touches of your own to the Quilt Rack. Check out the Designer's Notebook on page 40 for details on how to do incise carving.

You'll need some specialty carving tools and carbon paper to complete the carving, but I think you'll find the effort worth it (see Sources, page 126).

EXPLODED VIEW

OVERALL DIMENSIONS:
28W x 9D x 32H

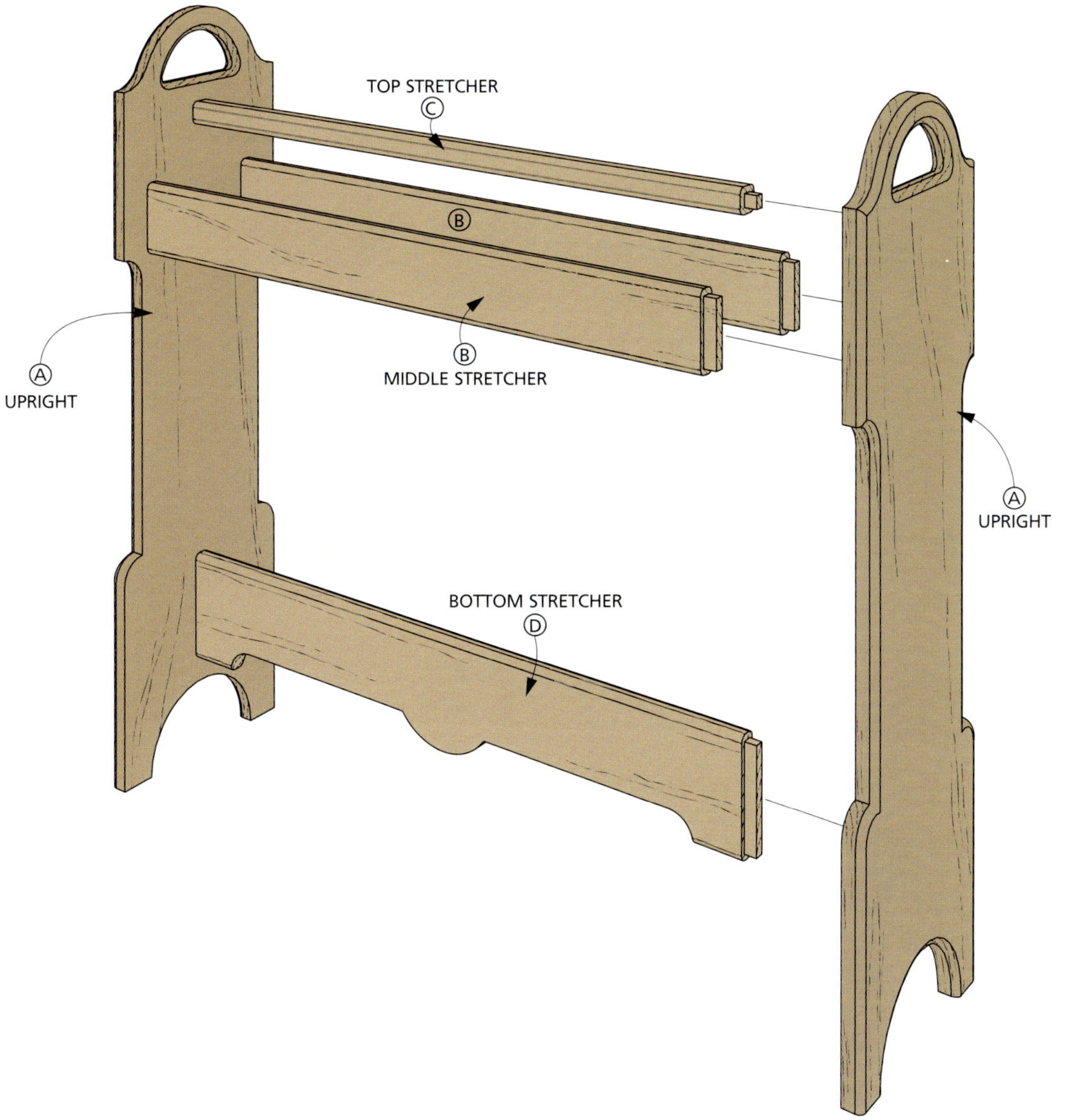

TOP STRETCHER
C
B
B
MIDDLE STRETCHER
A
UPRIGHT
A
UPRIGHT
BOTTOM STRETCHER
D

MATERIALS LIST

WOOD

A	Uprights (2)	$\frac{3}{4}$ x 9 - 32
B	Middle Stretchers (2)	$\frac{3}{4}$ x 3 - 27$\frac{3}{8}$
C	Top Stretcher (1)	1 x 1 - 27$\frac{3}{8}$
D	Bottom Stretcher (1)	$\frac{3}{4}$ x 4$\frac{1}{2}$ - 27$\frac{3}{8}$

CUTTING DIAGRAM

¾ x 3½ - 72 CHERRY (3 Boards @ 1.75 Bd. Ft. Each)
A
A
¾ x 5½ - 96 CHERRY (3.7 Bd. Ft.)
B
B
D
C
C

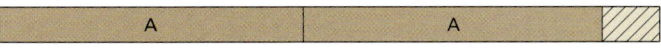

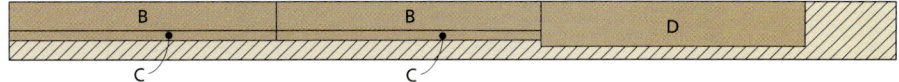

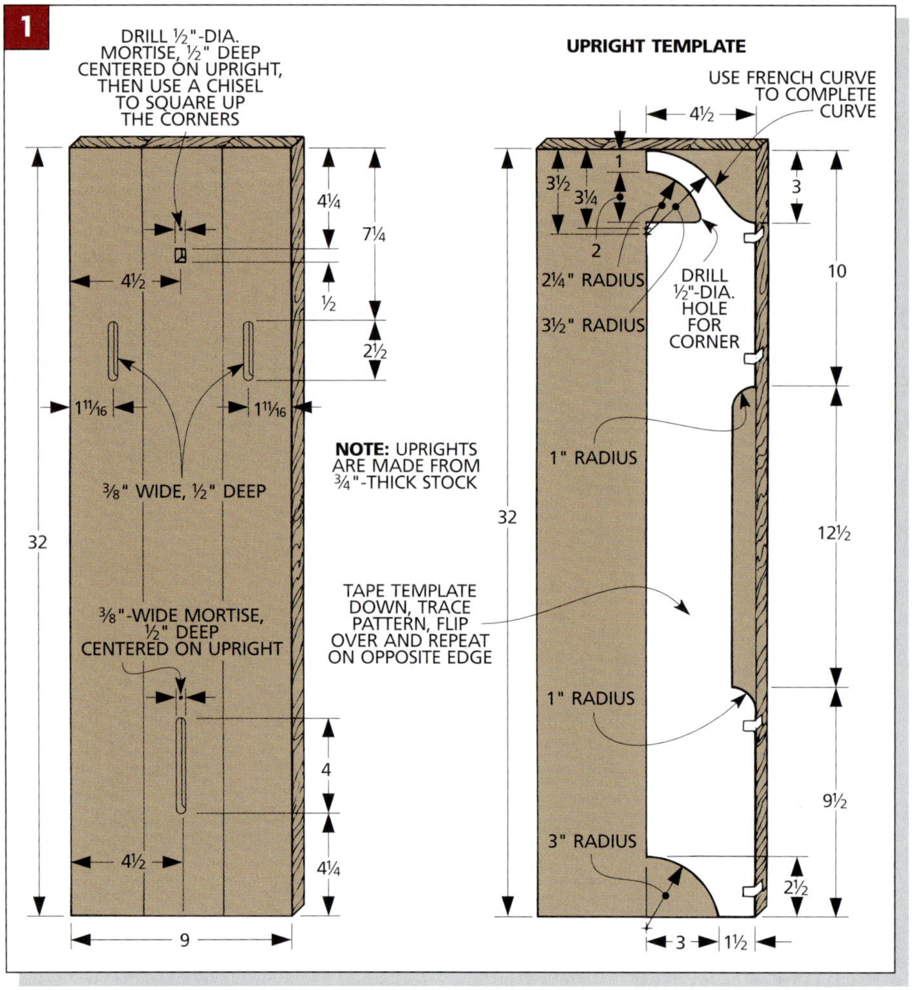
1
DRILL ½"-DIA. MORTISE, ½" DEEP CENTERED ON UPRIGHT, THEN USE A CHISEL TO SQUARE UP THE CORNERS
4½
4¼
7¼
½
2½
1¹¹⁄₁₆
1¹¹⁄₁₆
⅜" WIDE, ½" DEEP
32
⅜"-WIDE MORTISE, ½" DEEP CENTERED ON UPRIGHT
4
4½
4¼
9
NOTE: UPRIGHTS ARE MADE FROM ¾"-THICK STOCK
UPRIGHT TEMPLATE
USE FRENCH CURVE TO COMPLETE CURVE
4½
1
3½
3¼
2
3
2¼" RADIUS
3½" RADIUS
DRILL ½"-DIA. HOLE FOR CORNER
10
1" RADIUS
32
12½
TAPE TEMPLATE DOWN, TRACE PATTERN, FLIP OVER AND REPEAT ON OPPOSITE EDGE
1" RADIUS
9½
3" RADIUS
2½
3
1½

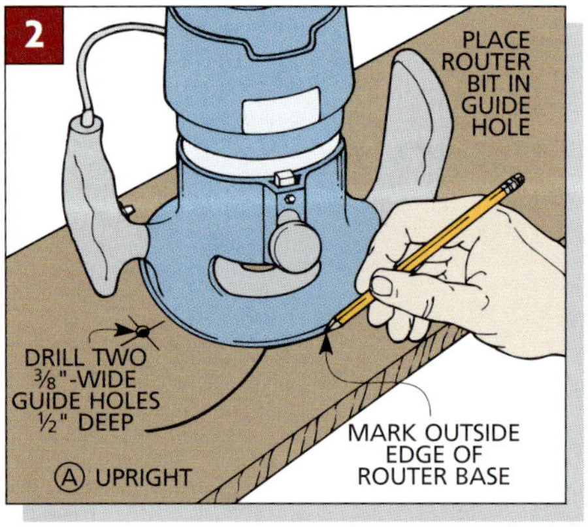
2
PLACE ROUTER BIT IN GUIDE HOLE
DRILL TWO ⅜"-WIDE GUIDE HOLES ½" DEEP
MARK OUTSIDE EDGE OF ROUTER BASE
Ⓐ UPRIGHT

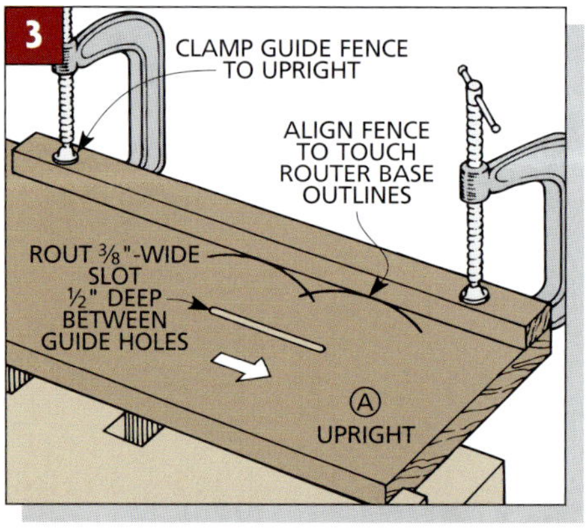
3
CLAMP GUIDE FENCE TO UPRIGHT
ALIGN FENCE TO TOUCH ROUTER BASE OUTLINES
ROUT ⅜"-WIDE SLOT ½" DEEP BETWEEN GUIDE HOLES
Ⓐ UPRIGHT

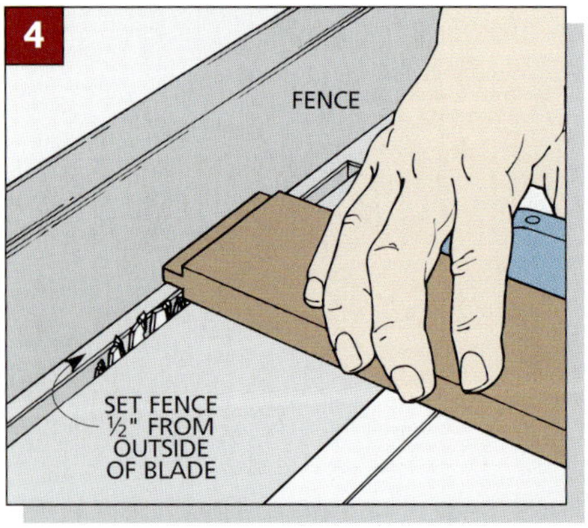
4
FENCE
SET FENCE ½" FROM OUTSIDE OF BLADE

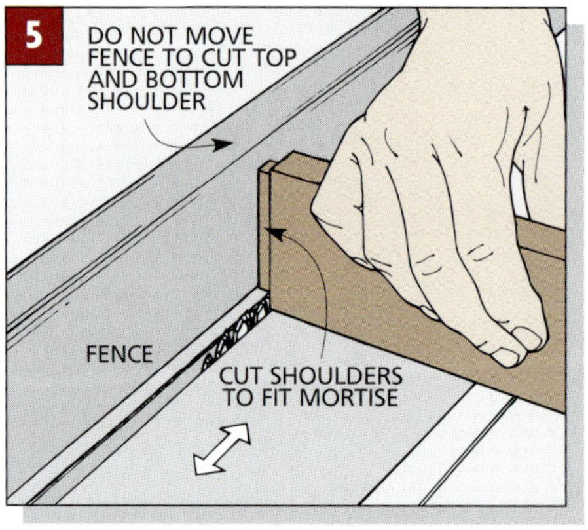
5
DO NOT MOVE FENCE TO CUT TOP AND BOTTOM SHOULDER
FENCE
CUT SHOULDERS TO FIT MORTISE

UPRIGHTS

Start building the Quilt Rack by edge-gluing together $3/4$"-thick cherry stock to form blanks for the two uprights.

BLANKS. To create the uprights (A), first cut three pieces of stock (for each upright) to rough length (33") and rip them to rough width ($3^1/4$") *(Fig. 1)*. Then glue and clamp the pieces together to make two oversize blanks.

Once the glue has completely set up, plane the blanks flat and trim them to length (32"). Now rip each blank to width (9"), taking equal amounts off both edges.

MORTISES

You need to cut four mortises in each blank for the stretchers. Start by marking the position of these mortises on each blank *(Fig. 1)*. Then use a guide fence and a router to cut the three long ones.

POSITION FENCE. To position the fence, first drill $3/8$" dia., $1/2$"-deep pilot holes to mark the ends of the mortises for a bottom stretcher and two center stretchers.

Then, mount a $3/8$" straight bit in the router and place the bit in one of the pilot holes. Trace around the edge of the router base with a pencil to mark its outside arc *(Fig. 2)*. Repeat the process with the router positioned in the second pilot hole.

Next, clamp the guide fence to the workpiece so the edge of the fence just touches the two circles *(Fig. 3)*.

ROUT MORTISES. With the bit set to cut about $1/4$" deep, rout the mortises in two passes to reach the full depth ($1/2$") for the three long mortises on each upright.

The mortise for the top stretcher can be added by simply drilling a $1/2$"-dia. hole, $1/2$" deep and squaring up the corners with a sharp chisel.

Note: The top stretcher would tend to twist if this mortise was not squared up.

UPRIGHT PROFILE

So the profile can be cut exactly the same on all four edges, I made a template from a piece of posterboard *(Fig. 1)*.

Cut out the template with a razor knife, tape it down, and mark the profile on one half of each upright. Then flip it over and repeat the process on the other half.

CUT OUT PROFILE AND HANDLE. Use a jig saw (or band saw) to remove the waste for the profile. (I made the cuts just a little "wide" of the pencil marks so I could sand the profile to the exact size later.)

To make the handles in the tops of the uprights, first drill two $\frac{1}{2}$"-dia. holes, one in each corner of the handle *(Fig. 1)*. Then cut out the remaining shape of the handle with a jig saw. Again, leave the lines intact to allow for sanding later.

SAND EDGES. Use a 1" sanding drum in the drill press to sand the curved edges at the top and bottom of the upright.

Then, to sand the straight edges, I mounted a notched fence to the drill press and used it as a guide to sand the edges straight (see the Shop Tip below).

On the bottom curve of the waste section, I used a sanding block to smooth out the profile. And finally, to sand the handle opening, I switched to a $\frac{1}{2}$"-dia. sanding drum on the drill press.

ROUND OVER EDGES. To complete the uprights, I rounded over the outside edges with a $\frac{1}{4}$" roundover bit. (The inside edges are left square.)

However, the edges on *both* sides of the handle opening are rounded over.

STRETCHERS

To join the two uprights and support the quilt, four stretchers are mounted in the mortises. Cut all four to rough length (29"). Rip the two middle stretchers (B) to width (3"). The bottom stretcher (D) is ripped to $4\frac{1}{2}$" wide *(Fig. 6b)*.

TOP STRETCHER. The top stretcher (C) is made from two glued-up pieces of $\frac{3}{4}$"-thick stock and ripped 1" square.

TRIM TO FINAL LENGTH. After all the stretchers are ripped to their final width, trim them to length ($27\frac{3}{8}$") *(Fig. 6)*.

TENONS

Next, $\frac{1}{2}$"-long tenons are cut on the ends of each stretcher to fit the mortises in the uprights. I used the table saw to cut the tenons, gradually raising the blade to cut away equal amounts of waste from each face. This produces a tenon that's centered on the thickness of the stock *(Fig. 4)*. (It should be snug, but not tight.)

Then complete the tenons by cutting shoulders on the top and bottom edges to fit the length of the mortise *(Fig. 5)*. Finally, I rounded over the edges of the tenons on the center and bottom stretchers with a file to fit the routed mortise. But remember to leave the tenon for the top stretcher square.

BOTTOM STRETCHER. After the tenons are cut, I cut a profile on the bottom stretcher *(Fig. 6a)*. This is just a matter of drawing a $2\frac{1}{2}$" radius at the center of the stretcher, and a 1" radius near each end. Then it's cut and sanded to shape.

ROUND OVER SHOULDERS. Finally, round over all four edges of each stretcher using a $\frac{1}{4}$" roundover bit on the router table *(Fig. 6)*.

Note: If you plan on doing the relief carving on the uprights and the stretcher, now is the time to do it, before you add any finish. The Designer's Notebook on page 40 has tips on doing this.

FINISH. After you've completed the stretchers, lightly sand the surface. (Especially if you did any carving on the Quilt Rack. This removes any traces of oil left from your hands and any smudges from the carbon paper.) Then glue the stretchers into the uprights.

To finish the rack, apply two coats of tung oil sealer. When the second sealer coat is dry, finish sand with 220-grit sandpaper and apply three coats of medium luster polymerized tung oil. ■

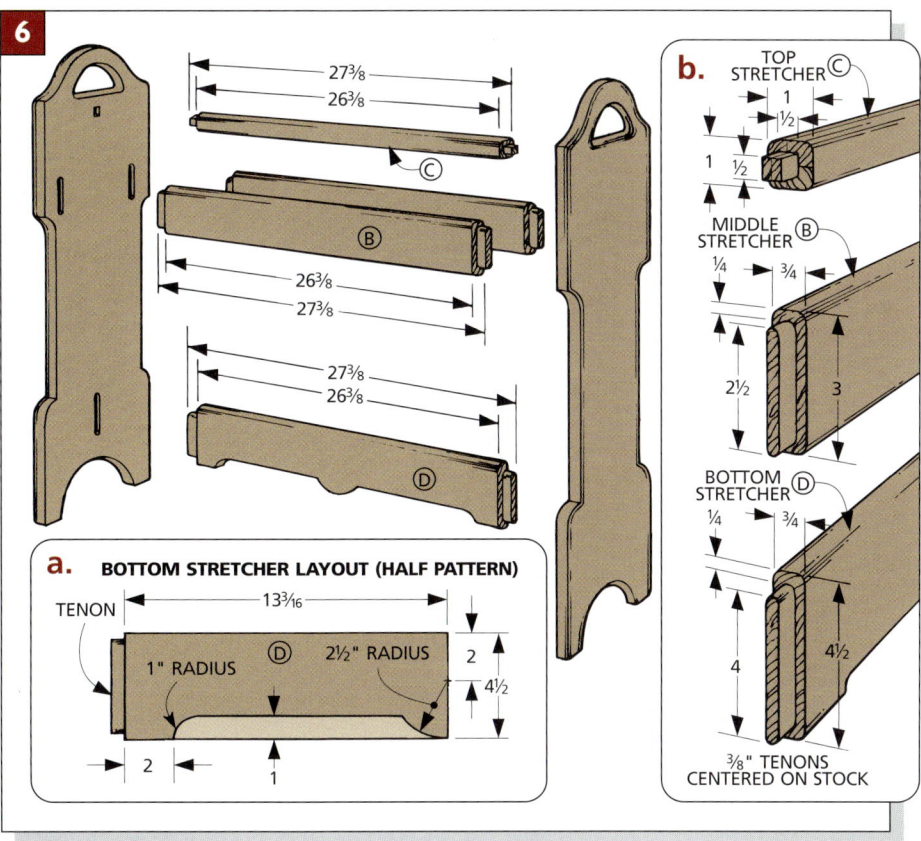

6

a. BOTTOM STRETCHER LAYOUT (HALF PATTERN)

TENON — $13\frac{3}{16}$
1" RADIUS — D — $2\frac{1}{2}$" RADIUS — 2
$4\frac{1}{2}$
2 — 1

b. TOP STRETCHER C — 1 — $1\frac{1}{2}$ — 1 — $\frac{1}{2}$
MIDDLE STRETCHER B — $\frac{1}{4}$ — $\frac{3}{4}$ — $2\frac{1}{2}$ — 3
BOTTOM STRETCHER D — $\frac{1}{4}$ — $\frac{3}{4}$ — 4 — $4\frac{1}{2}$
$\frac{3}{8}$" TENONS CENTERED ON STOCK

$27\frac{3}{8}$ — $26\frac{3}{8}$ (C)
$26\frac{3}{8}$ — $27\frac{3}{8}$ (B)
$27\frac{3}{8}$ — $26\frac{3}{8}$ (D)

SHOP TIP ... Drum Sander Fence

To sand the straight edges of the "waste" section on the uprights, I turned to the same 1"-dia. sanding drum I used to sand the curved edges.

But if you've ever tried sanding a straight line with a drum sander, you know how hard that is to do. That's where this fence comes in.

All you need is a plywood auxiliary fence with a small cutout to provide a little clearance for the drill press chuck. Just clamp the fence in place (see drawing). Then the straight edge on each end of the stretcher guides the workpiece in a straight line along the fence.

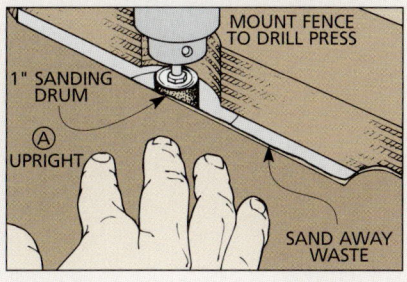

MOUNT FENCE TO DRILL PRESS
1" SANDING DRUM
Ⓐ UPRIGHT
SAND AWAY WASTE

DESIGNER'S NOTEBOOK

Carving an incise pattern on the Quilt Rack is fun — and easier to do than you would think. It gives the project a country look without detracting from the beauty of the quilt on display.

CONSTRUCTION NOTES:

■ The carving method I used is called incised line carving. There are four basic tools used to carve the vine and leaf design: a 60° 3mm V-parting tool (a 2mm would work just as well); a 5mm, #3 gouge; a 5mm (or 6mm) skew-cut chisel; and a 1mm veiner. (For sources of carving tools, see page 126.)

■ To duplicate the design on the uprights and bottom rail, first transfer the designs *(Figs. 1 and 2)* to a large piece of paper.

Note: Full-size patterns are available from *Woodsmith Project Supplies*. For information on ordering these patterns, see Sources on page 126.

■ Tape one edge of the pattern in position and slide a piece of carbon paper between the pattern and the wood (carbon down). Then use a sharp pencil to trace the pattern on the wood.

■ Start by cutting (incising) a centerline for the branches using the point of the skew chisel *(Fig. 3)*. Then, using the incised line as a guide, use the V-parting tool *(Fig. 4)* to carve out a groove for the branches. (The #3 gouge can be used to smooth out any rough areas on either side.) The V-grooves for the branches are about ³⁄₃₂" wide on the surface of the wood and approximately ¹⁄₈" deep.

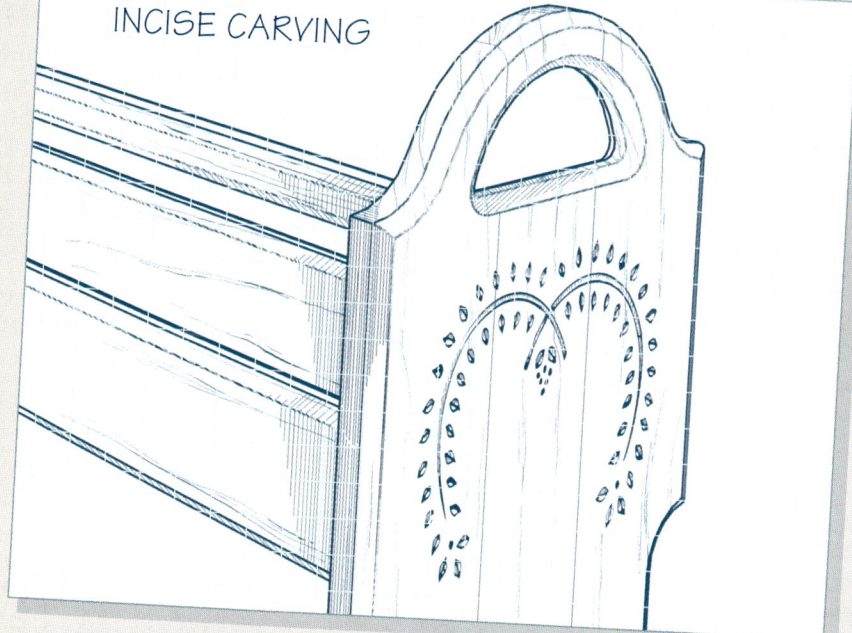

INCISE CARVING

■ To make the leaf patterns, begin by incising the center line for each leaf. Then you can use the 5mm #3 gouge to carve out the oval shape on either side of the leaf's centerline.

I found it best to start carving well inside the marked pattern lines with the first gouging cuts. Then gradually work out from the center (wider and deeper) to form the leaf *(Fig. 5)*. The leaves are ³⁄₁₆" wide on the surface and ¹⁄₈" deep.

■ Finally, the tiny seed pods are carved by holding the 1mm veiner straight up and down and rotating it in a continual circular motion (almost like drilling) until a depth of about ¹⁄₈" is achieved *(Fig. 6)*.

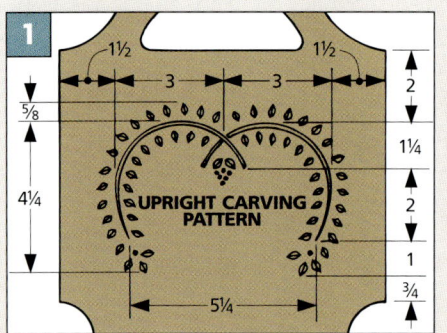

1
UPRIGHT CARVING PATTERN
1½ 1½
3 3
⅝
4¼
5¼
2
1¼
2
1
¾

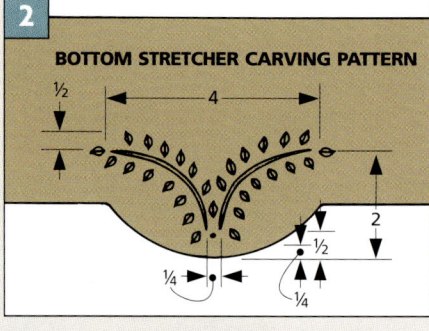

2
BOTTOM STRETCHER CARVING PATTERN
½ 4
¼ ½ ¼
2

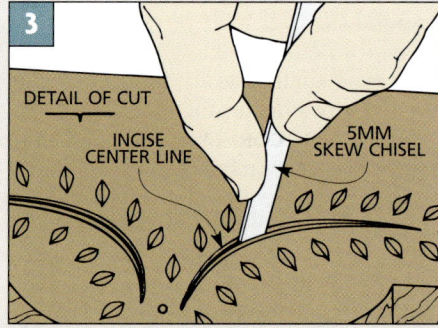

3
DETAIL OF CUT
INCISE CENTER LINE
5MM SKEW CHISEL

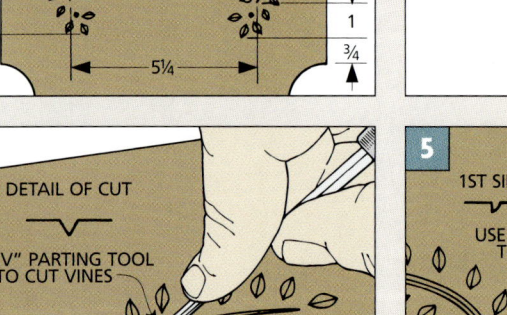

4
DETAIL OF CUT
USE "V" PARTING TOOL TO CUT VINES

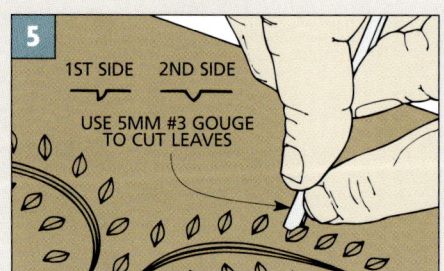

5
1ST SIDE 2ND SIDE
USE 5MM #3 GOUGE TO CUT LEAVES

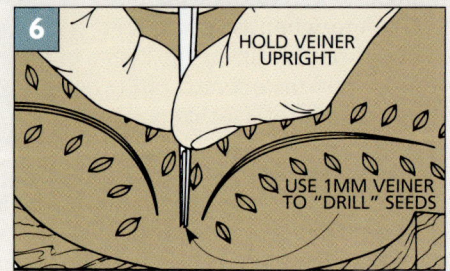

6
HOLD VEINER UPRIGHT
USE 1MM VEINER TO "DRILL" SEEDS

Cheval Mirror

Reflected in this project are the handsome styling and classic lines of another era. Special hardware allows the mirror to pivot in its frame. The joinery consists of splines in grooves and slots.

One of the biggest problems with a wall-mounted, full-length mirror is that it's never at the right height. No matter where it's hung on the wall, it's almost impossible to keep from looking either "headless" or "legless" or both. To remedy this problem, I built a Cheval Mirror — a full-length mirror that swivels on a stand.

This mirror consists of an arched-top frame that's attached to a two-post stand. I found that building the frame for the mirror was the most fun. That's because the top is arched and the bottom corners are also rounded. These assemblies are made with several mitered segments that are then cut to a round shape.

JOINERY. The mitered segments are joined to each other with splines that fit in grooves. The grooves are open to the inside of the frame and stopped on the other end. This way the splines can't be seen from the outside edge of the frame. The grooves are routed with the help of a jig that makes cutting them automatic.

A variation on this joint is used to secure the stretcher on the stand between the uprights, and to fasten the legs to the uprights. Here, instead of a groove, the jig is used to cut a mortise in each piece. The spline then serves as a "loose" tenon, tying the two pieces together.

ROUNDING CORNERS. Cutting the arch for the top of the mirror involves using a router on a trammel to cut the inside and outside edges. For the lower corners, I decided to use a cardboard template to lay out the curves. This ensures that both profiles are identical.

ALIGNING ENDS. Probably the biggest challenge when working with a half-round assembly like the top of the frame is getting the ends perfectly aligned. If the miter cuts are off even slightly, the ends will either be splayed out or toed in. So the uprights on the frame won't be parallel. But don't let that worry you. There's an easy way to compensate for this that guarantees the ends of the arch align.

EXPLODED VIEW

OVERALL DIMENSIONS:
24¹⁄₈W x 18D x 63H

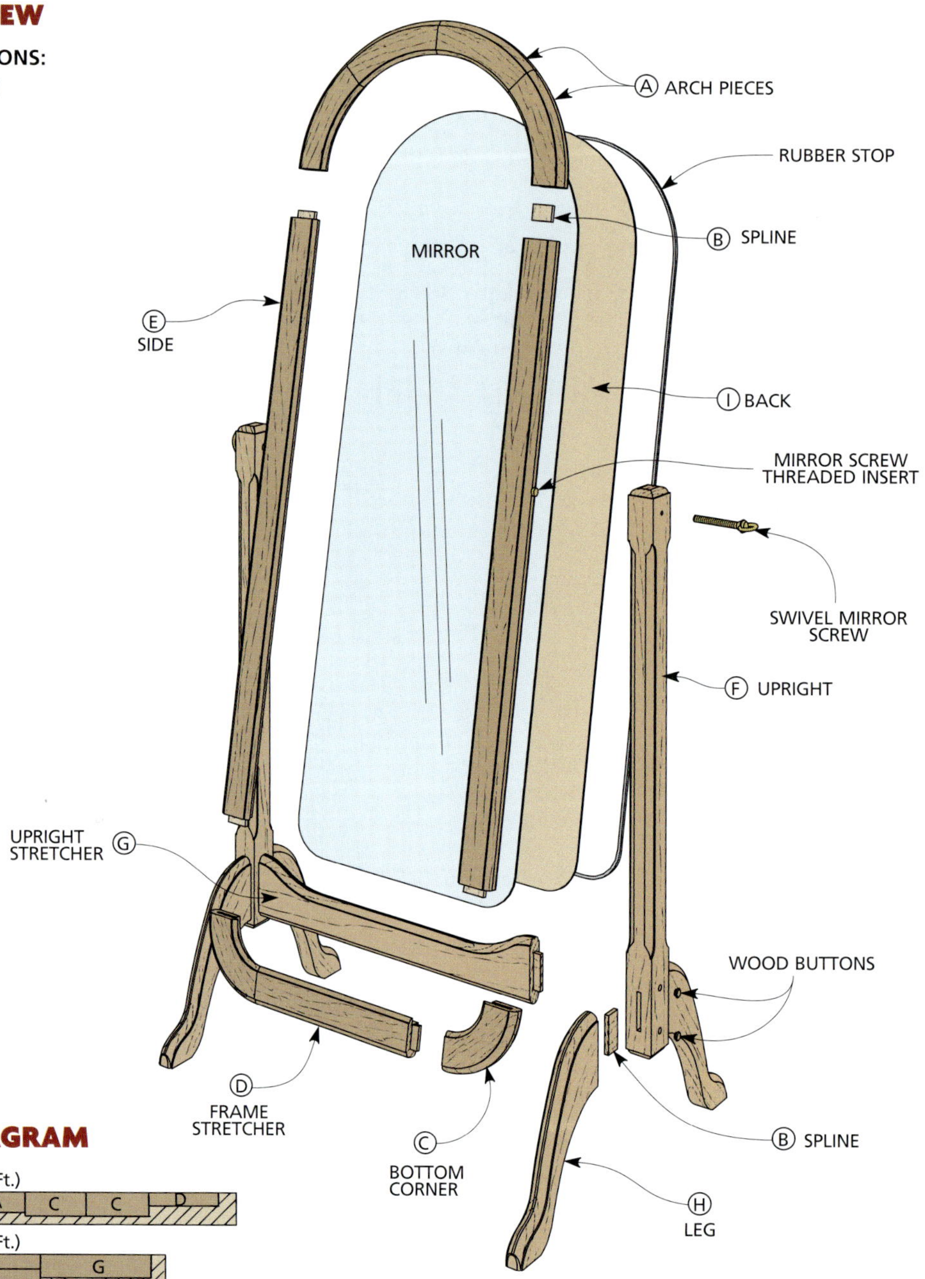

ARCH PIECES — (A)

RUBBER STOP

(B) SPLINE

(E) SIDE

(I) BACK

MIRROR

MIRROR SCREW THREADED INSERT

SWIVEL MIRROR SCREW

(F) UPRIGHT

UPRIGHT STRETCHER (G)

WOOD BUTTONS

FRAME STRETCHER (D)

BOTTOM CORNER (C)

(B) SPLINE

(H) LEG

CUTTING DIAGRAM

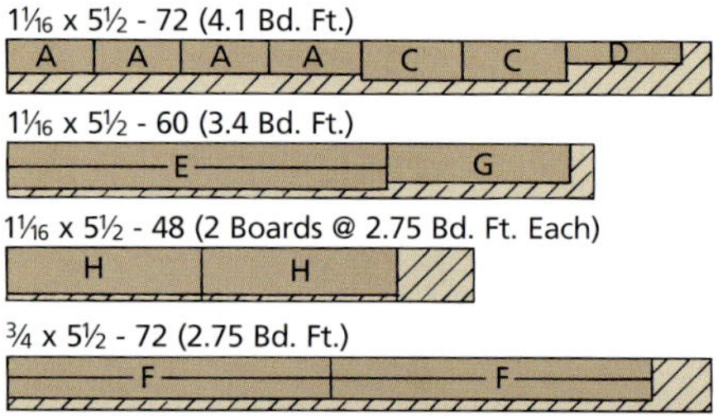

1¹⁄₁₆ x 5½ - 72 (4.1 Bd. Ft.)

| A | A | A | A | C | C | D | |

1¹⁄₁₆ x 5½ - 60 (3.4 Bd. Ft.)

| E | | G | |

1¹⁄₁₆ x 5½ - 48 (2 Boards @ 2.75 Bd. Ft. Each)

| H | H | |

¾ x 5½ - 72 (2.75 Bd. Ft.)

| F | F | |

NOTE: SPLINES (B) CUT FROM WASTE
ALSO NEED: ONE 24" x 48" PIECE OF ⅛" HARDBOARD FOR PART I

MATERIALS LIST

WOOD

A	Arch Pieces (4)	1¹⁄₁₆ x 3½ - 8¾
B	Splines (15)	¼ x 2¼ rgh. - 1
C	Bottom Corners (2)	1¹⁄₁₆ x 4 - 10³⁄₈
D	Frame Stretcher (1)	1¹⁄₁₆ x 2¼ - 11½
E	Sides (2)	1¹⁄₁₆ x 2¼ - 38¼
F	Uprights (2)	1½ x 2 - 33
G	Upright Stretcher (1)	1¹⁄₁₆ x 4 - 20⅞
H	Legs (4)	1¹⁄₁₆ x 5 - 20 rgh.
I	Back (1)	⅛ hdbd. - 16¾ x 48 rgh.

HARDWARE SUPPLIES

(2) 2⅝" swivel mirror screws and inserts
(12 ft.) Rubber stop
(1 pkg.) ⅜", 20-gauge brads
(4) ½" wood buttons
(1) ⅛"-thick mirror, 16¾" x 48" rough

ARCHED TOP

Construction of the mirror begins with the frame. It consists of nine pieces: four segments that make up an arched top; a three-sided bottom; and two straight sides that connect the top and bottom. I started with the arched top.

The top consists of four arch pieces (A) cut from 5/4 oak (1¹⁄₁₆" thick). The segments are mitered and then joined with splines *(Fig. 1)*. To make these pieces, start by ripping a board 3½" wide and 37" long *(Fig. 1)*. Then cut four 9"-long pieces from the board.

MITERING. To form the arch, the ends of all four pieces are mitered at 22½° so their final length is 8¾" from long point

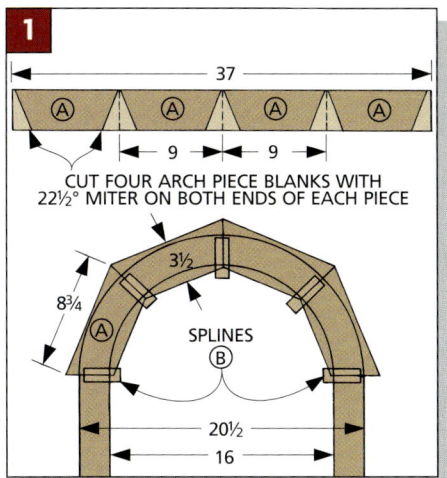

1

37
9 | 9
CUT FOUR ARCH PIECE BLANKS WITH
22½° MITER ON BOTH ENDS OF EACH PIECE

3½
8¾
SPLINES
B
20½
16

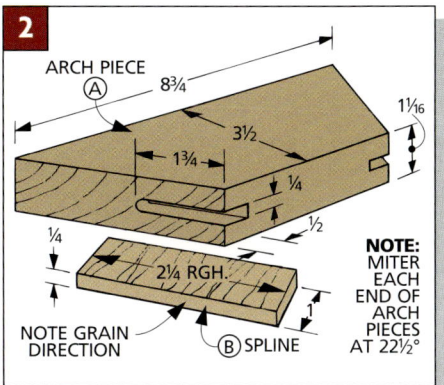

2

ARCH PIECE
A
8¾
3½
1³⁄₁₆
1¾
¼
½
¼
2¼ RGH.
1
NOTE GRAIN
DIRECTION
B SPLINE
NOTE: MITER EACH END OF ARCH PIECES AT 22½°

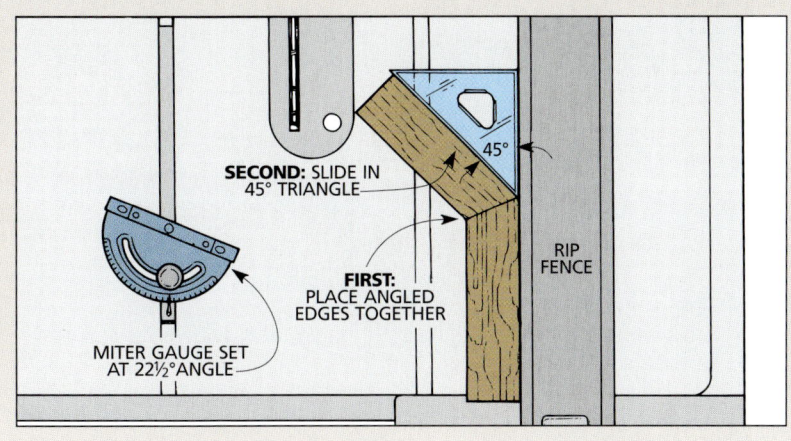

3

SCRAP PLYWOOD BASE
ROUTER
ROUT IN CLOCKWISE DIRECTION
TRAMMEL
PIVOT POINT
8
10¼
2¼
20½

to long point *(Fig. 2)*. (The Shop Tip below shows how to set your miter gauge to cut an accurate 22½° miter.)

ROUT GROOVES. The next step is to rout 1¾"-long grooves in the mitered ends of all four pieces *(Fig. 2)*. These accept splines that tie the pieces together. While this could be done on the router table, I found it was more accurate to use the slotting jig shown on page 46.

Then hardwood splines (B) are cut to fit the slots. Note that the grain of the spline runs at a right angle to the joint *(Fig. 2)*. This produces the strongest joint. (For a safe way to cut these small pieces, see the Shop Tip on page 44.)

ASSEMBLY. After the splines are cut to fit, the four pieces are glued up, two sections at a time. To do this, apply a light coat of glue to the miters and in the slots. Then insert the splines and hold two pieces together for two or three minutes. Clamps are not needed; hand pressure alone will produce a good joint.

Then glue the two sub-assemblies to each other the same way.

TRIM ENDS. At this point, the arch *should* form a half-circle, with the open mitered ends perfectly aligned in a straight line. Unfortunately, this rarely is the case. Usually, when a straightedge is butted across the ends of the arch, only the toes or the heels of the miters touch the straightedge.

Correcting any error on the ends of the arch is important. Unless they're perfectly aligned, the long sides of the mirror frame will either be toed in or toed out. The Shop Tip on page 44 shows how to trim the arch to prevent this.

Note: If you need to trim the ends of your arch, leave it attached to the plywood after you're done. You'll need the plywood for the next step.

ROUTING THE ARCH

To round off this mitered assembly, two radius cuts are made using a router with a trammel attachment.

When doing this, it's best to fasten the arch to a piece of plywood, and clamp the plywood to a workbench *(Fig. 3)*. I put carpet tape under the arch itself (trying to keep it out of the waste areas) so the arch would stay secure during the routing operation.

When using a trammel attachment, the pivot point must be at the same height as the workpiece itself. So I attached a small piece of 5/4 scrap to the plywood to serve as a base *(Fig. 3)*.

Then locate the pivot point by using a straightedge to extend the joint lines to the base. The point where these lines meet marks the location for the pivot hole for the trammel attachment.

INSIDE RADIUS. To rout the inside arc, set the trammel attachment to an 8" radius *(Fig. 3)*. Be sure to measure from the pivot hole to the *outside* edge of the router bit. Then rout the inside radius of the arch, moving in a clockwise direction in several shallow passes *(Fig. 3)*.

OUTSIDE RADIUS. Next, reset the trammel attachment to rout a 10¼" radius on the outside edge of the frame. (This time, measure from the pivot point to the *inside* edge of the bit.)

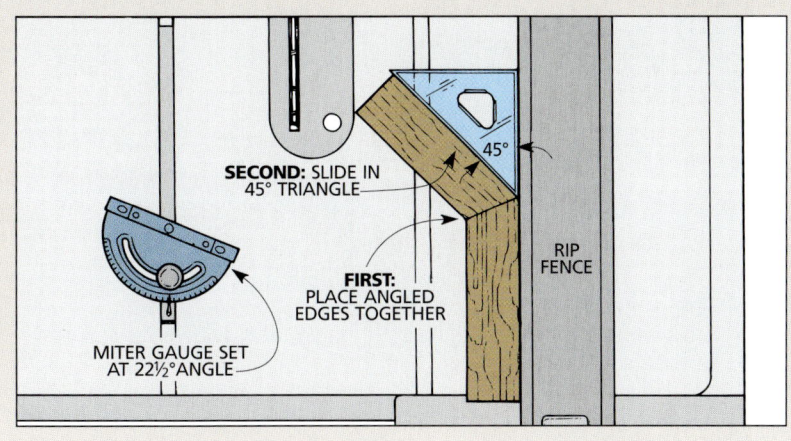

SHOP TIP . . . . *22½° Miters*

Setting a miter gauge to exactly 22½° can be difficult. But here's a trick to make this job easier.

Set your gauge to 22½° as indicated by the markings on the head of the gauge. Then make a test cut through a piece of scrap.

To check the accuracy of the setup, place the long side of one piece against the rip fence. Next, place the mitered end of the second piece against the mitered end of the first (see drawing). Check the angle between the second piece and the rip fence with a plastic triangle (available at office supply and art stores). An accurate cut creates a 45° angle.

SECOND: SLIDE IN 45° TRIANGLE
45°
FIRST: PLACE ANGLED EDGES TOGETHER
RIP FENCE
MITER GAUGE SET AT 22½° ANGLE

SHOP TIP ...... *Cutting Splines*

Once the grooves are cut in the frame pieces, the splines have to be cut to fit them. The key here is to cut the splines so they have a good friction fit in the groove.

For greatest strength, the splines should be cut so the grain runs across the joint line (see drawing). The way I do this is with two cuts on the end of a blank.

Before making the first cut, set the rip fence so the spline's thickness will equal the width of the grooves (see drawing).

For the second cut, set the rip fence about ¹⁄₃₂" beyond the bottom of the first cut, and guide the workpiece with the miter gauge to make a shallow cut on each face. Then simply snap off the splines and sand the ragged edge.

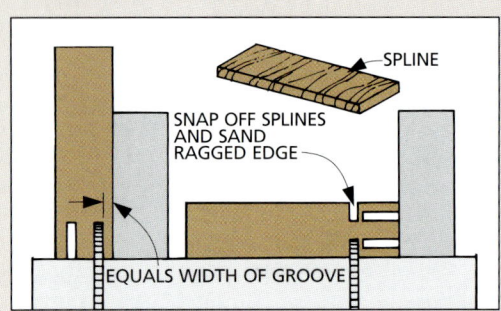

SPLINE

SNAP OFF SPLINES AND SAND RAGGED EDGE

EQUALS WIDTH OF GROOVE

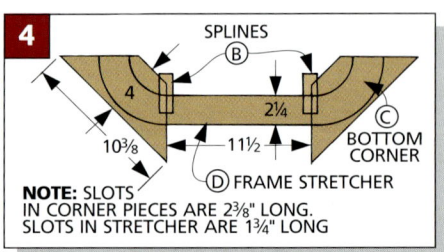

4

SPLINES

B

4

10³⁄₈   11½   2¼   C BOTTOM CORNER

D FRAME STRETCHER

NOTE: SLOTS IN CORNER PIECES ARE 2³⁄₈" LONG. SLOTS IN STRETCHER ARE 1¾" LONG.

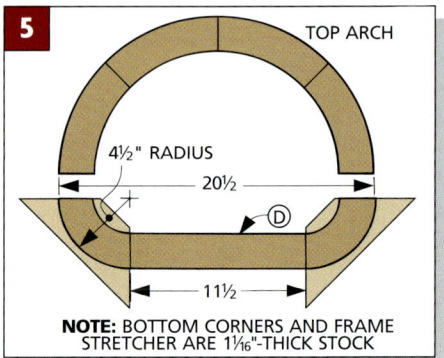

5

TOP ARCH

4½" RADIUS

20½

D

11½

NOTE: BOTTOM CORNERS AND FRAME STRETCHER ARE 1¹⁄₁₆"-THICK STOCK

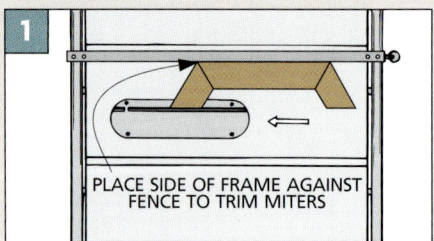

6

TRIM BOTTOM ASSEMBLY 4½" WIDE (SEE SHOP TIP BELOW)

4½

C   D   C

REMOVE "EARS" WITH HAND SAW

MIRROR BOTTOM

After the top arch was routed to shape, I worked on the bottom assembly. This assembly is different than the top arch. There are just three pieces. The first is a frame stretcher with square ends. The other two are mitered corner pieces on each end of the stretcher to make the transition from the horizontal stretcher to the vertical frame sides *(Fig. 4)*.

CUT PIECES. First, rip enough 5/4 stock to form two 4"-wide corners (C), and the 2¼"-wide frame stretcher (D) *(Fig. 4)*. Then both corner pieces are mitered at 45° on each end so they measure 10³⁄₈" long from point to point.

Next, determine the final length for the frame stretcher (D). To do this, measure the outside diameter of the top arch (mine was 20½"), then subtract 9" (to account for the 4½" radius that will be cut on each corner) *(Fig. 5)*. The result will be the finished length of the frame stretcher (11½" in my case).

ASSEMBLY. Once these three pieces are cut to size, you can start on the joinery. These pieces use the same slot and spline joint used on the top arch. But since the corner pieces aren't cut to finished shape yet, you'll need to rout the slots in them slightly longer (2³⁄₈") than the slots in the stretcher (1¾").

Now cut two more hardwood splines to fit the slots and glue the bottom assembly together *(Fig. 4)*.

TRIM MITERS. The next step is to true up the mitered ends that will be joined to the frame's long sides (B). To do this, first use a hand saw to remove the extra

"ears" extending below the bottom piece *(Fig. 6)*. Then sand the edge smooth. Finally, trim the mitered ends on the table saw so the assembly is 4½" wide *(Fig. 6* and the Shop Tip below).

TEMPLATE. After the mitered ends are trimmed, the arcs on each corner can be laid out. So that the corners would end up identical, I made a cardboard template with an inside radius of 2¼" and an outside radius of 4½" *(Fig. 7)*.

SHOP TIP .... *Trimming Half-Frames*

When making a mitered frame like those at the top and bottom of the Cheval Mirror, any error in the angle of the miters will show up when it's time to join the half-frames to the uprights. If the ends of the frame don't align perfectly, the uprights won't be parallel.

To compensate for this, you can trim the open ends of the half-frames on the table saw.

The flat edge of the frame stretcher on the three-piece bottom assembly can be run against the rip fence *(Fig. 1)*.

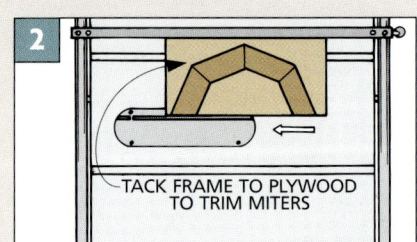

1

PLACE SIDE OF FRAME AGAINST FENCE TO TRIM MITERS

You'll need to mount the four-sided top assembly to a piece of scrap plywood first *(Fig. 2)*.

2

TACK FRAME TO PLYWOOD TO TRIM MITERS

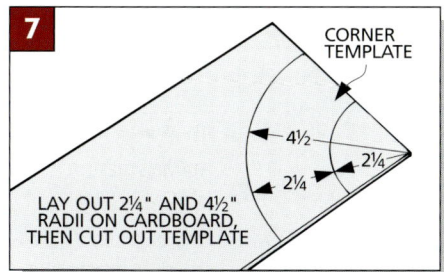

7 CORNER TEMPLATE

4½ 2¼ 2¼

LAY OUT 2¼" AND 4½" RADII ON CARDBOARD, THEN CUT OUT TEMPLATE

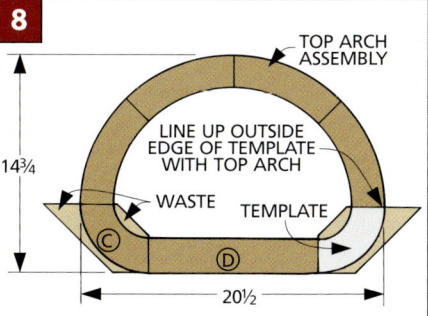

8 TOP ARCH ASSEMBLY

14¾

LINE UP OUTSIDE EDGE OF TEMPLATE WITH TOP ARCH

WASTE TEMPLATE

Ⓒ Ⓓ

20½

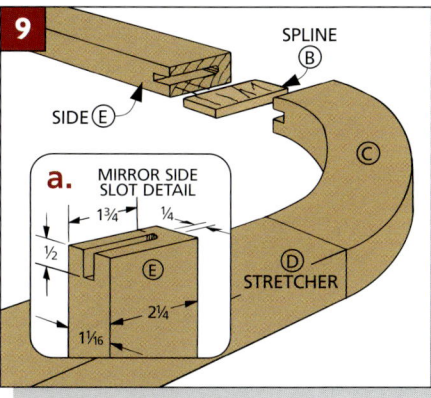

9 SPLINE Ⓑ

SIDE Ⓔ

a. MIRROR SIDE SLOT DETAIL

1¾ ¼

½

Ⓔ

2¼

1¹⁄₁₆

Ⓒ

Ⓓ STRETCHER

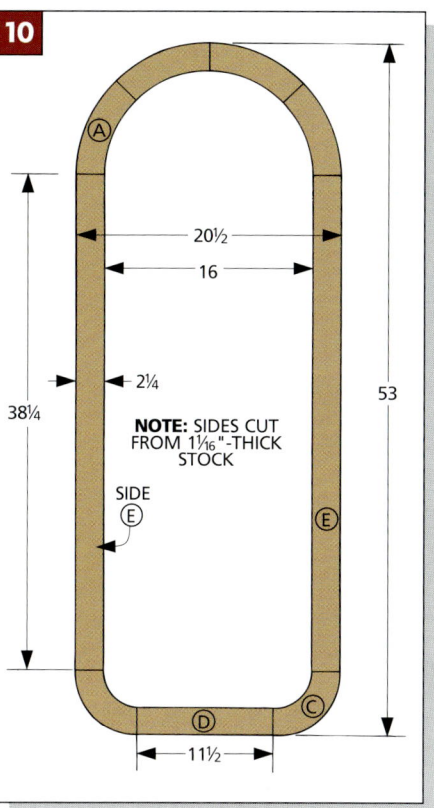

10

Ⓐ

20½

16

2¼

38¼

NOTE: SIDES CUT FROM 1¹⁄₁₆"-THICK STOCK

SIDE Ⓔ

Ⓔ

53

Ⓓ Ⓒ

11½

To transfer the curves onto the corner pieces, butt the bottom assembly against the top arch *(Fig. 8)*. Then position the template so that its outside edge lines up with the outside edge of the top arch, and the template is flush with the mitered edge that's butted against the top arch.

After the radius is traced on both corner pieces, the corners can be cut out on a band saw. Then, to sand the edges of the corners smooth, I chucked a drum sander in the drill press.

SIDES. Next, the frame's long sides (E) are added. To determine the length of these sides, butt the bottom assembly against the top arch, and measure their combined height *(Fig. 8)*. Then subtract this measurement from the 53" final height of the frame *(Fig. 10)*. (The sides of my mirror were 38¼" long.)

Cut both sides 2¼" wide, and to final length. Then use the slotting jig to rout

slots for splines on both ends of each piece *(Fig. 9)*. After cutting some more splines, the entire mirror frame can be assembled and set aside to dry.

PROFILE. Once the glue has dried, the edges of the frame are dressed up with a

series of roundover cuts. And a rabbet is routed along the back inside edge to accept the mirror. This is all covered in the Technique box below.

TECHNIQUE .... *Routing a Molded Edge*

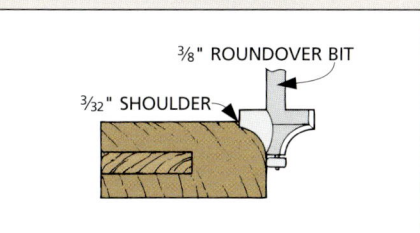

3/8 " ROUNDOVER BIT

3/32 " SHOULDER

1 *The first step is to rout the outside edge of the face side of the frame. Use a 3/8" roundover bit and leave a 3/32" shoulder.*

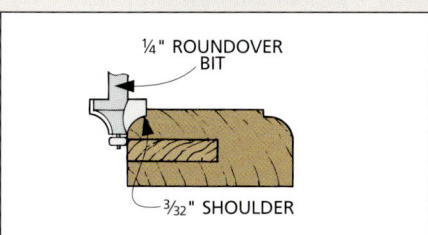

¼" ROUNDOVER BIT

3/32 " SHOULDER

2 *Then switch to a ¼" roundover bit to rout the inside edge of the frame. Here again, leave a 3/32" shoulder.*

All four edges of the mirror frame are routed to dress it up and create a space for the mirror (see drawing below). The front edges each have a roundover with a shoulder that "raises" a field. But note that different sizes of bits are used for these roundovers *(Steps 1 and 2)*.

Next, the back outside edge is eased with a ¼" roundover bit *(Step 3)*.

The last step is to rout a rabbet on the back inside edge *(Step 4)*. The rabbet holds the mirror, the backing board, and the rubber stop strip that holds them in place (refer to *Fig. 29* on page 49).

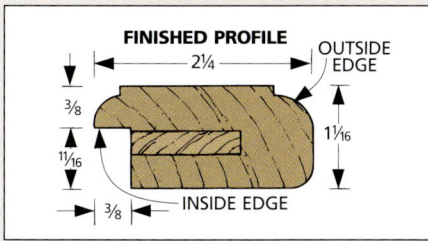

FINISHED PROFILE OUTSIDE EDGE

2¼

3/8

1¹⁄₁₆

11/16

3/8

INSIDE EDGE

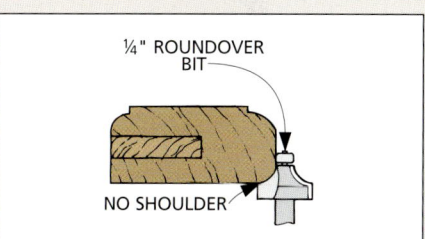

¼" ROUNDOVER BIT

NO SHOULDER

3 *The outside edge on the back side of the frame is also routed with the same ¼" roundover bit, but there's no shoulder.*

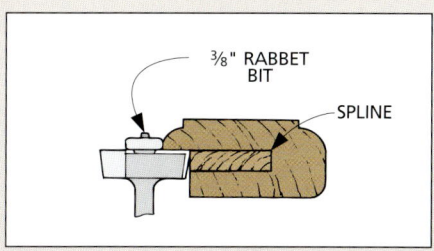

3/8 " RABBET BIT

SPLINE

4 *Finally, rout a 3/8" rabbet in very light passes. This rabbet should be just slightly deeper than the groove for the spline.*

The key to a slot and spline joint is to cut the grooves for the splines in the proper location. To do this accurately, I used a slotting jig that automatically centers the groove on the workpiece.

BUILDING THE JIG

The jig can be broken down into two major assemblies: the plywood base, and two adjustable wings *(Fig. 1)*.

The $1/2$" plywood base is cut $1\frac{1}{2}$" wider than the diameter of the router base and 13" long *(Fig. 1)*. Then $3/4$"-wide fences are glued to three sides of the base.

Note: The two side fences must be parallel to each other, and the distance between them must equal the diameter of your router's base.

Next, rout a $1/2$"-wide slot in the base. The slot starts $2\frac{1}{2}$" from the open end, and continues until the router base contacts the back fence *(Fig. 1)*.

WINGS. Next, two adjustable wings are added to the bottom of the base. These wings are $1/2$" plywood with solid-wood "pinchers" *(Fig. 1)*. The plywood pieces have two slots. Then they're glued and screwed to the pinchers.

Finally, screw threaded inserts into the base, and attach the wings with 1" panhead screws and washers *(Fig. 1)*.

SETUP

Before the jig can be used, the wings have to be adjusted for the thickness of the workpiece, while at the same time, keeping the workpiece centered under the slot in the base.

To accurately set up the jig, I made a setup block from the same stock as the workpiece itself. The block has a perfectly centered tongue on one edge. Cut this tongue by placing alternate sides of the block against the fence of the table saw *(Fig. 2)*. Nudge the rip fence until the tongue fits the groove in the jig.

Then to position the wings of the jig, place the setup block between the wings with the tongue in the groove *(Fig. 3)*. Clamp the wings against the sides of the setup block and tighten the four screws.

USING THE JIG

Positioning a workpiece in the jig is simple. All you need to do is lay out the slot on the workpiece. Place the workpiece in the jig so the ends of the layout lines match up with the end of the slot closest to the back fence. Then clamp the entire assembly in a vise *(Fig. 4)*.

Finally, position the router on the jig with the router bit in the groove, just ahead of the workpiece. Start the router and feed it into the workpiece until the base contacts the end of the jig.

MORTISES. To use the jig for routing mortises (used when joining the mirror's legs and stretcher to the uprights), clamp a stop to the open end of the base. Then make a plunge cut to start the cut, and slide the router back and forth between the stops to cut the mortise.

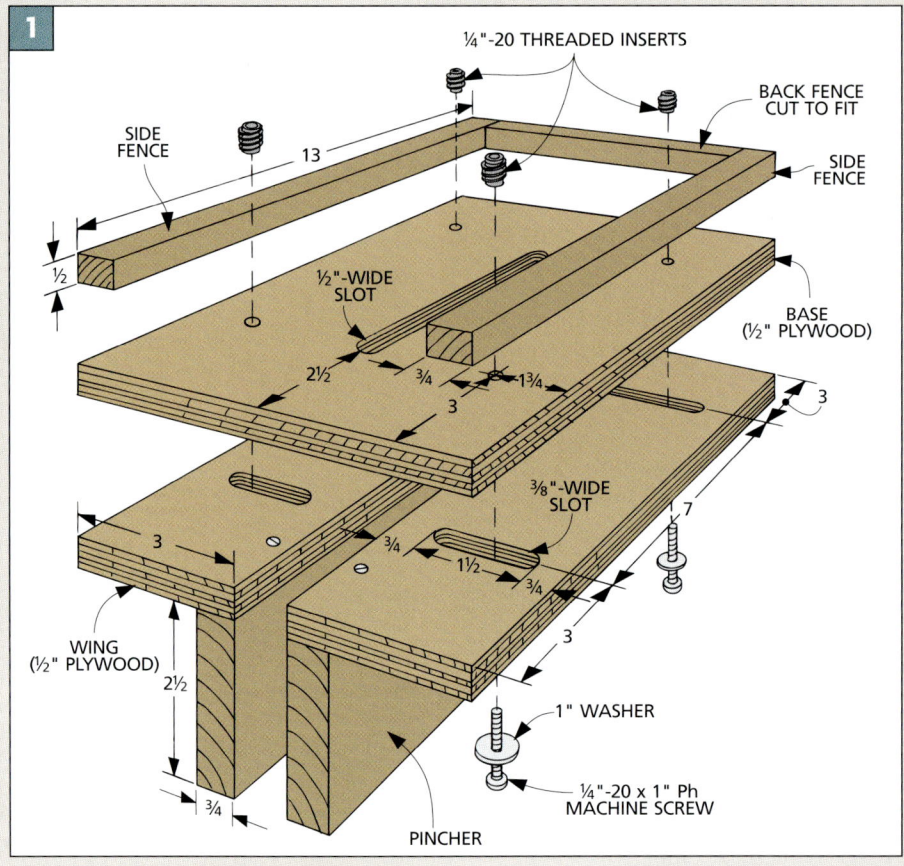

1

¼"-20 THREADED INSERTS

SIDE FENCE

13

BACK FENCE CUT TO FIT

SIDE FENCE

½

½"-WIDE SLOT

2½   ¾   3   1¾

3

BASE (½" PLYWOOD)

3

⅜"-WIDE SLOT

WING (½" PLYWOOD)

3   ¾   1½   ¾

2½

7

3

1" WASHER

¾

PINCHER

¼"-20 x 1" Ph MACHINE SCREW

2   ALTERNATE SIDES AGAINST FENCE TO CUT TONGUE CENTERED ON STOCK

1   FENCE   x

2   FENCE   x

3   FENCE   x

3   BASE   CENTERED TONGUE IN GROOVE

PINCHER

SETUP BLOCK

4   CLAMP WORKPIECE AND JIG IN VISE

VISE

WORKPIECE

UPRIGHTS

At this point, the mirror frame looked sharp enough by itself that I was tempted to just hang it on the wall. But I decided that the swivel stand was still a good idea.

The first step in building the mirror stand is to laminate two pieces of stock for each $1^1/2$"-thick upright (F) *(Fig. 11)*. Then the blanks are cut to final size.

MORTISES. A mortise and spline joint is used to join both the stretcher and the legs to the uprights. This joint is similar to a mortise and tenon, except mortises are cut in both pieces, rather than in only one piece. Then the two pieces are joined with a spline, which acts as a tenon.

Using the same slotting jig I used to rout slots for the top and bottom assemblies, I routed a mortise centered on each $1^1/2$"-wide face of each upright *(Fig. 11)*. These mortises are for attaching the legs.

Then I routed another mortise (for the stretcher) centered on one of the 2"-wide faces of each upright *(Fig. 11a)*.

MOLDING THE UPRIGHTS. After the mortises are complete, all four edges of the uprights receive a stopped roundover. These $3/8$" roundovers are cut so that the small ($3/32$") shoulders end up on the 2"-wide faces *(Fig. 12)*.

Routing these stopped roundovers requires two different setups on the router table. The first step is to attach a long auxiliary fence to the router table *(Step 1 in Fig. 14)*. Then stop blocks are clamped at both ends of the fence.

To rout the first edge, place the bottom end of the upright against the right stop. Then swing the top end of the upright into the bit, and immediately start sliding the upright toward the left stop.

Next, rotate the upright so the opposite 2"-wide face is down on the router table and the top end of the upright is still on the left. Then rout this edge.

At this point, only two diagonal edges have been routed *(Fig. 14a)*. Routing the remaining two edges requires reversing the position of the stop blocks, and flipping the upright end for end *(Step 2 in Fig. 14)*. Rout the remaining two edges in the same manner as the first two.

ROUT ENDS. After completing the edges, round over the top and bottom ends of the uprights *(Fig. 15)*.

DRILL HOLES. The mirror swivels on a pair of ornate thumbscrews and threaded inserts (refer to *Fig. 30* on page 49).

In order to mount the screws, drill a $1/4$"-dia. hole through the 2"-wide side of

the uprights *(Fig. 16)*. While I was at it, I also drilled two $3/8$"-dia. stopped holes at the bottom of the uprights to accept decorative buttons *(Fig. 16)*.

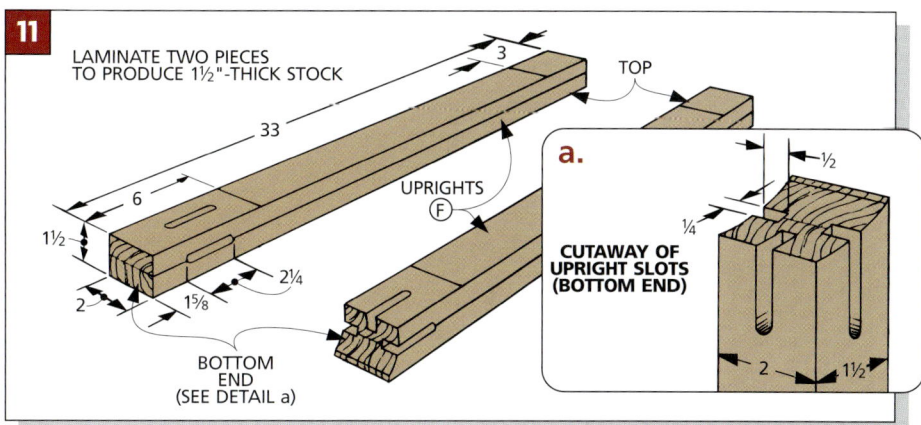

11 LAMINATE TWO PIECES TO PRODUCE $1^1/2$"-THICK STOCK — 33 — 3 — TOP — 6 — UPRIGHTS (F) — $1^1/2$ — 2 — $1^5/8$ — $2^1/4$ — BOTTOM END (SEE DETAIL a)

a. CUTAWAY OF UPRIGHT SLOTS (BOTTOM END) — $1/2$ — $1/4$ — 2 — $1^1/2$

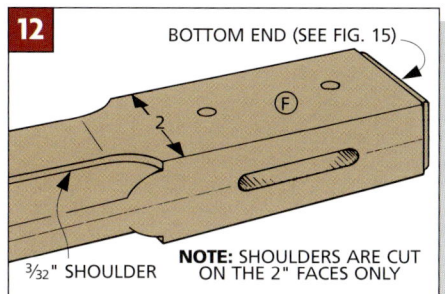

12 BOTTOM END (SEE FIG. 15) — (F) — 2 — $3/32$" SHOULDER — **NOTE:** SHOULDERS ARE CUT ON THE 2" FACES ONLY

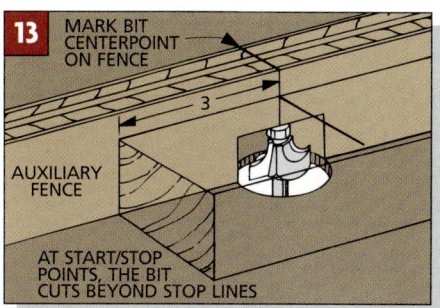

13 MARK BIT CENTERPOINT ON FENCE — 3 — AUXILIARY FENCE — AT START/STOP POINTS, THE BIT CUTS BEYOND STOP LINES

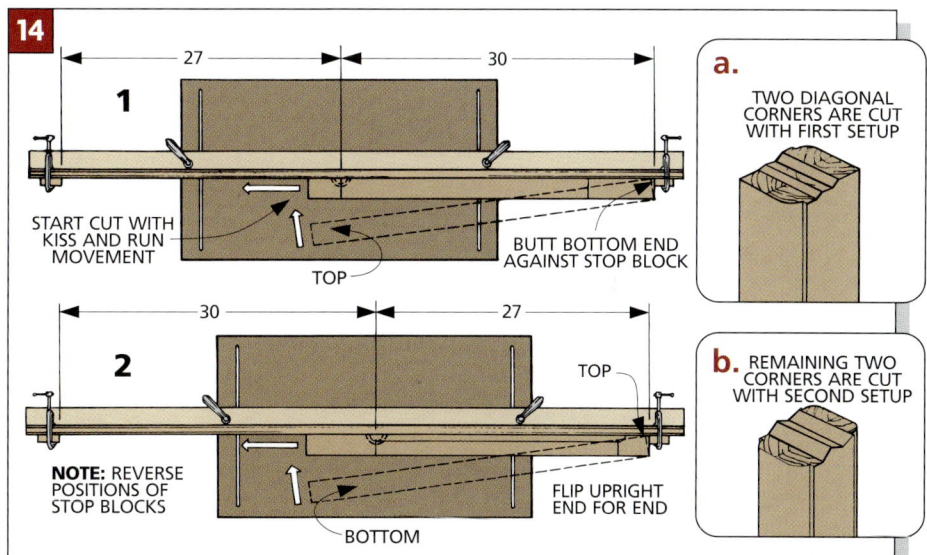

14 **1** — 27 — 30 — START CUT WITH KISS AND RUN MOVEMENT — TOP — BUTT BOTTOM END AGAINST STOP BLOCK

2 — 30 — 27 — TOP — **NOTE:** REVERSE POSITIONS OF STOP BLOCKS — FLIP UPRIGHT END FOR END — BOTTOM

a. TWO DIAGONAL CORNERS ARE CUT WITH FIRST SETUP

b. REMAINING TWO CORNERS ARE CUT WITH SECOND SETUP

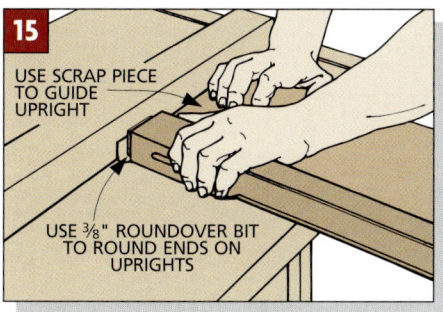

15 USE SCRAP PIECE TO GUIDE UPRIGHT — USE $3/8$" ROUNDOVER BIT TO ROUND ENDS ON UPRIGHTS

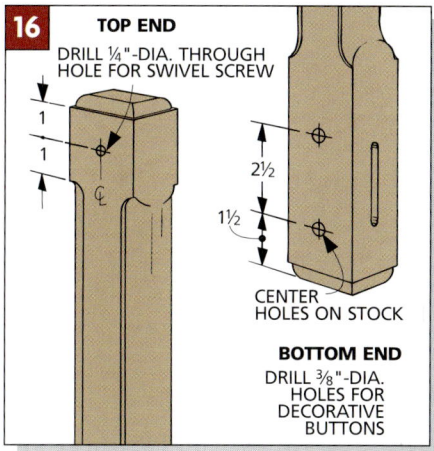

16 TOP END — DRILL $1/4$"-DIA. THROUGH HOLE FOR SWIVEL SCREW — 1 — 1 — $2^1/2$ — $1^1/2$ — CENTER HOLES ON STOCK

BOTTOM END — DRILL $3/8$"-DIA. HOLES FOR DECORATIVE BUTTONS

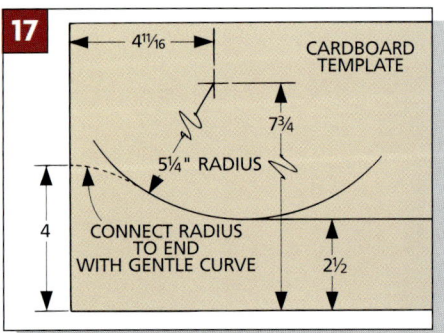

17
4¹¹⁄₁₆
CARDBOARD TEMPLATE
7³⁄₄
5¼" RADIUS
4
CONNECT RADIUS TO END WITH GENTLE CURVE
2½

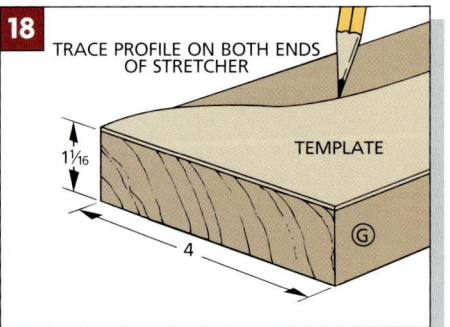

18
TRACE PROFILE ON BOTH ENDS OF STRETCHER
TEMPLATE
1¹⁄₁₆
4
(G)

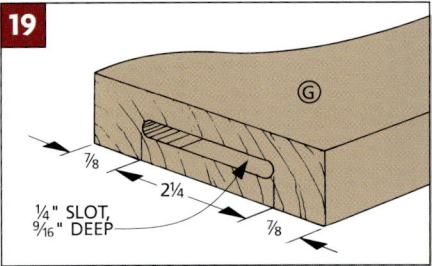

19
(G)
⅞
2¼
⅞
¼" SLOT, ⁹⁄₁₆" DEEP

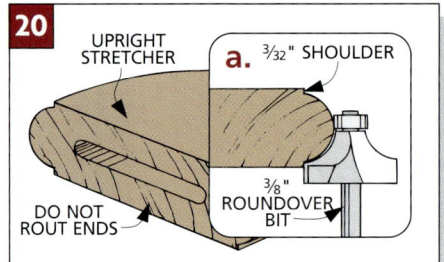

20
UPRIGHT STRETCHER
a. ³⁄₃₂" SHOULDER
DO NOT ROUT ENDS
³⁄₈" ROUNDOVER BIT

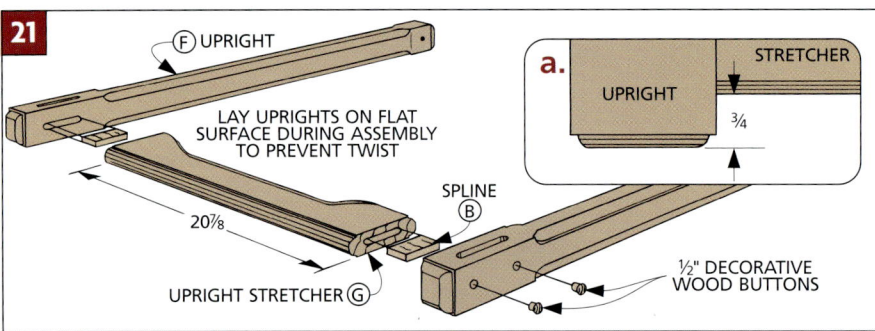

21
(F) UPRIGHT
LAY UPRIGHTS ON FLAT SURFACE DURING ASSEMBLY TO PREVENT TWIST
a.
STRETCHER
UPRIGHT
¾
20⅞
UPRIGHT STRETCHER (G)
SPLINE (B)
½" DECORATIVE WOOD BUTTONS

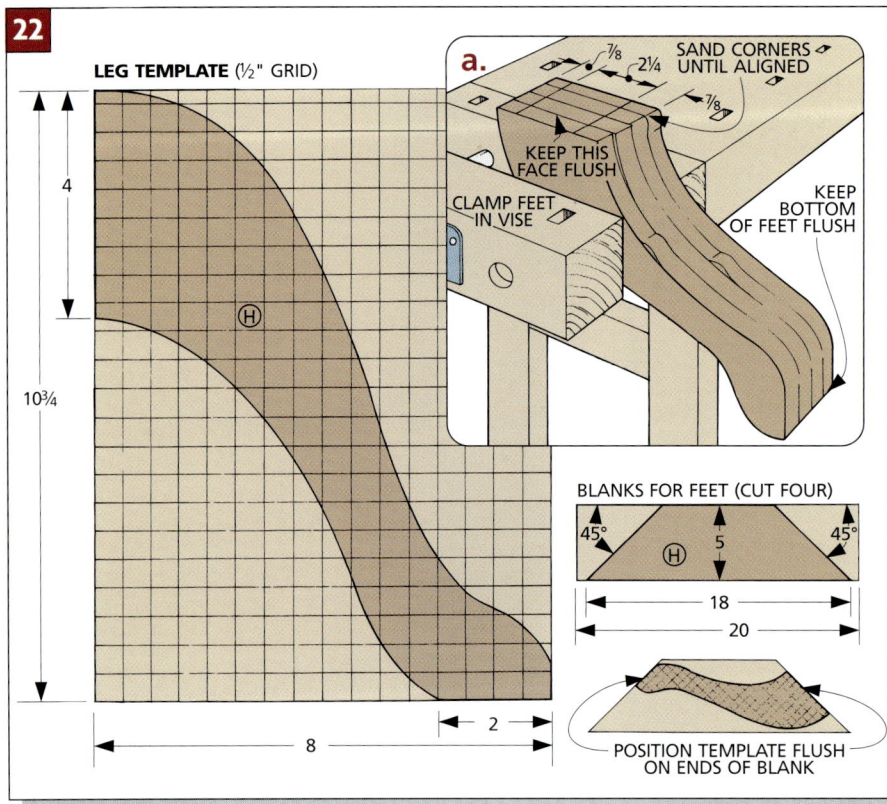

22
LEG TEMPLATE (½" GRID)
4
(H)
10¾
8
2
a.
⅞ 2¼
SAND CORNERS UNTIL ALIGNED
⅞
KEEP THIS FACE FLUSH
CLAMP FEET IN VISE
KEEP BOTTOM OF FEET FLUSH
BLANKS FOR FEET (CUT FOUR)
45°
(H)
5
45°
18
20
POSITION TEMPLATE FLUSH ON ENDS OF BLANK

STRETCHER

A single stretcher is used to join the two uprights on the mirror stand. To determine the correct length of the upright stretcher (G), you have to take into account the width of the mirror frame. But you also need to figure in the thickness of the flange on each of the threaded inserts that will be installed in the uprights (refer to *Fig. 30*). (The length of my stretcher ended up being 20⅞".)

The upright stretcher (G) is cut from 5/4 stock to a width of 4". Next, I made a template to lay out the curve at each end of the stretcher (*Figs. 17 and 18*). After the profile has been cut on the band saw, sand the edges smooth.

Again, rout ¼" x 2¼" slot mortises in the ends of the stretchers (*Fig. 19*), and cut hardwood splines to fit. Then the top and bottom edges of the stretcher are routed using a ⅜" roundover bit, set to leave a ³⁄₃₂" shoulder (*Fig. 20a*).

ASSEMBLY. Finally, finish-sand the uprights and the stretcher. Then assemble these pieces so the bottom edge of the stretcher is ¾" from the bottom of both uprights (*Fig. 21a*).

LEGS

To help eliminate waste, and to prevent weak spots due to improper grain direction, the four curved legs of the mirror stand are cut at an angle on four 5"-wide blanks. Miter both ends on each piece at 45°, so they measure 18" from long point to long point (*Fig. 22*).

Cutting all four legs to exactly the same shape requires using a template (*Fig. 22*). To make the template, first copy the profile onto a piece of cardboard and cut it out. Then trace the shape onto each of the leg blanks and band saw the blanks to rough shape.

Next, clamp the four legs together and sand them to a uniform shape. As you sand, check the lower curves where the legs will meet the uprights (*Fig. 22a*). These ends must all align so the legs can be positioned correctly later.

After the legs are cut to size, rout ¼" wide, 2¼"-long mortises on the end of each leg that attaches to the uprights (*Fig. 23*). (Again, I used the slotting jig on page 46 for this job.)

MOLDING. Now, using a ⅜" roundover bit on the router table, rout only the top edge on all four legs (*Fig. 23*). Here again, leave a ³⁄₃₂" shoulder on the roundover.

ASSEMBLY. After the legs are routed, they're sanded and glued to the uprights. You'll need to cut splines to fit the mortises, then glue the legs ³/₄" from the bottom of the uprights *(Fig. 24)*. You can use handscrews and pipe clamps, or hand pressure to clamp the legs in position.

FINAL FITTING

At this point, both the mirror frame and the stand are just about complete. However, the two assemblies can't be put together until a couple of threaded inserts are installed in the frame.

POSITION THE FRAME. To install the inserts, place a ³/₄"-thick spacer block between the mirror frame and the upright stretcher *(Fig. 25)*. With the frame held in this position, press an awl through the hole in an upright and mark one side of the mirror frame *(Fig. 26)*.

To be sure the insert on the other side of the frame is located in exactly the same position, measure from the mark to the bottom of the frame *(Fig. 25)*. Then transfer this measurement to the other side of the frame.

My inserts required ³/₈"-dia. holes drilled ⁷/₈" deep. The holes are centered on the flat spot on the outside edge of the frame *(Fig. 27)*.

Note: As I was installing the inserts, I decided to coat the outside threads with epoxy to help prevent them from rotating in the hole when the mirror is pivoted.

MIRROR BACK. The ¹¹/₁₆"-deep rabbet that was routed on the back of the mirror frame provides room for a ¹/₈"-thick mirror, a ¹/₈"-thick hardboard back, and a flexible rubber stop.

To make the back (I), rip a piece of hardboard to the same width as the distance between the rabbets on the back of the mirror frame. Then lay the frame over the hardboard, and trace the inside rabbeted profile of the top arch and both bottom corners *(Fig. 28)*. Using a jig saw, cut the hardboard to fit the frame.

At this point, I took the unfinished mirror frame to a local glass store and had them measure for and cut a piece of ¹/₈"-thick mirror to fit the frame.

FINISH. Before installing the mirror, I stained the frame and stand. Three coats of an oil finish were used as a topcoat.

MOUNTING THE MIRROR. Once the topcoat is dry, you are ready to mount the mirror. I laid the frame face-down on my bench with a blanket underneath to protect the finish and the mirror. Then

place the mirror in the frame. Next the hardboard back (I) is placed on top of the mirror, and the whole works is held in place with a flexible rubber stop that's tacked in place *(Fig. 29)*.

Finally, you can mount the frame in the stand by screwing the mirror screws into the threaded inserts *(Fig. 30)*. The mirror can be held in a tilted position by just tightening the screws. ∎

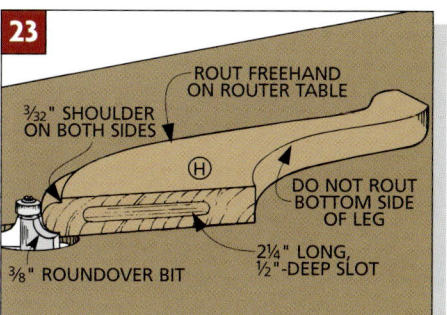

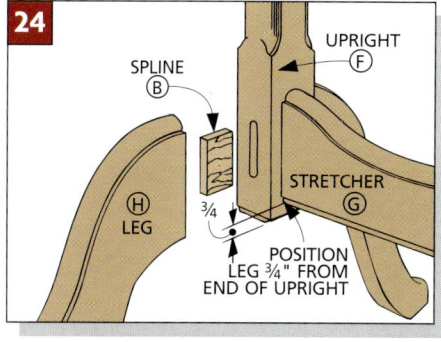

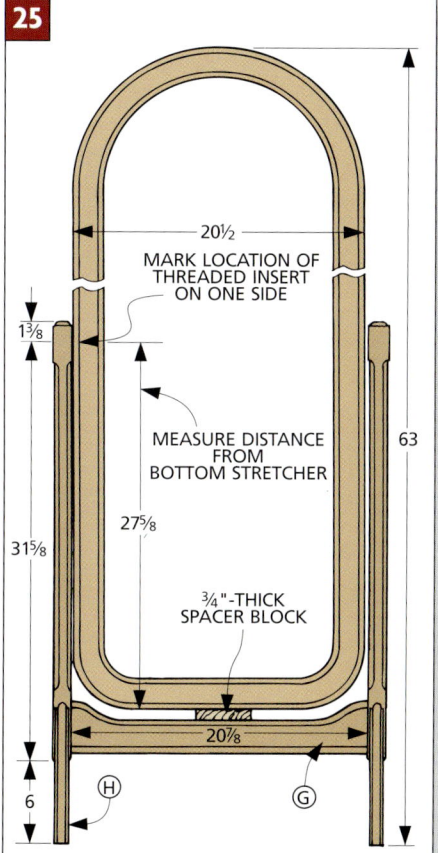

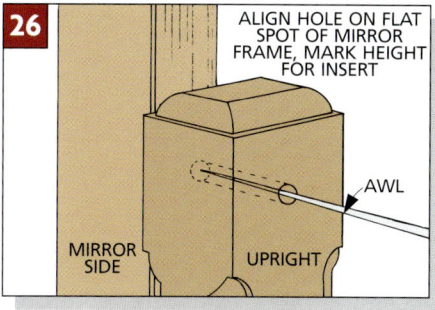

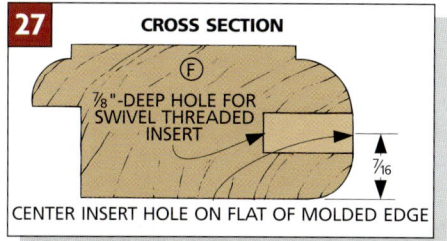

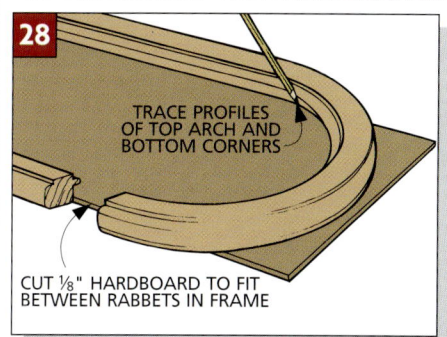

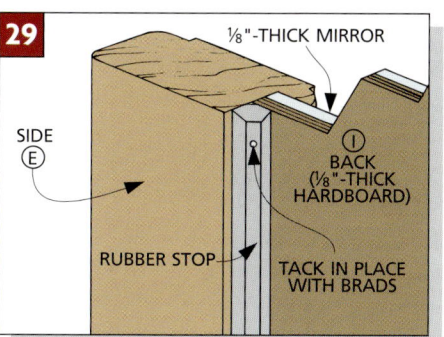

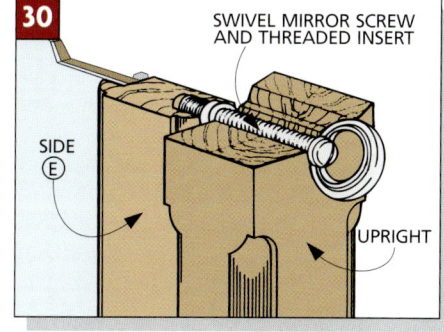

Under-Bed Storage Box

This handy storage box will help you turn the unused space under your bed into a convenient storage area for clothes and such. Hidden wheels let you roll it back and forth for quick and easy access.

When I was growing up, I remember one summer I kept a box under my bed that was filled with all my "childhood treasures." Many nights, I would pull the box out and sift through the contents.

I still store things under my bed, but these days it's much less exciting stuff (blankets, clothing, and shoes, mostly). And as I'm getting older, it's getting harder to the haul the box out. Which is why I like this project.

At first glance, it looks like this box is floating above the floor. But in reality, it's resting on wheels. You just can't see them. That's because the wheels are concealed in narrow "pockets" hidden at each end of the box.

The point of all this is that the wheels make it a lot easier to pull the box out from under the bed. Then after you've taken out (or put away) your things, the whole box rolls back under the bed, out of sight. And it's a lot kinder on my back.

DOVETAIL JOINERY. The corners of the Under-Bed Storage Box are joined with machine-cut dovetails. If you've never used a dovetail jig before, this is a good project to start with. If dovetails don't interest you, I'm also providing an alternate joint for the corners of the box. You can read more about this in the Joinery box on page 52.

By the way, if you're new to routing machine-cut dovetails, take a minute to read the Joinery article that starts on page 56. It explains in detail the ins and outs of using a half-blind dovetail jig.

MATERIALS. My box is made from hard maple, a straight-grained and very strong hardwood, but you could just as easily use low-cost pine or Baltic birch plywood.

SMALL STORAGE BOX. If you have treasures of your own that you'd like to take special care of, consider building the box featured in the Designer's Notebook on page 55. It's just the right size to fit safe and sound inside the large storage box.

EXPLODED VIEW

OVERALL DIMENSIONS:
36W x 24⅛D x 6⅝H

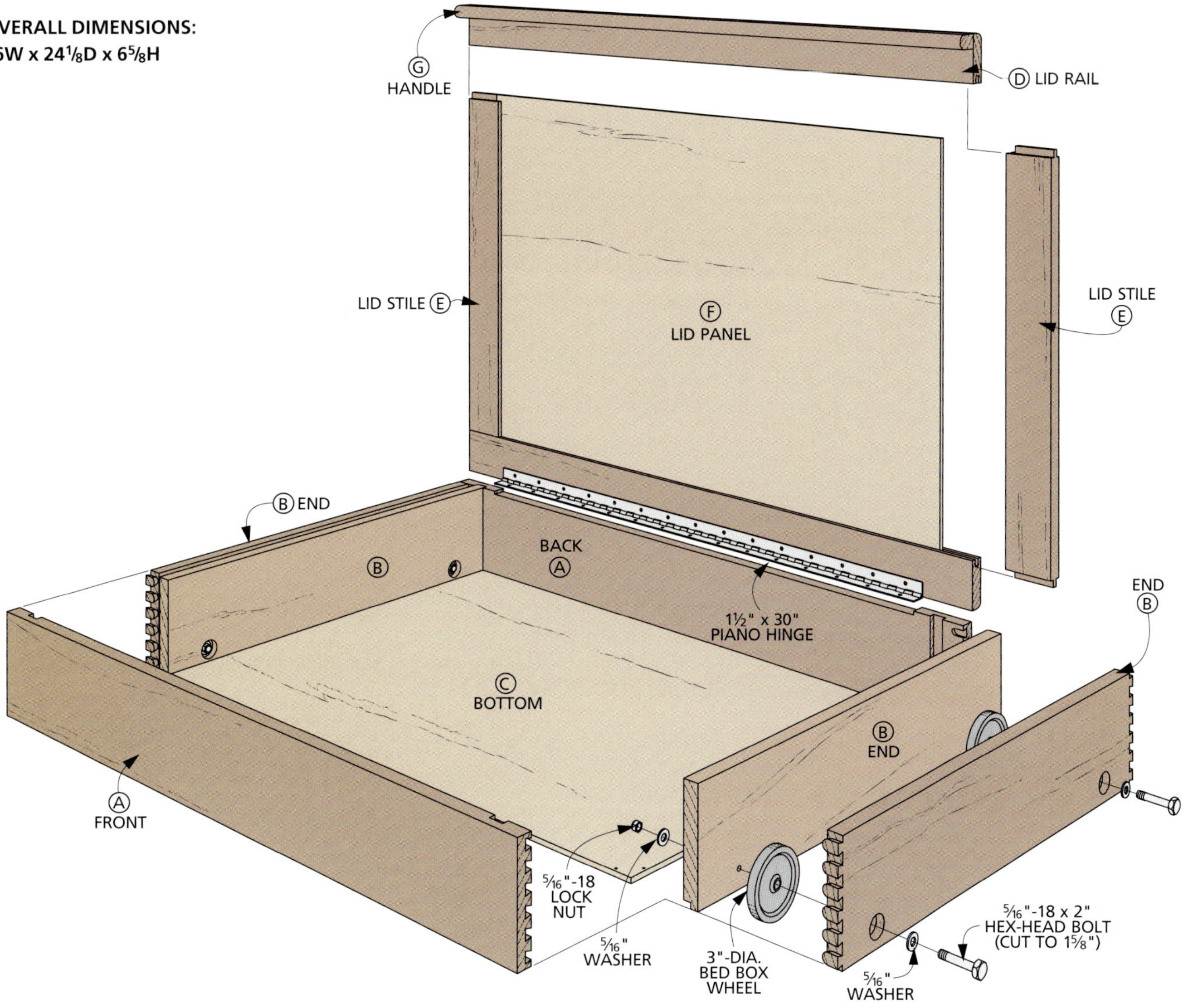

G HANDLE

D LID RAIL

LID STILE E

F LID PANEL

LID STILE E

B END

BACK A

B

END B

END B

1½" x 30" PIANO HINGE

C BOTTOM

A FRONT

⁵⁄₁₆"-18 LOCK NUT

⁵⁄₁₆" WASHER

3"-DIA. BED BOX WHEEL

⁵⁄₁₆" WASHER

⁵⁄₁₆"-18 x 2" HEX-HEAD BOLT (CUT TO 1⅝")

CUTTING DIAGRAM

¾ x 5½ - 96 HARD MAPLE (Two Boards @ 3.7 Bd. Ft. Each)

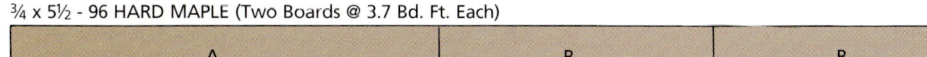

| A | B | B | |

¾ x 5½ - 84 HARD MAPLE (3.2 Bd. Ft.)

G

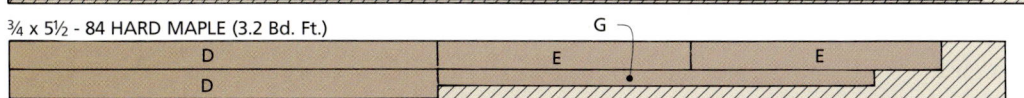

| D | E | E | |
| D | | | |

ALSO NEED: ONE 48" x 48" SHEET OF ¼" BIRCH PLYWOOD

MATERIALS LIST	
WOOD	**HARDWARE SUPPLIES**
A Front/Back (2) ¾ x 5¼ - 36	(20) No. 6 x ¾" Fh woodscrews
B Ends (4) ¾ x 5¼ - 23⅛	(4) ⁵⁄₁₆"-18 x 2" hex-head bolts
C Bottom (1) ¼ ply - 23¼ x 32¾	(4) ⁵⁄₁₆"-18 lock nuts
D Lid Rails (2) ¾ x 2½ - 36	(8) ⁵⁄₁₆" washers
E Lid Stiles (2) ¾ x 2½ - 21¼	(4) 3"-dia. bed box wheels
F Lid Panel (1) ¼ ply - 21¼ x 31¾	(1) 1½" x 30" piano hinge w/ screws
G Handle (1) ¾ x 1¼ - 36	

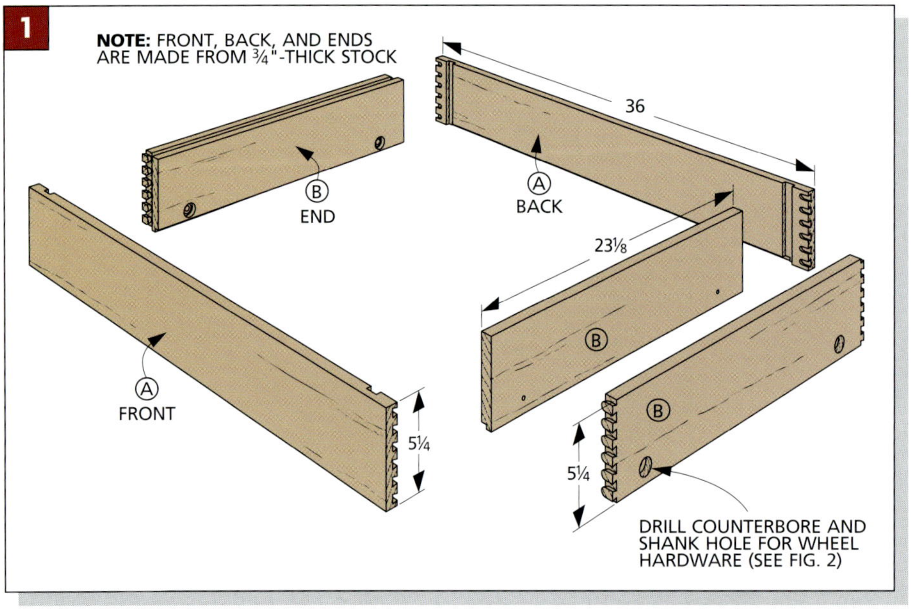
1
NOTE: FRONT, BACK, AND ENDS ARE MADE FROM ¾"-THICK STOCK
B END
36
A BACK
23⅛
A FRONT
B
B
5¼
5¼
DRILL COUNTERBORE AND SHANK HOLE FOR WHEEL HARDWARE (SEE FIG. 2)

CUT PIECES. To build the box frame, I began by planing all my stock to a uniform thickness (3/4"). (This is important for the dovetail jig to work properly.) Then I cut the front and back (A) and the ends (B) to size *(Fig. 1)*.

DRILL HOLES. Before starting on the dovetails, I drilled the holes in the end pieces for the wheel hardware *(Fig. 1)*. It's easier to drill the holes at this point, before the box is assembled. You just have to position the holes carefully so they will line up exactly when the box is assembled. To do this, I used a drill press with a fence and a stop block.

I started by drilling the counterbores first. After laying out the hole locations on all four pieces, I set up a stop block on the fence of my drill press *(Fig. 2)*. Then I drilled a 1"-dia. counterbore on one end of each piece *(Fig. 2a)*.

Now, without moving the fence or stop block, drill a hole through each piece using a 5/16"-dia. bit *(Fig. 2b)*. When you're finished with these holes, set up the stop block on the opposite side of the

BOX CONSTRUCTION

The Under-Bed Storage Box frame is made up of six pieces — a front and back and four end pieces *(Fig. 1)*. Two of these ends are dovetailed to join with the front and back. But the other two will fit into dadoes cut near the ends of the front and back pieces. This double-wall construction creates the cavity for the wheels.

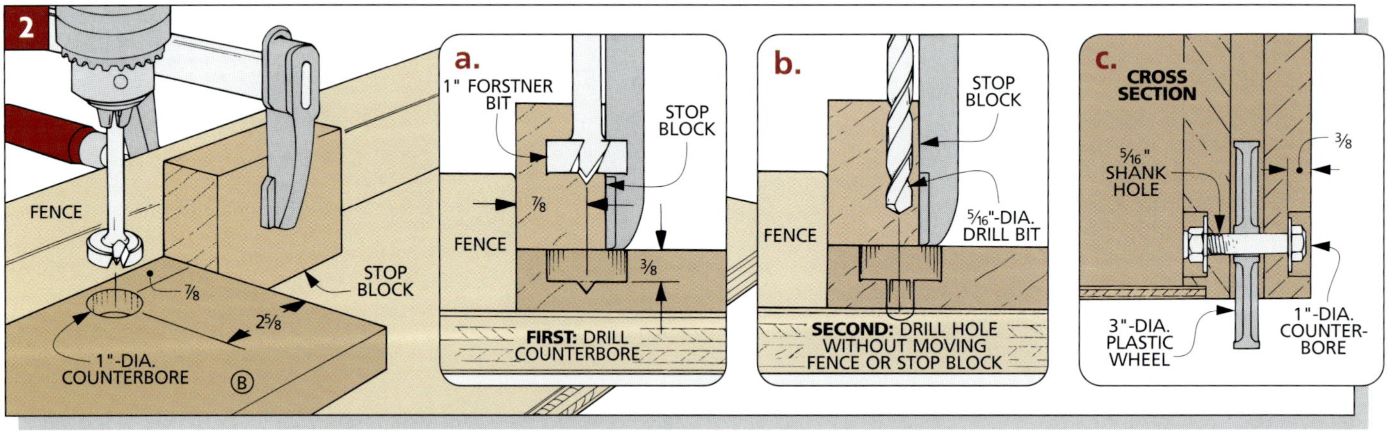
2
FENCE
⅞
2⅝
1"-DIA. COUNTERBORE
B
STOP BLOCK
a.
1" FORSTNER BIT
STOP BLOCK
FENCE
⅞
⅜
FIRST: DRILL COUNTERBORE
b.
STOP BLOCK
FENCE
5/16"-DIA. DRILL BIT
SECOND: DRILL HOLE WITHOUT MOVING FENCE OR STOP BLOCK
c.
CROSS SECTION
5/16" SHANK HOLE
⅜
3"-DIA. PLASTIC WHEEL
1"-DIA. COUNTER-BORE

JOINERY . . . . Rabbets

Dovetails provide extra strength when you need it and they look great. But if you don't have a dovetail jig, you can use rabbet joints to connect the ends of the box with the front and back.

All you have to do is cut rabbets on the edges of the front and back pieces to match the width of the ends (detail 'a'). (Make sure your dadoes are the same depth as your rabbets so the holes for the wheels line up correctly.) Then just assemble the box with glue and counterbored screws, plugging the screw holes with wood plugs (see drawing).

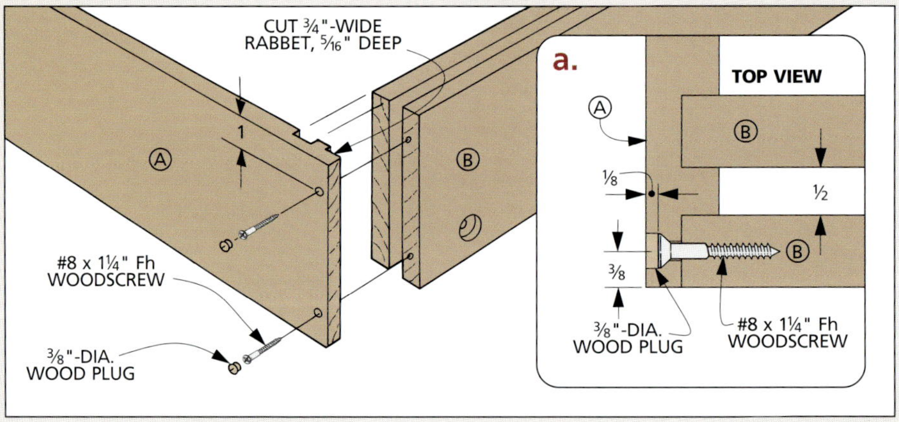
CUT ¾"-WIDE RABBET, 5/16" DEEP
1
A
B
#8 x 1¼" Fh WOODSCREW
⅜"-DIA. WOOD PLUG
a.
TOP VIEW
A
B
⅛
½
⅜
B
⅜"-DIA. WOOD PLUG
#8 x 1¼" Fh WOODSCREW

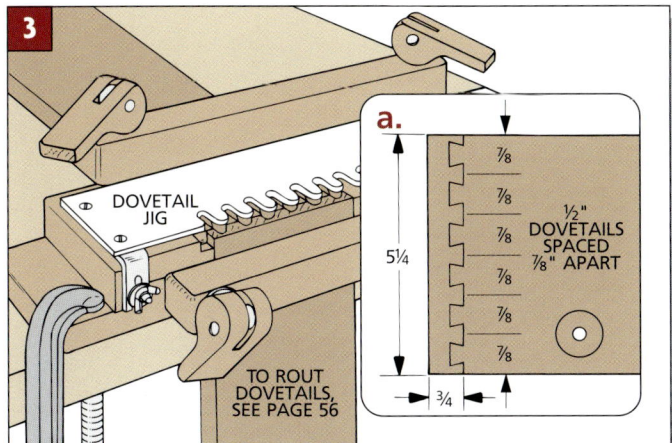

3

a.

DOVETAIL JIG

TO ROUT DOVETAILS, SEE PAGE 56

5¼

¾

⅞
⅞
⅞
⅞
⅞
⅞

½" DOVETAILS SPACED ⅞" APART

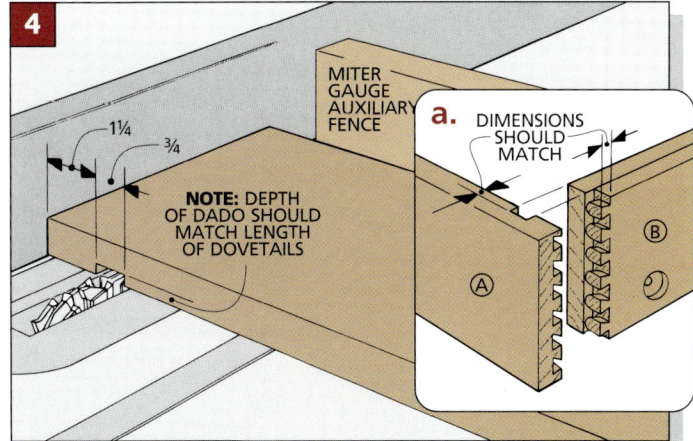

4

MITER GAUGE AUXILIARY FENCE

1¼   ¾

NOTE: DEPTH OF DADO SHOULD MATCH LENGTH OF DOVETAILS

a. DIMENSIONS SHOULD MATCH

Ⓐ

Ⓑ

bit and repeat the procedure to drill the holes and counterbores on the opposite ends of the workpieces.

ROUT DOVETAILS. Once the holes for the wheel hardware are drilled, you can rout the dovetails on the front, back, and two ends *(Figs. 3 and 3a)*. As you set up to rout the dovetails, make sure the counterbores for the wheel hardware will end up on the outside faces *(Fig. 2c)*.

If you don't want to use half-blind dovetails for your storage box, you can use a basic rabbet joint. (See the Joinery box on the preceding page.)

CUT DADOES. The interior end pieces are joined to the front and back with a simple dado joint *(Fig. 4)*. The width of the dado should match the thickness of your stock. (I made mine ¾" wide.) But to determine the depth of the dadoes, you'll need to measure the length of the dovetails on the end piece *(Fig. 4a)*. This way, all four end pieces will fit between the front and back of the box.

Once you have the dadoes cut to size, you're ready to glue and assemble the box. I glued up the dovetailed pieces first. Then I slid the two interior end pieces into the dadoes and clamped the box together.

BOTTOM. The box frame is almost complete, but the ¼"-thick plywood bottom (C) still needs to be added. Once the glue dries, turn the box upside-down and start by routing a ⅜"-wide rabbet around the large opening in the bottom of the box *(Figs. 5 and 5a)*. The depth of this rabbet should match the thickness of the plywood bottom.

When you're routing across the front and back pieces, you may need to clamp a support block flush with the pieces to support the router base *(Fig. 5)*. (The double-wall ends should provide enough support for the base while you're routing across the ends.)

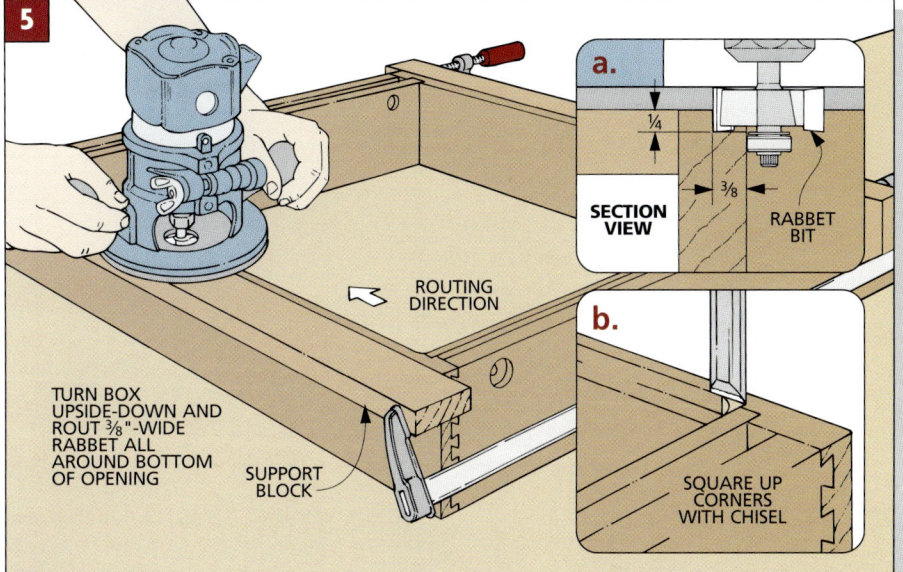

5

ROUTING DIRECTION

TURN BOX UPSIDE-DOWN AND ROUT ⅜"-WIDE RABBET ALL AROUND BOTTOM OF OPENING

SUPPORT BLOCK

a.

SECTION VIEW

¼   ⅜

RABBET BIT

b.

SQUARE UP CORNERS WITH CHISEL

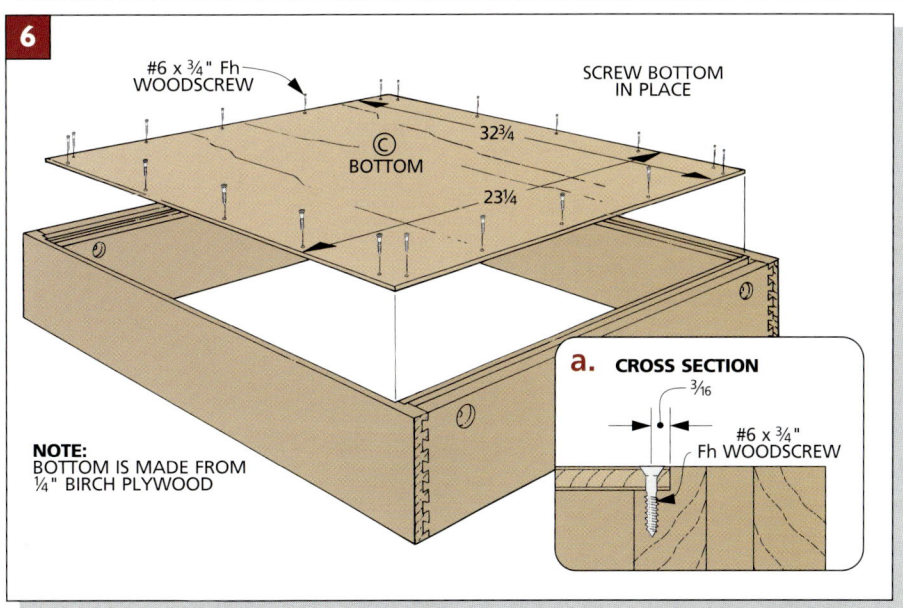

6

#6 x ¾" Fh WOODSCREW

SCREW BOTTOM IN PLACE

Ⓒ BOTTOM

32¾

23¼

NOTE: BOTTOM IS MADE FROM ¼" BIRCH PLYWOOD

a. CROSS SECTION

3/16

#6 x ¾" Fh WOODSCREW

The router leaves the corners of the rabbet rounded. So I squared them up with a sharp chisel *(Fig. 5b)*.

Finally, I cut the plywood bottom to size (23¼" x 32¾") and screwed it in place *(Figs. 6 and 6a)*.

7

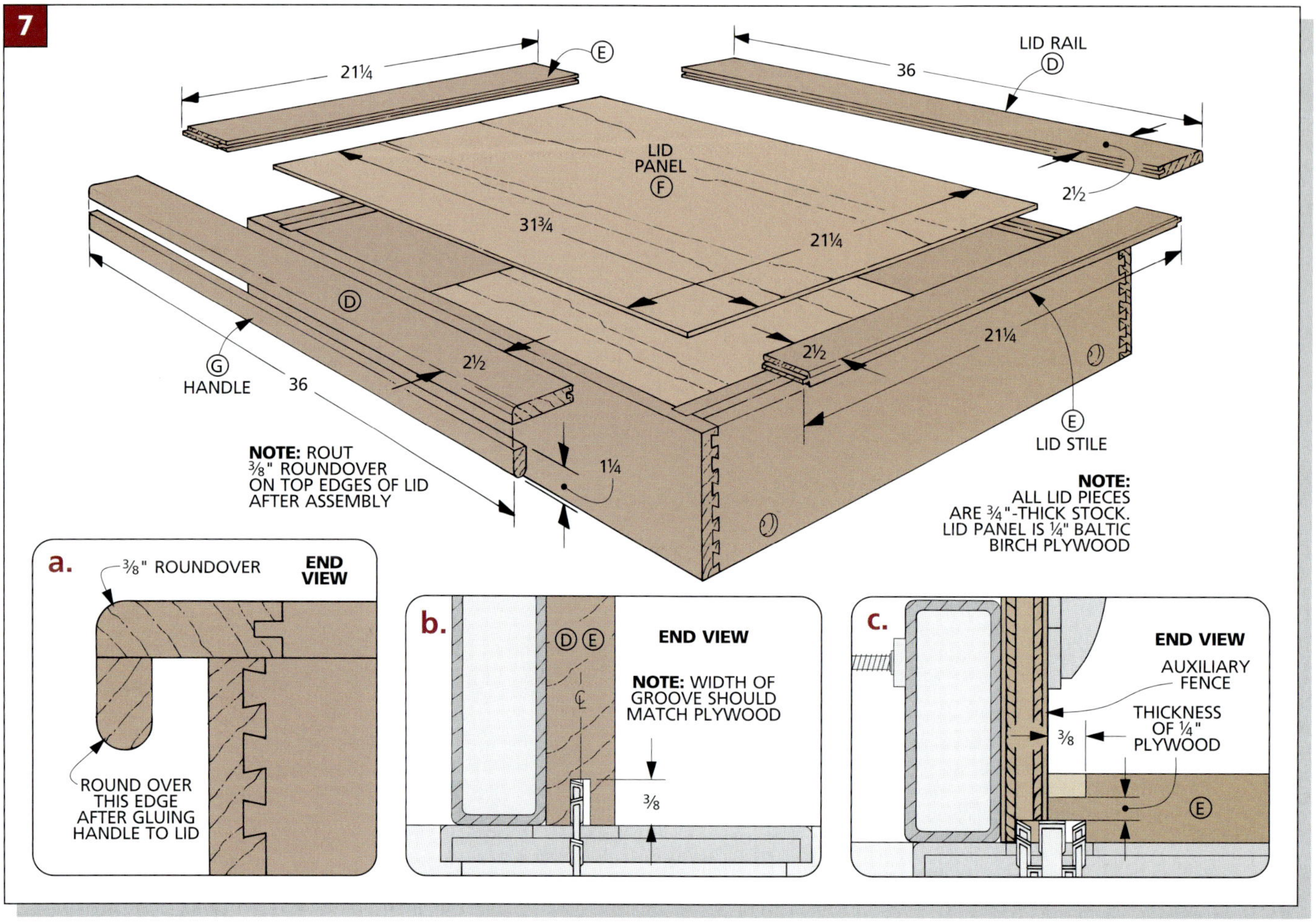

21¼ Ⓔ

LID RAIL Ⓓ
36

LID PANEL Ⓕ

31¾   21¼

2½

Ⓓ   21¼

Ⓖ   36
HANDLE

2½   2½

Ⓔ
LID STILE

1¼

NOTE: ROUT ⅜" ROUNDOVER ON TOP EDGES OF LID AFTER ASSEMBLY

NOTE: ALL LID PIECES ARE ¾"-THICK STOCK. LID PANEL IS ¼" BALTIC BIRCH PLYWOOD

a.   ⅜" ROUNDOVER   **END VIEW**

ROUND OVER THIS EDGE AFTER GLUING HANDLE TO LID

b.   Ⓓ Ⓔ   **END VIEW**

NOTE: WIDTH OF GROOVE SHOULD MATCH PLYWOOD

⅜

c.   **END VIEW**

AUXILIARY FENCE

THICKNESS OF ¼" PLYWOOD

⅜

Ⓔ

LID CONSTRUCTION

With the box completed, you can start working on the lid for the Under-Bed Storage Box, which is nothing more than a plywood panel in a hardwood frame. It's designed to be flush with the box on the ends and back, but it overhangs the front 1½". This provides room for a handle that's added later.

CUT LID FRAME. To make the lid, I began by cutting the frame pieces to size (*Fig. 7*). The lid frame is made up of two rails (D) and two stiles (E).

GROOVES AND TENONS. Once these pieces are all cut to size, you can cut a centered groove along one edge of each piece to hold the plywood panel (*Fig. 7b*).

To center the groove on the thickness of the rails and stiles, cut the groove in two passes, flipping the workpiece end for end between passes.

STUB TENONS. With the grooves cut in all four frame pieces, stub tenons can be cut on the ends of the stiles. These are sized to fit the grooves in the rails. You can make them on the table saw by burying a dado blade in a plywood fence that is

clamped to the rip fence (*Fig. 7c*). I found it easier to "sneak up" on the thickness of the stub tenon by raising the blade a little at a time between passes.

After cutting the lid panel (F) from ¼" plywood, the lid can be glued up. Then the edges are eased by routing a ⅜" roundover on the top.

ADD HANDLE. The last piece to add before attaching the lid is a handle. The handle (G) is a strip of hardwood running along the front edge of the lid (*Fig. 7*).

To make the handle, I cut a piece of stock to match the length of the lid (36").

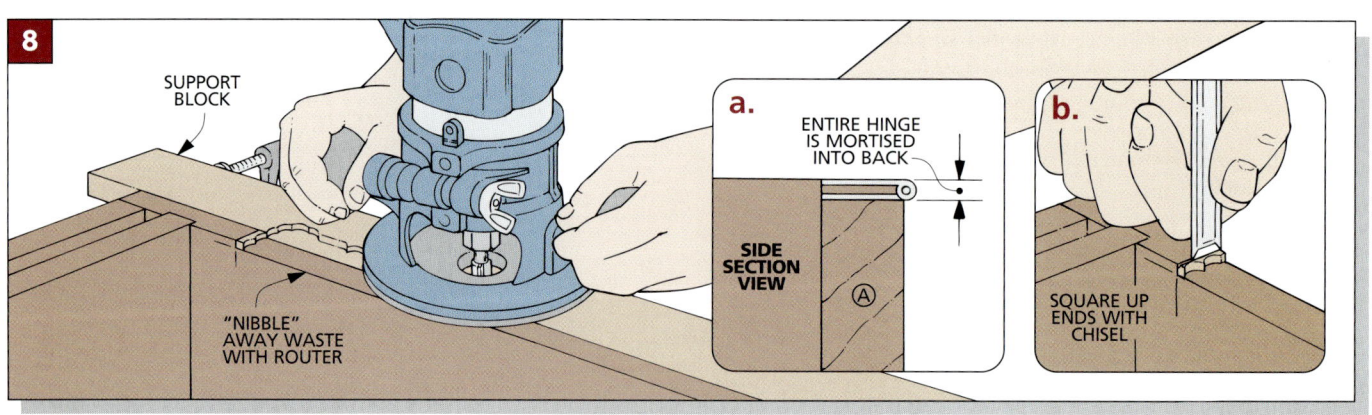

8   SUPPORT BLOCK

a.   ENTIRE HINGE IS MORTISED INTO BACK

SIDE SECTION VIEW   Ⓐ

b.   SQUARE UP ENDS WITH CHISEL

"NIBBLE" AWAY WASTE WITH ROUTER

The finished handle has a roundover routed on the front and back edges *(Fig. 7a)*. But I had to create this profile in two steps. First I rounded over just one edge of the handle (the inside edge). But before rounding over the front edge, I glued the handle to the lid. (It's easier to position the clamps while the front edge is still partially square.)

HINGE MORTISE. The lid is attached to the box with a piano hinge. It's mortised into the back of the box and screwed to the surface of the lid *(Fig. 8a)*.

To create the mortise for the hinge, I used a straight bit in my router *(Fig. 8)*. To provide some support for the router base, I clamped a scrap piece to the back of the box, flush with the top. Then I "nibbled away" the waste, working from one end to the other *(Fig. 8)*. Use a chisel to square off the mortise ends *(Fig. 8b)*.

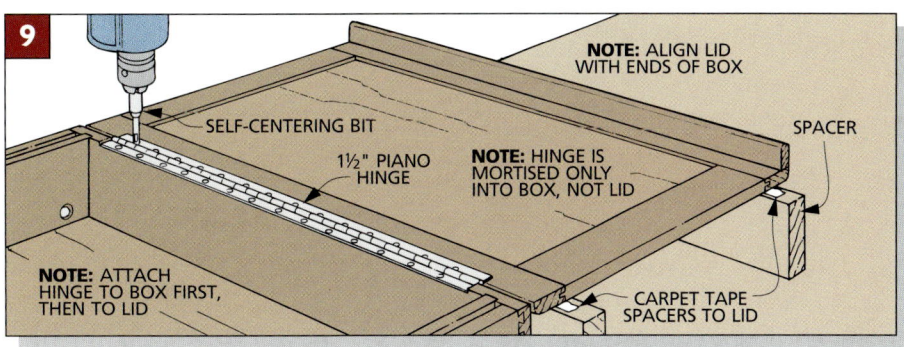

9

NOTE: ALIGN LID WITH ENDS OF BOX

SELF-CENTERING BIT

SPACER

1½" PIANO HINGE

NOTE: HINGE IS MORTISED ONLY INTO BOX, NOT LID

NOTE: ATTACH HINGE TO BOX FIRST, THEN TO LID

CARPET TAPE SPACERS TO LID

FINISH. Now it's time to apply a finish. (I used a wipe-on oil finish.) After the finish dries, the lid can be attached. First, screw the hinge into the mortise. I used spacer blocks to position the lid so that it was flush with the top of the box *(Fig. 9)*. Then simply screw the hinge to the lid.

ADD WHEELS. Finally, all that's left is to add the four bed box wheels (see Sources, page 126). Hex bolts serve as wheel "axles," and $5/16$"-18 lock nuts and washers hold everything together (refer to *Fig. 2c* on page 52).

Note: To make the axles for the wheels, I cut 2"-long bolts down to $1^5/8$". I used 2" bolts (instead of shorter ones) so each wheel has a smooth, unthreaded portion to ride on. ∎

DESIGNER'S NOTEBOOK
Protect your keepsakes in this Small Storage Box.

CONSTRUCTION NOTES:

■ To build the storage box, first cut the front (H), back (H), and sides (I) to size from $1/2$"-thick hardwood (see drawing).
■ For this small box, I used a simple tongue and dado joint to hold the sides in place. All this requires is cutting a dado near the ends of the front and back (see detail 'a' in drawing). Then cut a rabbet on the ends of the side pieces to make a tongue that fits the dado.
■ Next, cut a $1/4$"-deep groove in the front, back, and side pieces to hold a $1/4$" plywood bottom (see drawing).
■ Now, dry-assemble the box parts and measure the inside to determine the size of the bottom (J). Don't forget to add $1/2$" to the length and the width to account for the grooves you cut earlier.
■ Cut a piece of $1/2$"-thick hardwood to size for the lid (K) (see drawing). Then drill

a $1^1/2$"-dia. hole in the lid for a finger hold and add a $1/4$" roundover on the top edges of the lid and on each edge of the finger hole.
■ To complete the box, rout a shallow mortise on the back to hold a piano hinge flush with the top edge of the box sides and front (refer to

SMALL STORAGE BOX

Figs. 8 and 8a on the facing page) and screw lid in place. (This allows the lid to lie flat on top of the box.)

MATERIALS LIST
NEW PARTS
H Sm. Box Front/Back (2) $1/2$ x $4^3/8$ - 32
I Small Box Sides (2) $1/2$ x $4^3/8$ - $4^1/2$
J Small Box Bottom (1) $1/4$ ply - $4^1/2$ x $31^1/2$
K Small Box Lid (1) $1/2$ x 5 - 32
HARDWARE SUPPLIES
(1) $1^1/2$" x 30" piano hinge w/ screws

SMALL BOX SIDE

NOTE: BOTTOM IS $1/4$" PLYWOOD. ALL OTHER PARTS ARE $1/2$"-THICK STOCK

$1/2$" PIANO HINGE (30" LONG)

ROUT $1/4$" ROUNDOVER AROUND TOP OF LID

$1^1/2$"-DIA. FINGERHOLE WITH $1/4$" ROUNDOVERS ON TOP AND BOTTOM

32

SMALL BOX LID

SMALL BOX BACK

5

H SMALL BOX FRONT

32

31½

$4^1/2$

$4^1/2$

$4^3/8$

J SMALL BOX BOTTOM

$4^1/2$

I

a. H

I

$1/4$

$1/4$

MEASURE OPENING CUT-TO-FIT

$1/4$" x $1/4$" GROOVE FOR BOTTOM

Cutting half-blind dovetails is easy when you have the right tools for the job. I can still remember the first time I used a router and a dovetail jig. I don't know if it was the high-powered scream of the router, the shower of chips, or the rhythmic motion of moving the router in and out around the template, but I was definitely hooked. For the next few months, I used half-blind dovetails on just about every project I made.

Although that initial excitement has subsided a little, I still think a dovetail jig is a great accessory for any shop. For speed and accuracy, it's really hard to beat.

But there's more to cutting dovetails than simply flipping the switch on your router. The jig and router each require careful setup. Plus, you'll need a couple of scrap test pieces to "fine-tune" the fit. Fortunately, the setup steps aren't too difficult. All it takes is a little patience and some perseverance.

JIGS. There are several kinds of jigs on the market designed to cut dovetails. One of the more common types cuts "half-blind" dovetails (see photo above).

Note: Half-blind dovetails are often used on drawers where you don't want the dovetails to be visible from the front. Another benefit is the ability to "show-off" the joint with contrasting woods

All half-blind dovetail jigs work in the same fashion (see the photos below).

The two workpieces are clamped in the jig at a right angle to each other. Then a comb-like template is placed over the workpieces. A bushing on the router base

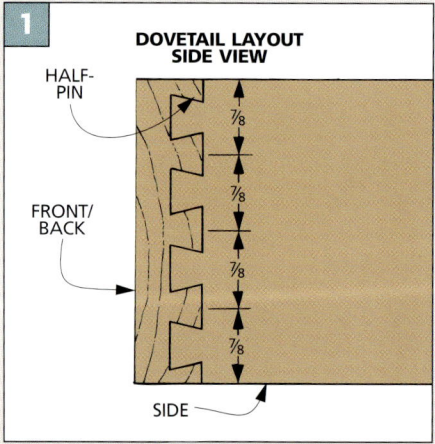

1

DOVETAIL LAYOUT
SIDE VIEW

HALF-PIN

FRONT/BACK

$\frac{7}{8}$

$\frac{7}{8}$

$\frac{7}{8}$

$\frac{7}{8}$

$\frac{7}{8}$

SIDE

(or sometimes a pilot bearing on the router bit) guides a dovetail-shaped bit around the "fingers" of the template. This way, both the pins and the tails are cut at the same time *(Figs. 2a and 2b)*.

The template controls the spacing of the dovetails. Most templates are designed to cut $\frac{1}{2}$"-wide dovetails spaced $\frac{7}{8}$" apart. So it's best to plan your projects so the width (height) of the drawers is always a multiple of $\frac{7}{8}$". (As is the case with all the dovetail projects in this book.) This way, you'll always end up with a joint that is symmetrical — with a perfect half-pin on both the top and the bottom *(Fig. 1)*.

TEST CUTS. The template may control the spacing of the dovetails, but there are still a couple of adjustments that you'll have to make to control the fit of the joint. And since you don't want to risk ruining your finished drawer, you'll need to practice on a couple of test pieces that are the same width and thickness as your drawer pieces. Then once you get the settings just right, you can rout the dovetails on your actual workpieces.

SETTING UP THE JIG. Essentially, there are three different adjustments that you'll need to be concerned with when setting up the dovetail jig.

First, a "stepped" stop on each end of the jig is used to create an offset between two workpieces. This also positions them from side-to-side underneath the tem-

Clamp Pieces in Jig. *After adjusting both workpieces underneath the dovetail jig template, tighten down the cams on the clamping bars to hold the workpieces securely in place.*

Rout Dovetails. *The template guides the router in and out as the dovetails and pins are routed simultaneously. This ensures you'll end up with a perfectly-aligned joint every time.*

Test Fit. *With the pieces removed from the jig, test the fit of the joint. The tails should slide halfway into the sockets. If needed, a soft mallet can then be used to drive the joint home.*

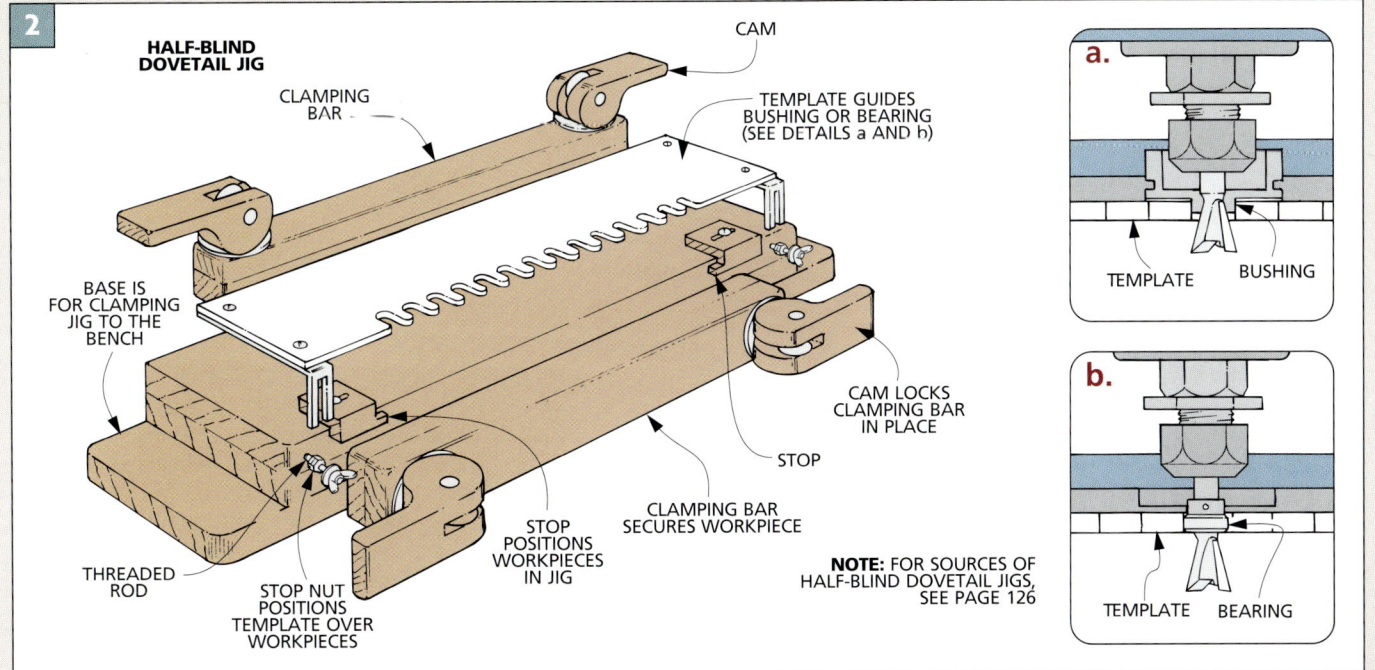

2

HALF-BLIND DOVETAIL JIG

CLAMPING BAR

CAM

TEMPLATE GUIDES BUSHING OR BEARING (SEE DETAILS a AND h)

BASE IS FOR CLAMPING JIG TO THE BENCH

CAM LOCKS CLAMPING BAR IN PLACE

STOP

STOP POSITIONS WORKPIECES IN JIG

CLAMPING BAR SECURES WORKPIECE

THREADED ROD

STOP NUT POSITIONS TEMPLATE OVER WORKPIECES

NOTE: FOR SOURCES OF HALF-BLIND DOVETAIL JIGS, SEE PAGE 126

a.

TEMPLATE   BUSHING

b.

TEMPLATE   BEARING

---

plate *(Fig. 2 and Step 1 below)*. (On some dovetail jigs, this offset is created by using two separate stops.) This stop ensures that the dovetails are centered on the width of the workpieces (leaving equal-sized half-pins at the top and bottom of each piece) *(Fig. 1)*.

When you're making a drawer or box, half the joints are cut on the left side of the jig and half are cut on the right side. (This way, the bottom of the workpiece is always against a stop.) So you'll have to set the stop at each end independently (see *Step 1* at right).

The second adjustment to make is to the template. Two stop nuts on the threaded rods control the front-to-back positioning of the template, which affects the depth of the sockets *(Steps 2 and 3)*. (The sockets are the spaces into which the dovetail pins fit.)

And finally, raising or lowering the height of the dovetail bit in the router controls the fit of the dovetails *(Step 4)*.

Later, you'll fine-tune each of these adjustments. For now, you just want to get them "close" and make your first test cut.

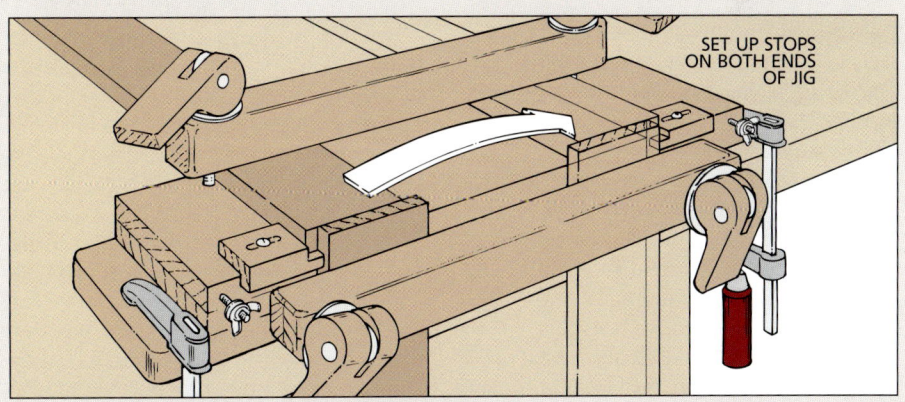

SET UP STOPS ON BOTH ENDS OF JIG

1 The stops on the ends of the jig are used to create a ⁷⁄₁₆" offset between the two workpieces and to position them from side-to-side beneath the template. You'll need to adjust each end of the jig independently, since half the dovetail joints are cut on the left and half are cut on the right.

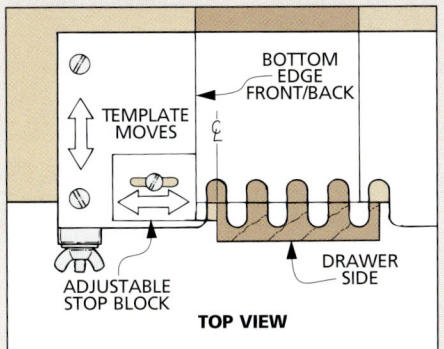

BOTTOM EDGE FRONT/BACK

TEMPLATE MOVES

ADJUSTABLE STOP BLOCK

DRAWER SIDE

TOP VIEW

2 With the test pieces in the jig, adjust the stop so the edge of the front piece is centered in the first notch or opening of the template.

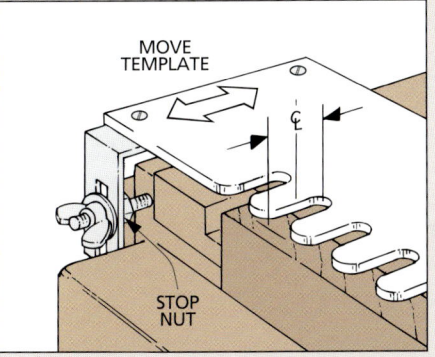

MOVE TEMPLATE

STOP NUT

3 A stop nut on each end of the jig should be adjusted in or out so the fingers of the template are centered over the "joint line" between the two test pieces.

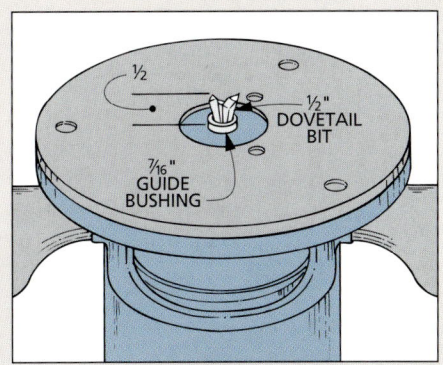

½

½" DOVETAIL BIT

⁷⁄₁₆" GUIDE BUSHING

4 Mount a ⁷⁄₁₆" guide bushing onto the router. Then to start with, raise the bit ½" from the router base. It may have to be adjusted slightly later on.

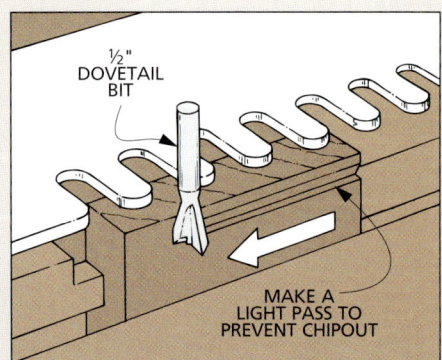

½" DOVETAIL BIT

MAKE A LIGHT PASS TO PREVENT CHIPOUT

5 *To prevent chipout on the drawer side, start by making a light pass, routing from right to left. This skim cut will then establish a clean shoulder line.*

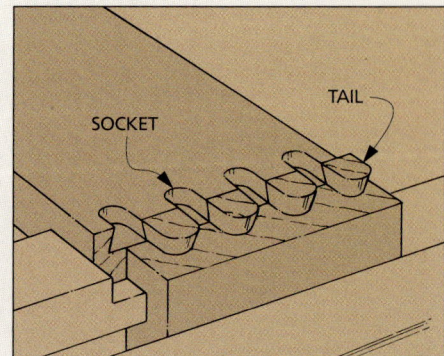

MOVE ROUTER IN AND OUT

6 *Next, move the router from left to right in and out of the notches. Push the router into each notch until the bushing hits the back of the notch.*

SOCKET   TAIL

7 *Finally, you can carefully remove the template (but not the workpieces) and check to make sure that all of the dovetails and sockets are uniform.*

ROUT TEST PIECES

Once you have the initial settings in place, you're ready to start making your test cuts to set the adjustments. To do this, place a test side under the clamping bar on the front of the jig and a test front under the clamping bar on top of the jig. (See the Shop Tip below for a way to get a solid grip on the workpieces.)

Make sure that both workpieces are tight against the stops. Plus, the end of the side piece should be flush with the top face of the front piece. (This is also important when it comes to routing dovetails in your actual workpieces.)

ADD TEMPLATE. Next, mount the template on the jig. Hold it down flat on the workpieces while you tighten the wing nuts. Also, make sure the template is resting flat and isn't flexed by the workpieces (especially if it's plastic).

ROUT THE TEST PIECES. Now the pieces can be routed. To prevent chipout, start

by making a light scoring pass from right to left along the jig *(Step 5).*

Note: It's normally not a good idea to rout in this direction (this is called back-routing). Just be sure to get a tight grip, go slow, and take a light pass.

After the initial scoring cut, start gently moving the router in and out of the fingers, beginning on the left-hand side *(Step 6).* You should be able to feel the guide bushing stop at the back of each notch.

Let the bushing and the template guide the router. You want to keep the bushing in contact with the edge of the template, but you don't need to force it.

When you're routing the dovetails, be careful to keep the router base flat on the template at all times. Accidentally tipping the router or lifting it up could damage your dovetails or your template.

REMOVE TEMPLATE. When you've finished routing the dovetails in the test pieces, remove the template to examine the dovetails. It's a good idea to leave the pieces in the jig until after you've checked, to make sure that you've routed every pin and socket cleanly *(Step 7).* This way, if you miss a spot, simply replace the template and clean up the area you missed.

TEST FIT. Now you can remove the test pieces from the jig and see how they fit. Before fitting the pieces together, though, take a second to blow out any chips in the sockets and lightly sand off any wood fibers remaining on the pieces *(Step 8).*

Slide the pieces together to see how they fit *(Step 9).* You should be able to slide the dovetails about halfway into the sockets by hand. Then a light tap or two with a mallet should fully seat the tails.

Don't worry if the fit isn't perfect. Chances are you'll have to make some adjustments to the jig or the router bit. (See "Testing the Fit" on the next page.)

The important thing is to avoid trying to adjust everything at once. Instead, focus on one thing at a time and keep making test cuts until you get it right.

Note: To re-use your test pieces, simply trim the dovetails off the ends.

Once you're satisfied with the fit of the cuts you made on the left side, cut a test joint on the right side of the jig as well to make sure the stop on this end is positioned correctly. (You shouldn't have to change the bit setting or the stop nuts for the template.) Now you're ready to rout the dovetails on your actual pieces.

WOOD FIBERS

DUST

8 *Before testing the fit of the joint, blow out any remaining wood chips and sand off any "whiskers" that are still attached to the pieces.*

9 *The dovetails should easily fit into the sockets about half way. A couple of taps with a dead-blow mallet should drive them in the rest of the way.*

ROUT DRAWER PIECES

The procedure for routing dovetails on the final workpieces is the same one that you used for routing your test pieces. But this is where all your patience in adjusting the jig pays off. Now it's just a matter of clamping each piece in the jig and routing the dovetails. The trick is keeping all the drawer pieces organized.

LAY OUT JOINTS. To help keep things straight, I like to start by laying out all four drawer pieces on top of my bench, with the *inside* faces up *(Fig. 3a)*. Then I number the matching corners (starting at the left front corner) and label each piece (front, back, or side). Finally, label or mark the bottom edge of each piece.

When you've got all the pieces labeled, you're ready to start routing the first corner. There are two main things to remember when placing the pieces in the jig. First, the pieces are always inserted so the *inside* faces out. And second, the bottom edges should always be against the stops. This means that you have to cut half the joints on the left side of the jig and half on the right side.

Note: To help me keep track of which corner goes where, I also label the ends

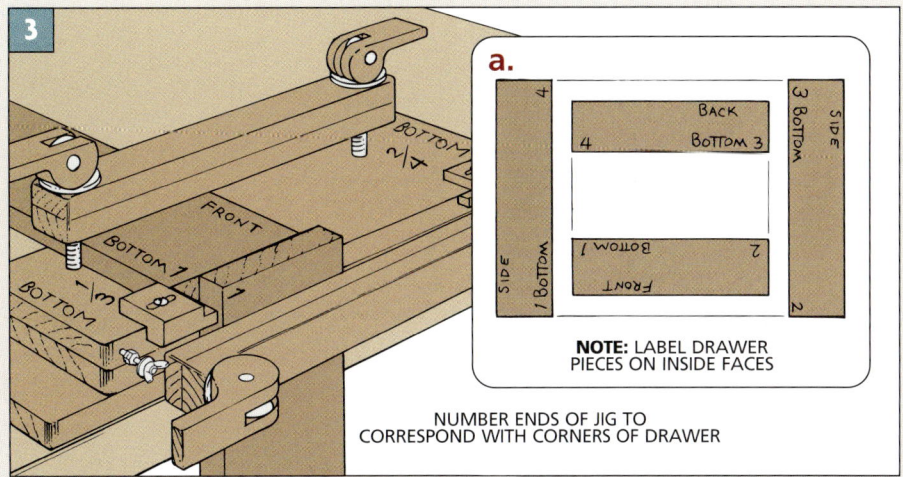

a.

NOTE: LABEL DRAWER PIECES ON INSIDE FACES

NUMBER ENDS OF JIG TO CORRESPOND WITH CORNERS OF DRAWER

of the jig with markings similar to those on the workpieces *(Fig. 3)*.

ROUT FIRST CORNER. To rout the first corner, place the drawer side in the front of the jig and the drawer front on the top, just like you did with the test pieces. Make sure the pieces are against the stops and the clamps are tightened securely. Then rout the dovetails.

At this point, you've routed the dovetail joint at the left front corner of the drawer (Number 1). Next, rout the right rear corner joint (Number 3) using the

same procedure. (Place the drawer back piece on the top of the jig.) The other two joints (Numbers 2 and 4) are routed with the pieces tight against the stop block on the right side of the jig.

When routing on the right side of the jig, follow the same procedure. Make a light scoring pass from right to left and then move the router in and out of the notches from left to right.

Now it's just a matter of repeating this process to cut the half-blind dovetails on any remaining drawers.

TESTING THE FIT

Setting up to rout machine-cut dovetails is always a trial and error effort. There's usually lots of fiddling around with test pieces and adjusting of the jig to get a perfect fit. The following are some troubleshooting techniques to try.

TOO LOOSE. If the joint is so loose that the pieces wiggle around when they're put together, the depth of cut is too shallow (left photo). Increase the depth of cut $1/32$" and try again.

TOO TIGHT. If a trial cut is so tight that the pieces can't be tapped together, the

router bit is extended out too far from the router base. Decrease the depth of cut about $1/32$" and try again.

TOO DEEP. If the pins on the drawer sides go too far into the sockets on the drawer front, the sockets are too deep (middle photo). To correct this, move the template forward (toward you) by turning the stop nuts on the studs counterclockwise. (Be sure to adjust the nuts equally on both ends of the jig.)

TOO SHALLOW. If the pins don't go far enough into the sockets, move the tem-

plate back (away from you) by turning the stop nuts clockwise.

OFFSET. If the top edges of the two pieces aren't flush when you assemble the joint, the problem is either with the offset of the stop blocks (it should be $7/16$") or the fact that the pieces weren't tight against the stops (right photo).

OTHER PROBLEMS. Other problems are usually caused by the pieces not being clamped down in the jig so they are flush across the top, or because they move out of position as they're being routed.

Too Loose. *If the dovetail joint is too loose, you can increase the depth of cut.* **Too Tight.** *But if the joint is too tight, you will need to decrease the depth of cut.*

Too Deep. *If the pins go deep in the socket, move the template forward a bit.* **Too Shallow.** *If the pins are not deep enough, move the template back.*

Offset. *If the drawer sides don't align at the top or bottom of the front or back, the workpieces may not have been pushed tight against the stops.*

Jewelry Case

This beautiful case was obviously built with its contents in mind. It has a rich appearance that says you are proud to store your fine jewelry inside. A rose inlay in the top adds a touch of elegance.

Fine jewelry deserves a fine home. The challenge is to build a case for your jewelry that has a delicate, yet rich appearance — in keeping with its contents. That's what I tried to do with this Jewelry Case.

In one respect, this case is only a four-sided box that's joined with miter and spline joints. But there are two things that make this case a little more than that. The first is the gently curved profile cut in the sides. In technical terms, it's a parabolic cove. In woodworking terms, it's an eye-catching detail that's cut on the table saw. All you need to cut this type of cove is a posterboard template for setting up your table saw. After the coves are cut the sides are joined with splined miters for a finished look.

INLAID TOP. The second "extra" is an inlaid marquetry top. Adding this touch is fairly simple, too. The inlaid top is really a pre-made piece. To add it, I left room in the lid frame for a plywood panel with a piece of inlay veneer glued to it.

That's just one way to dress up the lid. You could also build a lid from solid wood and then mortise in an inlay. I'll show you how to add a "pattern" inlay in the Designer's Notebook on page 72.

TRAYS. Another nice feature of the Jewelry Case is the trays. Instead of just throwing your fine jewelry in a jumble inside the case, I've designed it for two trays with dividers to keep everything straight. A lower tray fits snug in the bottom of the case and an upper tray (half as big as the lower tray) gives you even more storage space for your valuables.

HALF-MORTISE LOCK. And what Jewelry Case would be complete without a lock to keep its contents secure? The Technique article on page 64 gives you step-by-step instructions for installing the half-mortise lock.

NO COVES. I left off the coves and streamlined the look for a Jewelry Box that's a lot easier to build (see page 70).

EXPLODED VIEW

OVERALL DIMENSIONS:
12⁷⁄₈W x 8⁷⁄₈D x 4³⁄₈H

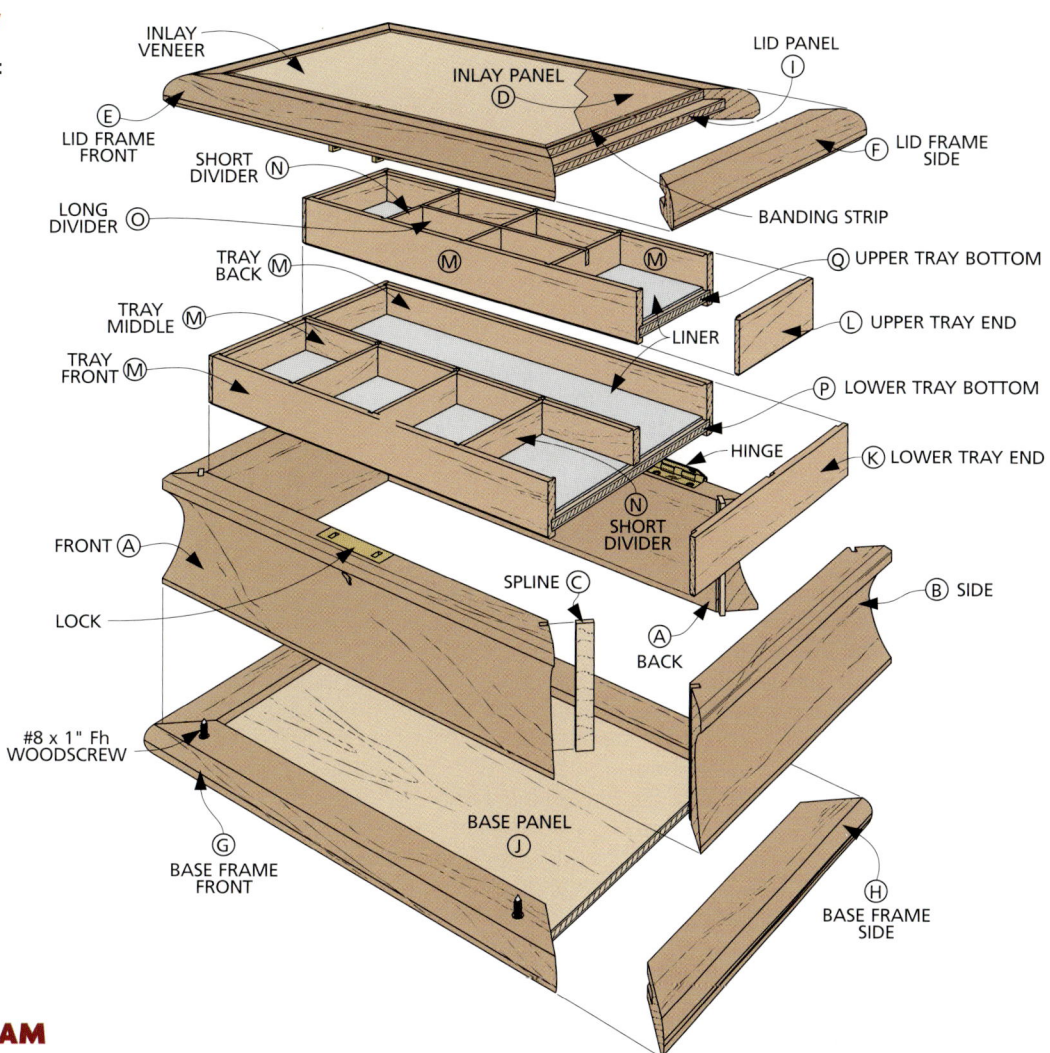

INLAY VENEER

INLAY PANEL (D)

LID PANEL (I)

LID FRAME FRONT (E)

LID FRAME SIDE (F)

BANDING STRIP

SHORT DIVIDER (N)

LONG DIVIDER (O)

TRAY BACK (M)

TRAY MIDDLE (M)

TRAY FRONT (M)

(M) (M)

UPPER TRAY BOTTOM (Q)

UPPER TRAY END (L)

LINER

LOWER TRAY BOTTOM (P)

LOWER TRAY END (K)

HINGE

SHORT DIVIDER (N)

FRONT (A)

LOCK

SPLINE (C)

(A) BACK

(B) SIDE

#8 x 1" Fh WOODSCREW

BASE FRAME FRONT (G)

BASE PANEL (J)

BASE FRAME SIDE (H)

CUTTING DIAGRAM

³⁄₄ x 5½ - 60 WALNUT (2.3 Bd. Ft.)

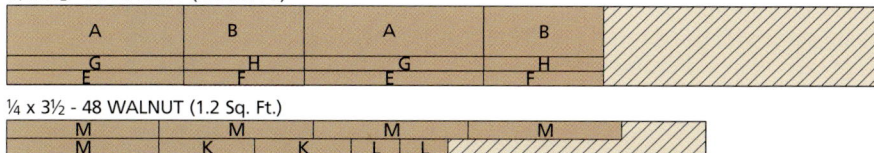

A	B	A	B
G	H	G	H
E	F	E	F

¼ x 3½ - 48 WALNUT (1.2 Sq. Ft.)

M	M	M	M
M	K	K	L	L	M

NOTE: CUT PARTS C, N, AND O FROM WASTE SECTION OF ¾"-THICK STOCK

¼" PLYWOOD - 24 x 36

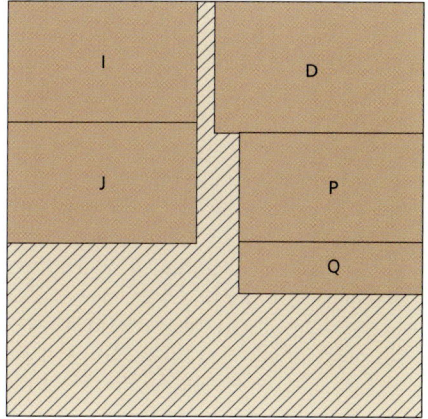

I	D
J	P
	Q

MATERIALS LIST

WOOD

A Front/Back (2)   ¾ x 2¾ - 12¼
B Sides (2)   ¾ x 2¾ - 8¼
C Splines (4)   ⅛ x ⅜ - 2¾
D Inlay Panel (1)   ¼ ply - 9 rgh. x 12 rgh.
E Lid Frame Fr./Bk. (2)   ¾ x 1 - 12¼
F Lid Frame Sides (2)   ¾ x 1 - 8¼
G Base Frame Fr./Bk (2)   ¾ x 1¼ - 12⁷⁄₈
H Base Frame Sides (2)   ¾ x 1¼ - 8⁷⁄₈
I Lid Panel (1)   ¼ ply - 7 x 11
J Base Panel (1)   ¼ ply - 7⅛ x 11⅛
K Lower Tray Ends (2)   ¼ x 1¼ - 6¹¹⁄₁₆
L Upper Tray Ends (2)   ¼ x 1¼ - 3¹³⁄₃₂
M Tray Fr./Bk./Middle (5)   ¼ x 1¼ - 10¹¹⁄₁₆
N Short Dividers (6)   ⅛ x ¾ - 3⁵⁄₃₂

O Long Divider (1)   ⅛ x ¾ - 5⅜
P Lower Tray Btm. (1)   ¼ ply - 6⁷⁄₁₆ x 10¹¹⁄₁₆
Q Upper Tray Btm. (1)   ¼ ply - 3⁵⁄₃₂ x 10¹¹⁄₁₆

HARDWARE SUPPLIES

(4) No. 8 x 1" Fh woodscrews
(1 pr.) 1½" x 1" brass-plated hinges
(4) ⅜"-dia. walnut button plugs
(1) Rose pattern inlay veneer (6¼" x 10¼")
(1) ¹⁄₃₂"-thick banding strip (¼" x 36")
(1 pc.) Posterboard (¹⁄₁₆" x 6³⁄₁₆ - 10⁵⁄₁₆")
(1 pc.) Posterboard (¹⁄₁₆" x 2²⁵⁄₃₂ - 10⁵⁄₁₆")
(1 pc.) Fabric tray liner (12" x 24")
(1) ⅛"-thick mirror (6½" x 10½")
(1) Half-mortise lock w/ key

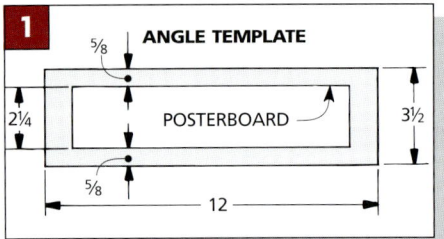

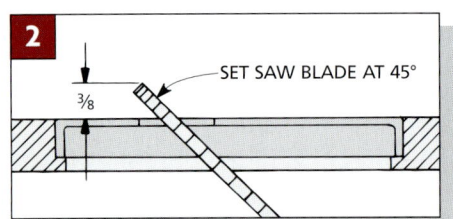

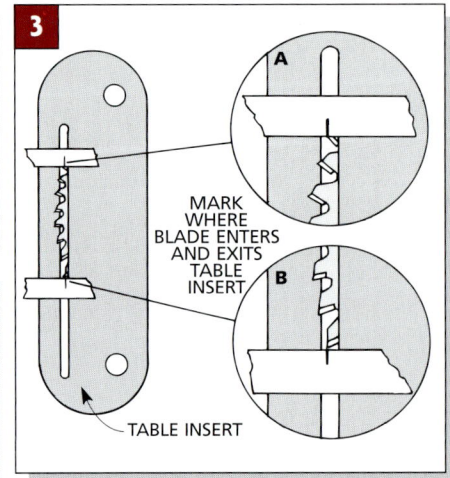

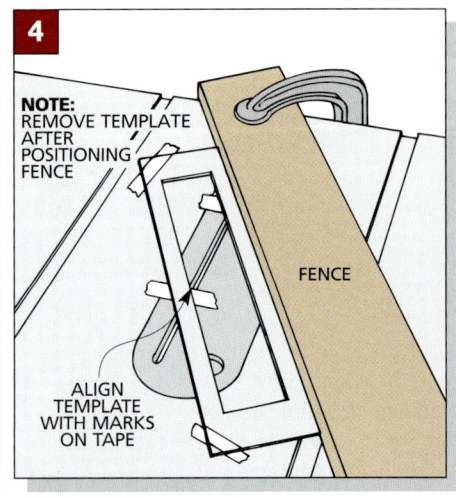

CUT SIDES & COVES

Start work on the case by cutting the sides to rough size. This means cutting two pieces of $3/4$"-thick stock to size ($3\frac{1}{2}$" x 28"). (I used walnut.) Each piece yields one front or back (A) and one side (B) with some left over.

TEMPLATE. Next, set up the saw to cut the parabolic cove in these two pieces. To do this, you need a template to set the position of the guide fence.

To make the template, cut a rectangular hole in some posterboard *(Fig. 1)*. The critical measurements are the width of the opening ($2\frac{1}{4}$"), and the distance between the opening and the outside edge of the template ($5/8$").

SET UP. After making the template, tilt the blade to a 45° angle and raise it to a height of $3/8$" *(Fig. 2)*. (The tilt is the secret to the parabolic cove.)

Now use the template to position an auxiliary rip fence. It helps here to place masking tape over the table insert and mark where the blade enters and exits *(Fig. 3)*. Then simply twist the template until the edges touch the marks on the masking tape and tape it down *(Fig. 4)*.

Now slide the fence (I used a piece of straight 1x4 scrap stock) up against the edge of the template. This will position the fence $5/8$" from the blade and at the proper angle to make the cove cut.

CUT COVE. After clamping the fence in position, remove the template and lower the blade so it's only $1/16$" high. Slide a piece of scrap along the fence to get a feel for this operation. When you're comfortable, slide the workpiece slowly over the blade to cut a cove.

Now raise the blade (in $1/16$" increments) and make repeated passes until the blade is at full height ($3/8$"). At this height the cove will be $2\frac{1}{4}$" wide *(Fig. 5)*.

SMOOTH THE COVE. To get the smoothest cut, make the last pass very slowly. Even with this, the cove will have lots of tiny ridges. I found that a gooseneck scraper and a specially-made foam sanding block do a good job of cleaning the cove right up. For more on how to make a cove sanding block, see the Shop Tip on the next page.

SPLINED MITER JOINTS

After the coves have been scraped and sanded smooth, cut the workpieces to get a 13" and 9" length out of each piece. These four pieces are then mitered to length to get a front and back piece (A) and two end pieces (B) *(Fig. 6)*.

CUT TO LENGTH. To miter these pieces to length, I added an auxiliary fence to the miter gauge and used a stop block to make sure the matching pieces were cut to exactly the same length.

Start by cutting a 45° miter on one end of each workpiece. Then clamp a stop block to the auxiliary fence to cut the front piece (A) to final length ($12\frac{1}{4}$") *(Figs. 6 and 8)*. As soon as the front piece is cut, cut the back piece (A) with the stop block in the same position. (I set the stop so the first cut leaves the pieces a little long. Then I nudged the stop over and cut each piece to length.)

Now repeat the procedure to miter the end pieces (B) to final length ($8\frac{1}{4}$").

GROOVE FOR SPLINE. The case front, back, and sides are joined with the aid

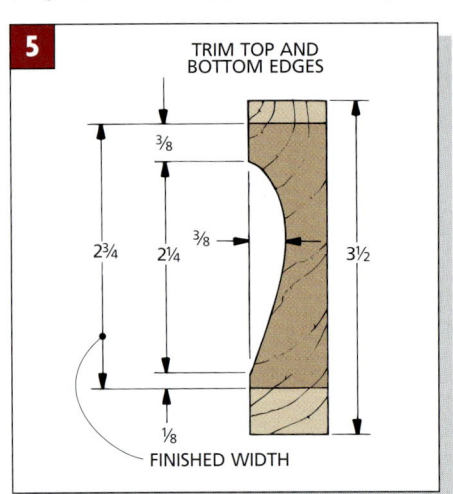

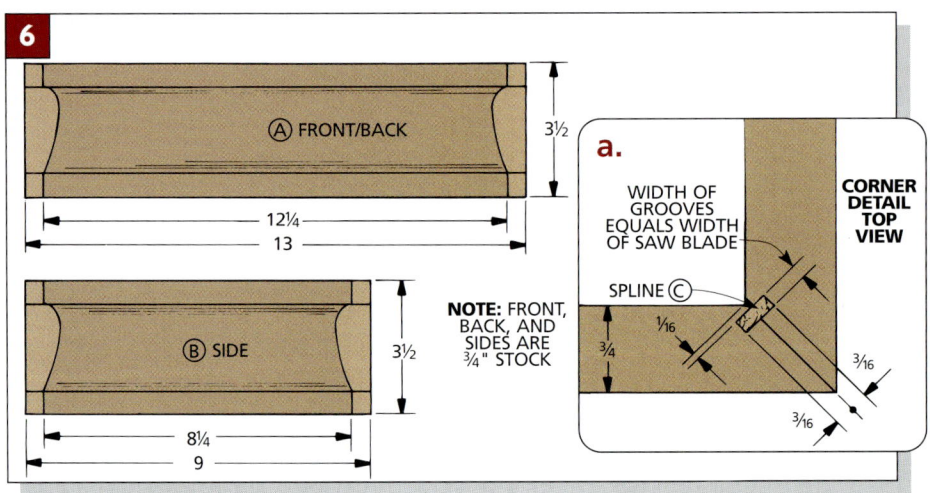

of splines. (Splines add strength to the miters and keep all four of the pieces aligned as they're clamped together.)

To make this joint, you have to cut a $3/16$"-deep groove in each mitered end *(Fig. 9a)*. Keep the saw blade at a 45° angle and slide the rip fence over to use as a stop. Position the fence to cut the groove $1/16$" from the inside corner of each piece *(Fig. 9)*.

Note: It helps here to use a piece of cutoff cove as a test piece to make sure that when you cut the groove it doesn't cut through into the cove.

TRIM TO WIDTH. After the grooves are cut, the four sides can be trimmed to final width ($2^3/4$"). To do this, trim a little off both edges so there's a $3/8$"-wide border at the top of the cove and a $1/8$"-wide border below the cove *(Fig. 5)*.

SPLINES. The last step is to cut the splines. Since the splines will show on the top edge of the case, I decided to make them out of walnut (using scrap left over from making the sides).

The four splines (C) are cut so the grain runs across the joint line for more strength. Set the blade a little over $3/8$" high (the combined depth of the grooves in the mitered ends), and set the fence $1/8$" from the blade (the thickness of the saw blade kerf) *(Step 1 in Fig. 10a)*.

Now stand the workpiece on end and make cuts on both ends. Then re-adjust the fence to cut off the splines *(Step 2)* so they're a tad less than $3/8$" wide to leave room for glue in the grooves.

After the splines are cut, carefully test-fit them in the grooves. Then band-clamp the sides together to make sure the case is square. But don't glue the sides together yet — the lock has to be mortised in the front piece first.

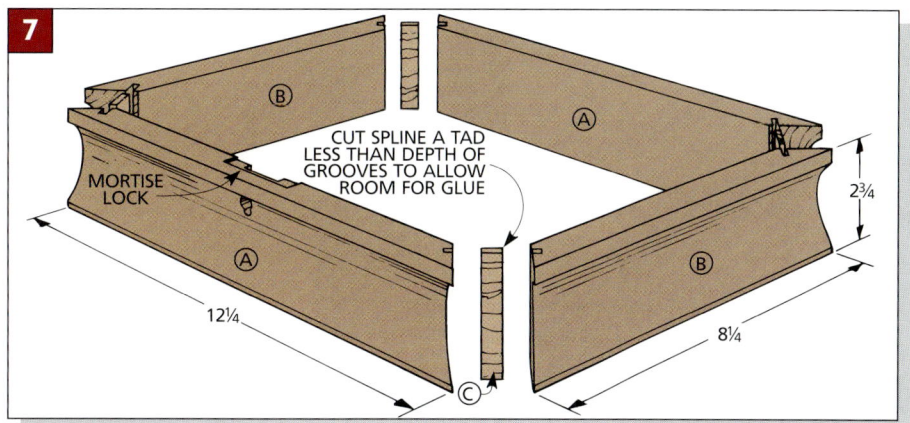

7

MORTISE LOCK

CUT SPLINE A TAD LESS THAN DEPTH OF GROOVES TO ALLOW ROOM FOR GLUE

B A A B C

$12^1/4$ $8^1/4$ $2^3/4$

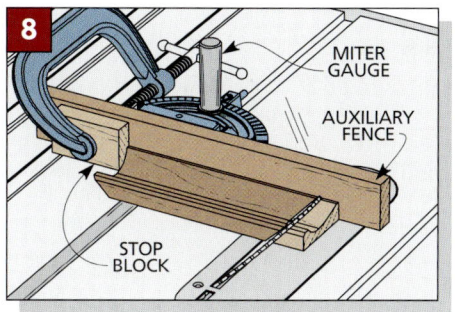

8

MITER GAUGE

AUXILIARY FENCE

STOP BLOCK

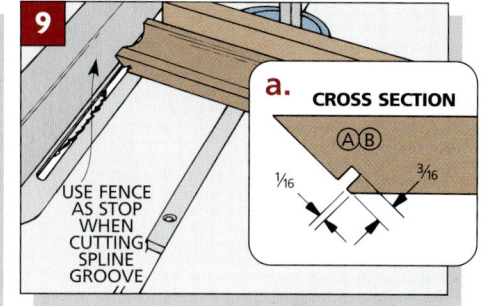

9

USE FENCE AS STOP WHEN CUTTING SPLINE GROOVE

a. CROSS SECTION

A B

$1/16$ $3/16$

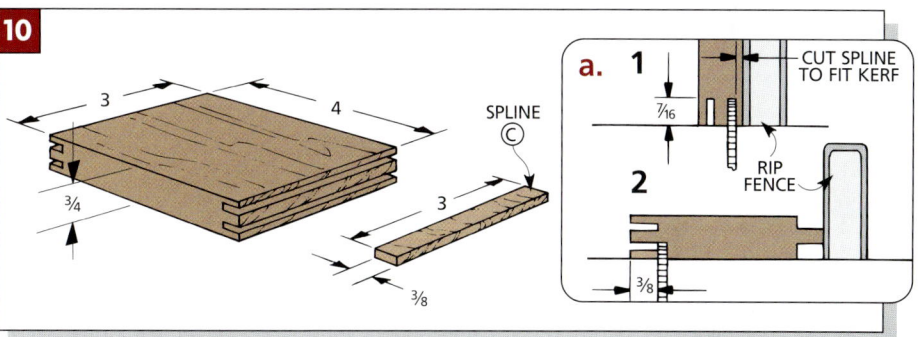

10

3 4 3

$3/4$ $3/8$

SPLINE C

a. 1 CUT SPLINE TO FIT KERF

$7/16$ RIP FENCE

2 $3/8$

ASSEMBLE THE CASE. The lock requires a stepped-mortise to make room for the lock plate. This isn't difficult to do, but it does take a little care when positioning and laying out the lock body and the catch plate. (Refer to the Technique on page 64 for a step-by-step procedure.)

After it's cut and the lock plate is mounted, assemble the case by gluing and clamping the mitered sides together.

SHOP TIP · *Cove Sanding Block*

The best sanding block is one that matches the shape to be sanded. So I made a custom sanding block from rigid foam insulation for the cove in the Jewelry Box.

First, trace the profile on the end of the foam (left photo). Then cut the foam to rough shape on the band saw (middle photo). Finally, shape the foam to the desired profile using the piece to be sanded (right photo).

Trace Profile. *Trace the outline of the cove onto a small block of thick foam insulation board.*

Rough Cut Profile. *Next, use a band saw (or hand saw and file) to cut the profile to rough shape.*

Sand Profile. *Smooth the profile by rubbing it across a piece of sandpaper stuck to the piece.*

TECHNIQUE ...... *Half-Mortise Lock*

The Jewelry Case wouldn't be complete without a lock. Since a neat lock installation adds a touch of craftsmanship to the case, I treated it as a project in itself.

LAYOUT

The first step is positioning the lock mechanism on the front of the case.

MARK LOCK POSITION. Begin by marking the exact center of the lock on top of the lock plate. Next, mark the center of the case on the top surface of the case front. Then, with the lock upside down against the inside of the case front, align the center marks *(Step 1 below)*.

With the lock held in place, press the flat side of a chisel against the plate and nick the edges of the case front on either side of the lock *(Step 1)*. Then, with a sharp pencil, trace the outline of the lock plate on the inside of the case front.

SCORE LOCK POSITION. After the lock outline is marked, it must be scored to provide clean edges on the finished mortise. This is a two-part operation that requires a chisel (or a marking knife) and a combination square.

First, I score the outlines of the sides of the lock plate. Set the combination square so the rule projects the height (depth) of the lock plate *(Step 2)*. Next, press the back edge of the chisel into one of the nicks and slide the square over tight against the chisel *(Step 3)*.

When the combination square is butted against the chisel, hold it tight. Then move the chisel so the point is on the penciled line marking the bottom of the lock *(Step 3)*. Next score the outline of the side by drawing the cutting edge away from the penciled bottom line to the edge of the case front. Repeat the process on the opposite side.

To score the bottom outline, the combination square and chisel are used together like a cutting gauge *(Step 4)*.

To do this, begin by pressing the square tight against the top of the case front. Next, hold the chisel edge against the bottom of the rule. Then pull the square and the chisel across the top edge to score the lock plate bottom outline between the two side outlines.

The lock plate has a lip that "folds" over the top edge of the case front. To score the outline of the lip on the top edge, just reset the combination square and repeat *Steps 2, 3, and 4*.

MORTISE LOCK IN PLACE

After the outline is marked, a stepped mortise is created within it. This is a two-part process that forms a shoulder to support the lock plate and a recess for the locking mechanism. I used a chisel and a router with a ¼" straight bit to do this.

MORTISE LOCK PLATE. The first step is to mortise the case front so the surface of the lock plate is flush with the inside of the case front. Begin by setting the router so the bit projects to cut as deep as the thickness of the plate (not the mechanism). Then, rout out the waste almost to the scored outline *(Step 5)*.

After the bulk of the waste has been routed out, the rest is removed to the scored outline with a chisel *(Step 6)*. First, chisel down around the scored perimeter to the depth of the routed surface. Then, pare away the remaining waste with the back of the chisel pressed flat against the routed surface.

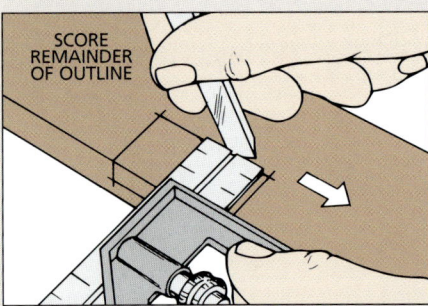

1 *Align center of lock plate with center of case front. Use a chisel to nick the edges of case front to mark width of plate. Then trace the outline of the plate with a pencil.*

2 *Set combination square for use as marking gauge. Place lock upright on flat surface and lock the square's rule to exactly match the height of the lock plate.*

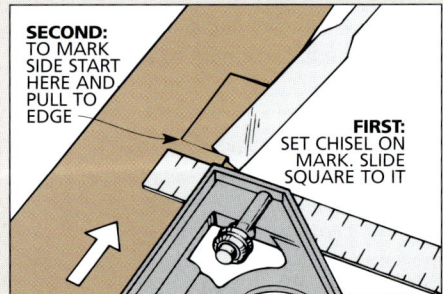

3 *Score outline of lock plate by placing chisel in "nick" on edge. Next, slide square until it contacts the chisel. Then score from pencil line to edge.*

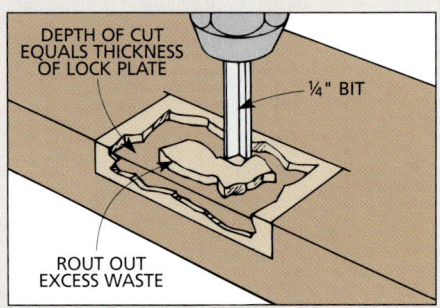

4 *Use square and chisel together as marking gauge. Press square against top of case front. Then slide square and chisel to score bottom line of lock plate.*

5 *Use router with ¼" bit to rough out waste to thickness of lock plate. Be careful to keep the bit from gouging the scored perimeter lines.*

6 *Remove waste to outline. First, chisel straight down on outline to depth of routed surface. Then pare to outline with chisel back pressed flat on surface.*

MORTISE FOR LOCK MECHANISM. After the lock plate mortise is finished, another mortise is cut to allow room for the lock mechanism. Begin by setting the router bit so it projects slightly higher than the thickness of the lock mechanism *(Step 7)*.

Next, draw an outline centered inside the lock plate mortise that allows room for the mechanism *(Step 8)*. Then, rout almost to the line and finish by paring right up to the outline with a chisel.

LOCATE KEYHOLE

The last step for installing the lock mechanism is to locate and drill the keyhole. Begin by pressing the lock into the mortise so the "key pin" leaves a dimple in the bottom of the mortise *(Step 9)*.

Using the dimple as a centerpoint, drill a $1/4$" hole with a brad point bit from the inside of the case *(Step 10)*. To prevent chipout, stop drilling as soon as the point of the bit breaks through the outside surface of the cove. Then finish the hole from the outside of the case front.

To complete the keyhole, use a $1/8$" bit to drill a second hole centered $3/16$" down from the first hole *(detail 'a' in Step 11)*. The shoulder left between the two holes can be cleaned up with a file or razor knife to form the keyhole shape.

ASSEMBLE BOX. Before the lock installation can be completed, the case has to be assembled and the hinges installed (refer to pages 66 and 67). The hinging action of the lid controls the alignment of the lock mechanism and the catch plate.

INSTALL CATCH PLATE

After the case is assembled, the catch plate is installed. Locating the position of the catch plate is easy because it has two points on either end to mark its position.

POSITION PLATE. First, place the catch plate in the lock *(detail 'a' in Step 12a)*. Then close the lid and press it tight so the points on the catch plate mark the lid.

Now remove the catch plate and position it on the marks made by the points. Tap the catch plate flush against the lid, and score the outline of the catch plate with a chisel *(Step 13)*.

MORTISE CATCH PLATE. To cut the mortise within the scored outline, first set a $1/8$" straight bit to rout to the thickness of the catch plate. Then rout the waste almost to the outline *(Step 14)*, and finish by paring to the outline.

Finally, press the catch plate into the mortise and install the screws.

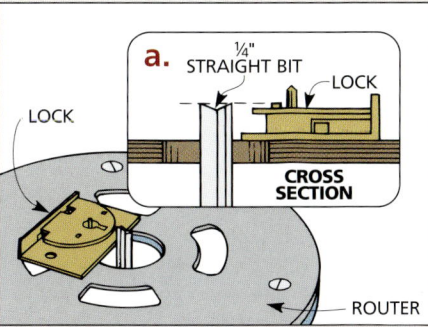

7 Set depth of cut to rough out waste for lock mechanism. Bit projects slightly higher than total thickness of lock mechanism, but not as high as key pin.

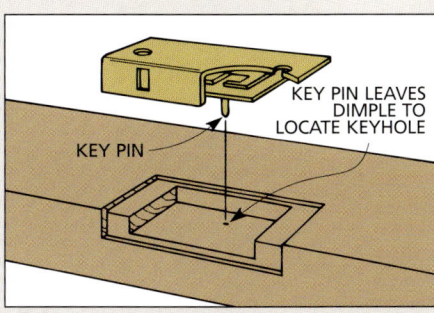

9 To mark the position of the keyhole, press the lock tightly into the finished mortise. The key pin in the lock mechanism will leave a "dimple" to mark the keyhole.

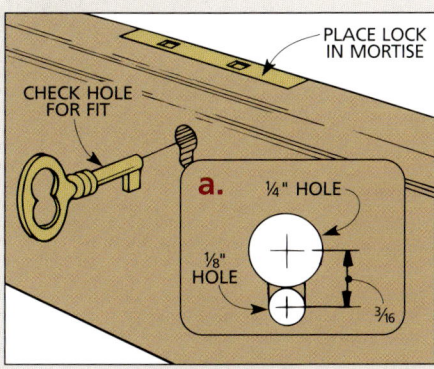

11 Finish keyhole by boring a $1/8$"-dia. hole centered $3/16$" below the first hole. Then pare or file away shoulder between holes to form final keyhole shape.

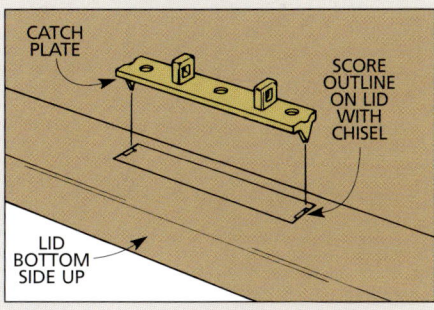

13 To mark the mortise for the catch plate, tap catch plate into the lid using point impressions for reference. Then score an outline with the corner of a chisel.

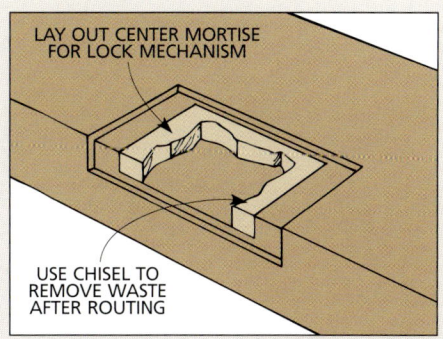

8 Lay out location of lock mechanism mortise within lock plate mortise. Pare out waste almost to outline with router. Then clean up to outline with chisel.

10 Bore main hole for keyhole with $1/4$" brad point bit. Use "dimple" left by key pin for center point. Stop when point breaks through, finish from face side.

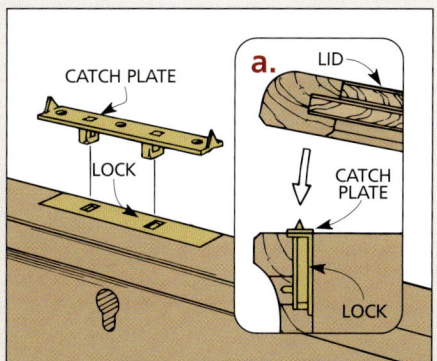

12 To position catch plate in lid, place catch plate in lock mechanism. Then press the lid down on catch plate. Two points on catch plate will mark location.

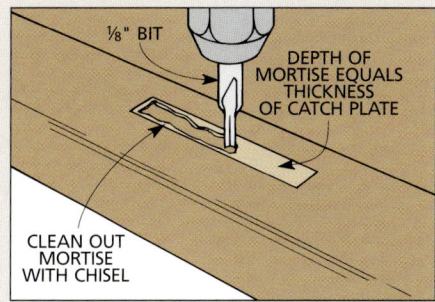

14 To cut the mortise, rout the waste almost to the outline with a $1/8$" bit set to thickness of plate. Remove remaining waste to the outline with a chisel.

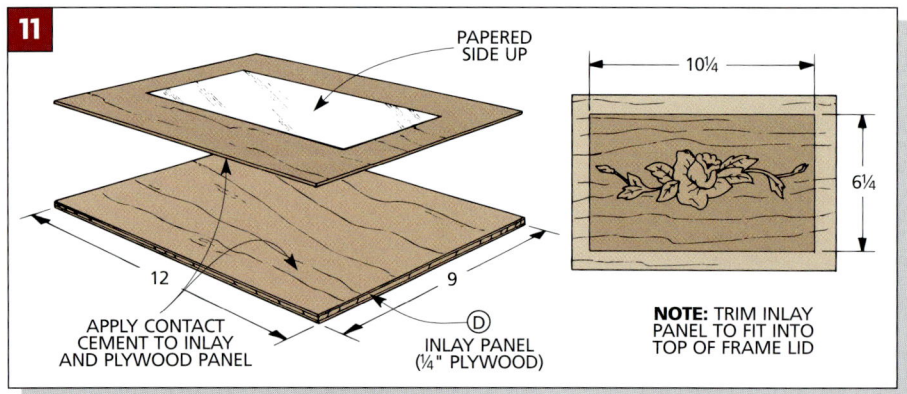

11

PAPERED SIDE UP

12

9

APPLY CONTACT CEMENT TO INLAY AND PLYWOOD PANEL

Ⓓ INLAY PANEL (¼" PLYWOOD)

10¼

6¼

NOTE: TRIM INLAY PANEL TO FIT INTO TOP OF FRAME LID

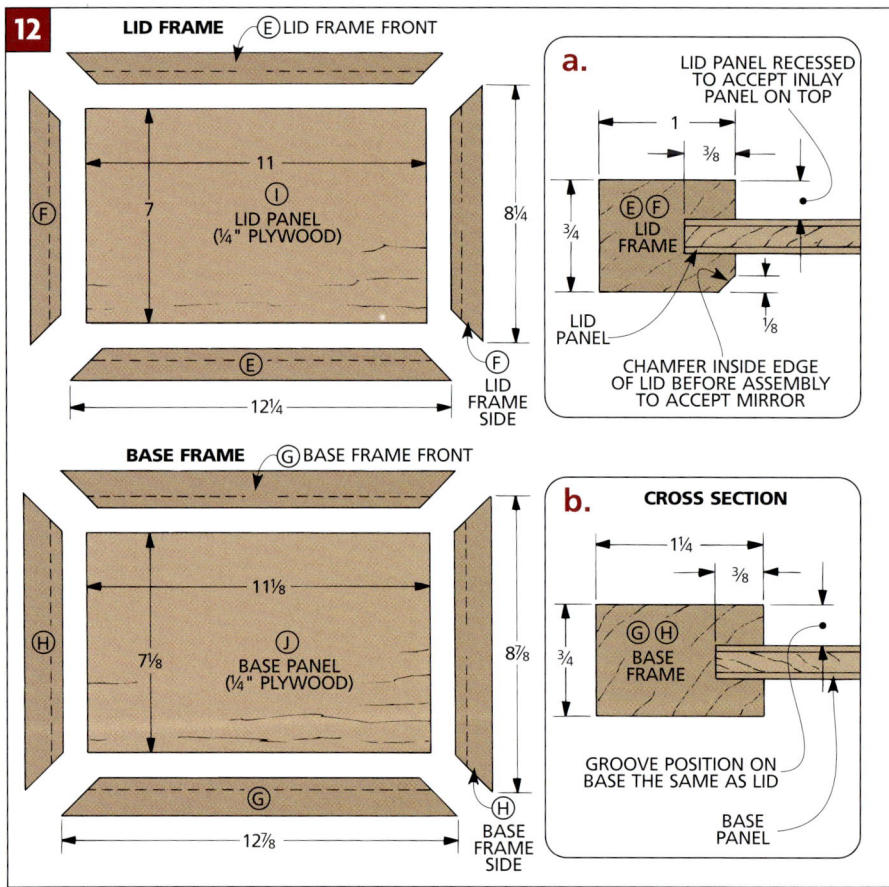

12

LID FRAME Ⓔ LID FRAME FRONT

Ⓕ

11

7

Ⓘ LID PANEL (¼" PLYWOOD)

8¼

Ⓔ

Ⓕ LID FRAME SIDE

12¼

a.

LID PANEL RECESSED TO ACCEPT INLAY PANEL ON TOP

1

⅜

¾

ⒺⒻ LID FRAME

LID PANEL

⅛

CHAMFER INSIDE EDGE OF LID BEFORE ASSEMBLY TO ACCEPT MIRROR

BASE FRAME Ⓖ BASE FRAME FRONT

Ⓗ

11⅛

7⅞

Ⓙ BASE PANEL (¼" PLYWOOD)

8⅞

Ⓖ

12⅞

Ⓗ BASE FRAME SIDE

b. **CROSS SECTION**

1¼

⅜

¾

ⒼⒽ BASE FRAME

GROOVE POSITION ON BASE THE SAME AS LID

BASE PANEL

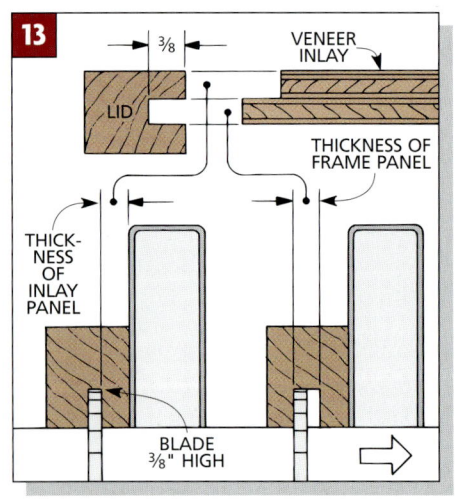

13

⅜

VENEER INLAY

LID

THICKNESS OF FRAME PANEL

THICK-NESS OF INLAY PANEL

BLADE ⅜" HIGH

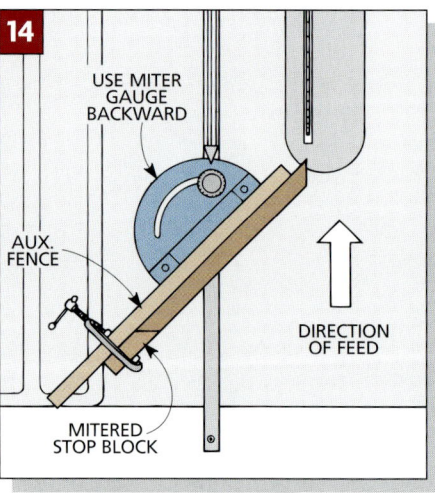

14

USE MITER GAUGE BACKWARD

AUX. FENCE

DIRECTION OF FEED

MITERED STOP BLOCK

MARQUETRY INLAY FOR LID

The next step is to build walnut frames for the lid and base. Then to dress up the lid, I also added a panel with a marquetry inlay (see photo on page 60).

ADDING AN INLAY. Adding the rose inlay is easy. The one I used came as a pre-made piece — the rose was already inlaid into a surrounding piece of walnut veneer (see page 126 for sources). (To install a patterned inlay into a hardwood top, see the Designer's Notebook on page 72.)

To mount the inlay, apply contact cement to a ¼" plywood inlay panel (D) and to the inlay itself (*Fig. 11*).

Note: The inlay comes with a paper backing. Apply the contact cement to the other side so that the papered side is up when it's mounted (*Fig. 11*).

Use a roller to press the inlay onto the plywood panel. Then moisten the paper backing to loosen the glue and scrape the paper off.

LID & BASE FRAMES

Next, I made the lid and base frames. Start by cutting two strips of ¾"-thick stock for the lid frame front and back (E) and sides (F) (1" x 24", enough for one front or back and one side), and two other strips for the base frame front and back (G) and sides (H) (1¼" x 24").

GROOVE. Before mitering these pieces, I cut a groove on one edge for the plywood lid and base panels. The set-up for the groove in the lid is identical for the one in the base, but the exact position of this groove is critical on the lid frame. That's because it has to be positioned so the rose inlay panel can be mounted flush with the surface of the frame.

Set up the saw so the distance between the fence and the blade is equal to the thickness of the inlay panel (and veneer) (*Fig. 13*). Make one pass on all four strips.

Next, widen the groove to accept the plywood panel by moving the fence away from the blade and making another pass on each piece (*Fig. 13*).

FRAME PIECES. After the grooves are complete, cut each strip into two rough-length pieces (9" long and 14" long) to get the eight pieces needed for the frames.

Next, miter these pieces to final length. The pieces for the lid frame are mitered to length to equal the outside dimensions of the case. But the pieces for the base frame are ⅝" longer than the outside dimensions of the case (*Fig. 12*).

As when mitering the case sides, I added an auxiliary fence and stop block to the miter gauge. It also helps if you reverse the gauge in the table slot so that as the miter is cut, the blade pushes the workpiece against the stop *(Fig. 14).*

There's one final step before cutting the plywood panels and assembling the frames. I routed a chamfer on the inside edges of the top frame to leave a shoulder for the mirror that's mounted later on the inside face of the lid panel *(Fig. 17).*

PLYWOOD PANELS. Now the 1/4" plywood lid and base panels (I, J) can be cut to fit the lid and base frames. Dry-assemble the frames to get the inside measurements and add the depth of the grooves. Then cut the panels to this size, and glue the frames together.

BANDING STRIP. When the top frame is dry, the inlay panel can be added by trimming it to fit in the frame. Then I added a solid-wood banding strip between the frame and the inlay panel *(Fig. 16).*

To do this, I routed a rabbet around the perimeter of the inlay panel that's equal to the width and thickness of the banding strip *(Fig. 15).* (I used the router table and a 1/2" straight bit to cut the rabbet.) Then glue the panel in the frame and the strip in the rabbet *(Fig. 16).*

ROUND EDGES. To complete the frames, round over the outside edges. On the top frame I used a 1/2" roundover bit to rout the top edge *(Step 1 in Fig. 17).* Then I routed a 45° chamfer on the outside bottom edge *(Step 2).*

Note: This chamfer is more than just decoration — it's needed for clearance on the back edge where the hinges are mounted. Also, while the chamfer bit is in place, go ahead and chamfer the top outside edges of the case *(Fig. 19).*

The bottom frame is routed with a 1/2" roundover bit set to create a softened bullnose profile *(Steps 1 and 2 in Fig. 18).*

MOUNT LID & BASE TO CASE

At this point the lid and base frames are ready to be mounted to the case.

MOUNT HINGES. To mount the lid, I mortised the lid and case back and used brass hinges set so the outside of the knuckle lines up with the outside edge of the case and the lid frame *(Fig. 20a).*

Note: With the hinges mounted this way, the lid won't fall back when opened. It opens to about 120° and stays there.

After the lid is hinged, add the catch plate for the lock (see page 64).

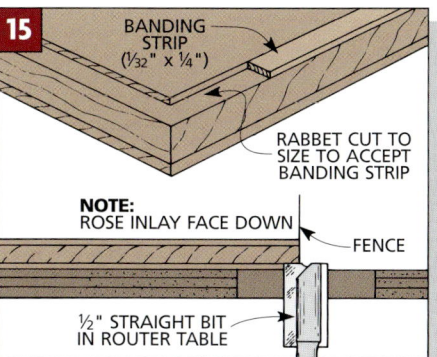

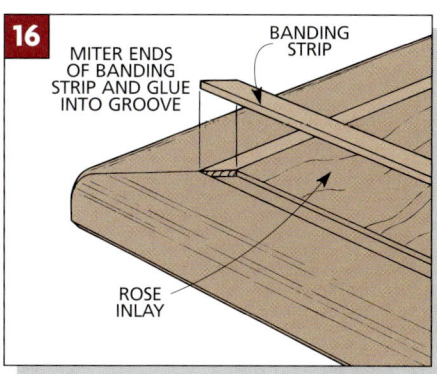

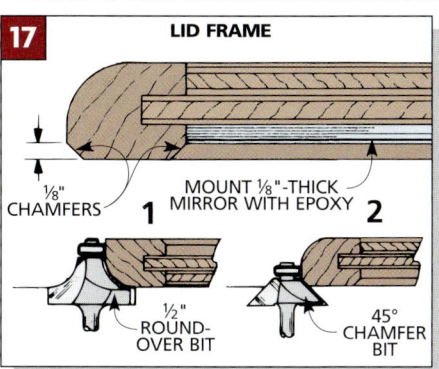

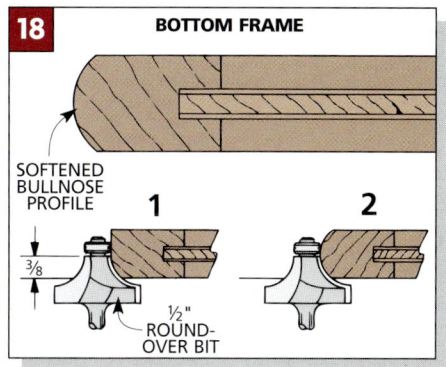

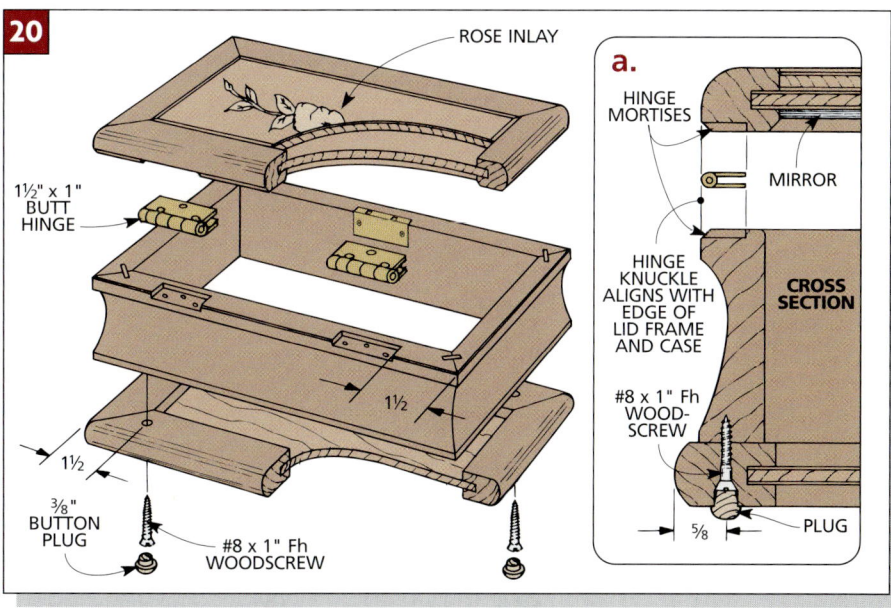

To mount the base frame, first glue and screw it to the sides. Then I added button hole plugs, with a spot of glue in the screw holes, to act as "feet" *(Fig. 20).*

MIRROR. Finally, I cut a mirror to fit inside the recess in the lid frame. Later, to make sure it stayed put, I mounted it with epoxy after the case was finished.

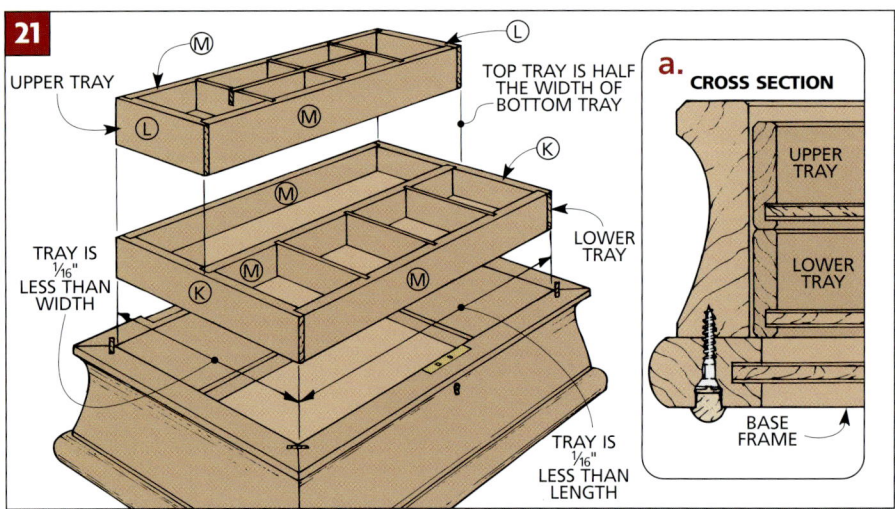

21

UPPER TRAY

TOP TRAY IS HALF THE WIDTH OF BOTTOM TRAY

a. CROSS SECTION

UPPER TRAY

LOWER TRAY

TRAY IS 1/16" LESS THAN WIDTH

LOWER TRAY

BASE FRAME

TRAY IS 1/16" LESS THAN LENGTH

BASE FRAME

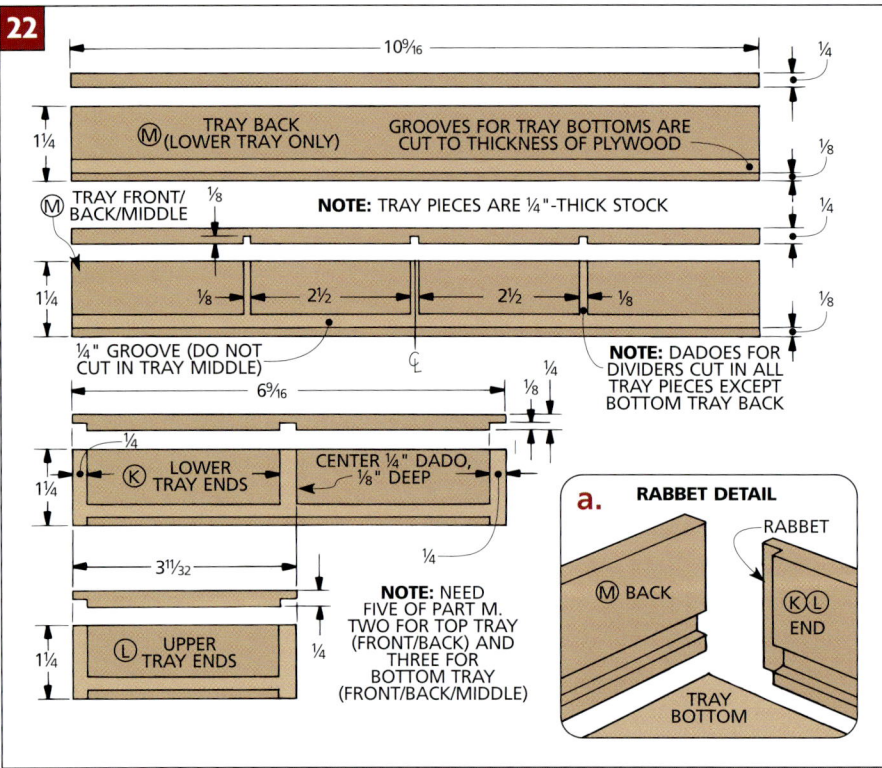

22

10⁹/₁₆

1/4

1¼

M TRAY BACK (LOWER TRAY ONLY)

GROOVES FOR TRAY BOTTOMS ARE CUT TO THICKNESS OF PLYWOOD

1/8

1/4

M TRAY FRONT/ BACK/MIDDLE

1/8

NOTE: TRAY PIECES ARE 1/4"-THICK STOCK

1¼

1/8

2½

2½

1/8

1/8

1/4" GROOVE (DO NOT CUT IN TRAY MIDDLE)

₵

NOTE: DADOES FOR DIVIDERS CUT IN ALL TRAY PIECES EXCEPT BOTTOM TRAY BACK

6⁹/₁₆

1/4

1/8

1/4

1/4

K LOWER TRAY ENDS

CENTER 1/4" DADO, 1/8" DEEP

1¼

3¹¹/₃₂

1/4

a. RABBET DETAIL

RABBET

L UPPER TRAY ENDS

1/4

1¼

NOTE: NEED FIVE OF PART M. TWO FOR TOP TRAY (FRONT/BACK) AND THREE FOR BOTTOM TRAY (FRONT/BACK/MIDDLE)

M BACK

K L END

TRAY BOTTOM

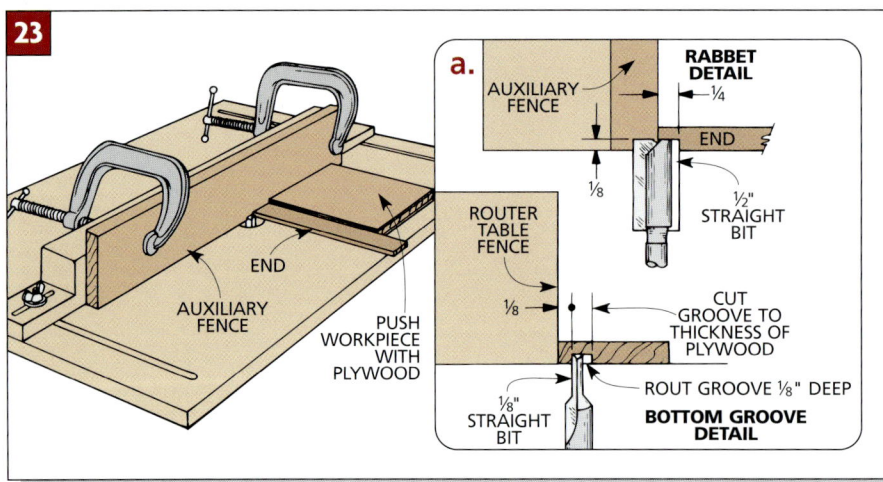

23

END

AUXILIARY FENCE

PUSH WORKPIECE WITH PLYWOOD

a.

AUXILIARY FENCE

RABBET DETAIL

1/4

END

1/8

1/2" STRAIGHT BIT

ROUTER TABLE FENCE

1/8

CUT GROOVE TO THICKNESS OF PLYWOOD

ROUT GROOVE 1/8" DEEP

1/8" STRAIGHT BIT

BOTTOM GROOVE DETAIL

TRAYS

I decided to build two trays, each with several small compartments. The large tray is sized to fit the entire bottom of the case. A smaller tray rests right on top of the bottom tray and slides back and forth over it *(Fig. 21)*.

Both trays consist of an outside frame made from 1/4"-thick walnut. Inside these frames are a series of dividers.

OUTSIDE FRAMES. Start by cutting four pieces of 1/4"-thick stock for the outside frames (for both trays) to a rough length of 14". (This is plenty for the nine 1/4"-thick pieces needed for the trays.)

Rip these four pieces to a rough width of 1³/₈". (Cutting the rabbets and dadoes may chip out the edges, so I rip them to final width after they've been cut.)

Then from these workpieces, cut the nine pieces for the two trays *(Fig. 22)*. I started with the four end pieces for both trays. The lower tray end pieces (K) for the bottom tray are cut to length 1/16" less than the inside front-to-back measurement of the assembled case. The upper tray end pieces (L) are a little more than half this length.

JOINERY. Next, cut 1/8" deep, 1/4"-wide rabbets at both ends of all four end pieces (K, L) to accept the tray front and back pieces (M) *(Fig. 22a)*. I cut the rabbets in the end pieces on the router table with a 1/2" straight bit *(Fig. 23)*.

Note: To support these narrow pieces as the rabbets are cut, I clamped a zero-clearance auxiliary fence to the front of the router table fence. And when cutting the rabbets, I used a piece of scrap plywood to support and push the pieces through the bit *(Fig. 23)*.

After the rabbets are cut, a 1/4"-wide dado for the tray middle (M) is cut in the center of the two lower tray end pieces (K). I used a 1/8" straight bit, cutting each dado in two passes.

TRIM TO SIZE. After the rabbets and dadoes are cut, the tray front, back, and middle pieces (M) are cut to length so when the tray is assembled it's 1/32" less than the inside width of the case.

Next, rip the tray front and back pieces to width (1¼"). (The tray middle is ripped to final width later.) This width leaves a 1/4" space at the top of the case when the trays are stacked *(Fig. 21a)*.

BOTTOMS. Finally, cut a groove 1/8" up from the bottom edge of all pieces (except the tray middle) to accept a 1/4" plywood bottom. I did this on the router table, making two passes with a $\frac{1}{8}$" straight bit *(Fig. 23)*. Once the groove is cut, dry-assemble the trays and measure for the bottoms (O, P) *(Figs. 24 and 25)*.

DIVIDERS

To make the compartments in each tray, I cut $\frac{1}{8}$"-thick "egg-crate" dividers. The same basic procedure is used to cut these dividers as was used on the tray pieces.

First, cut a piece of $\frac{3}{4}$"-thick stock to a width of $\frac{3}{4}$" and to rough length of 12". Then resaw it into three strips $\frac{1}{8}$" thick to make the short and long dividers (N, O) *(Figs. 24 and 25)*.

CUT DADOES AND CROSS-LAPS. To mount the dividers to the tray frame, cut $\frac{1}{8}$" dadoes on three tray frame front and back pieces and on the tray middle *(Fig. 22)*. Then the short dividers on the top tray are interlocked by cutting cross-lap joints *(Fig. 25)*.

Note: The dividers as well as the tray middle are trimmed to a final width later to allow for the thickness of the velvet lining. So make the lining first before trimming them down *(Figs. 26 and 27)*.

LINING THE TRAYS

The bottoms of both trays are lined with fabric. I prefer to mount the fabric to a piece of posterboard that's cut to size so it's $\frac{1}{16}$" less (in both directions) than the inside dimensions of the tray *(Fig. 26)*. Then cut the fabric so it's 1" larger than the posterboard in both dimensions.

To mount the fabric, cut the corners to within $\frac{1}{8}$" of the posterboard *(Fig. 26)*. Then apply rubber cement to the out-side border of the posterboard and the fabric overlap and fold the tabs over, stretching the fabric tight.

EARRING BLOCKS. I also made two ear-ring blocks out of chunks of foam covered with velvet *(Fig. 27)*.

FINISHING. I finished the case with brushing lacquer (see the Finishing article on page 71). You could also finish it with rubbing varnish on the case and tung oil on the trays.

TRIM TO SIZE. After the trays have been lined, trim the short (N) and long (O) dividers to width and length.

ASSEMBLY. When all pieces are cut to size, assemble the two trays by gluing the four sides to the plywood bottoms. (Don't glue the tray middle or the dividers in place, so they can be removed if you want to make bigger compartments.) ■

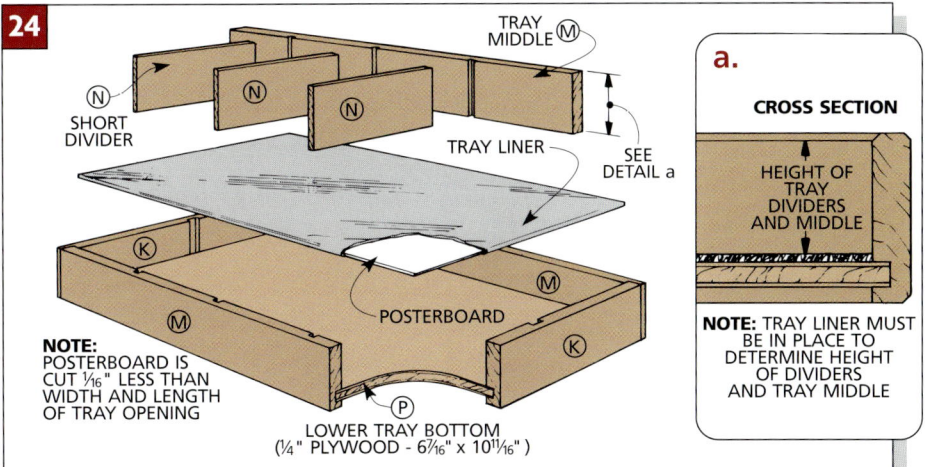

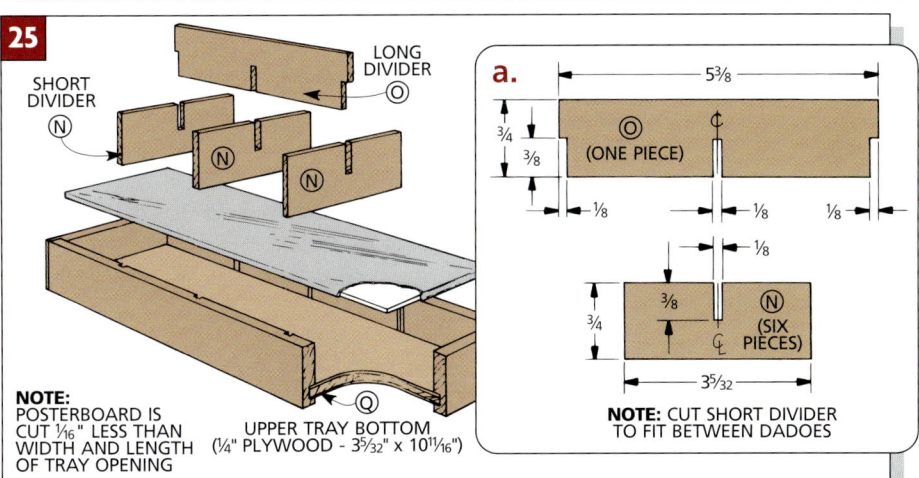

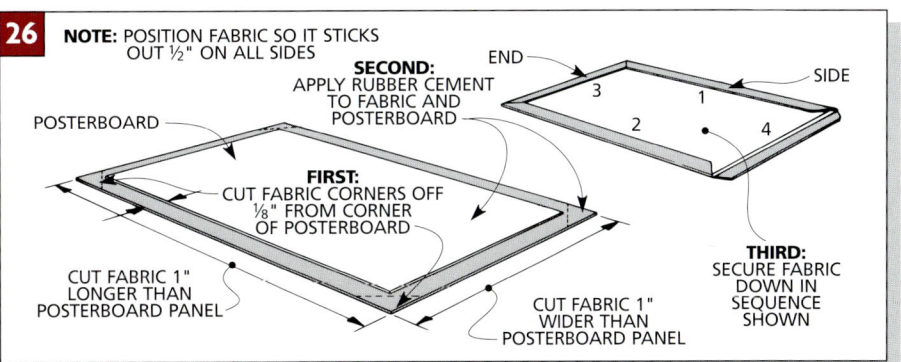

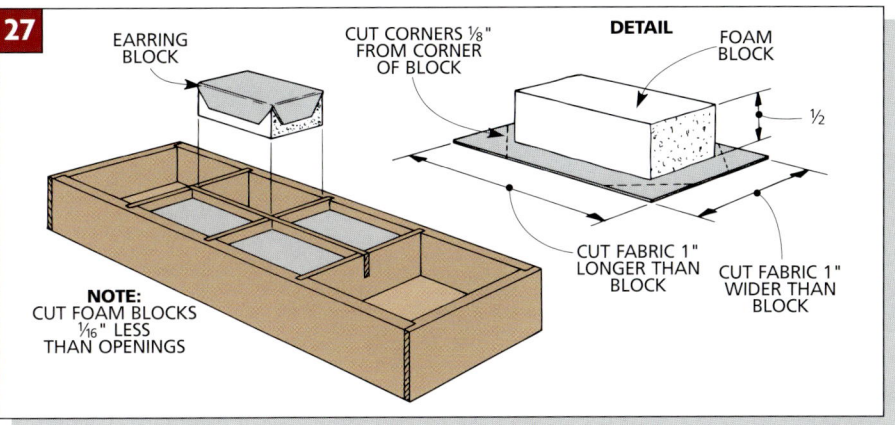

DESIGNER'S NOTEBOOK

By resizing the lower frame and eliminating the cove detail, you end up with an attractive Jewelry Box that's very easy to build. To dress up the lid, you could use plastic laminate, veneer, or leather.

CONSTRUCTION NOTES:

■ Construction of the Jewelry Case can be simplified a great deal by removing the parabolic cove on the front, back, and sides of the case.

The great thing is it's still a nice-looking case with lots of room for storage. The reason for that has to do with the trays. This case still has all the room on the inside of the original.

■ Begin by ripping the blanks for the front (A), back (A), and sides (B) to width from two extra-long pieces of ³⁄₄"-thick stock (see drawing).

■ Once that's complete, rout a ¹⁄₈" chamfer on the the outside edges of these blanks (see drawing).

■ Now, miter the blanks to length and cut the grooves for the splines. Then cut the splines from scrap to fit the grooves. Finally, add the lock before gluing these pieces together.

■ Next, build the mitered lid and base frame as before, only this time the base frame front (G), back (G), sides (H), and panel (J) are cut to match the size of the lid frame (see drawing).

■ With the frames built, now you can dress up the lid. My feeling is that a marquetry inlay would be out of place in this contemporary style of case. But there are plenty of other options that would look nice to fill the lid frame. I used a piece of hardwood veneer, or you could use plastic laminate or leather.

Note: Yellow glue works great to attach hardwood veneer. For plastic laminate, I like to use contact cement. But for a piece of leather, I've found that a slow-setting adhesive, like liquid hide glue, works best. You want to have plenty of time to position the leather.

■ Now that the inlaid panel has been added to the lid frame, you can round over the outside edges and chamfer the outside bottom edge as before.

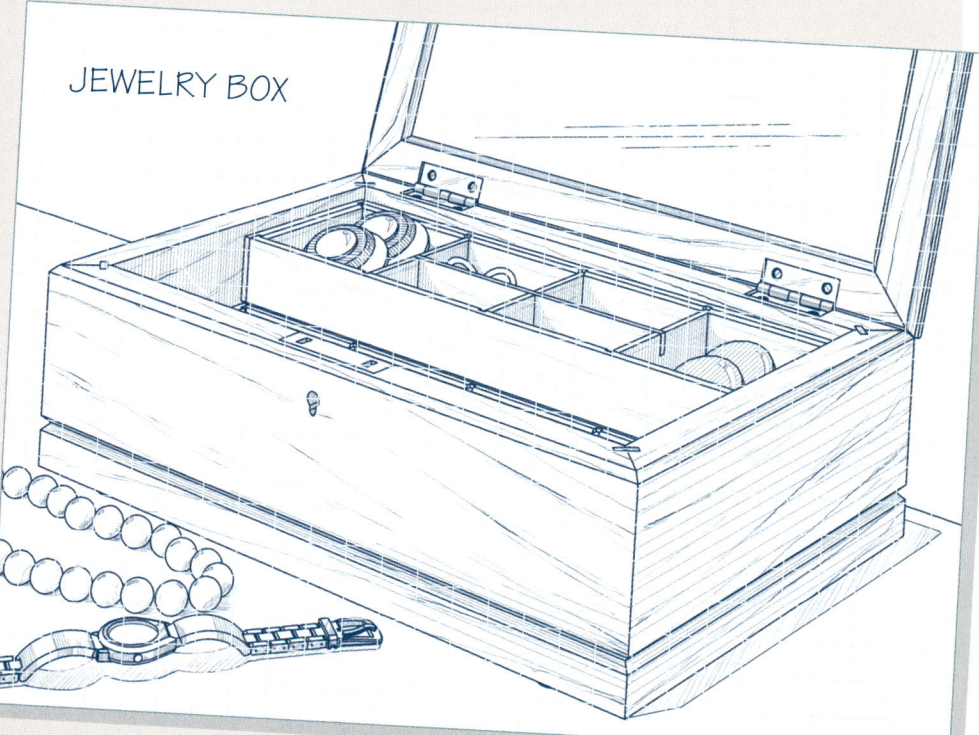

JEWELRY BOX

■ But with the base frame, instead of routing a bullnose profile, you'll want to leave the bottom outside edges square. Then, to match the look at the top of the Jewelry Box, I routed a ¹⁄₈" chamfer on the outside top edge of the base frame. This chamfer mirrors the one you routed on the bottom of the case (see detail 'a').

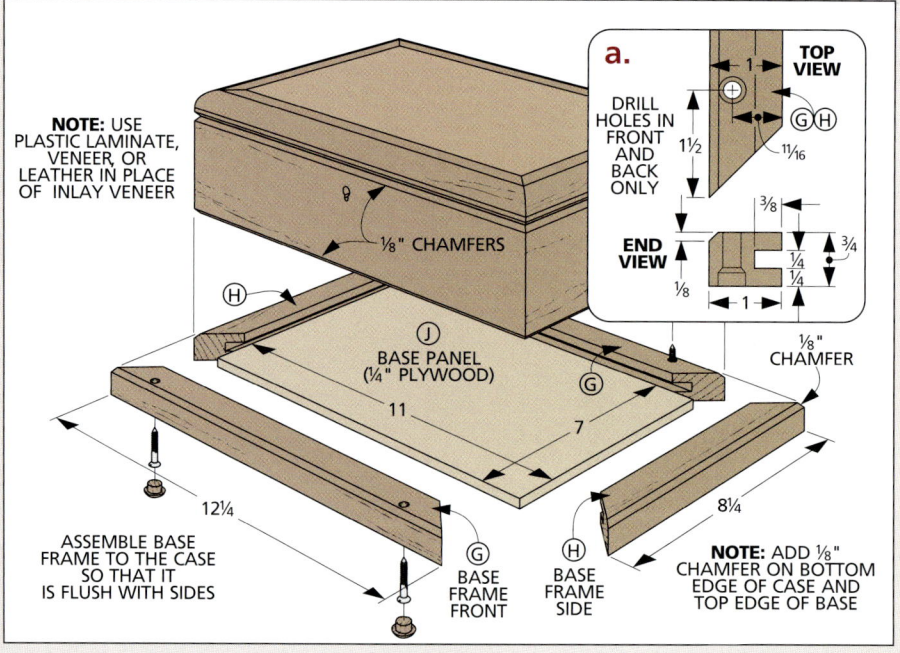

NOTE: USE PLASTIC LAMINATE, VENEER, OR LEATHER IN PLACE OF INLAY VENEER

¹⁄₈" CHAMFERS

J
BASE PANEL (¹⁄₄" PLYWOOD)

11

7

G

H

12¼

ASSEMBLE BASE FRAME TO THE CASE SO THAT IT IS FLUSH WITH SIDES

G
BASE FRAME FRONT

H
BASE FRAME SIDE

8¼

NOTE: ADD ¹⁄₈" CHAMFER ON BOTTOM EDGE OF CASE AND TOP EDGE OF BASE

a.

TOP VIEW

DRILL HOLES IN FRONT AND BACK ONLY

1

1½

G H

11⁄16

END VIEW

³⁄₈

¾

¼

¼

¹⁄₈

1

¹⁄₈" CHAMFER

MATERIALS LIST

CHANGED PARTS

G	Base Frame Fr./Bk. (2)	³⁄₄ x 1 - 12¼
H	Base Frame Sides (2)	³⁄₄ x 1 - 8¼
J	Base Panel (1)	¼ ply - 7 x 11

Some woodworkers feel varnish isn't worth the effort. They have even stronger feelings when using brushing lacquer. Brushing lacquer's major advantage over varnish — it dries quicker — is also its biggest disadvantage.

It dries so quickly that you can't really brush it on. Or at least you can't do much brushing after the liquid is on the surface. It's more like flowing it on. But when the job is complete, the results definitely make the extra work worth it.

FILL & SEAL

The process starts with filling and sealing so the lacquer won't collapse into the pores of the wood. This step is especially important for open-grained woods.

On the walnut Jewelry Case, I started by brushing a coat of shellac on the flower inlay and maple border with a small artist's brush. The shellac sealed these parts and prevented the color of the filler from staining them.

WOOD FILLER. Next, I applied a coat of paste wood filler, brushing on with the grain and wiping off across the grain. And since I only cared that the box was smooth, I didn't apply filler to the trays.

After the first coat of filler has dried, apply a second thin coat to fill the pores.

SEALER. When the second coat was dry, I sanded lightly to flatten the surface. Then I thinned down some five pound cut shellac (three parts denatured alcohol to one part shellac) and brushed it over the entire box and trays to seal the filler and the wood.

APPLYING THE LACQUER

After the shellac has a chance to dry, lightly sand the box and trays with 320 to 400-grit sandpaper. This should leave a flat, smooth surface for the lacquer.

BRISTLE BRUSH. The solvents in lacquer would quickly dissolve a foam brush, so I use a soft, natural hair, high-quality bristle brush.

To apply brushing lacquer, pour it into a separate jar and then dunk the brush in halfway up the bristles. The object is to fill up the bristles with lots of lacquer — this is called "fully charging" the brush.

FLOWING ON. Then hold the brush at a low angle to the workpiece (if possible

keep the workpiece horizontal) and allow the lacquer to flow out of the brush. Don't brush it back, just flow on a thin coat.

As you work, it starts drying and if you try to brush it out even thinner, there will be brush marks. Instead of brushing it out, keep refilling the brush. One fill of the brush might not last more than twelve inches. Anytime you feel the brush start to drag, fill it up again.

Unlike varnish, don't be tempted to go back over and fill in missed spots since the surrounding area may already be setting up. If you miss a spot, go on, and then cover the spot with the next coat.

SECOND COAT. Though it may feel dry right away, it's best to wait a couple of hours before applying a second coat.

Since lacquer coats dissolve into each other, it isn't necessary to sand between coats. But leveling with 280-grit non-clogging sandpaper will flatten out brush marks. And then rub with 0000 steel wool to leave a uniform, dead-flat surface.

If you thought the first coat was difficult to flow on, the second is usually worse. It's flowed on like the first, but it starts to dissolve the first coat as it's being applied. If the brush isn't kept completely full of lacquer, it "catches" like a dull razor on two day's growth. This can create brush marks and a washboard effect.

SOME SOLUTIONS

This may all sound like brushing lacquer isn't worth the trouble, but there are some things you can do to make it easier.

If the lacquer seems to be too thick, I've found that occasionally dipping the brush into lacquer thinner before dipping it in the lacquer helps it flow better.

THIN IT DOWN. Sometimes I even thin down the lacquer itself. (I thin the first coat about 50/50.) To determine exactly how much to thin takes some trial and error. If it's hard to brush, it's not thin enough. If there are runs or brush marks or it takes too many coats to build up the finish, there's too much thinner.

RUNS AND DRIPS. After each coat dries, I carefully rub any runs and drips level with a little thinner on a fingertip. Then I allow the surface to dry and lightly sand before applying another coat.

RUBBING SMOOTH

Flow on at least three coats of brushing lacquer and then wait 48 hours before rubbing the finish smooth.

Why so long? Because slow solvent evaporation can cause the lacquer film to shrink down into the pores of the wood.

One nice thing about lacquer: I find it's easier to rub smooth than varnish is.

GLOSSY FINISH. For a glossy finish, I start by leveling the surface with 600-grit wet/dry sandpaper and rubbing oil. (Use 400-grit first if the surface has brush marks or rough spots.)

Spread a thin coat of rubbing oil on the surface and sprinkle some pumice on top. Now lightly mix the oil and pumice to a creamy paste with a rag or felt pad and start rubbing with the grain.

Next, clean the surface and then follow the same rubbing procedure with rottenstone and oil. Rottenstone burnishes the surface and brings it to a fine high-gloss, polished appearance.

SATIN FINISH. For a satin finish you need a surface with a little deeper scratch pattern. To obtain this, I just rub 0000 steel wool in the direction of the grain and then buff with a soft cloth. For a little bit more gloss, something between satin and glossy, work some paste wax into the steel wool and rub with the grain. Then buff it to a fine luster.

DESIGNER'S NOTEBOOK

The style of inlay you use will determine how the lid is constructed. Here, instead of building a lid with a wood frame and plywood panel, I used an oval-shaped inlay that's recessed in solid wood.

CONSTRUCTION NOTES:

■ Patterned inlays come in various shapes and are actually surrounded by a rectangular piece of veneer that serves as a "container" to hold the small pieces of wood that make up the pattern. There's also a piece of brown paper tape on one side to hold all the pieces in place after the manufacturing process. This means they have to be mounted a little differently.

Start by building a solid-wood lid (R) from ³/₄"-thick stock *(Fig. 1)*. You won't need any of the lid frame parts (D, E, F). But the same roundover is added to the top of the lid and chamfers are also added to the bottom *(Figs. 1a and 1b)*.

■ Before the inlay can be mounted to the lid, it has to be separated from the surrounding layer of protective veneer.

Use a pair of scissors to cut away most of the protective veneer — to within about ¹/₄" of the pattern *(Step 1 on next page)*. Then switch to a razor knife and carefully cut around the outside of the pattern and through the paper tape *(Step 2)*.

■ After the outside veneer is trimmed off, sand the edges to get them as smooth as possible. Use fine-grit sandpaper attached to a sanding block — but instead of moving the block, hold it steady and move the inlay edge across the sandpaper.

■ The inlay must be mounted in a shallow recess in the surface of the lid. The recess is cut to the same shape as the inlay.

■ To make this recess, first mark the outline of the inlay. It's often difficult (especially on dark woods) to see the marked outline, so I glued a plain sheet of white paper to the top of the workpiece with spray adhesive.

■ To center the inlay on the workpiece, draw cross hatch reference lines on the paper *(Step 3)*. Then center the inlay over the cross hatch lines.

■ Next, the inlay is pinned to the piece so its outline can be marked on the paper.

Special marquetry pins (with thin, flat points that don't damage the pattern of the inlay) are used for this, or you can hammer flat points on a couple of plastic-head push pins and use them *(Step 4)*.

■ Once the inlay is in place (with paper side up), draw the cross hatch reference lines across the brown paper tape. Then, to avoid confusion later, mark an "X" on the inlay and another on the paper pattern so when the inlay is removed it can be returned to the same position *(Step 4)*.

■ When the inlay is pinned down, you need to mark its outline on the paper. To do this, use a razor knife to make a light scoring cut around the inlay, undercutting along the edge to compensate for the width of the knife blade *(Step 4)*.

■ Then make two or three more scoring cuts to a depth approximately equal to the thickness of the inlay. These cuts define the outline of the inlay in the surface of the wood. Now remove the inlay, and peel up the section of white paper *(Step 5)*. What remains should be an exact pattern of the inlay. All that remains is to rout out this recess.

■ Use a router with a ¹/₈" or ¹/₄" straight bit to make the recess. It keeps the bottom of the inlay flat, smooth, and at a consistent depth. The object is to rout as close to the edge of the scored outline as possible without actually cutting into it.

Note: You may want to try this on some scrap wood a couple of times to get comfortable with the process.

MARQUETRY TOP

MATERIALS LIST

NEW PART

R Lid (1) ³/₄ x 8¹/₄ - 12¹/₄

Note: Do not need parts D, E, and F, rose inlay veneer, or banding strip

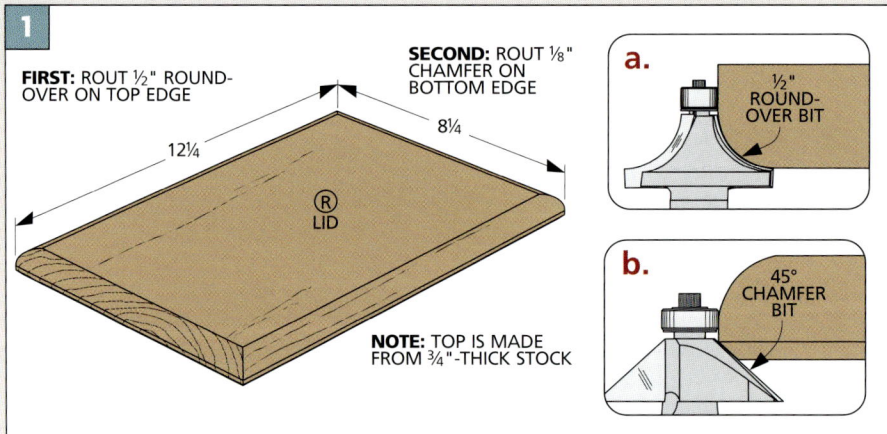

1

FIRST: ROUT ¹/₂" ROUND-OVER ON TOP EDGE

SECOND: ROUT ¹/₈" CHAMFER ON BOTTOM EDGE

12¹/₄

8¹/₄

Ⓡ LID

NOTE: TOP IS MADE FROM ¾"-THICK STOCK

a. ½" ROUND-OVER BIT

b. 45° CHAMFER BIT

■ Set the depth of cut to just a little over half the thickness of the inlay (Step 6). This shallow depth of cut means the inlay will stick up above the surface of the workpiece just a tad so it can be sanded flush with the surface later.

■ Routing such a shallow depth doesn't generate much sawdust or many wood chips, so I get down close to the router — especially when routing near the scored outline (Step 7). (Remove the router's chip shield to get a better view and always wear protective eyewear.)

■ As the recess is routed, rotate the workpiece to keep the edge of the white paper pattern in sight. You should be able to get close enough to the score marks so just

a small sliver of wood remains. Then clean out this sliver with a razor knife or small chisel (Step 8).

■ Once the sliver is removed, the inlay should just pop right into the recess. If it doesn't, you may have to trim the recess and the edges of the inlay to get the two to mate perfectly.

■ When everything fits, you're ready to glue the inlay in place. Contact cement is usually recommended, but a slower drying glue (like yellow or white glue) is easier to work with and works fine.

■ Apply a light coat of glue on the back of the inlay and another on the bottom of the recess. A very light coat is all that's needed. If there's too much glue, the

excess won't have any place to go when the inlay is clamped, and it may buckle.

■ Carefully place the inlay in the recess and cover it with a piece of waxed paper. Then place a piece of scrap wood on top and clamp this "sandwich" in a vise while the glue sets up.

■ Before the inlay can be sanded flush with the top of the workpiece, you must remove the paper tape. To do this, lightly moisten the brown paper tape and gently scrape it off with a cabinet scraper or putty knife (Step 9).

■ After the paper backing is completely removed, use fine grit sandpaper (in a sanding block) to sand the surface of the inlay flush with the workpiece.

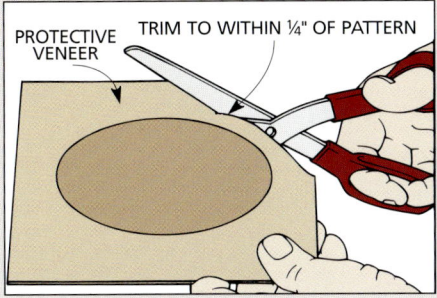

1 *Most patterned marquetry inlays are surrounded with a piece of protective veneer. Use scissors to remove most of it to within ¼" of the pattern.*

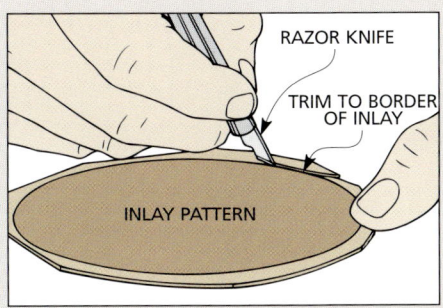

2 *Switch to a razor knife to trim off the rest of the protective veneer. Then sand the edge of the pattern on a sanding block to get the edges as smooth as possible.*

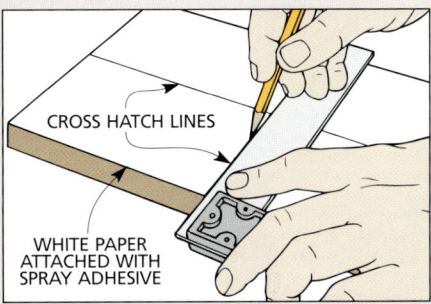

3 *Use spray adhesive or a thin coat of rubber cement to "glue" a piece of white paper to the workpiece. Then draw cross hatch lines to center the inlay.*

4 *Pin the inlay to surface with flattened push pins. Then lightly score around the inlay with a razor knife, undercutting the edges slightly. Make repeated cuts.*

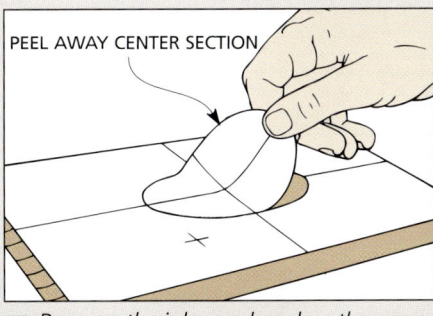

5 *Remove the inlay and peel up the paper. The outline of the white paper should create an exact duplicate of the inlay that's easy to see when routing.*

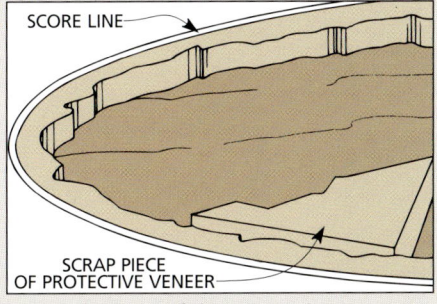

6 *Use a piece of the protective veneer as a gauge to determine the depth of cut for the router bit. Set the depth to a little over half the thickness of the inlay.*

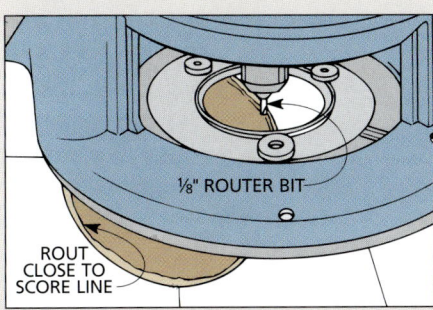

7 *Use protective eyewear and get down close to the action. Rout out the inlay's recess — getting as close to the outline as possible. Rotate the workpiece often.*

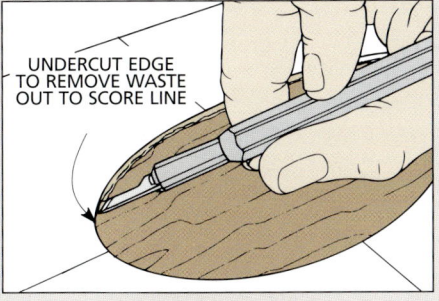

8 *Use a sharp razor knife to trim away the sliver of wood left after routing. Undercut the edge of the recess slightly, and trim the inlay's edge to get a good fit.*

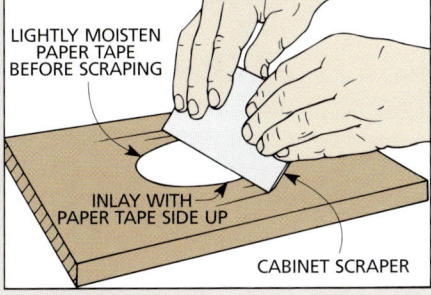

9 *Glue and clamp the inlay in place. Then lightly moisten the paper backing and gently scrape the paper off. Finally, sand the inlay flush with the surface.*

CLASSIC CHERRY SET

Classic styling is the hallmark of this bedroom set. And you'll find numerous ways to customize the cabinets without losing that style. From something as simple as different drawer pulls, to an alternate design for the kickboards, to door and drawer options, and even a cabinet that can be built as one dresser or two separate units, this versatile set provides plenty of ways to make it your own.

Night Stand — 76

Technique: Routing Inside Chamfers. 80
Technique: Edge Jointing Basics 82
Designer's Notebook: Door 85

Lingerie Dresser — 86

Designer's Notebook: Apron Cutout 90
Technique: Routing Stopped Chamfers 91
Technique: Blind Nailing 93
Designer's Notebook: Pulls 94
Designer's Notebook: Double-Deep Drawers 95
Technique: Raised Panels 96

Classic Cherry Bed — 98

Shop Info: Spokeshaves 103
Technique: Tenons on Long Rails 104
Shop Jig: Dado Routing Guide 105
Technique: Through Mortises 106
Technique: Drum Sander Thicknessing. 108
Designer's Notebook: Twin and Full Size. 110
Hardware: Bed Rail Fasteners 111

Chest-on-Chest — 112

Joinery: Rabbetted Tongue and Groove 115
Shop Tip: Clamp Position 116
Shop Tip: Sanding Chamfers 117
Designer's Notebook: Solid-Wood Top. 120
Technique: Installing Inserts 124
Designer's Notebook: Kickboard Base 125

Night Stand

When you set out to build a classically-styled cabinet, it seems only natural to include classic joinery and details— like raised panel drawers dovetailed at the front and back, and frame and panel sides.

While I was working on this Night Stand, a few people wandered into the shop to check the progress. They all had the same initial comment: "It's so small."

But its scale in the shop can be deceiving. Put it alongside a bed, sofa, or chair, and it takes on all the proper proportions. And its scale from a creative standpoint is no different than the challenges offered by a full-sized dresser.

This Night Stand is designed to complement the two other cabinets in this section — the Lingerie Dresser (page 86) and the Chest-on-Chest (page 112).

If you were to stretch some of the Night Stand's parts, you'd end up with one of those projects (almost). So if you plan on making one (or both) of the other cabinets also, this is a good place to start.

BACK DESIGN. The only major difference in the design of the Night Stand compared to the other two cabinets is its finished back. The back is a frame and panel unit (like the sides), not just a piece of plywood screwed to the back of the case. That way it will look good sitting beside a chair, away from a wall.

JOINERY. Although most of the joinery is very traditional, I chose a slightly

unusual approach for joining the drawer rails (that support and separate the drawers) to the sides of the cabinet. Typically, these rails are joined to the cabinet sides with mortise and tenon joints. However, I designed the rails so they could be mounted with a tongue and dado arrangement.

MATERIALS. I chose black cherry for this project — including cherry plywood panels for the frame and panel sides. The drawer sides are made of poplar. Besides helping keep the cost down, the lighter color of the poplar adds a nice contrast for the dovetails on the drawer fronts.

EXPLODED VIEW

OVERALL DIMENSIONS:
20W x 16D x 22½H

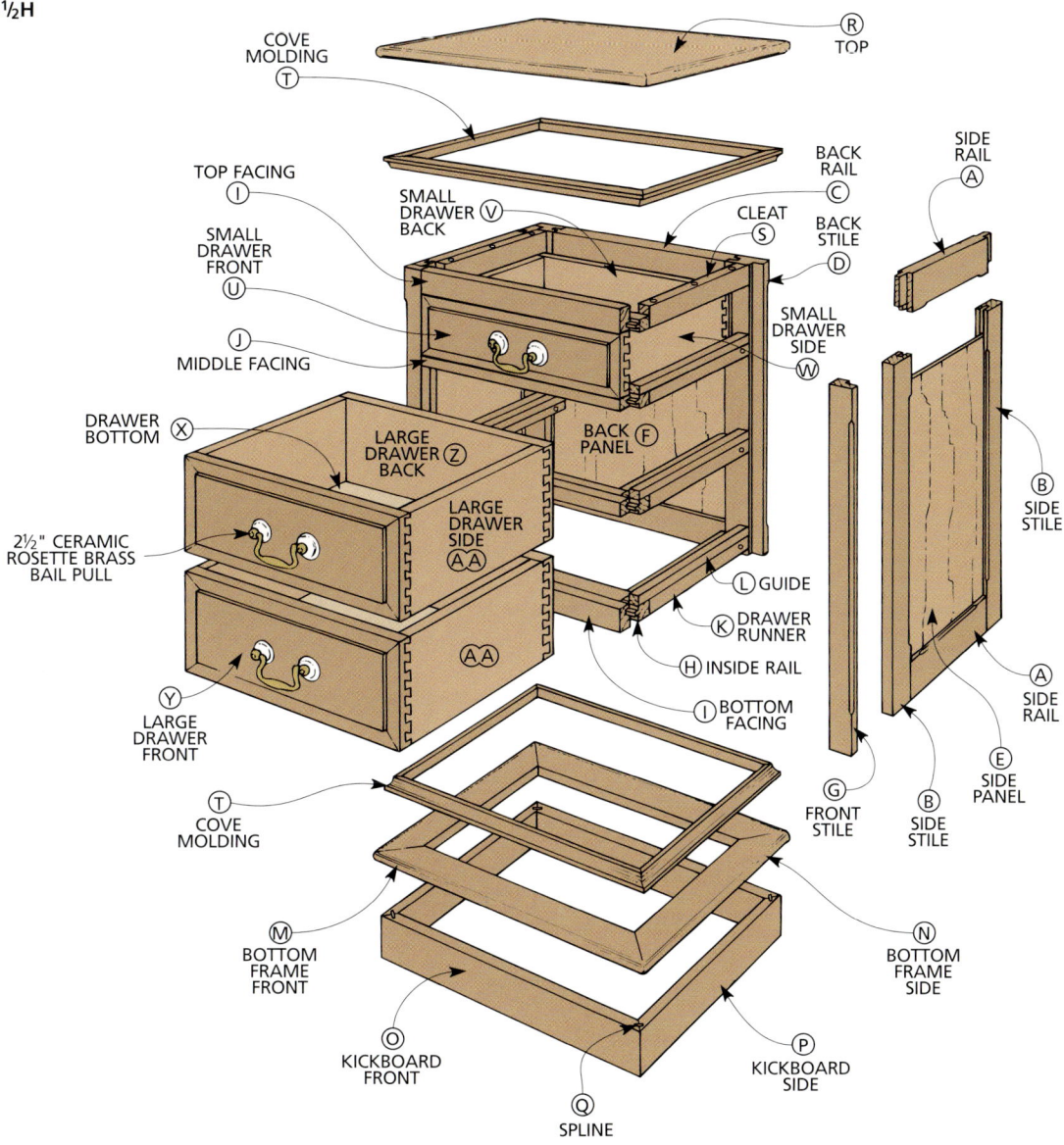

MATERIALS LIST

WOOD

A	Side Rails (4)	¾ x 2 - 10¾
B	Side Stiles (4)	¾ x 1½ -18⅝
C	Back Rails (2)	¾ x 2 - 14¾
D	Back Stiles (2)	¾ x 2 -18⅝
E	Side Panels (2)	¼ ply - 10⅝ x 15½
F	Back Panel (1)	¼ ply - 14⅝ x 15½
G	Front Stiles (2)	¾ x 1¼ - 18⅝
H	Inside Rails (4)	¾ x 1½ -16¼
I	Top/Btm. Facings (2)	¾ x 1⅜ - 15¼
J	Middle Facings (2)	¾ x ¾ - 15¼
K	Drawer Runners (6)	¾ x 1½ - 11
L	Drawer Guides (6)	½ x ½ - 12¼

M	Btm. Frame Fr./Bk. (2)	¾ x 1⅞ - 20
N	Btm. Frame Sides (2)	¾ x 1⅞ - 16
O	Kickboard Fr./Bk. (2)	¾ x 2⅜ - 19½
P	Kickboard Sides (2)	¾ x 2⅜ - 15½
Q	Splines (4)	⅛ x 2⅜ - ¹³⁄₁₆
R	Top (1)	¾ x 16 - 20
S	Cleats (2)	¾ x 1⅜ - 11
T	Cove Molding (8)	⅝ x ⅝ - 22 rough
U	Small Drwr. Front (1)	¾ x 3½ - 15¼
V	Small Drwr. Back (1)	½ x 3½ - 15¼
W	Small Drwr. Sides (2)	½ x 3½ - 12¼
X	Drawer Bottoms (3)	¼ ply - 12¹⁄₁₆ x 14¹¹⁄₁₆

Y	Large Drwr. Fronts (2)	¾ x 5¼ - 15¼
Z	Large Drwr. Backs (2)	½ x 5¼ - 15¼
AA	Large Drwr. Sides (4)	½ x 5¼ - 12¼
BB	Drawer Stops (3)	¼ x 1½ - 3

HARDWARE SUPPLIES

(12) No. 8 x 1¾" Fh woodscrews
(12) No. 8 x 1¼" Rh woodscrews
(12) No. 6 x 1" Fh woodscrews
(6 ft.) Nylon glide strip
(3) 2½" ceramic rosette brass bail pulls
(3) Plastic turnbuttons w/ screws

CUTTING DIAGRAM

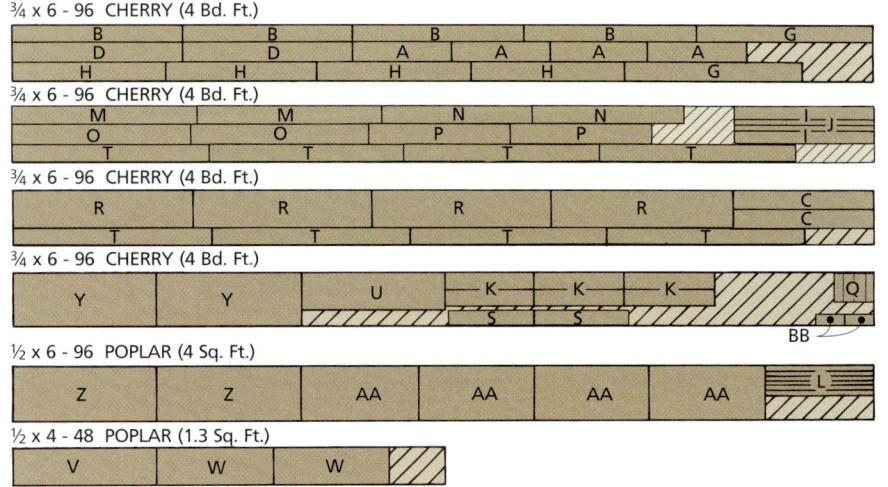

¾ x 6 - 96 CHERRY (4 Bd. Ft.)

¾ x 6 - 96 CHERRY (4 Bd. Ft.)

¾ x 6 - 96 CHERRY (4 Bd. Ft.)

¾ x 6 - 96 CHERRY (4 Bd. Ft.)

½ x 6 - 96 POPLAR (4 Sq. Ft.)

½ x 4 - 48 POPLAR (1.3 Sq. Ft.)

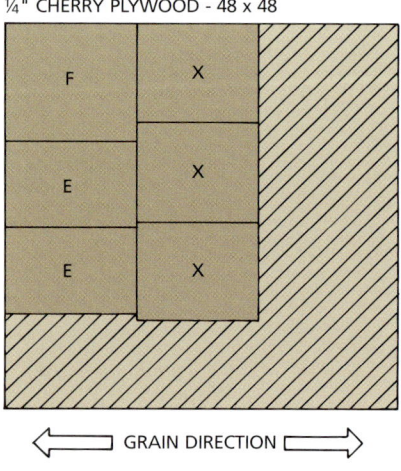

¼" CHERRY PLYWOOD - 48 x 48

⟵ GRAIN DIRECTION ⟶

BACK & SIDE FRAMES

The Night Stand is a case made up of three frame and panel units: two side units joined to a back unit that, together, form a "U-shaped" assembly.

Across the front of the case are four rails with attached facing strips which define the openings for three drawers.

I began work on the cabinet by making the two side frames and one back frame. Each unit consists of two rails and two stiles that surround a ¼" plywood panel.

RAILS AND STILES. Start by cutting four side rails (A) and two back rails (C) to size from ¾"-thick stock *(Fig. 1)*. Next, rip

four side stiles (B) and two back stiles (D) to finished width *(Fig. 1)*. Then cut all six stiles to the same length (18⅝").

GROOVE FOR PANELS. When the rails and stiles are cut to size, grooves are cut on the inside edges to accept the panels. Cut these grooves wide enough to accept the plywood panels and centered on the thickness of the pieces *(Fig. 1)*.

Note: Most hardwood plywood is slightly less than ¼" thick. So cut the grooves just wide enough to accept the actual thickness of the plywood.

TENONS. After cutting the grooves, I cut stub tenons on the ends of the rails to fit the grooves in the stiles.

The length of the tenons matches the depth of the grooves and they're centered on the thickness of the rails *(Fig. 1)*.

PANELS. With grooves and tenons cut, you're ready to dry-assemble the back frame and one side frame to take measurements for the plywood panels.

Now cut the panels (E, F) to size, allowing ⅟₁₆" clearance all around so the panels will fit inside the frames *(Fig. 1)*.

ASSEMBLE FRAMES. Next, the frames can be assembled around the panels. To do this, first glue the rails onto the panels. Then glue on the stiles. As you clamp each assembly together, make sure it stays square and flat.

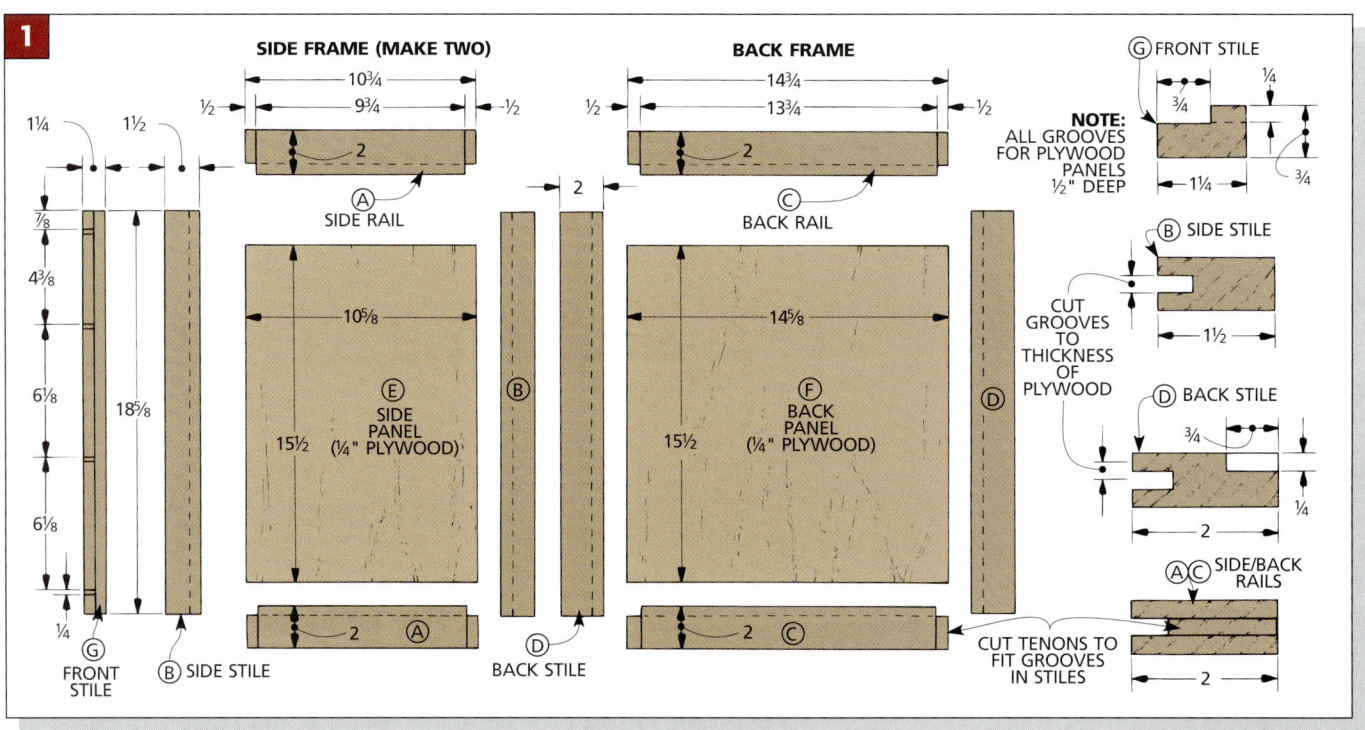

1

SIDE FRAME (MAKE TWO)

BACK FRAME

Ⓖ FRONT STILE

SIDE RAIL Ⓐ

BACK RAIL Ⓒ

NOTE: ALL GROOVES FOR PLYWOOD PANELS ½" DEEP

Ⓔ SIDE PANEL (¼" PLYWOOD)

Ⓕ BACK PANEL (¼" PLYWOOD)

Ⓑ SIDE STILE

CUT GROOVES TO THICKNESS OF PLYWOOD

Ⓓ BACK STILE

Ⓐ©Ⓒ SIDE/BACK RAILS

CUT TENONS TO FIT GROOVES IN STILES

FRONT STILE Ⓖ

Ⓑ SIDE STILE

Ⓓ BACK STILE

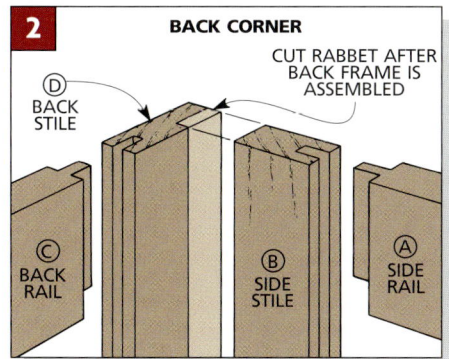

2 BACK CORNER

CUT RABBET AFTER BACK FRAME IS ASSEMBLED

Ⓓ BACK STILE

Ⓒ BACK RAIL

Ⓑ SIDE STILE

Ⓐ SIDE RAIL

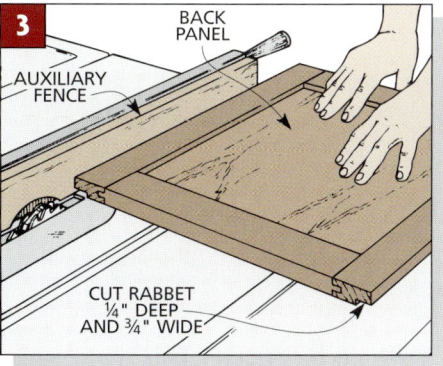

3 BACK PANEL

AUXILIARY FENCE

CUT RABBET ¼" DEEP AND ¾" WIDE

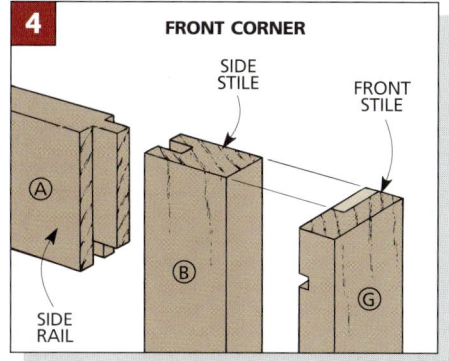

4 FRONT CORNER

SIDE STILE

FRONT STILE

Ⓐ

Ⓑ

Ⓖ

SIDE RAIL

RABBETS. The next step is to cut a shallow rabbet on the inside face of both back stiles *(Figs. 1 and 2)*. These accept the side stiles when the case is assembled *(Fig. 5a)*. I made these cuts on the table saw with a dado blade *(Fig. 3)*.

JOIN SIDES AND BACK. Now the case sides and back are ready to be assembled into a "U" shape *(Fig. 5)*.

Note: Check the inside corners for square after attaching the clamps.

FRONT STILES & RAILS

The front of the case is made up of a pair of vertical stiles glued to the front of the side frames *(Fig. 5)*. Then, rails and facing strips are added *(Fig. 7)*.

Start by ripping the front stiles (G) to width, then cutting them to the same length as the side frame *(Fig. 1)*.

DADOES. Next, to accept the inside rails that create the drawer openings, cut four ¼"-deep dadoes across the back of each front stile *(Fig. 1)*.

ATTACH STILES. Each front stile also has a rabbet along its back face *(Figs. 1 and 4)*. As with the back stiles, this rabbet accepts the side stile *(Fig. 5b)*. Plus it keeps the dadoes from showing on the side of the cabinet. Then glue the front stiles in place.

RAILS. To find the length of the inside rails (H), measure across the inside of the case at the back. Then cut two rabbets on the front edge of each rail to form tongues to fit the dadoes in the stiles *(Fig. 6)*.

FACING STRIPS. After the rails are glued in place, the facing strips (I, J) can be ripped to width *(Fig. 7a)*.

A groove is cut on the back face of each strip to fit onto the tongue on the inside rails. The groove on the top and bottom facing (I) is offset and on the middle facing, it's centered *(Fig. 7a)*.

Finally, cut the facing strips to fit snug between the front stiles. Then glue and clamp them in place *(Fig. 7)*.

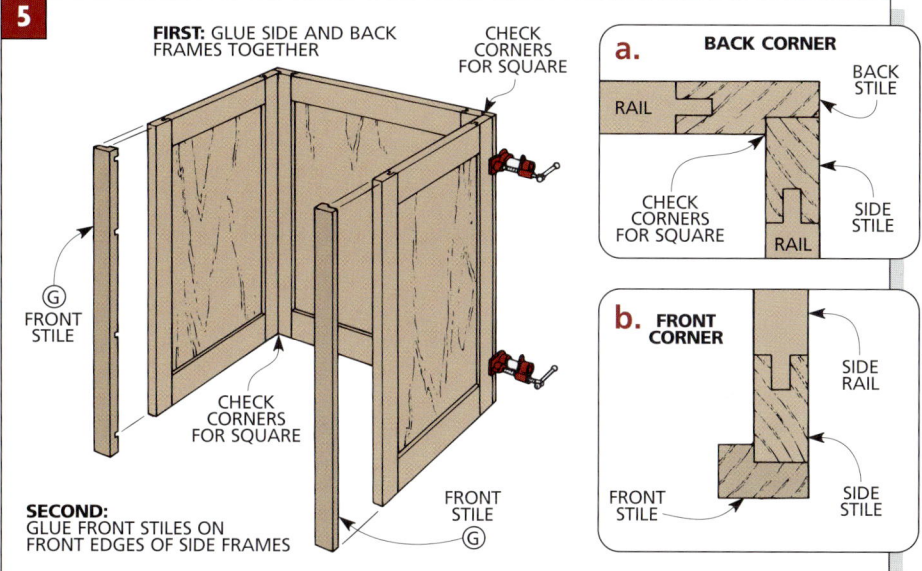

5 FIRST: GLUE SIDE AND BACK FRAMES TOGETHER

CHECK CORNERS FOR SQUARE

Ⓖ FRONT STILE

CHECK CORNERS FOR SQUARE

SECOND: GLUE FRONT STILES ON FRONT EDGES OF SIDE FRAMES

FRONT STILE Ⓖ

a. BACK CORNER

RAIL

BACK STILE

CHECK CORNERS FOR SQUARE

SIDE STILE

RAIL

b. FRONT CORNER

SIDE RAIL

FRONT STILE

SIDE STILE

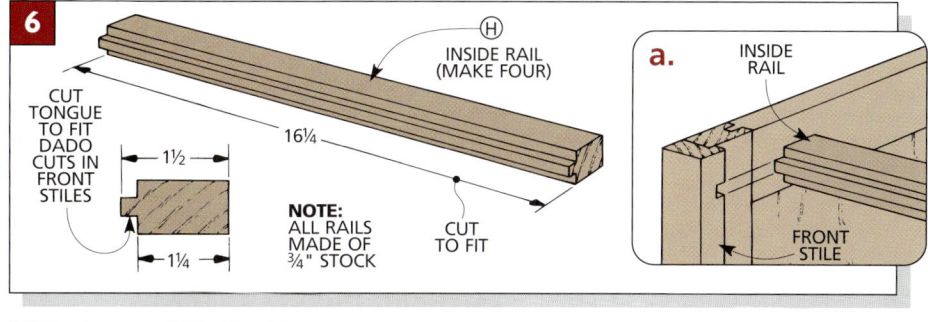

6 CUT TONGUE TO FIT DADO CUTS IN FRONT STILES

Ⓗ INSIDE RAIL (MAKE FOUR)

1½

1¼

16¼

NOTE: ALL RAILS MADE OF ¾" STOCK

CUT TO FIT

a. INSIDE RAIL

FRONT STILE

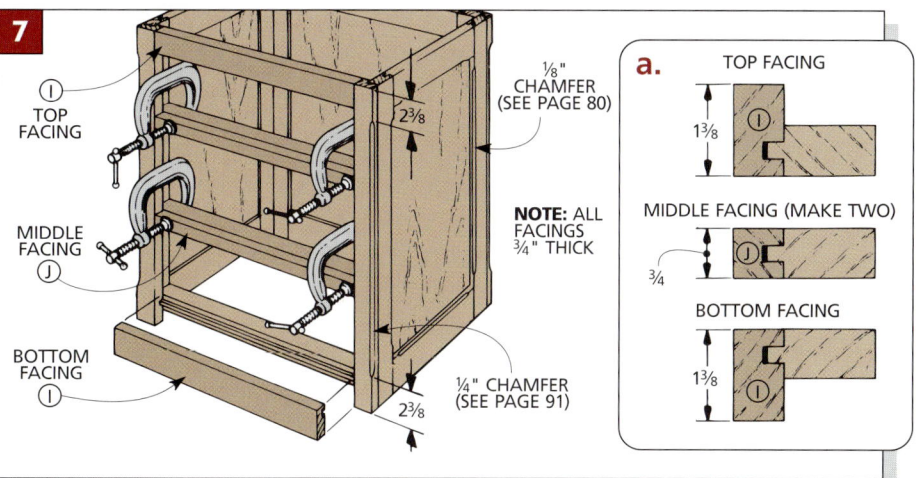

7 Ⓘ TOP FACING

MIDDLE FACING Ⓙ

BOTTOM FACING Ⓘ

⅛" CHAMFER (SEE PAGE 80)

2⅜

NOTE: ALL FACINGS ¾" THICK

¼" CHAMFER (SEE PAGE 91)

2⅜

a. TOP FACING

Ⓘ

1⅜

MIDDLE FACING (MAKE TWO)

Ⓙ

¾

BOTTOM FACING

Ⓘ

1⅜

Frame and panel units look more finished if the inside edges of the frame are lightly chamfered. But routing a chamfer on these edges is a problem if the unit is assembled — the panel interferes with the pilot bearing on a chamfer bit.

To get around this problem you can use a V-groove router bit instead. Since a V-groove bit has no pilot bearing, the panel can't interfere. Then, to substitute

for the pilot bearing, attach a shop-built edge guide to the router.

An edge guide does two things. First it keeps the bit a uniform distance from the frame edge. The guide also stops the router a uniform distance from the corners ($^3/_4$" for this guide).

To make the edge guide, replace the original router base with one made from $^1/_4$" hardboard *(Fig. 1)*. For the guide

itself, cut another piece of $^1/_4$" hardboard $1^1/_2$" wide and about 3" long *(Fig. 1)*. Align the edge of the guide with the center of the bit and center the guide on the bit *(Fig. 1a)*. Then glue it to the base.

Now just turn on the router and raise the bit until enough is exposed to cut a narrow chamfer along the edge of the frame. Keep the narrow edge of the guide pressed against the frame *(Fig. 2)*.

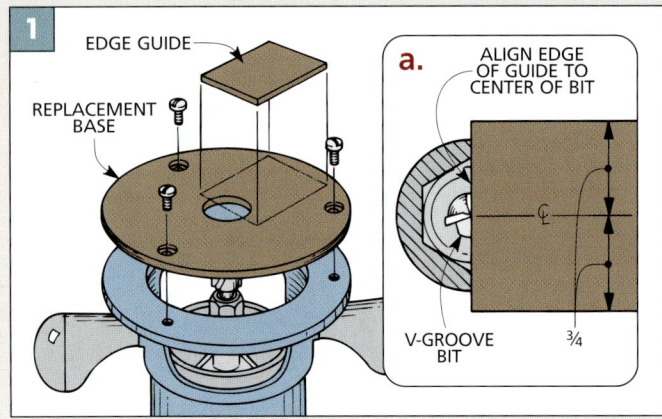

1 EDGE GUIDE · REPLACEMENT BASE · **a.** ALIGN EDGE OF GUIDE TO CENTER OF BIT · V-GROOVE BIT · $^3/_4$

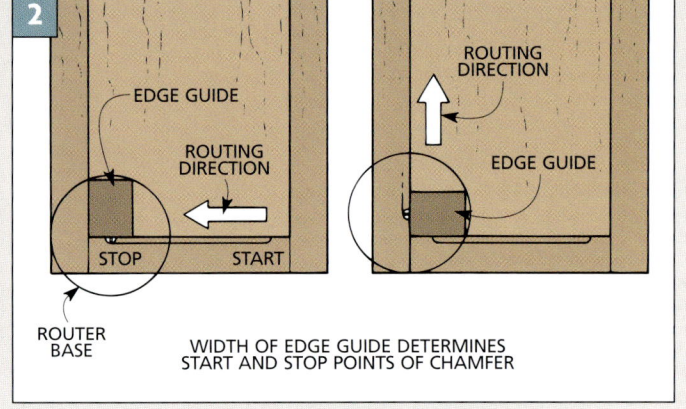

2 EDGE GUIDE · ROUTING DIRECTION · STOP · START · ROUTER BASE · ROUTING DIRECTION · EDGE GUIDE · WIDTH OF EDGE GUIDE DETERMINES START AND STOP POINTS OF CHAMFER

DRAWER SUPPORTS

Once the main case is complete, you can turn your attention to the drawer supports. Each support consists of a runner and a guide *(Fig. 8)*.

RUNNERS. The drawers are supported by the runners (K). To make the runners, rip six pieces of $^3/_4$" stock to width *(Fig. 8)*. Then cut these to length to fit between the back of the case and the back edge of the inside rails (H) *(Fig. 8a)*.

GUIDES. A drawer guide attached to each runner keeps each drawer centered in its opening as the drawer is moved in and out. The guides (L) fit between the back of the case and the back of the front stiles (G) *(Fig. 8a)*. Once they are cut to length, screw a guide to the top of a runner to make a drawer support *(Fig. 8)*.

When that's done, glue and screw the supports to the inside of the case, with the front ends of the drawer guides (L) glued to the top of the inside rails *(Fig. 8a)*.

CHAMFERS

To give the case a finished look, stopped chamfers are routed on the outside edges of the front and back stiles, and also around the inside edges of the side and back frames (refer to *Fig. 7* on page 79).

Similar chamfers are routed on all three cabinets in the Classic Cherry Set. So the Technique box above shows how to set up your router to rout the inside chamfers. Then you can refer to the Technique box on page 91 for details about routing the outside chamfers. And there's a tip on page 117 about touching up the ends of the chamfers so they're symmetrical.

BASE

With the basic case of the Night Stand complete, work can begin on the base. This consists of a bottom frame that's glued on top of a kickboard frame.

BOTTOM FRAME. The bottom frame is an open frame, with miters at each corner.

Start by cutting a bottom frame front (M), back (M), and two frame sides (N) to width *(Fig. 9)*. Then cut all four pieces to rough length (about 4" longer than the outside dimensions of the case).

Before cutting the pieces to final length, rout a bullnose edge on each piece. First, rout a $^1/_2$" roundover on the top edge *(Fig. 9b)*. Then, to rout the bottom edge, switch to a $^1/_4$" roundover bit raised $^3/_{16}$" above the router table.

After the bullnose has been routed, miter both ends of all the pieces so the lengths are $2^1/_4$" longer (from long point to long point) than the case.

Now just glue the miters together to form the frame. Hold the pieces on a flat surface until the glue sets. (I didn't bother

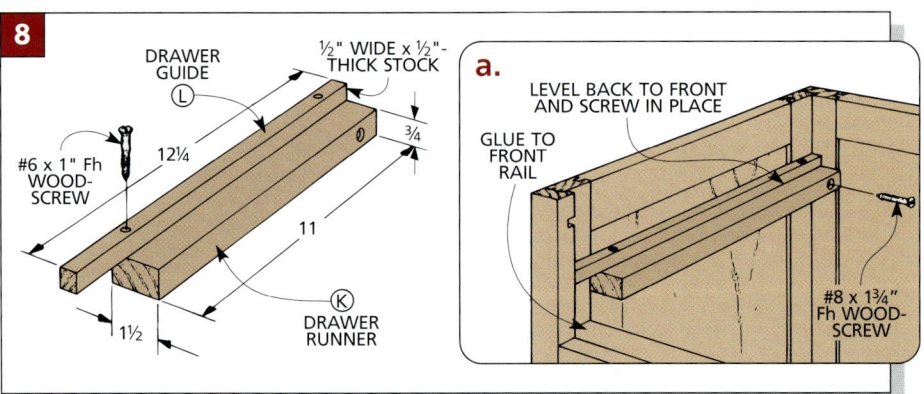

8 DRAWER GUIDE (L) · $^1/_2$" WIDE x $^1/_2$"-THICK STOCK · #6 x 1" Fh WOOD-SCREW · $12^1/_4$ · $^3/_4$ · 11 · $1^1/_2$ · (K) DRAWER RUNNER · **a.** LEVEL BACK TO FRONT AND SCREW IN PLACE · GLUE TO FRONT RAIL · #8 x $1^3/_4$" Fh WOOD-SCREW

to reinforce the miters with splines because the frame will be glued to the kickboard later.)

KICKBOARD. Next up is the kickboard. This consists of a kickboard front (O), back (O), and two sides (P) *(Fig. 9)*. Miter both ends of each piece so they're $1/2$" shorter than the bottom frame.

Note: You can dress up the kickboard with the cutout shown on page 90.

KERF AND SPLINE. I added splines (Q) to help keep the miters aligned while clamping, and to strengthen the joint. You'll need to cut a kerf in each miter, then cut splines to fit the kerfs *(Fig. 9c)*. I cut my splines $1/16$" shorter than the combined depths of the kerfs. That way, the miters will close tightly.

ASSEMBLY. At this point, you can glue the kickboard frame together. Then center and glue the bottom frame to the top of the kickboard *(Fig. 9)*.

Note: There's a trick to centering the bottom frame over the kickboard frame with an equal overhang all around. First, draw centerlines on all four pieces of each frame *(Fig. 9)*. Then simply line up all the marks and clamp the assembly in this position while the glue dries.

BASE TO CASE. To attach the base assembly to the cabinet case, the first thing to do is drill shank holes through the base frame *(Fig. 9a)*.

Now turn the case upside down and center the bottom frame on it. Then mark the location of the pilot holes through the shank holes. Finally, drill the pilot holes and screw the base to the cabinet.

CABINET TOP

To complete the cabinet, I started work on the solid-wood top (R). Begin by edge-gluing enough $3/4$" stock to make a blank 18" wide and 22" long. (The Technique article on page 82 shows how to prepare lumber before gluing up a panel.)

After the glue dries, plane the blank flat and trim it $2^1/4$" larger in each dimension than the top of the case *(Fig. 10)*.

ROUT EDGES. Next, rout the same bull-nose profile on all four edges as on the base frame — but for the top the profile is opposite that of the base. That is, the $1/2$" roundover is on the bottom edge.

ATTACH TOP. To fasten the top to the cabinet, I first glued a pair of cleats (S) inside the case *(Figs. 10 and 10b)*. Next, with the top lying on the bench and the case positioned on it upside down, center the case on the top.

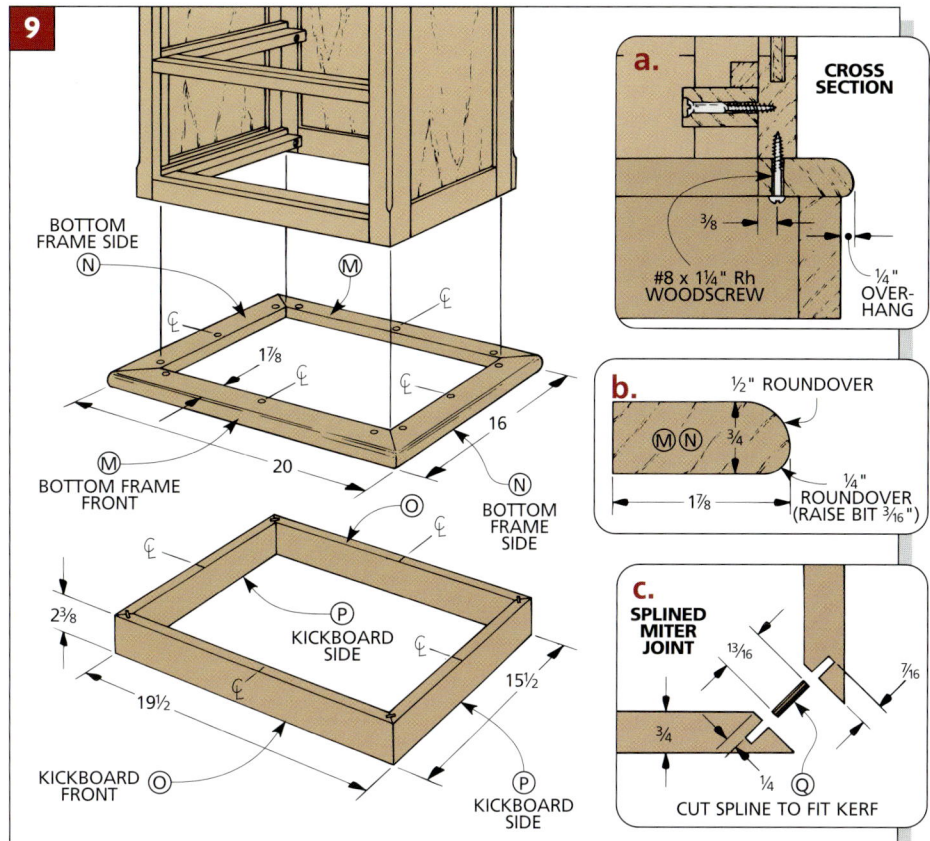

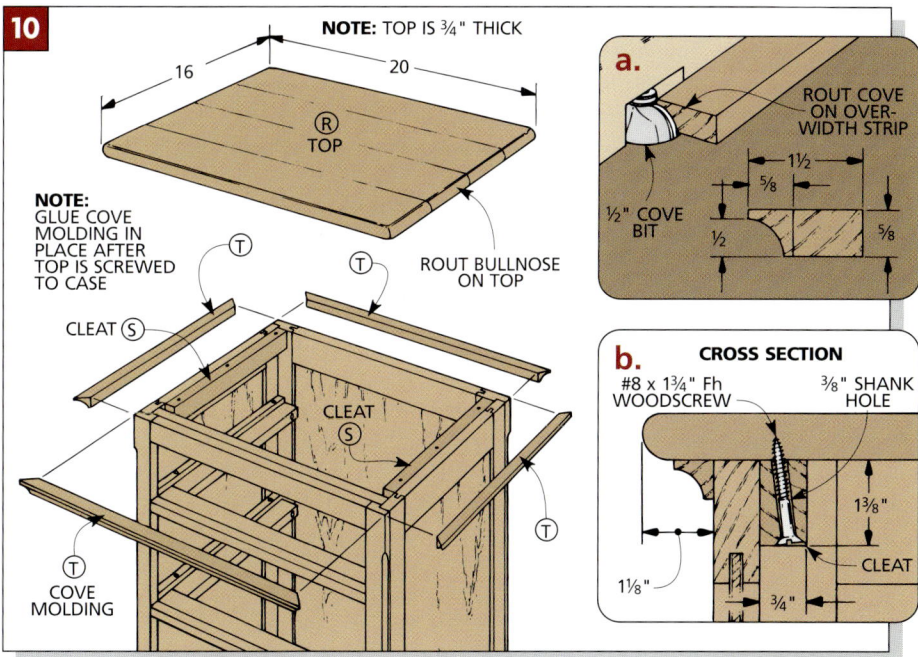

Then drill three screw holes through each cleat into the underside of the top *(Fig. 10b)*. (Use a drill bit collar so you don't drill through the top.)

Now enlarge the shank holes in the cleats to allow the top to move with changes in humidity. Then screw (don't glue) the top in place.

MOLDING. To dress up the cabinet, I glued cove molding strips (T) around the case where it's joined to the base and the top *(Figs. 10 and 10a)*. I started with an over-wide blank and routed a cove along one edge. After ripping the molding to finished width, the molding is mitered to fit around the cabinet.

TECHNIQUE ... *Edge Jointing Basics*

What's the secret to gluing up panels so the joints are strong and nearly invisible? The answer lies in preparing the edges. Boards with straight, smooth, square edges glue up into flat panels with strong joints that practically disappear.

BUYING WOOD

The job of making a tight joint and a good-looking panel actually starts at the lumber yard. I usually buy lumber for panels with both faces planed smooth. (This is called S2S, which is short for "surfaced two sides.") This makes it easier to select boards that have similar color and grain pattern.

WARPING. The next thing I look for is warp. Boards with bow (the face curls in a long "U" shape along its length) or twist (opposite corners curl up) can be difficult

to use for making panels. It's best to leave these alone.

But that doesn't mean you have to find boards that are perfectly straight and flat. Boards that are crooked (flat, but curved along their edges) or that are cupped ("U" shaped across their width, as viewed from an end) can be used. However, they'll need a lot of work to make them straight and flat enough for gluing-up.

I should mention that nearly all boards are a little warped. And you're seldom going to find perfect color and grain. So there's usually compromise involved when looking for lumber that looks good and can be cut straight and flat easily.

PREPARING WOOD

Once you've got the wood, how do you prepare it for edge-gluing?

The first thing I do is... nothing. I buy the wood early enough that it can sit in the shop for a couple of weeks. This lets the moisture content in the wood adjust to the conditions in the shop.

ROUGH CUTTING. After the wood has been sitting for a while, you can begin

preparations. Start by cutting your boards about 3" longer than finished length. I do this for a couple of reasons.

First, if you're jointing the edges of the board on a jointer or planing them on a planer, there might be a snipe (a slightly deeper cut) at the end of the board. Also, when gluing up several boards, it's nearly impossible to keep the ends aligned.

Finally, if the wood splits or the joint opens up, it's almost always at the ends. By using boards that are longer than finished length, you can cut out any of these problems after the panel is glued-up.

WIDTH. As a rule of thumb, I usually rip the boards to between 3" and 5" wide. The reason is, I've found boards over 5" wide are more likely to cup.

PREPARING THE EDGE

An edge properly prepared for gluing has three characteristics — it's straight, 90° to both faces of the board, and smooth.

Here's why. Straight edges make strong joints. But a wavy edge creates an uneven glue line where some of the

joint is starved for glue and some has too much to create a strong bond.

An edge needs to be 90° to the faces so the panel will glue up flat. If it's not, the boards may slide apart during clamping or they won't stay flat in the clamps.

Finally, mating edges need to be smooth so the glue can bond properly. When the edges are rough, the glue bonds to the raised fibers, and then the fibers can tear loose if the joint is stressed.

So how do you make an edge like this? You can use a variety of tools.

HAND PLANE

Traditionally, a long hand plane called a jointer was the tool of choice. ("Jointing" is the process of preparing one board or edge to be joined to another.)

A jointer plane has a long sole, usually well over 20". So as it's passed over a wavy edge the plane iron (blade) only cuts off the high spots. (A shorter plane will ride along the wavy edge and won't provide a flat surface.)

1 PLANE MATING EDGES TOGETHER

POSITION BOARDS IN VISE FACE SIDES OUT

a. FACE SIDE — FACE SIDE

NOTE: BEVEL EXAGGERATED FOR CLARITY

ANGLES OF MATING EDGES MATCH

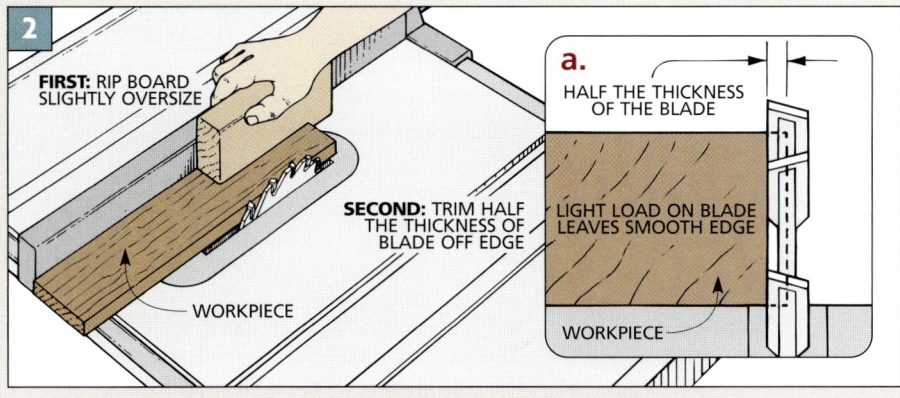

2

FIRST: RIP BOARD SLIGHTLY OVERSIZE

SECOND: TRIM HALF THE THICKNESS OF BLADE OFF EDGE

WORKPIECE

a.

HALF THE THICKNESS OF THE BLADE

LIGHT LOAD ON BLADE LEAVES SMOOTH EDGE

WORKPIECE

MATING EDGES. One of the biggest challenges with hand planing is getting a perfect 90° angle between the edge and the face. One solution is to not worry about being perfect. Instead, tighten both boards into a vise with the mating edges up and the face sides of the boards out (*Fig. 1*). Now plane both boards at the same time. Any variation from 90° on one edge is cancelled out by the variation on the other edge (*Fig. 1a*).

JOINTER

Certainly the best tool for the job today is a sharp, well-adjusted power jointer. But one of the biggest problems with a jointer is chipout.

To avoid chipout along the edge, feed the work so the grain on the face of the board points down and toward the back end of the board. Then the knives will pull the fibers down and out of the workpiece rather than dig up into it.

TABLE SAW

If you don't have a jointer, a table saw can be set up to do the job. In fact, for a long time, a table saw was all I ever used. With a sharp blade and a well-adjusted saw, you may never need a jointer.

Jointing on the table saw is simple. But before trying this, check to be sure the blade is clean, 90° to the table, and parallel with the rip fence. I use a sharp, carbide-tipped combination blade.

SKIM CUT. To get a smooth edge, I use a skim cut technique. Start by ripping the edge, leaving the piece about $1/16''$ oversize. Then rip the edge a second time, taking only half the thickness of the blade off the edge (*Fig. 2a*).

To check if an edge is properly jointed, place the edge on something that you know is straight and flat, like your saw table. If there's a light behind the workpiece, it will show under any gaps.

But the best method is to place the mating edges together, and put the boards on a flat surface. Any gaps will show along the joint.

ROUTER TABLE

There are several ways you can use a router to cut a straight, smooth glue edge. The first way involves using your router table like a jointer (*Fig. 3*).

A jointer has separate infeed and outfeed tables that are offset from each other. To create the same effect on the router table, I attached a piece of plastic laminate to the left (outfeed) side of the router

table fence. The router bit removes stock like the knives of a jointer, and the laminate supports the newly-cut edge.

Before attaching the laminate to the fence, file a slight bevel on the edge of the laminate by the bit opening. That way it won't catch the leading corner of the workpiece (*Fig. 3a*). Then I used double-sided carpet tape to attach the plastic laminate to the fence so one end aligns with the bit opening (*Fig. 3*).

Next mount a straight bit in the router table. (If your router will accept it, a $1/2''$ shank bit works better than a $1/4''$ shank bit since the thicker shank helps cut down on vibration.) Then adjust the fence so the surface of the laminate is aligned with the outermost edge of the bit (*Fig. 3a*).

Now turn on the router and push the workpiece along the fence from right to left. For the best edge, move the board in a smooth, non-stop pass.

This method has a couple of limitations. First, the thickness of the stock to be jointed is limited to the length of the bit's cutting edge. Also, since the length of the fence is fairly short, it's difficult to joint long pieces.

HAND-HELD ROUTER

You can also use a hand-held router and a flush trim bit to prepare an edge for glue-up. The key is a guide fence with a perfectly straight edge.

Since most flush trim bits have a bearing on the bottom of the bit, the guide fence has to be clamped to the bottom side of the workpiece while the router rides on the top (*Fig. 4*).

If the edge is rather rough, you can take several passes to remove the waste and get the workpiece close to a finished edge. Then for the final pass, trim just a small amount ($1/16''$ or less) off the edge of the workpiece (*Fig. 4*).

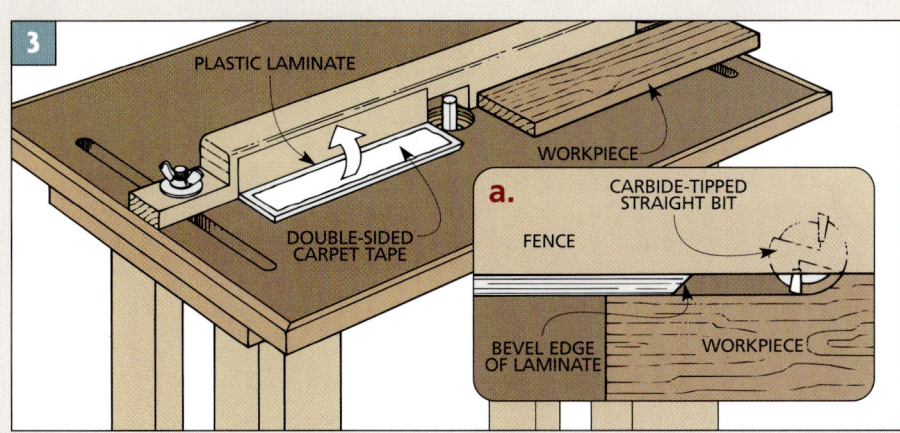

3

PLASTIC LAMINATE

WORKPIECE

DOUBLE-SIDED CARPET TAPE

a.

CARBIDE-TIPPED STRAIGHT BIT

FENCE

BEVEL EDGE OF LAMINATE

WORKPIECE

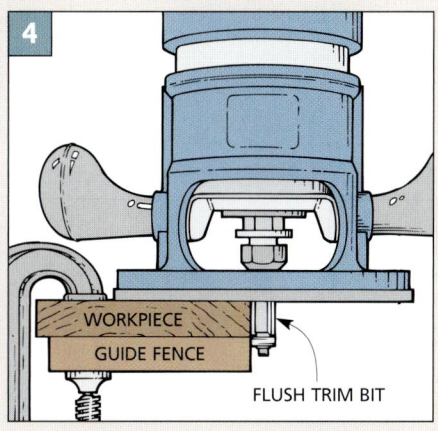

4

WORKPIECE

GUIDE FENCE

FLUSH TRIM BIT

DRAWERS

When the molding strips are in place, the last thing to make is the drawers.

DRAWER PARTS. Begin by cutting the drawer fronts (U, Y) from ³⁄₄" stock so they're ¹⁄₈" smaller in both dimensions than the drawer openings *(Fig. 11)*.

Next, cut the drawer backs (V, Z) to the same dimensions as the fronts, but from ¹⁄₂"-thick stock. (I used poplar for the sides and backs of the drawers.) Then cut the drawer sides (W, AA) from the same ¹⁄₂" stock. The drawer sides are cut to the same width as the fronts, and to a uniform length of 12¹⁄₄".

JOINERY. Once all the drawer pieces are cut to size, rout half-blind dovetail joints on each corner *(Fig. 11a)*. (If you're not familiar with how to do this, see the Joinery article on page 56.)

Next, cut a groove along the lower inside edge of each drawer piece to fit the thickness of the plywood to be used for the drawer bottoms *(Fig. 11a)*.

DRAWER BOTTOMS. Now cut the plywood drawer bottoms (X) to fit in the grooves in the bottom of the drawers.

Note: Before assembling the drawers, cut a notch centered on the bottom edge of each drawer back *(Fig. 11)*. This notch lets the drawer slide over a drawer stop that's added later *(Fig. 12)*.

RAISE THE PANELS. To complete the drawer fronts, I made chamfer cuts around the edges to create the effect of a raised panel *(Fig. 11b)*. These cuts can be made on the table saw or with a straight bit in a router table. Both methods are covered in the Technique article beginning on page 96.

When the drawer fronts have been chamfered, drill counterbored holes for the drawer pulls *(Fig. 13)*. The drawer pulls are centered on the drawer fronts.

ASSEMBLY. Now glue the drawers up square with the plywood bottoms in place.

DRAWER STOPS & HARDWARE

After the drawers have been assembled, there are a few details that remain before the Night Stand is complete.

GLIDE STRIPS. To help the drawers slide more smoothly, I added self-adhesive nylon glide strips to the drawer runners *(Figs. 12 and 13)*. And there's another benefit to adding these strips — they raise the drawers off the facing strips and create a continuous, evenly-spaced gap around the drawer front.

DRAWER STOPS. Then, to stop the fronts of the drawers flush with the cabinet facing strips, I glued a drawer stop (BB) to each front inside rail *(Fig. 12)*. Size the stops smaller than the notch on the bottom of the drawer back so the drawers can slide into the openings.

TURNBUTTONS. Then, to prevent the drawers from being pulled all the way out, I screwed turnbuttons to the inside of the front rails *(Fig. 14)*.

FINISH. To complete the project, I applied a urethane/oil combination finish to the entire Night Stand.

Finally, after the finish dries, mount the drawer pulls *(Fig. 13)*. (You may need to trim the length of the screws so they're flush with the inside of the drawer.) ■

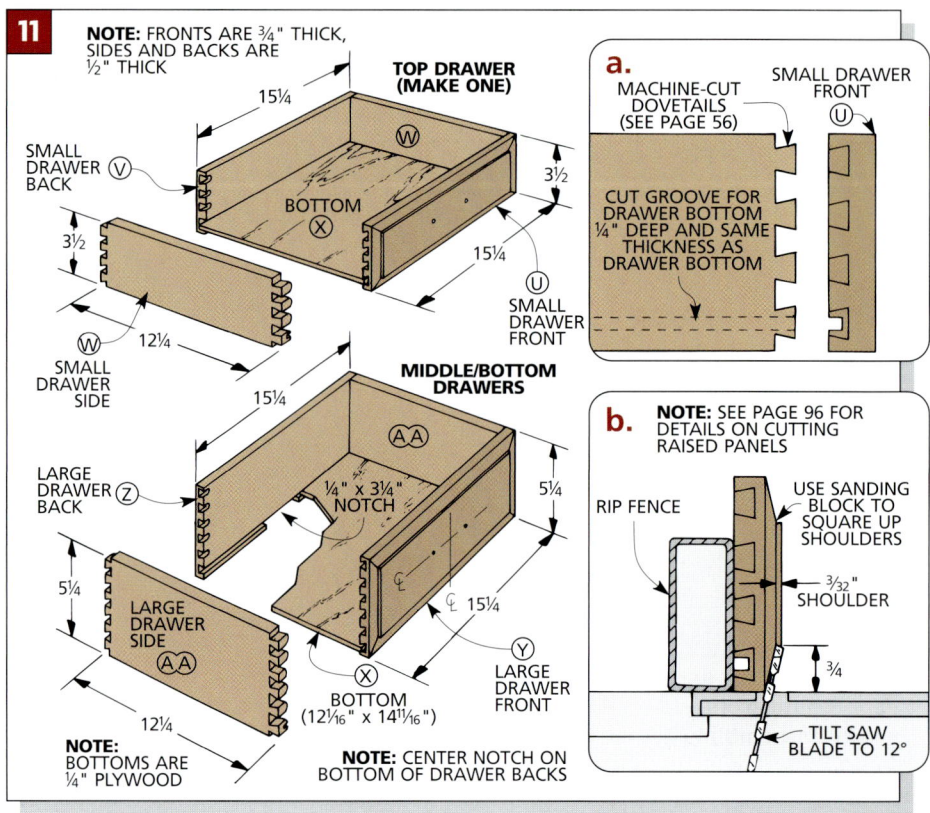

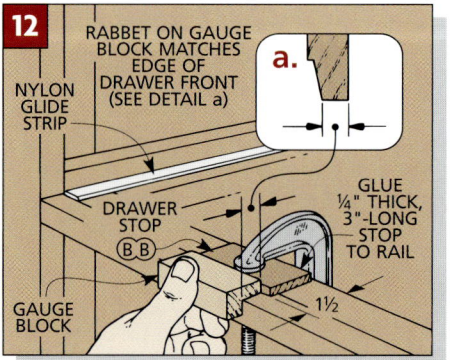

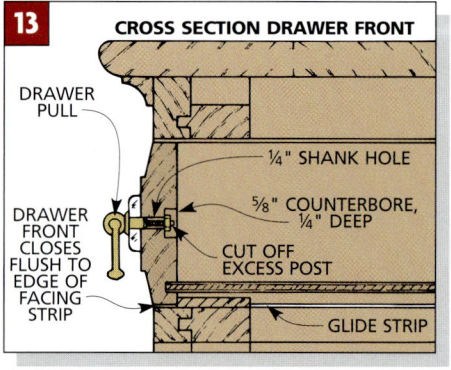

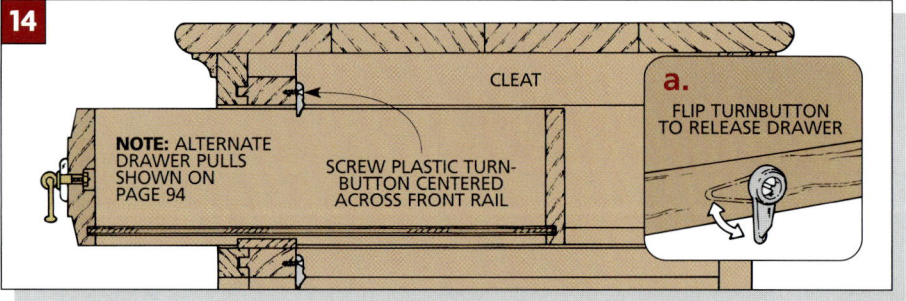

DESIGNER'S NOTEBOOK

By combining the space for the two lower drawers, you can have a storage area for larger items. A frame and panel door reflects the look of the side panels and the chamfer around the drawer front.

CONSTRUCTION NOTES:

■ The sides and back of the cabinet are built as before. But there is a change in the dadoes cut in the front stiles (G). Go ahead and cut the dadoes for the top two rails as before. Don't cut a dado for the third rail. And the position of the lowest dado has changed to make space for a bottom panel. It's ¹/₂" above the bottom edge of the front stile *(Fig. 1)*.

■ You'll only need three inside rails and the facings (I, J) for them. Also, do not install the guides (L) on the two lowest drawer runners (there is no drawer). To secure the lower drawer runners, drive a screw in the front and back *(Fig. 1)*.

■ After assembling the cabinet, install the bottom (CC). This is two layers of ¹/₄" plywood glued together *(Fig. 1)*.

   Note: You can cut all the plywood parts for this version of the Night Stand from a 48" x 48" sheet of ¹/₄" plywood.

■ Now cut the door stiles (DD) and door rails (EE) to length *(Fig. 2)*.

■ Just as with the side panel assemblies, cut a centered groove on the frame pieces and cut stub tenons on the rails to fit the grooves. Then dry-assemble the frame and measure for the door panel (FF).

■ With all the pieces cut to size, you can glue up the door.

■ The chamfer around the outside edge of the door frame is just like the one on the drawer front.

■ The stopped chamfers routed on the inside of the door frame are the same as on the side panels *(Fig. 2)*.

■ Now mount the hinges to the front stile of the cabinet.

   Note: You can hinge the door from whichever side you prefer.

   Hold the door in place and transfer the hinge positions to the door. Then cut ¹/₁₆"-deep mortises for the hinges and screw them in place *(Fig. 2)*. (I chose polished brass hinges so they would match the brass on the pulls.)

■ Finally, install on the door a pull that matches the drawer pull. Center the pull on the length of the stile. Then mount the door in the cabinet.

DOOR

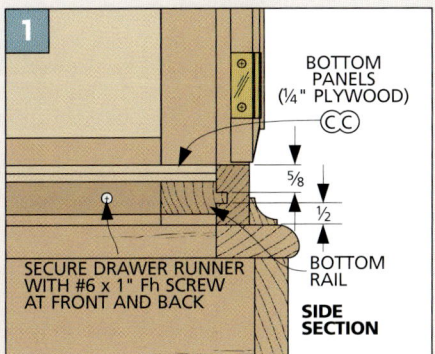

BOTTOM PANELS (¹/₄" PLYWOOD) — CC

⁵/₈ · ¹/₂

SECURE DRAWER RUNNER WITH #6 x 1" Fh SCREW AT FRONT AND BACK

BOTTOM RAIL

SIDE SECTION

MATERIALS LIST

CHANGED PARTS

H	Inside Rails (3)	³/₄ x 1¹/₂ - 16¹/₄
J	Middle Facing (1)	³/₄ x ³/₄ - 15¹/₄
K	Runners (4)	³/₄ x 1¹/₂ - 11 rgh.
L	Guides (2)	³/₄ x ¹/₂ - 12¹/₄ rgh.
X	Drawer Bottom (1)	¹/₄ ply - 12¹/₁₆ x 14¹¹/₁₆
BB	Drawer Stop (1)	¹/₄ x 1¹/₂ - 3

NEW PARTS

CC	Bottom Panels (2)	¹/₄ ply - 12¹/₄ x 16¹/₄
DD	Door Stiles (2)	³/₄ x 2 - 11³/₈
EE	Door Rails (2)	³/₄ x 2 - 11¹/₈
FF	Door Panel (1)	¹/₄ ply - 11⁵/₈ x 7⁷/₈

Note: Do not need parts Y, Z, AA.

HARDWARE SUPPLIES

(4) No. 6 x 1" Fh woodscrews
(2 ft.) Nylon glide strip
(1) 2¹/₂" ceramic rosette drawer pull
(1) Drawer turnbutton
(1 pr.) 1¹/₂" x 1¹/₄" brass butt hinges w/ screws
(1) 1" ceramic knob

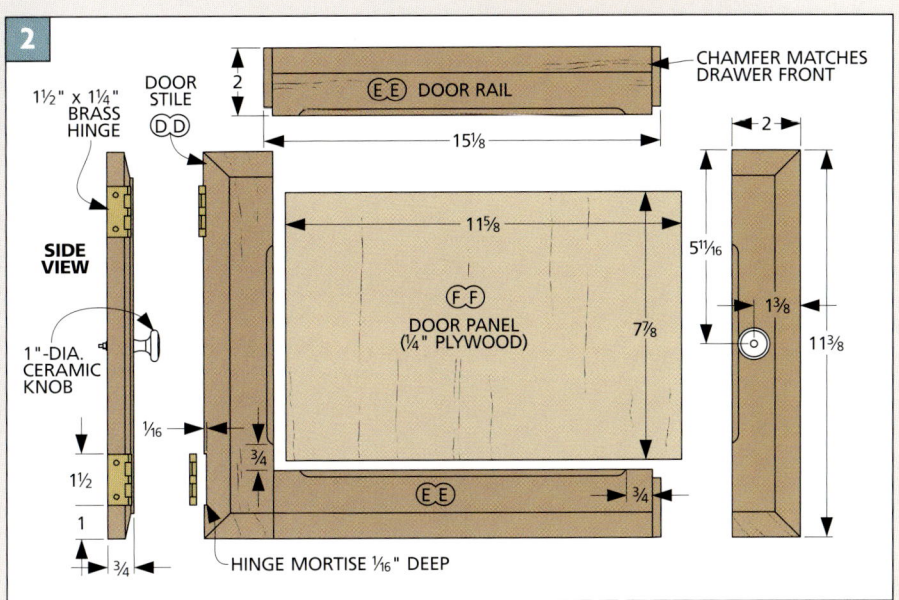

1¹/₂" x 1¹/₄" BRASS HINGE

DOOR STILE DD

SIDE VIEW

1"-DIA. CERAMIC KNOB

1/16

1¹/₂

1

³/₄

HINGE MORTISE ¹/₁₆" DEEP

2 · EE DOOR RAIL · CHAMFER MATCHES DRAWER FRONT

15¹/₈

11⁵/₈

FF DOOR PANEL (¹/₄" PLYWOOD)

³/₄ · 7⁷/₈

EE · ³/₄

2

5¹¹/₁₆

1³/₈

11³/₈

Lingerie Dresser

The second cabinet in this set is tall and elegant. The drawers are all the same size so construction is quick. Or you can add double-deep drawers — without changing the appearance of the cabinet.

After a look at the Night Stand on page 76, it's easy to see the design details that this dresser shares with it. In fact, if you cover up the bottom four drawers of the Lingerie Dresser, what remains is pretty much the Night Stand. But besides the size, there are a few other changes in the construction.

SIDE PANELS. One of the main differences between this piece and the other two cabinets in the Classic Cherry Set is in the construction of the sides. Instead of one frame with a long panel, a center rail is added so there are two side panels in each frame. This makes the frame sturdier and breaks up (both visually and physically) what would be a large panel.

SIMPLER CONSTRUCTION. Another difference is in back. While the Night Stand has a "finished" back so it can sit anywhere in a room, this cabinet is meant to be placed against a wall. So the back face doesn't have to be as "dressy." As a result, some of the construction is simpler.

For example, the back is just a plywood panel instead of a frame and panel (like the sides). And the molded base is mitered only at the front corners, but left square at the back corners. Likewise, the cove molding extends only around the front and sides, not the back. So again, you just need to cut miters at the front.

DESIGN OPTIONS. I've included a number of design options with this dresser, two of which can be adapted to change the look of all three cabinets in the set. The first of those is a simple change of pulls. Some ideas are on page 94.

The second option that works with all three cabinets is a cut-out profile for the base instead of the solid base shown. Details about this are in the Designer's Notebook on page 90.

And for the Lingerie Dresser, if larger drawers suit you better, the Designer's Notebook on page 95 shows how to combine the four lower drawers into two larger ones — while still maintaining the illusion of seven individual drawers.

EXPLODED VIEW

OVERALL DIMENSIONS:
21½"W x 16⅛"D x 49⅞"H

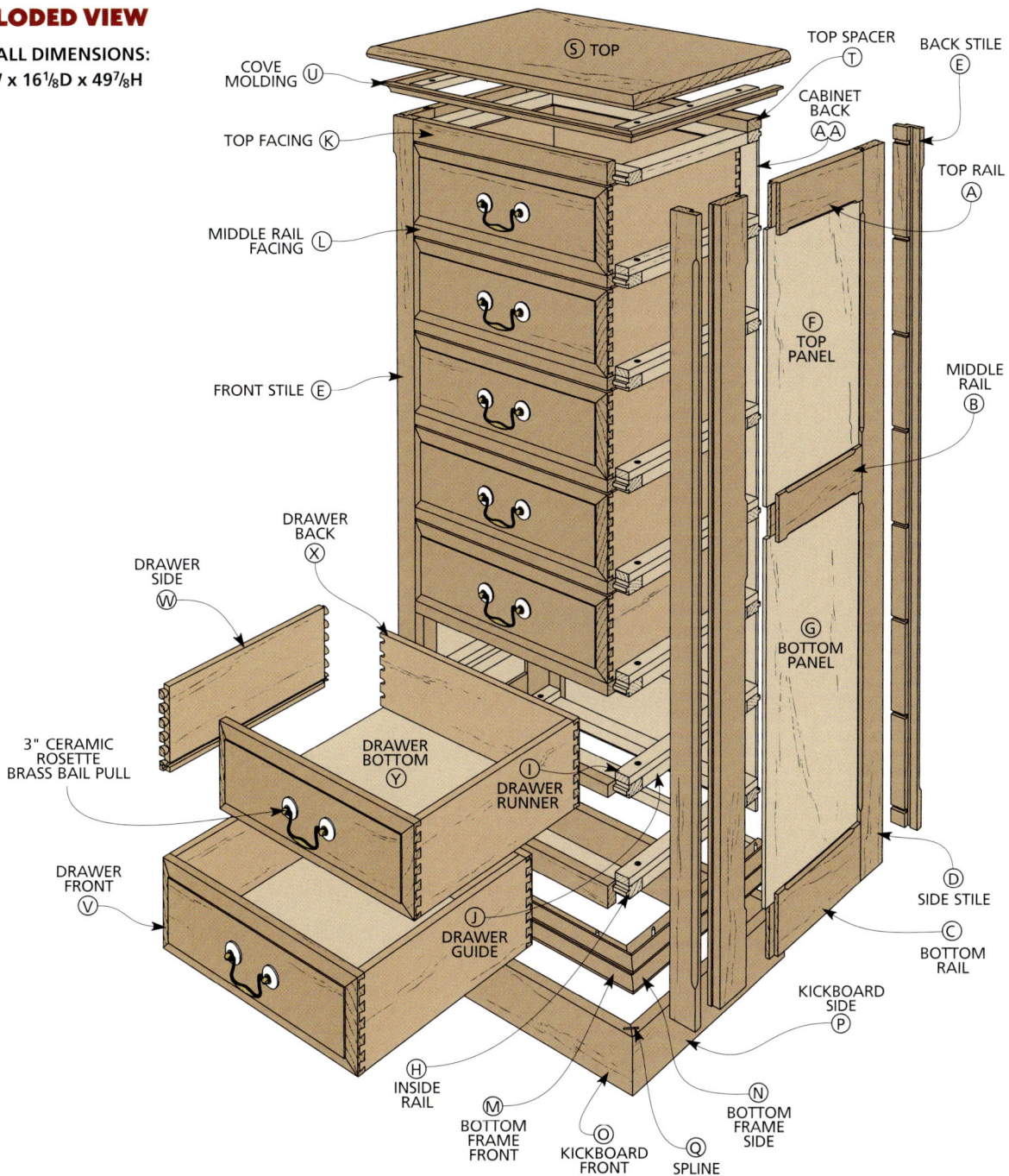

COVE MOLDING (U)

TOP FACING (K)

MIDDLE RAIL FACING (L)

FRONT STILE (E)

DRAWER BACK (X)

DRAWER SIDE (W)

3" CERAMIC ROSETTE BRASS BAIL PULL

DRAWER FRONT (V)

DRAWER BOTTOM (Y)

DRAWER RUNNER (I)

DRAWER GUIDE (J)

INSIDE RAIL (H)

BOTTOM FRAME FRONT (M)

KICKBOARD FRONT (O)

SPLINE (Q)

BOTTOM FRAME SIDE (N)

KICKBOARD SIDE (P)

(S) TOP

TOP SPACER (T)

CABINET BACK (AA)

BACK STILE (E)

TOP RAIL (A)

TOP PANEL (F)

MIDDLE RAIL (B)

BOTTOM PANEL (G)

SIDE STILE (D)

BOTTOM RAIL (C)

MATERIALS LIST

WOOD

A	Top Rails (2)	¾ x 3 - 10
B	Middle Rails (2)	¾ x 2¾ - 10
C	Bottom Rails (2)	¾ x 3⅝ - 10
D	Side Stiles (4)	¾ x 2⅝ - 44⅞
E	Front/Back Stiles (4)	¾ x 1¾ - 44⅞
F	Top Panels (2)	¼ ply - 9¹⁵⁄₁₆ x 15¹⁵⁄₁₆
G	Bottom Panels (2)	¼ ply - 9¹⁵⁄₁₆ x 21⁷⁄₁₆
H	Inside Rails (16)	¾ x 1½ - 17¾
I	Dwr. Runners (16)	¾ x 1½ - 11
J	Dwr. Sd. Guides (16)	½ x 1¹⁄₃₂ - 13½
K	Top/Btm. Facings (2)	¾ x 1⅜ - 15¾
L	Mdl. Rail Facings (6)	¾ x ¾ - 15¾

M	Bottom Frame Fr. (1)	¾ x 2⅜ - 21½
N	Btm. Frame Sides (2)	¾ x 2⅜ - 16⅛
O	Kickboard Ft./Bk. (2)	¾ x 3½ - 21
P	Kickboard Sides (2)	¾ x 3½ - 15⅞
Q	Splines (4)	⅛ x 3½ - ¹³⁄₁₆
R	Bottom Spacer (1)	¾ x ⁹⁄₁₆ - 16¾
S	Top (1)	¾ x 16⅛ - 21½
T	Top Spacer (1)	⅝ x 1¾ - 15¾
U	Cove Molding	⅝ x ⅝ - 120 ln. in.
V	Drawer Fronts (7)	¾ x 5¼ - 15⅝
W	Drawer Sides (14)	½ x 5¼ - 13¾
X	Drawer Backs (7)	½ x 5¼ - 15⅝
Y	Drawer Bottoms (7)	¼ ply - 15⅛ x 13⅝

Z	Drawer Stops (7)	¼ x 1½ - 3
AA	Cabinet Back (1)	¼ ply - 16¾ x 44⅞

HARDWARE SUPPLIES

(20) No. 6 x ½" Fh woodscrews
(48) No. 8 x 1" Fh woodscrews
(7) No. 8 x 1½" Rh woodscrews
(6) No. 8 x 1¾" Fh woodscrews
(18) ⅝" x 19 gauge brads
(7) 3" ceramic rosette brass bail pulls
(14 ft.) Nylon glide strip
(7) Plastic turnbuttons w/ screws

CUTTING DIAGRAM

¾ x 7½ - 72 CHERRY (3.75 Bd. Ft.)

A	B	C	D
A	B	C	D

¾ x 7½ - 96 CHERRY (5 Bd. Ft.)

D
D E E
D E E

¾ x 7½ - 96 CHERRY (2 Boards @ 5 Bd. Ft. Each)

| H | H | I | I | J J |
| H | H | I | I | J J |

¾ x 7½ - 96 CHERRY (5 Bd. Ft.)

K | M | | O | P | R
L | N | Q | O | P |
L | N | | | | T

¾ x 7½ - 96 CHERRY (5 Bd. Ft.)

| S | S | S | V | V |
U

¾ x 7½ - 96 CHERRY (5 Bd. Ft.)

| V | V | V | V | V | Z Z Z Z |
| | | | | | Z Z Z Z |
U

¾ x 6 - 84 POPLAR (2 Boards @ 3.5 Bd. Ft. Each)

| W | W | W | W | W | W |

¾ x 6 - 96 POPLAR (4 Bd. Ft.)

| X | X | X | X | X | X |

¾ x 6 - 48 POPLAR (2 Bd. Ft.)

| X | W | W |

ALSO NEED: ONE 48" x 96" SHEET OF ¼" CHERRY PLYWOOD FOR PARTS F, G, Y, AND AA

SIDE FRAMES

I began building the dresser by assembling the two side frames. Each side frame consists of three rails, two stiles, and two ¼" plywood panels.

RAILS. The first thing to do is to cut six rails from ¾"-thick stock. Note that the top rails (A), middle rails (B), and bottom rails (C) are all different widths (*Fig. 1*). But they're all the same length (10").

STILES. The stiles are also ¾" thick. The four side stiles (D) are $2\frac{5}{8}$" wide while the two front (E) and two back stiles (E) are $1\frac{3}{4}$" wide (*Fig. 1*). All eight pieces are $44\frac{7}{8}$" long.

JOINERY

After all of the rails and stiles are cut to finished size, the joints that hold them together can be cut.

GROOVE FOR PANELS. Start by cutting a ½"-deep groove on the edge of each rail and side stile (D) to accept the plywood panels (*Fig. 1*). Center the groove on the thickness of each workpiece.

Cut the grooves on only the *inside* edge of the top and bottom rails (A, C) and the side stiles (D). Then cut a groove on *both* edges of the middle rails (B).

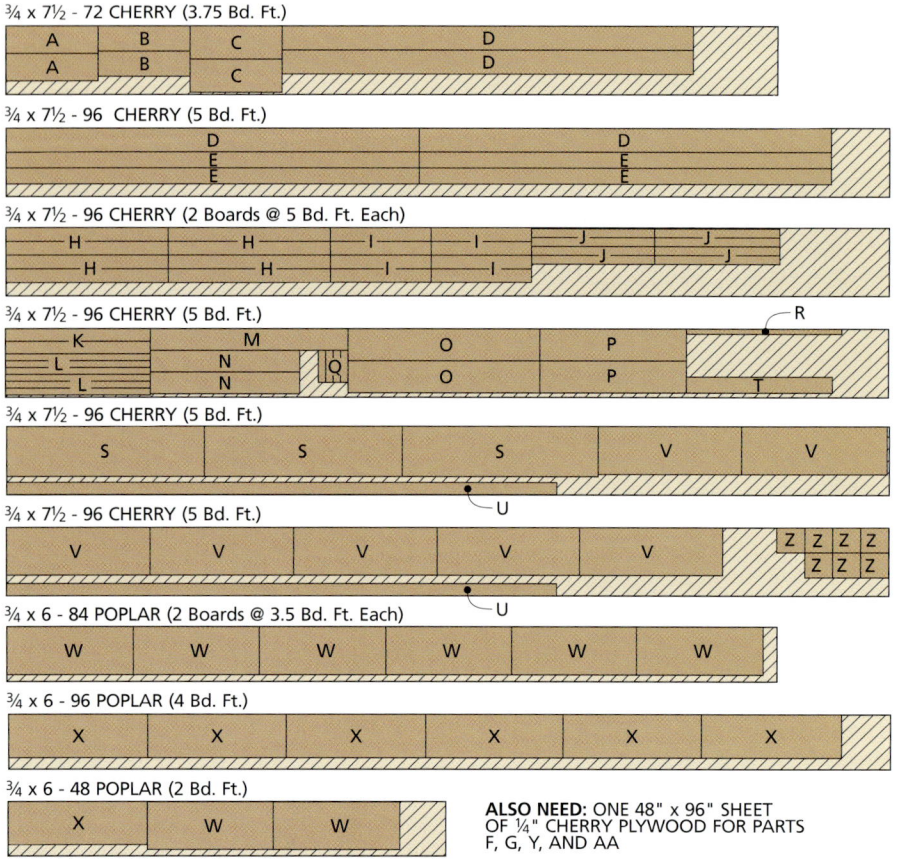

1

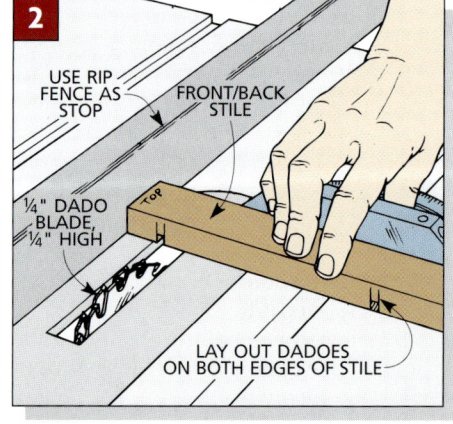

3

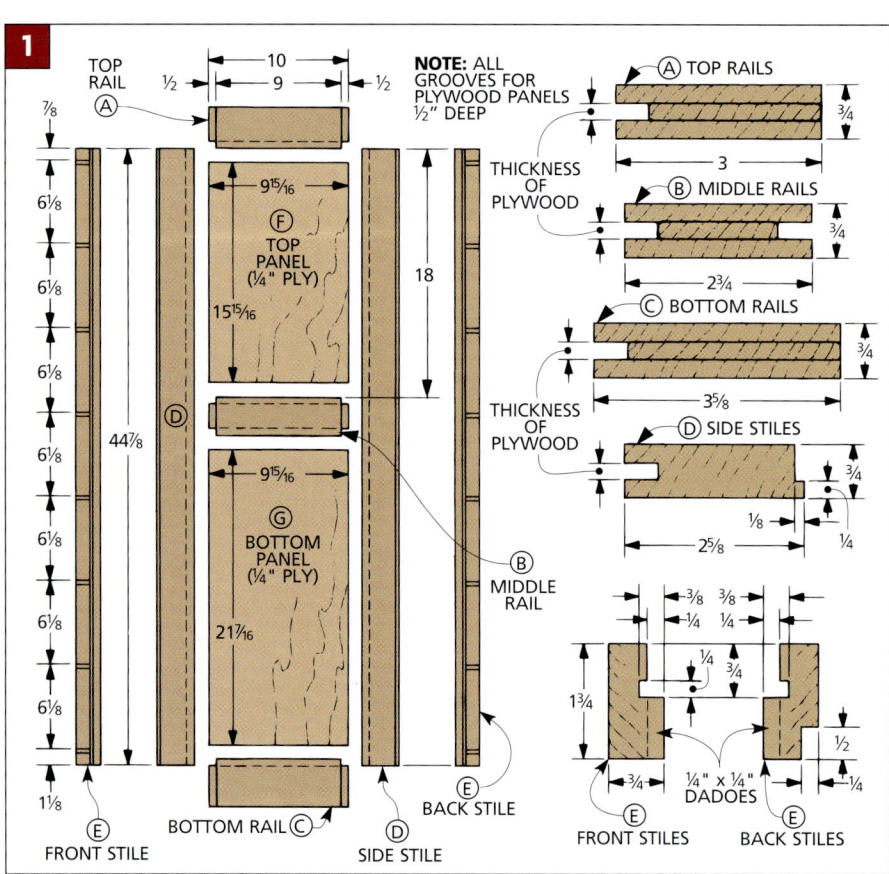

2

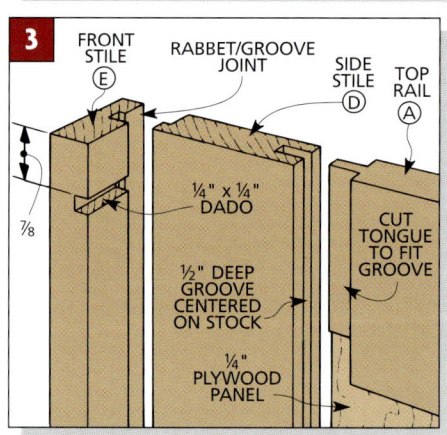

Note: The panels are made from ¼" plywood. But most hardwood plywood actually measures slightly less than ¼" thick. So cut the grooves just wide enough to accept the actual thickness of the plywood panels.

STUB TENONS. After cutting the grooves, I cut stub tenons on the ends of all six rails to fit into the grooves on the stiles. The length of the tenons matches the depth of the grooves (½").

DADOES. Next, I switched over to work on the front and back stiles (E). The first step here is to lay out the position of eight ¼"-wide dadoes *(Fig. 1)*. (These dadoes will hold part of the assemblies that support the drawers.)

Note: Mark the top of each piece so the dadoes can be lined up later *(Fig. 2)*.

The first dado is ⅞" from the top end. Then seven more dadoes are laid out every 6⅛". This should all come out so there's 1⅛" between the *top* of the last dado and the bottom of the stile *(Fig. 1)*.

Once the dadoes are laid out, raise the dado blade ¼" above the table and set the rip fence as a stop ⅞" from the inside of the blade *(Fig. 2)*. Now check that the blade matches up with the layout line and cut the dado. Then turn the workpiece end for end, check that the blade matches up with the line on that end, and cut another dado.

After cutting the end dadoes on all four pieces, move the fence 7" from the blade and cut the second dado in each piece. Repeat the process to cut the remaining dadoes.

CORNER JOINT. When all the dadoes are cut, you can begin work on the corner joint that holds the front and back stiles (E) to the side stiles (D) *(Fig. 3)*.

The first step is to cut a ¼" wide by ⅜"-deep groove down the inside face of the front and back stiles (E). (This groove is cut on the face with the eight dadoes.) Position the fence so the distance to the *outside* of the blade equals the thickness of the side stile (D) *(Step 1 in Fig. 4)*.

If you went ahead and cut a tongue on the edge of the side stile to fit into this groove, the eight dadoes would be exposed. (You would see eight "holes" on the sides of the dresser.)

To prevent this, I cut a rabbet the same depth as the dadoes on the inside face of each front and back stile. That way, when the side stile fits into the rabbet, it hides the dadoes *(Fig. 3)*.

RABBET. To cut the rabbet, raise the dado blade above the table. Then stand each front and back stile on edge and trim a section off the inside face *(Step 2 in Fig. 4)*. After this cut is made, the dadoes should have disappeared along the outside edges of the stiles.

BACK RABBET. Next, lower the dado blade to ½" above the table and cut a rabbet on the back stiles for the ¼" plywood back. (Note the position of this rabbet in *Step 3*.)

TONGUE. The last step is to make a tongue on the side stiles to fit the groove in the front and back stiles. To make the cut, lay the stile flat on the saw. Then sneak up on the blade height and rip fence position until you have a tongue that fits snugly into the groove *(Step 4)*.

ASSEMBLY

Once the tongues are cut to fit the grooves, dry-assemble the frames to take measurements for the top panels (F) and bottom panels (G). As you measure, allow for ¹⁄₁₆" of clearance on the height and width of the panels *(Fig. 1)*. This way, the rails and stiles will seat tightly when the sides are assembled.

Once the panels are cut to size from ¼" plywood, the frames can be assembled. I did this in two steps. First, I glued up the corner pieces to make four L-shaped assemblies.

Start by gluing a side stile to a front stile — making sure the eight dadoes face in *(Fig. 5)*. Check the inside corner to be sure it's perfectly square.

PANELS, RAILS, AND CORNERS. When all four corners are assembled, the second step is to glue them to the rails and panels to make a side frame *(Fig. 5)*.

Note: Before I actually glued up these frames, I double-checked to make sure I had two mirrored sides. Also, check to see that the "TOP" label on all four stiles is actually on the top.

Once everything is lined up, glue each side assembly together checking that the pieces lie flat against the pipe clamps and the ends are flush.

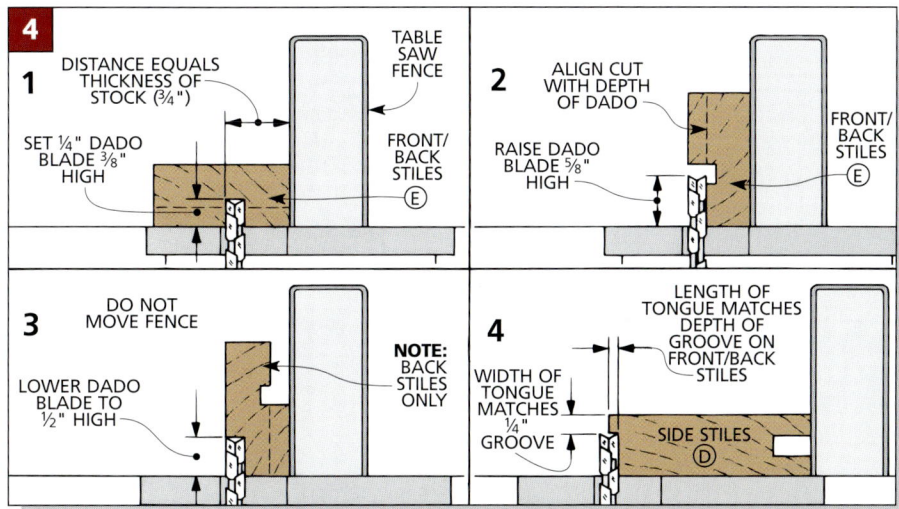

4

1 DISTANCE EQUALS THICKNESS OF STOCK (¾") — TABLE SAW FENCE — FRONT/BACK STILES (E) — SET ¼" DADO BLADE ⅜" HIGH

2 ALIGN CUT WITH DEPTH OF DADO — FRONT/BACK STILES (E) — RAISE DADO BLADE ⅝" HIGH

3 DO NOT MOVE FENCE — NOTE: BACK STILES ONLY — LOWER DADO BLADE TO ½" HIGH

4 LENGTH OF TONGUE MATCHES DEPTH OF GROOVE ON FRONT/BACK STILES — WIDTH OF TONGUE MATCHES ¼" GROOVE — SIDE STILES (D)

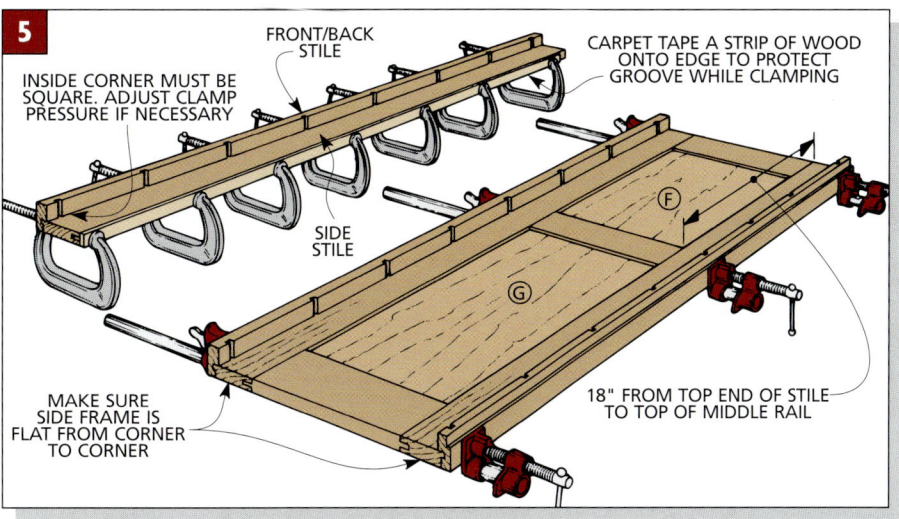

5

FRONT/BACK STILE — CARPET TAPE A STRIP OF WOOD ONTO EDGE TO PROTECT GROOVE WHILE CLAMPING — INSIDE CORNER MUST BE SQUARE. ADJUST CLAMP PRESSURE IF NECESSARY — SIDE STILE — (F) — (G) — MAKE SURE SIDE FRAME IS FLAT FROM CORNER TO CORNER — 18" FROM TOP END OF STILE TO TOP OF MIDDLE RAIL

DESIGNER'S NOTEBOOK

This cutout on the apron "lifts" the cabinet visually.

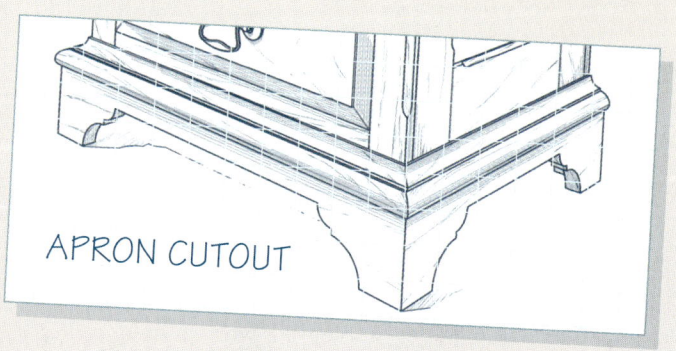

APRON CUTOUT

CONSTRUCTION NOTES:

■ This cutout profile can be used on any of the cabinets in the cherry set. The layout is the same for the Lingerie Dresser and Chest-on-Chest (page 112) *(Fig. 1)*. The apron on the Night Stand (page 76) is not as wide, so the dimensions are different *(Fig. 2)*.

■ To make sure the profiles match on all sides, make a hardboard template of the profile. Then fasten the template to the apron with double-sided tape and use a flush trim bit in the router to bring the end close to finished shape.

■ After routing around the template, square up the two inside corners (where the bit won't reach) with a chisel.

■ To cut the straight line between the profiles, cut away most of the waste at the band saw. Then fasten a straight piece of scrap to the apron and again use a flush trim bit in the router to trim away the remaining waste.

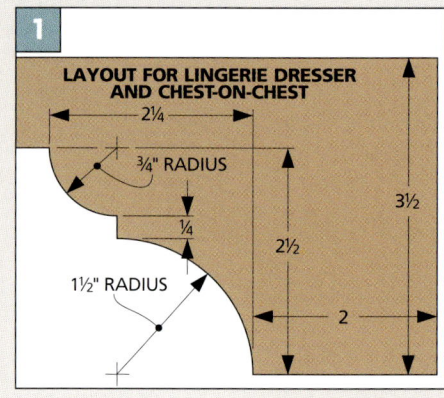

1 LAYOUT FOR LINGERIE DRESSER AND CHEST-ON-CHEST

2¼
¾" RADIUS
¼
2½
3½
1½" RADIUS
2

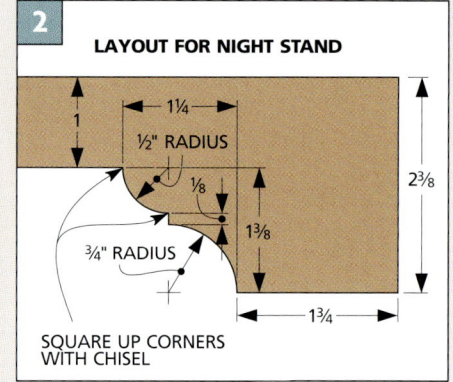

2 LAYOUT FOR NIGHT STAND

1
1¼
½" RADIUS
⅛
2⅜
1⅜
¾" RADIUS
1¾
SQUARE UP CORNERS WITH CHISEL

RAILS

While the side frames were drying, I began work on the rails.

INSIDE RAILS. One set of inside rails bridges the front of the cabinet to create the openings for the drawers. And along the back, the rails also support the drawer guides that are made next.

Start by cutting 16 inside rails (H) to a width of 1½" and finished length of 17¾" *(Fig. 6)*. (When in place, this should yield an opening of 15¾" between the face stiles.) After the rails are trimmed to size, cut rabbets on the front edge to create a tongue that fits into the dadoes on the front and back stiles *(Fig. 6)*.

ASSEMBLY. Once the rails fit in the dadoes, assembly can begin. Lay one side frame face down on a flat surface and glue a rail into each top and bottom dado *(Fig. 7)*. Then glue the other side frame to the other end of the rails.

Note: I placed a piece of squared-up plywood inside each end temporarily to hold the assembly square *(Fig. 7)*.

After the glue sets on this assembly, add the remaining rails.

DRAWER GUIDES

Next, drawer guides are mounted to the rails. These guides are made from two pieces — a runner (I) and a drawer guide (J) *(Fig. 8)*. The drawer guide bridges between the rails in front and back and keeps the drawer tracking straight when it's pulled out of the dresser. The runner sits below the guide, flush with the top of the rails and supports the drawer.

To make these assemblies, first cut 16 drawer runners (I) to a width of 1½". Then trim them to length to fit between the front and back inside rails on the cabinet (11" in my case) *(Fig. 8)*.

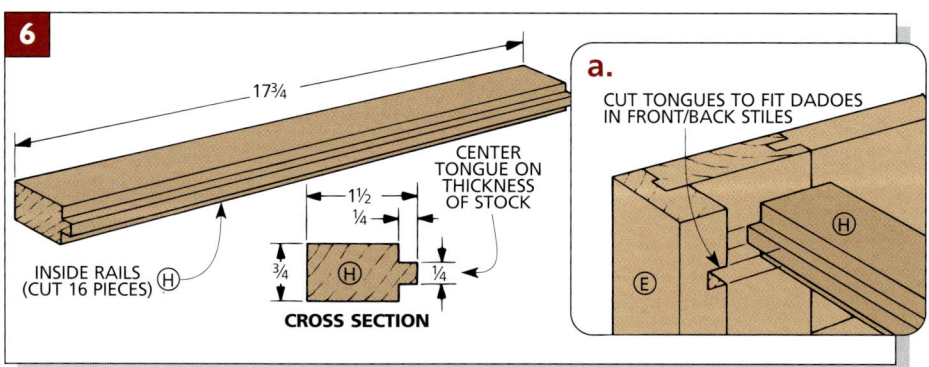

6
17¾
INSIDE RAILS (H) (CUT 16 PIECES)
1½
¼
¾
H
¼
CENTER TONGUE ON THICKNESS OF STOCK
CROSS SECTION

a. CUT TONGUES TO FIT DADOES IN FRONT/BACK STILES
H
E

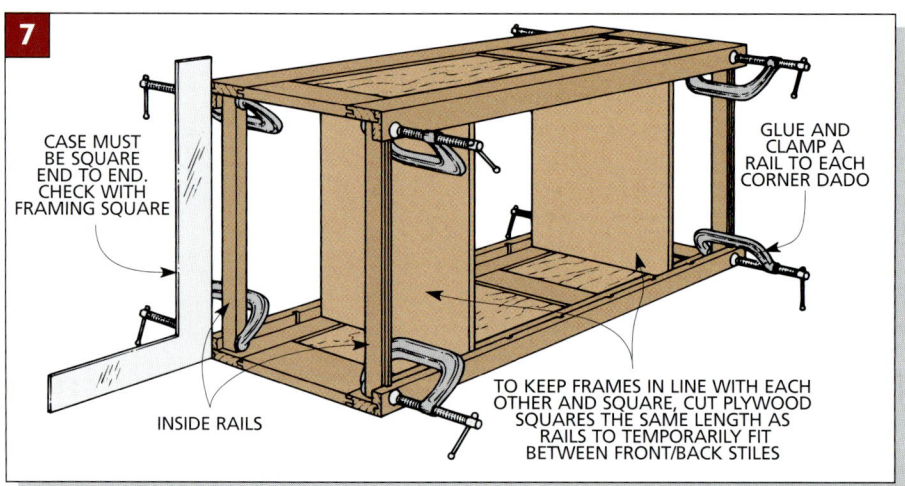

7
CASE MUST BE SQUARE END TO END. CHECK WITH FRAMING SQUARE
GLUE AND CLAMP A RAIL TO EACH CORNER DADO
INSIDE RAILS
TO KEEP FRAMES IN LINE WITH EACH OTHER AND SQUARE, CUT PLYWOOD SQUARES THE SAME LENGTH AS RAILS TO TEMPORARILY FIT BETWEEN FRONT/BACK STILES

Next, cut 16 drawer guides (J). To determine their width, measure from the inside corner of the side of the cabinet to the edge of the front stile. Then add $1/32"$ to provide clearance between the drawer and the front stile (*Fig. 8a*). As for their length, the guides are $2^1/2"$ longer than the runners ($13^1/2"$).

Now screw a drawer guide to the top of a runner to make a complete drawer guide unit (*Fig. 8*). The drawer guide hangs over the runner by $1^1/4"$ on each end so it can be glued to the top of the front and back rails (*Fig. 8b*).

FACING STRIPS

After all of the drawer guides are glued in place, work can begin on the front facing strips. There are two different sizes of facing strips (*Fig. 9a*). The top and bottom strips (K) are wider ($1^3/8"$) than the six middle strips (L) ($3/4"$). But all of the strips are made from $3/4"$ stock and cut to a rough length of 16".

CUT THE GROOVES. Each facing strip has a $1/4"$-deep groove cut on the back face to fit onto the tongue on the front inside rails (*Fig. 9*). Note that the groove on the top and bottom strips (K) is offset on the width (*Fig. 9a*). The groove on the six middle strips (M) is centered on the thickness of the stock.

CUT TO LENGTH. Once the grooves are cut, all the facing strips can be cut to length to fit between the front stiles and then glued in place (*Fig. 9*).

CHAMFERS. Next, I routed stopped chamfers on the four corners. (See the Technique box below. And refer to page 80 to rout the inside chamfers.)

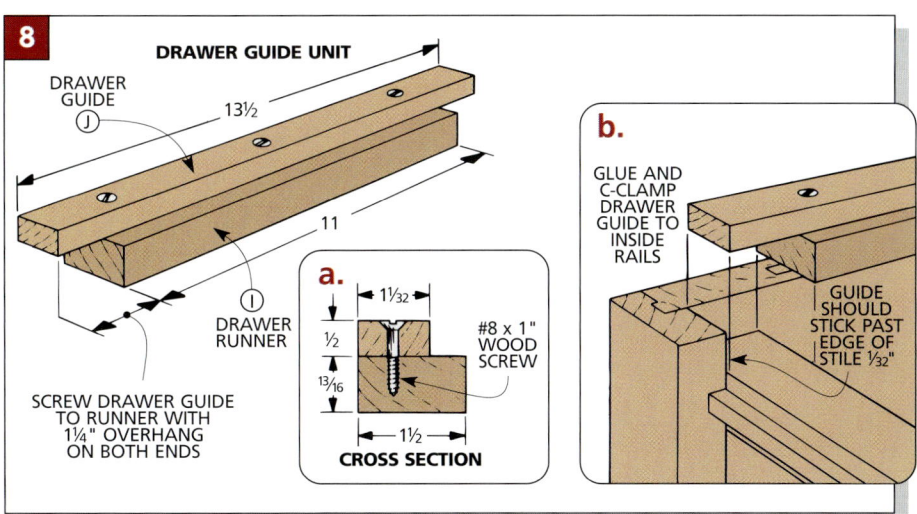

8 DRAWER GUIDE UNIT

DRAWER GUIDE (J) 13½ 11

(I) DRAWER RUNNER

SCREW DRAWER GUIDE TO RUNNER WITH 1¼" OVERHANG ON BOTH ENDS

a. 1½2 ½ 13⁄16 1½ #8 x 1" WOOD SCREW **CROSS SECTION**

b. GLUE AND C-CLAMP DRAWER GUIDE TO INSIDE RAILS

GUIDE SHOULD STICK PAST EDGE OF STILE ½2"

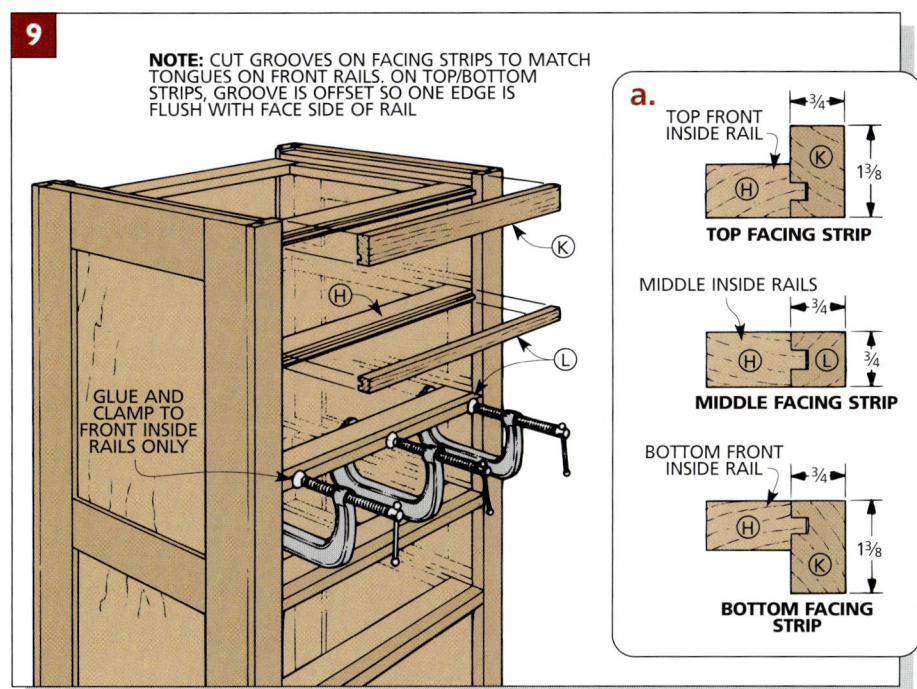

9 NOTE: CUT GROOVES ON FACING STRIPS TO MATCH TONGUES ON FRONT RAILS. ON TOP/BOTTOM STRIPS, GROOVE IS OFFSET SO ONE EDGE IS FLUSH WITH FACE SIDE OF RAIL

GLUE AND CLAMP TO FRONT INSIDE RAILS ONLY

(K) (H) (L)

a. TOP FRONT INSIDE RAIL ¾ (K) 1⅜ (H) **TOP FACING STRIP**

MIDDLE INSIDE RAILS ¾ (H) (L) ¾ **MIDDLE FACING STRIP**

BOTTOM FRONT INSIDE RAIL ¾ (H) (K) 1⅜ **BOTTOM FACING STRIP**

TECHNIQUE .... Routing Stopped Chamfers

Sharp outside corners on a cabinet are likely to be damaged by a bump. And bumping into a sharp corner can be painful. So to soften the corners and add a decorative touch to the cabinets in this set, I routed stopped chamfers.

For the best appearance, the start and stop points of the chamfers should align. To accomplish this, cut a couple of $2^1/2"$-wide stop blocks and clamp them flush with the top and bottom of the cabinet (see drawing). The pilot bearing on the router bit will bump into the block, stopping the cut at the proper spot.

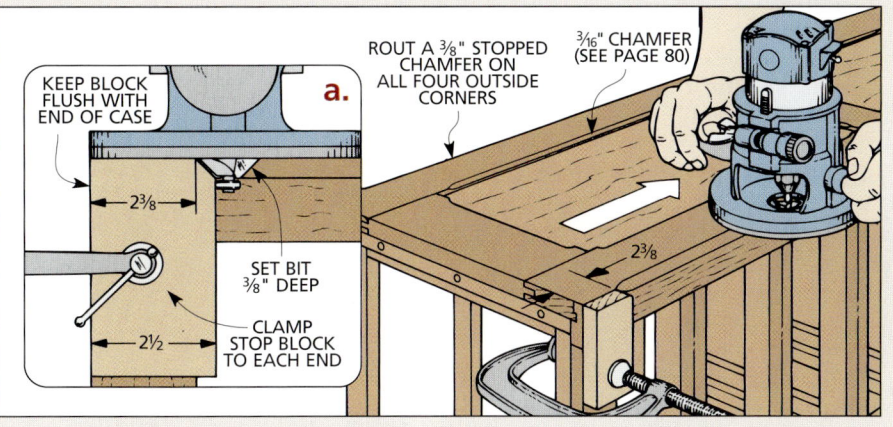

KEEP BLOCK FLUSH WITH END OF CASE

2⅜ 2½

SET BIT ⅜" DEEP

CLAMP STOP BLOCK TO EACH END

ROUT A ⅜" STOPPED CHAMFER ON ALL FOUR OUTSIDE CORNERS

a.

3⁄16" CHAMFER (SEE PAGE 80)

2⅜

At this point, work can begin on the base. The base consists of a bottom frame mitered at the front corners and glued on top of a kickboard frame.

BOTTOM FRAME. Start by cutting a bottom frame front (M) and two bottom frame sides (N) to width (2³⁄₈") *(Fig. 10)*. Then rough cut the front to a length of 23" and sides to a length of 18".

Before cutting the pieces to final length, rout a bullnose edge on the pieces. Start by routing a ¹⁄₂" roundover on the top edge *(Step 1 in Fig. 10b)*. Then, for the bottom edge, use a ¹⁄₄" roundover bit raised ³⁄₁₆" above the table *(Step 2)*.

After the bullnose has been routed, miter the front piece (M) on both ends so the length is 2¹⁄₄" longer (from long point to long point) than the width of the cabinet. (In my case the frame front was 21¹⁄₂".) Now, miter each side piece (N) on one end only and cut them 1¹⁄₈" longer than the depth of the cabinet (16¹⁄₈").

Next, glue the front miters and hold them on a flat surface until the glue sets.

KICKBOARD. For the kickboard frame, start by cutting a kickboard front (O), back (O), and two sides (P) to a width of 3¹⁄₂" *(Fig. 11)*. Then miter both ends of the kickboard front and back so the length of each piece is ¹⁄₂" shorter than the bottom frame (21").

Next, miter both ends of each kickboard side (P) so the length is ¹⁄₄" shorter than the bottom frame sides (15⁷⁄₈").

KERF AND SPLINE. To help keep the miters aligned while clamping, cut a kerf in each miter. Then resaw and plane a spline (Q) to fit each kerf *(Fig. 11a)*. Once the joints are cut, glue and clamp the kickboard frame together checking each corner for square.

ASSEMBLY. After the kickboard frame dries, glue the bottom frame to the top of the kickboard frame *(Fig. 12)*. The bottom frame is centered on the front and flush with the back. (This leaves a ¹⁄₄" overhang on the front and sides.)

SPACER. One final step is to glue a bottom spacer (R) to the top of the kickboard back *(Figs. 12 and 12a)*. This strip creates a ¹⁄₄" rabbet for the cabinet back.

BASE TO CASE. To attach the base to the case, drill shank holes through the top of the bottom frame. Next, turn the case upside down, and center the base assembly across the front, flush with the back. Then mark and drill the pilot holes, and screw the base to the case *(Fig. 13)*.

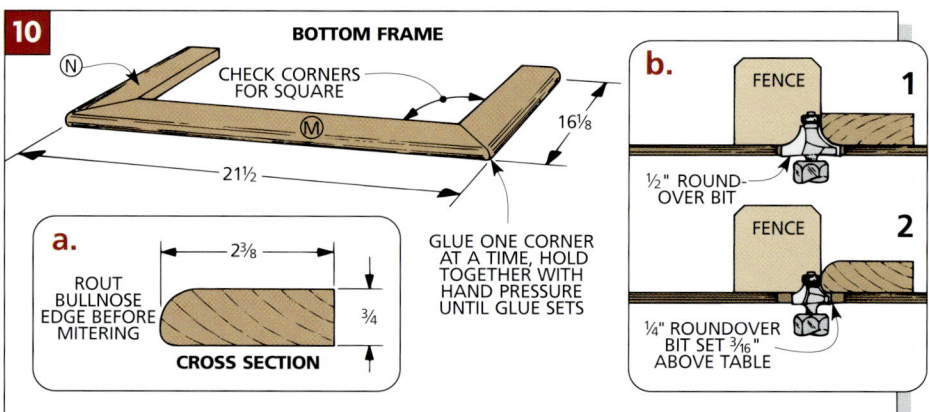

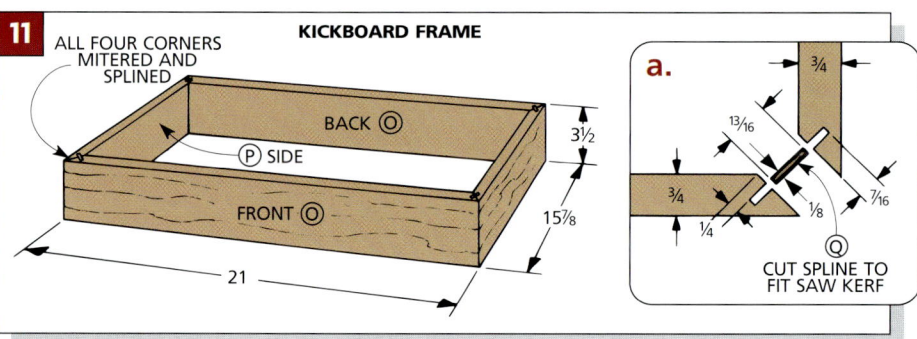

TOP

After the base was screwed to the bottom of the case, I started work on the top (S).

PANEL. Begin by edge-gluing a blank. After it's dry, cut it to finished size: 2¹⁄₄" longer than the cabinet's width and 1¹⁄₈" wider than its depth *(Fig. 14)*.

Next, rout the the sides and front of the panel (but not the back) creating the same bullnose profile as on the bottom frame — only this time, the ¹⁄₄" roundover is on the top *(Fig. 14b)*.

TOP SPACER. Before attaching the top, glue a top spacer (T) between the top back rail and the back of the case *(Fig. 14a)*.

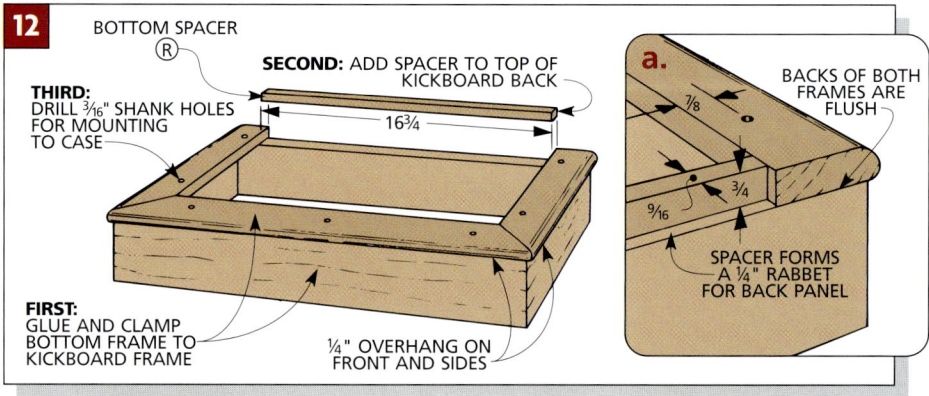

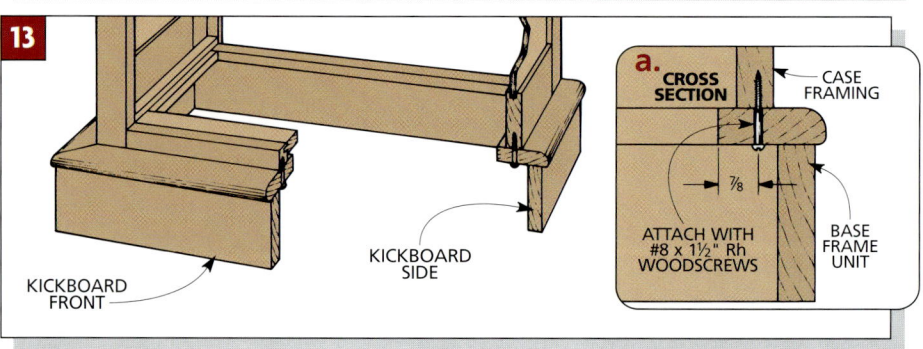

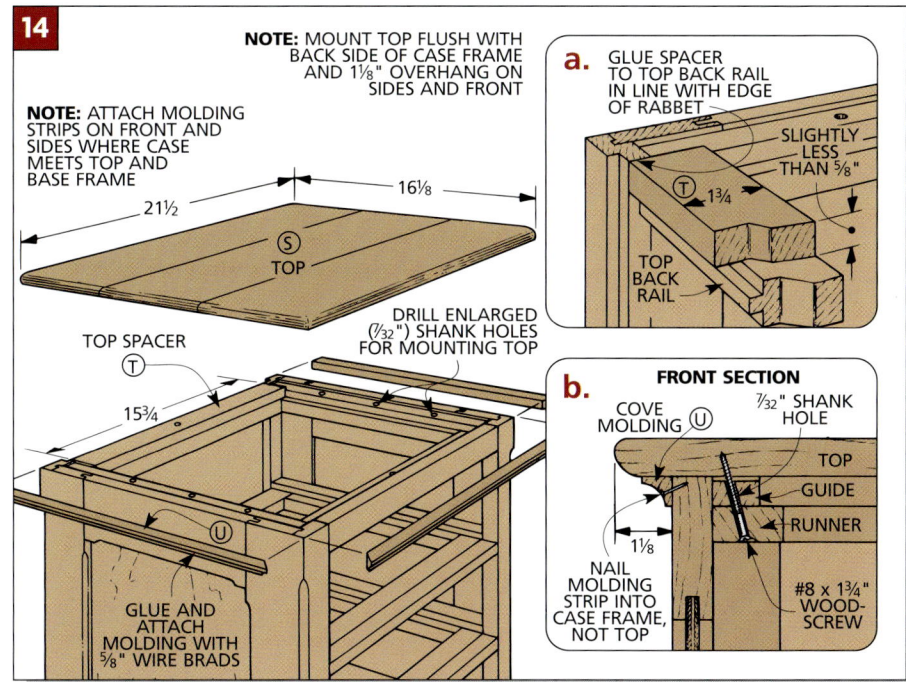

14

NOTE: ATTACH MOLDING STRIPS ON FRONT AND SIDES WHERE CASE MEETS TOP AND BASE FRAME

NOTE: MOUNT TOP FLUSH WITH BACK SIDE OF CASE FRAME AND 1⅛" OVERHANG ON SIDES AND FRONT

21½

16⅛

S
TOP

TOP SPACER
T

15¾

U

DRILL ENLARGED (7/32") SHANK HOLES FOR MOUNTING TOP

GLUE AND ATTACH MOLDING WITH ⅝" WIRE BRADS

a. GLUE SPACER TO TOP BACK RAIL IN LINE WITH EDGE OF RABBET

SLIGHTLY LESS THAN ⅝"

T 1¾

TOP BACK RAIL

b. FRONT SECTION

COVE MOLDING U

7/32" SHANK HOLE

TOP

GUIDE

RUNNER

1⅛

NAIL MOLDING STRIP INTO CASE FRAME, NOT TOP

#8 x 1¾" WOOD-SCREW

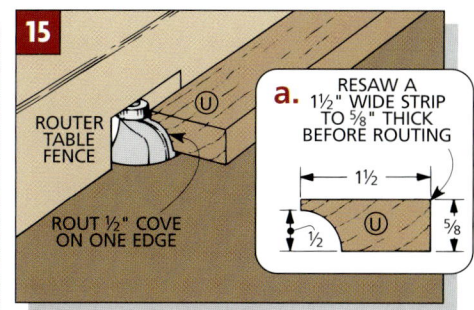

15

ROUTER TABLE FENCE

U

ROUT ½" COVE ON ONE EDGE

a. RESAW A 1½" WIDE STRIP TO ⅝" THICK BEFORE ROUTING

1½

½

U

⅝

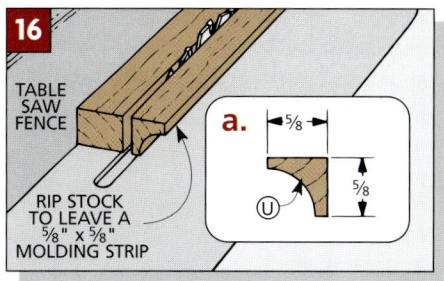

16

TABLE SAW FENCE

RIP STOCK TO LEAVE A ⅝" x ⅝" MOLDING STRIP

a. ⅝"

U

⅝

ATTACHING TOP.

To secure the top, first center the top on the case (flush in back) and clamp it down. Then drill holes up through the top rails and drawer guides *(Fig. 14b)*.

Now enlarge the shank holes so the top can expand and contract with changes in humidity. Then screw down the top.

MOLDING

To dress up the front and sides of the dresser, I added cove molding above the base and below the top *(Fig. 14)*.

The molding (U) starts with some overwidth blanks planed to ⅝" thick *(Fig. 15a)*. Rout a ½" cove on one edge

of an overwidth blank, taking several passes to cut the full depth of the cove *(Fig. 15)*. (This reduces the chances of chipout.) Then trim the molding off the outside edge of the workpiece *(Fig. 16)*.

Now you can miter the strips to fit around the front and sides of the cabinet. Finally, glue and nail each strip of molding to the case (but not to the top panel) *(Fig. 14b)*. And for a tip on hiding the nails, see the Technique below.

TECHNIQUE .... *Blind Nailing*

One problem with using nails (as when fastening the molding to the dresser) is hiding the nail heads.

A method that has been used by finish carpenters for years is blind nailing. To do this, you lift up a chip, set the nail, and then glue the chip back in place.

BLIND NAILER. To lift the chip, you can use a special tool called a "blind nailer." (See page 126 for sources.) It looks like a miniature plane that holds a small chisel for a blade (see photo).

CHISEL. A blind nailer quickly lifts a chip. But if you're careful, you can do the same thing with a ¼" (or smaller) chisel.

Start by holding the chisel parallel with the grain and with the bevel facing down *(Step 1 in Fig. 1)*. Then raise the back of the bevel slightly off the work surface and wiggle it forward. The goal is to curl up a chip without breaking it off.

Next, grip a brad with a pair of needle-nosed pliers and tack it most of the way

in *(Step 2 in Fig. 1)*. To prevent splitting the molding, use as thin a brad as possible. (I used ⅝" x 19 gauge brads.) Then set the brad just below the bottom of the chip with a nail set.

After the brad is set, spread a thin layer of glue under the chip with a toothpick and roll the curled chip down with your thumb *(Step 3 in Fig. 2)*.

Finally use a dowel to hold the chip until the glue sets *(Step 4 in Fig. 2)*.

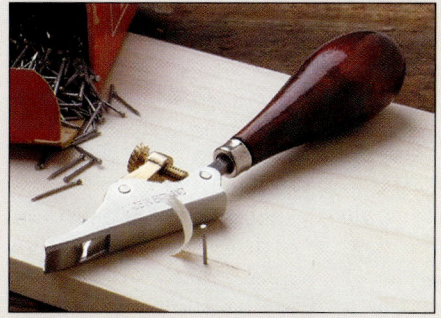

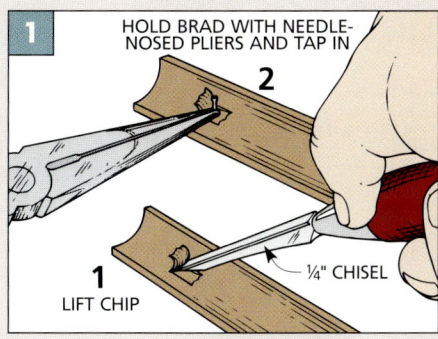

1

HOLD BRAD WITH NEEDLE-NOSED PLIERS AND TAP IN

2

1 LIFT CHIP

¼" CHISEL

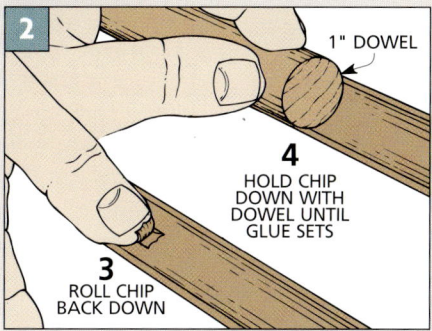

2

1" DOWEL

4 HOLD CHIP DOWN WITH DOWEL UNTIL GLUE SETS

3 ROLL CHIP BACK DOWN

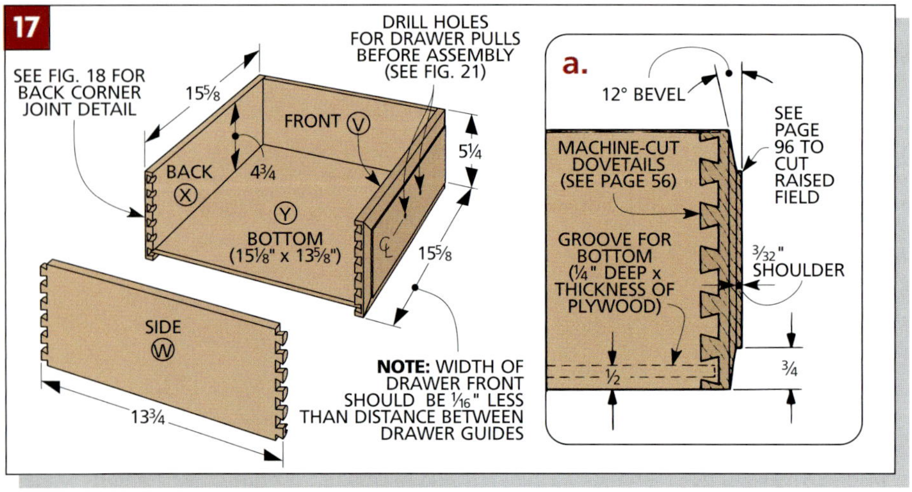
17
SEE FIG. 18 FOR BACK CORNER JOINT DETAIL
DRILL HOLES FOR DRAWER PULLS BEFORE ASSEMBLY (SEE FIG. 21)
15⅝
FRONT (V)
BACK (X)
4¾
5¼
BOTTOM (15⅛" x 13⅝")
(Y)
15⅝
SIDE (W)
13¾
NOTE: WIDTH OF DRAWER FRONT SHOULD BE 1⁄16" LESS THAN DISTANCE BETWEEN DRAWER GUIDES
a.
12° BEVEL
MACHINE-CUT DOVETAILS (SEE PAGE 56)
SEE PAGE 96 TO CUT RAISED FIELD
GROOVE FOR BOTTOM (¼" DEEP x THICKNESS OF PLYWOOD)
3⁄32" SHOULDER
½
¾

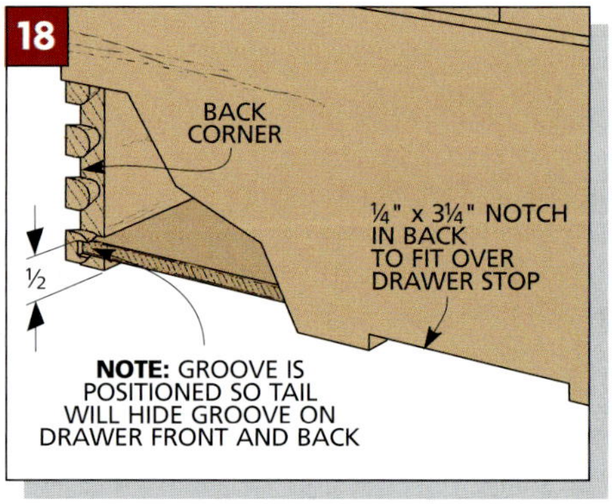
18
BACK CORNER
¼" x 3¼" NOTCH IN BACK TO FIT OVER DRAWER STOP
½
NOTE: GROOVE IS POSITIONED SO TAIL WILL HIDE GROOVE ON DRAWER FRONT AND BACK

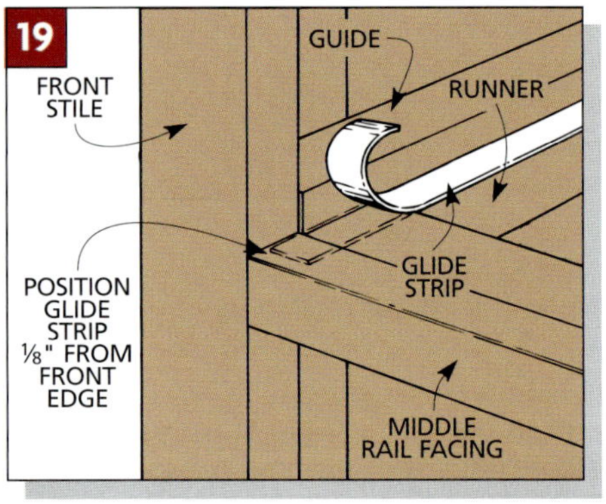
19
FRONT STILE
GUIDE
RUNNER
POSITION GLIDE STRIP ⅛" FROM FRONT EDGE
GLIDE STRIP
MIDDLE RAIL FACING

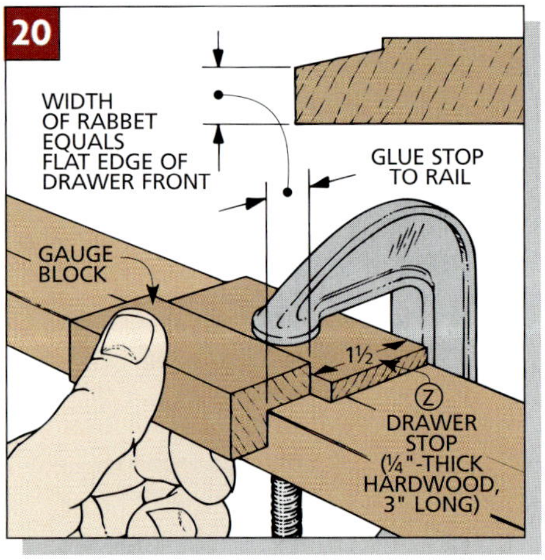
20
WIDTH OF RABBET EQUALS FLAT EDGE OF DRAWER FRONT
GLUE STOP TO RAIL
GAUGE BLOCK
1½
(Z) DRAWER STOP (¼"-THICK HARDWOOD, 3" LONG)

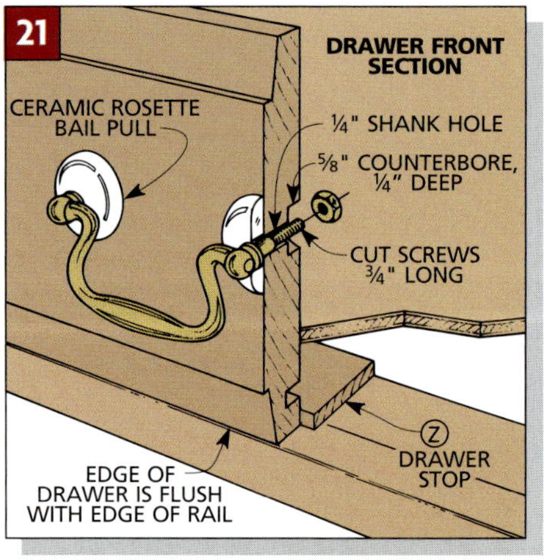
21
DRAWER FRONT SECTION
CERAMIC ROSETTE BAIL PULL
¼" SHANK HOLE
⅝" COUNTERBORE, ¼" DEEP
CUT SCREWS ¾" LONG
EDGE OF DRAWER IS FLUSH WITH EDGE OF RAIL
(Z) DRAWER STOP

DRAWERS

After the molding strips are in place, the only thing left is to make the drawers. And because all seven are the same size, construction goes quickly.

CUT THE PIECES. Begin by cutting seven $3/4$"-thick drawer fronts (V) to $5^1/4$" wide and $1/16$" less in length than the distance between the guides *(Fig. 17)*.

Next, the drawer sides (W) and drawer backs (X) are cut to size from $1/2$" stock *(Fig. 17)*. The backs are the same size as the drawer fronts.

Note: The sides and backs of drawers are seldom seen, so it's common to use a less expensive species of wood for these parts. I chose poplar.

DOVETAILS. Once all the pieces are cut to size, you can set up your dovetail jig and router to cut the joints *(Fig. 17a)*. (This process is covered in the Joinery article starting on page 56.)

BOTTOM. After cutting the dovetails, cut a $1/4$"-deep groove for the bottom panel on the inside edge of each drawer piece *(Fig. 18)*. The grooves are positioned so that they will be hidden by a pin on the drawer sides.

Then cut a $1/4$" plywood bottom (Y) to fit between the grooves *(Fig. 17)*.

RAISED FIELD. There are just a few more things to do before assembling the drawers. First, a raised field is cut on each drawer front. (There's more about this on page 96.) Then drill the counterbored holes for the bail pulls *(Fig. 22)*.

ASSEMBLY. Finally glue up the drawer around the bottom panel, checking that the assembly is square.

GLIDE STRIPS. There are a few details left to complete the drawers. To help the drawers glide smoothly and create a slight gap below each drawer, I added

DESIGNER'S NOTEBOOK

The appearance of a cabinet can be changed dramatically just by selecting a different type of pull.

PULLS

- One of the simplest ways to customize the appearance of the cabinets in the Classic Cherry Set is to choose a different style of drawer pull.
- An early-American style (left drawing) or two round knobs (right drawing) are two of a wide variety of options.

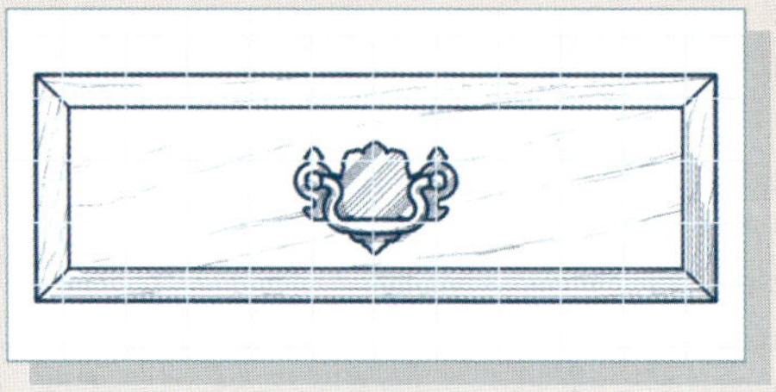

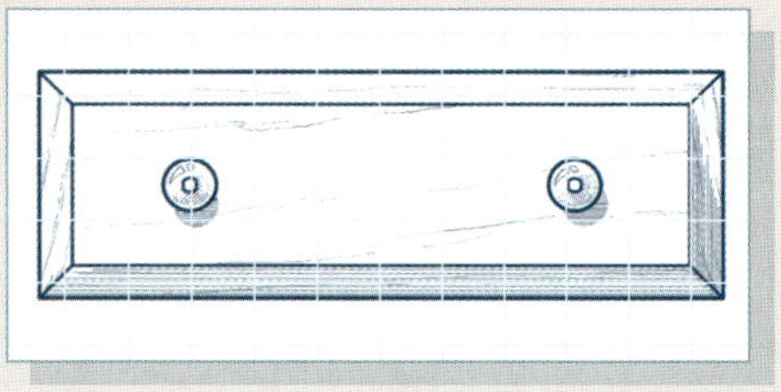

nylon glide strips to the drawer guides *(Fig. 19)*. (See Sources on page 126.)

DRAWER STOPS. Also, to position the chamfer on the drawer front flush with the front of the cabinet, I glued a $1/4$"-thick drawer stop (Z) to the top of each front rail *(Figs. 20 and 21)*. Then notch the drawer back to fit over the stop *(Fig. 18)*.

You also need to stop the drawers from being pulled all the way out. To do this I screwed a turnbutton to the back of the front rail above each drawer *(Fig. 22)*.

BACK. When the drawers are in place, cut a $1/4$" plywood back (AA) to fit in the back of the cabinet and screw it in place.

FINISH. The last thing to do is to apply a finish and then mount the pulls. ■

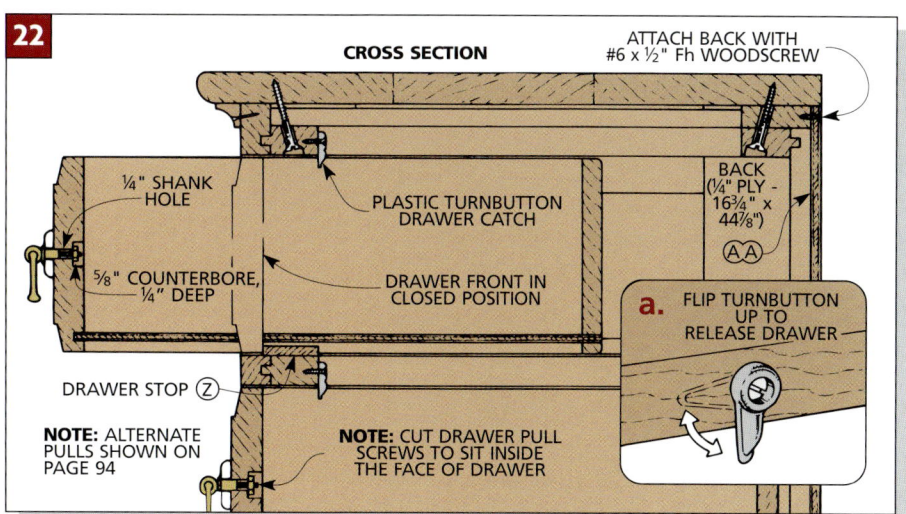

22

CROSS SECTION

ATTACH BACK WITH #6 x ½" Fh WOODSCREW

¼" SHANK HOLE

PLASTIC TURNBUTTON DRAWER CATCH

BACK (¼" PLY - 16¾" x 44⅞") AA

⅝" COUNTERBORE, ¼" DEEP

DRAWER FRONT IN CLOSED POSITION

a. FLIP TURNBUTTON UP TO RELEASE DRAWER

DRAWER STOP Z

NOTE: ALTERNATE PULLS SHOWN ON PAGE 94

NOTE: CUT DRAWER PULL SCREWS TO SIT INSIDE THE FACE OF DRAWER

DESIGNER'S NOTEBOOK

Disguise deep drawers with doubled-up drawer fronts.

CONSTRUCTION NOTES:

■ The first change comes when cutting the dadoes for the rails in the front stiles. Leave off the fifth and seventh dadoes, as counted from the top. After the rails are added, this will create two tall drawer openings at the bottom of the cabinet.

■ Because there are two fewer drawers, you'll need four fewer drawer guide assemblies (I, J), two fewer rails (H), and two fewer middle facing strips (L).

■ The tall drawer sides (BB) and backs (CC) are glued up from $1/2$"-thick stock. Then they are cut to the same length as before, but $11^3/8$" wide (see drawing).

■ The tall drawer fronts are made from two regular drawer fronts (V) glued together with a narrow spacer between them (see drawing). So you'll still need seven drawer fronts.

■ After cutting the drawer fronts to size, chamfer the front faces as before.

■ Now cut the $1/2$"-thick spacers (DD) to size. (The final width of the tall drawer fronts should be $11^3/8$".) At this point, you can glue up the two tall drawer fronts.

■ Once the dovetails are cut, assemble the drawers around the drawer bottoms.

DOUBLE-DEEP DRAWERS

MATERIALS LIST

CHANGED PARTS

H	Inside Rails (12)	$3/4$ x $1^1/2$ - $17^5/8$
I	Drawer Runners (12)	$3/4$ x $1^1/2$ - 11
J	Drawer Guides (12)	$1/2$ x $^{31}/_{32}$ - $13^1/2$
L	Mdl. Rail Facings (4)	$3/4$ x $3/4$ - $15^3/4$
W	Drawer Sides (6)	$1/2$ x $5^1/4$ - $13^3/4$
X	Drawer Backs (3)	$1/2$ x $5^1/4$ - $15^5/8$
Y	Drawer Bottoms (5)	$1/4$ ply - $15^1/8$ x $13^5/8$
Z	Drawer Stops (5)	$1/4$ x 1 - 3

NEW PARTS

BB	Tall Drawer Sides (4)	$1/2$ x $11^3/8$ - $13^3/8$
CC	Tall Drawer Backs (2)	$1/2$ x $11^3/8$ - $15^5/8$
DD	Spacers (2)	$1/2$ x $7/8$ - $15^5/8$

HARDWARE SUPPLIES

(30) No. 8 x 1" Fh woodscrews
(10 ft.) Nylon glide tape
(5) Plastic turnbuttons w/ screws

NOTE: SPACERS ARE MADE FROM SAME STOCK AS DRAWER FRONTS

DRAWER FRONT V

DRAWER FRONT V

15⅝

TALL DRAWER SIDE BB

TALL DRAWER BACK CC

5¼

11⅜

⅞

SPACER (½" THICK) DD

5¼

SIDE SECTION VIEW

NOTE: CUT CHAMFERS ON DRAWER FRONTS BEFORE GLUING TOGETHER WITH SPACER

NOTE: DRAWERS ARE JOINED WITH DOVETAILS AT FRONT AND BACK

Each cabinet in the Classic Cherry Set has drawers with a raised field. The fields are raised by cutting wide, shallow chamfers around the edges of the drawer front. Cutting these chamfers is a simple operation that can be done on either the table saw or the router table.

TABLE SAW METHOD

On the table saw, you're actually making two different kinds of cuts — two rip cuts (on the sides, with the grain) and two cross cuts (at the ends, across the grain).

So one of the first considerations is the type of blade to use. I found I got the best results with a carbide-tipped, 40 or 50 tooth, combination blade.

After the blade is mounted, attach a tall auxiliary plywood fence to the rip fence to help steady the panel *(Fig. 1)*. Then tilt the blade to an angle of 12°.

Next, raise the blade so the distance from the table to the highest point on the blade equals the width of the chamfered border (3/4") *(Fig. 1a)*.

Finally, adjust the rip fence so the blade cuts off enough to leave a 3/32"-high shoulder — to "raise" the field in the center of the panel *(Fig. 1a)*.

MAKE THE CUTS. Now it's just a matter of making the cuts. Hold the panel on end and cut the two ends first. Be careful to keep your fingers away from the path of the blade. Once the ends are complete, cut the two sides *(Fig. 1)*.

CLEAN UP CUT. After all four chamfers are cut, the downside of using the table saw becomes obvious — there are swirl marks from the saw blade on the chamfered edge. It's usually worse on the end grain, but all four edges will have to be sanded or scraped.

To sand the chamfers, I use a sanding block with a bevel on one side *(Fig. 2)*. The beveled edge of the block rides against the angled shoulder and squares it to the face of the raised field.

ROUTER TABLE METHOD

There is another way to cut the chamfers that will reduce the amount of sanding and scraping — cutting the chamfers on the router table. All this involves is a straight bit and a fence angled at 12° — a setup that costs almost nothing.

FENCE. The first step is to make the angled fence. Begin by cutting a 2x4 to length so that it will support the full length of the drawer front on each side of the bit.

Note: The angled fence will be screwed to the fence of the router table. So you may need to attach a wood auxiliary fence to your router table first.

CUT THE ANGLE. Next, an angled face and small support ledge are cut on the front of the fence. There are two steps in this process *(Fig. 3)*. First, tilt the saw blade to 12° and move the rip fence so it's 1/8" from the blade (measured at the tabletop level) *(Fig. 3a)*.

Since the cut is deep, I made it in two passes. Raise the blade about 2" above the table and make the first pass. Then raise the blade 3 1/8" above the table (leaving room for the 3/8"-high ledge) and make a second pass *(Fig. 3a)*.

Safety Note: Use push sticks and featherboards to keep your hands away from the blade.

CUT THE LEDGE. Next, to form the angled ledge, lower the blade and move the rip fence to the other side of the blade. Then set the fence 3/8" away from the blade (at the tabletop) and raise the blade so it cleans out the waste *(Fig. 3b)*.

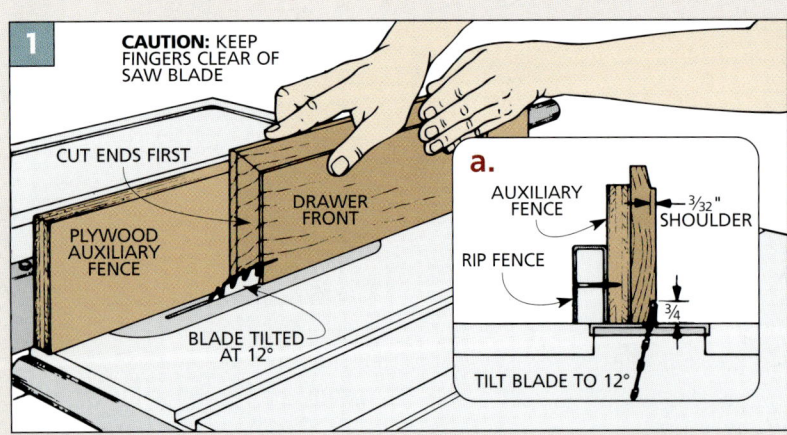

1 **CAUTION:** KEEP FINGERS CLEAR OF SAW BLADE

CUT ENDS FIRST

PLYWOOD AUXILIARY FENCE

DRAWER FRONT

BLADE TILTED AT 12°

a. AUXILIARY FENCE — 3/32" SHOULDER

RIP FENCE

3/4

TILT BLADE TO 12°

2 RAISED FIELD

a. BEVELED EDGE SQUARES UP SHOULDER

DRAWER FRONT

SANDING BLOCK

SWIRL MARKS FROM SAW TEETH

Note: To keep the workpiece from pinching down on the waste piece, I slipped a ⅛" hardboard spacer into the first kerf *(Fig. 3b)*.

NOTCH FOR BIT. After the ledge is cut, notch out a small opening in the ledge to fit around the router bit *(Fig. 4)*.

Now you can secure the angled auxiliary fence to the fence of the router table *(Fig. 4)*. (I screwed mine in place.)

FEATHERBOARD. After the angled fence was in place, I clamped a featherboard to the table to hold the panel tight to the fence *(Fig. 5)*. (The featherboard also acts as a bit guard when routing.)

I added a spacer block under the featherboard so it pressed tight against the center section of the raised panel (not the chamfered edge) *(Fig. 5)*. Also, I trimmed the end of the featherboard at a 12° angle to match the angle of the fence.

ROUTING THE RAISED PANELS

To rout the raised panels, I stood behind the fence and reached over it *(Fig. 5)*. Start by mounting a ½" straight bit in the router and raise it so the fluted cutting edge sticks ¾" above the ledge (the width of the chamfered edge) *(Fig. 4b)*.

ROUTING THE EDGES. I routed the chamfers in three passes, moving the fence toward the bit between each pass *(Steps 1, 2, and 3 in Fig. 5a)*. (You have to reset the featherboard with each pass.)

There are several things to keep in mind when routing. First, start by routing the ends of each workpiece, then clean up any chipout by routing the sides. Next, to keep the bit from pulling the drawer front through the jig, move it from your right to left *(Fig. 5)*. Finally, position your hands so you can feed the workpiece at a constant rate. If you stop in the middle, there may be a divot in the routed surface.

It's a good idea to work with a test piece the same thickness as the drawer fronts first. Then, on the last pass, sneak up on the final position of the fence to get the correct shoulder height (³⁄₃₂").

SANDING. Though routing creates a much cleaner chamfer than sawing, there's always a little bit of sanding left to do. Again, a beveled sanding block is just the ticket here *(Fig. 2)*.

FINAL THOUGHTS. The one limitation of this technique is that the width of the chamfered edge is limited to the length of the cutting edge on the router bit. So make sure you have a bit that can reach through the table and far enough above the ledge to cut the chamfer.

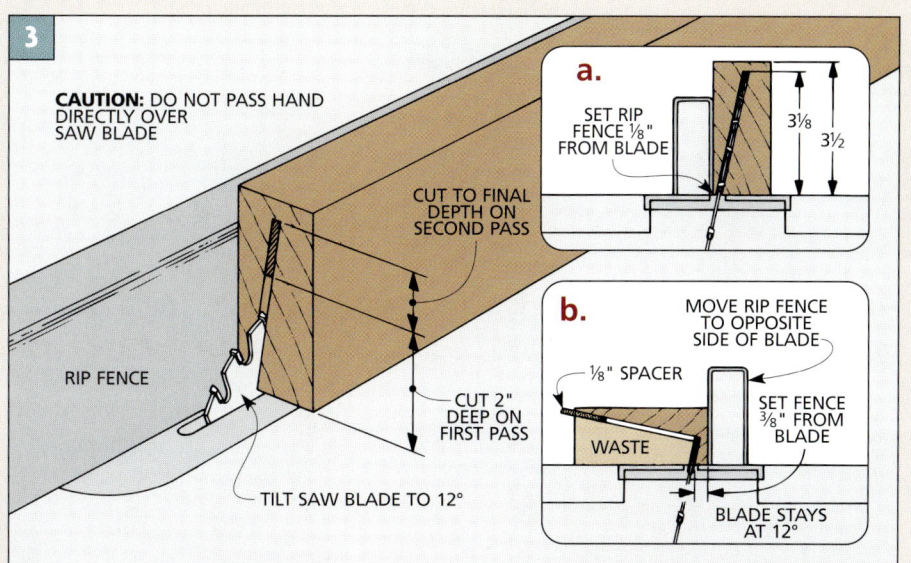

3

CAUTION: DO NOT PASS HAND DIRECTLY OVER SAW BLADE

CUT TO FINAL DEPTH ON SECOND PASS

RIP FENCE

CUT 2" DEEP ON FIRST PASS

TILT SAW BLADE TO 12°

a. SET RIP FENCE ⅛" FROM BLADE — 3⅛ — 3½

b. MOVE RIP FENCE TO OPPOSITE SIDE OF BLADE

⅛" SPACER

SET FENCE ⅜" FROM BLADE

WASTE

BLADE STAYS AT 12°

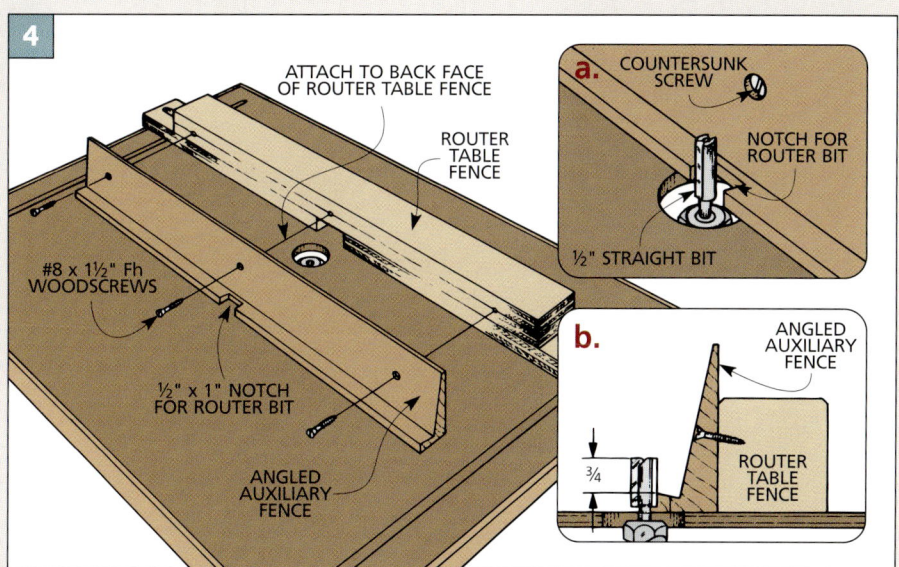

4

ATTACH TO BACK FACE OF ROUTER TABLE FENCE

ROUTER TABLE FENCE

#8 x 1½" Fh WOODSCREWS

½" x 1" NOTCH FOR ROUTER BIT

ANGLED AUXILIARY FENCE

a. COUNTERSUNK SCREW

NOTCH FOR ROUTER BIT

½" STRAIGHT BIT

b. ANGLED AUXILIARY FENCE

¾

ROUTER TABLE FENCE

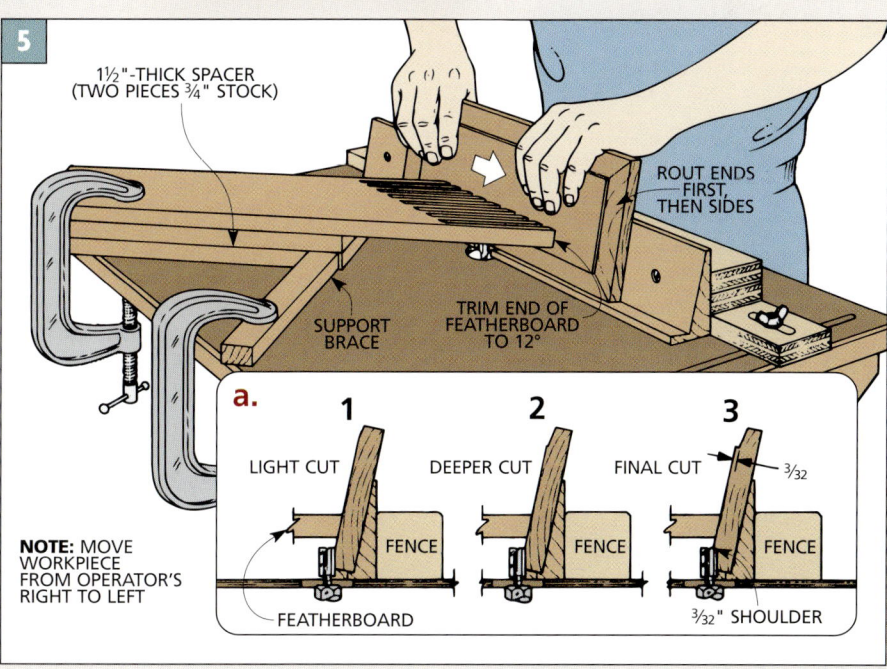

5

1½"-THICK SPACER (TWO PIECES ¾" STOCK)

ROUT ENDS FIRST, THEN SIDES

SUPPORT BRACE

TRIM END OF FEATHERBOARD TO 12°

NOTE: MOVE WORKPIECE FROM OPERATOR'S RIGHT TO LEFT

a.

1 LIGHT CUT — FENCE

2 DEEPER CUT — FENCE

3 FINAL CUT — ³⁄₃₂ — FENCE

FEATHERBOARD

³⁄₃₂" SHOULDER

Classic Cherry Bed

The moldings on this bed are the same as those of the cabinets in the set. And you won't lose any sleep figuring out how to make all the mortises for the slats. A simple jig and a hand-held router make it easy.

Several years back, I made a wish list of the pieces of bedroom furniture that I wanted to build. It included the three cabinets in this section. And the centerpiece of my list was this bed. So it's one that I've been wanting to build for a long time.

CHALLENGES. But I was anxious to build this project for another reason than simply wanting to cross it off my list. It involves some interesting woodworking challenges. Like cutting tenons on the ends of the five-foot-long headboard and footboard rails. And coming up with a way of making all the mortises for the slats. (I think the solution to that one is

particularly interesting. The Technique article on page 106 shows what I did.)

DETAILS. The bed features several of the same design details as the cabinets in the set. For starters, it's made of solid cherry. Second, the headboard and footboard both feature the same bullnose profile found on the base and top of each of the cabinets. So all the pieces look like they belong together.

KNOCK-DOWN FASTENERS. The bed uses knock-down fasteners to connect the rails to the headboard and footboard. They are extremely strong, and can be quickly disconnected without any tools so the bed can be moved or stored easily.

(These fasteners are available from *Woodsmith Project Supplies*. See page 126 for details and other sources.)

SIZE. The bed as shown fits a queen-size mattress and box spring. The design allows some space (1½") between the box spring and side rails, so you can tuck in the blankets and show off the rails.

However, if you want to build a twin-size or full-size bed, all you have to do is alter the length of the side rails and the width of the headboard and footboard. (That means the number of slats will change, as well.) I've provided dimensions for these changes in the Designer's Notebook on page 110.

EXPLODED VIEW

OVERALL DIMENSIONS:
71W x 88½D x 45H

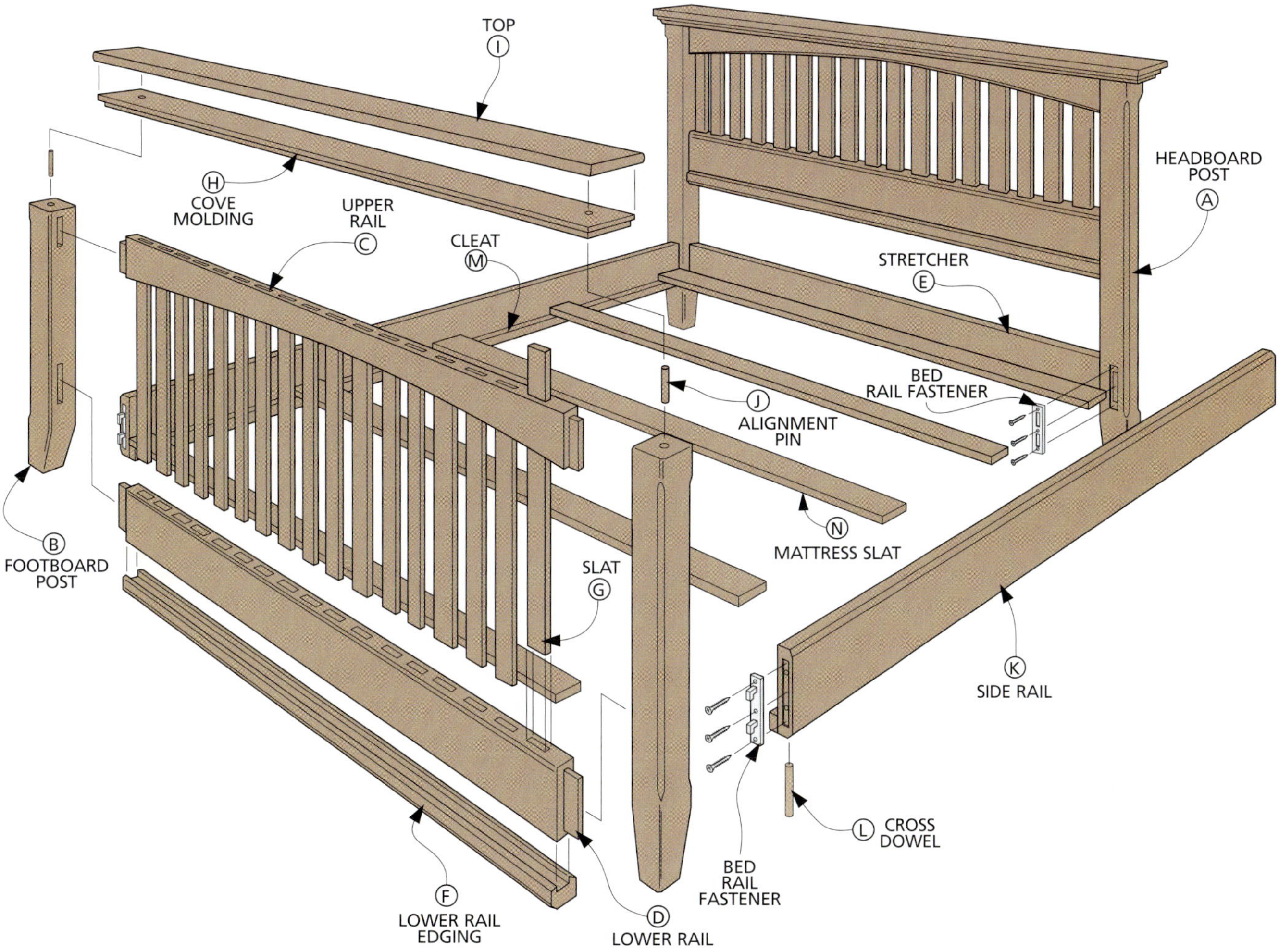

TOP
(I)

HEADBOARD
POST
(A)

(H)
COVE
MOLDING

UPPER
RAIL
(C)

CLEAT
(M)

STRETCHER
(E)

BED
RAIL FASTENER

(B)
FOOTBOARD
POST

(J)
ALIGNMENT
PIN

(N)
MATTRESS SLAT

SLAT
(G)

(K)
SIDE RAIL

(L) CROSS
DOWEL

BED
RAIL
FASTENER

(F)
LOWER RAIL
EDGING

(D)
LOWER RAIL

CUTTING DIAGRAM

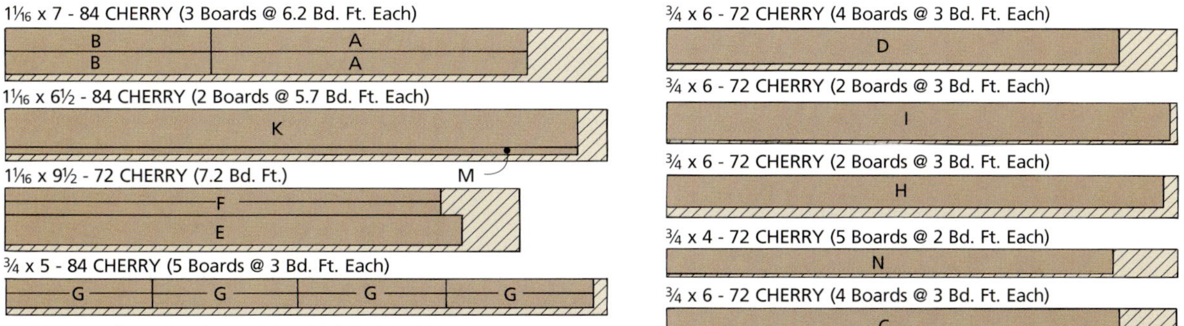

1¹⁄₁₆ x 7 - 84 CHERRY (3 Boards @ 6.2 Bd. Ft. Each)

B	A
B	A

1¹⁄₁₆ x 6½ - 84 CHERRY (2 Boards @ 5.7 Bd. Ft. Each)

K

1¹⁄₁₆ x 9½ - 72 CHERRY (7.2 Bd. Ft.)   M

F
E

¾ x 5 - 84 CHERRY (5 Boards @ 3 Bd. Ft. Each)

| G | G | G | G |

ALSO NEED: ½"-DIA. DOWEL, 36" LONG FOR PARTS J AND L

¾ x 6 - 72 CHERRY (4 Boards @ 3 Bd. Ft. Each)

D

¾ x 6 - 72 CHERRY (2 Boards @ 3 Bd. Ft. Each)

I

¾ x 6 - 72 CHERRY (2 Boards @ 3 Bd. Ft. Each)

H

¾ x 4 - 72 CHERRY (5 Boards @ 2 Bd. Ft. Each)

N

¾ x 6 - 72 CHERRY (4 Boards @ 3 Bd. Ft. Each)

C

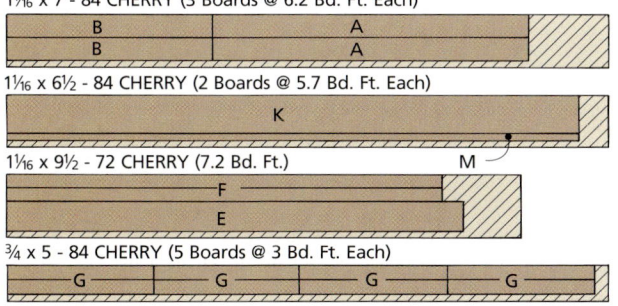

MATERIALS LIST

WOOD

A	Headboard Posts (2)	3 x 3 - 43½
B	Footboard Posts (2)	3 x 3 - 28½
C	Upper Rails (2)	1½ x 5 rgh. - 64
D	Lower Rails (2)	1½ x 5 rgh. - 64
E	Stretcher (1)	1¹⁄₁₆ x 4½ - 64
F	Lower Rail Edgings (2)	1¹⁄₁₆ x 2 - 61

G	Slats (34)	½ x 2 - 20³⁄₈
H	Cove Moldings (2)	¾ x 4³⁄₈ - 69⁷⁄₈
I	Tops (2)	¾ x 5½ - 71
J	Alignment Pins (4)	½ dowel x 1¹¹⁄₁₆
K	Side Rails (2)	1¹⁄₁₆ x 5½ - 80
L	Cross Dowels (4)	½ dowel x 4¾
M	Cleats (2)	1¹⁄₁₆ x ¾ - 80

N	Mattress Slats (5)	¾ x 3½ - 62⁵⁄₈

HARDWARE SUPPLIES
(4) 4" bed rail fasteners
(40) No. 8 x 1½" Fh woodscrews

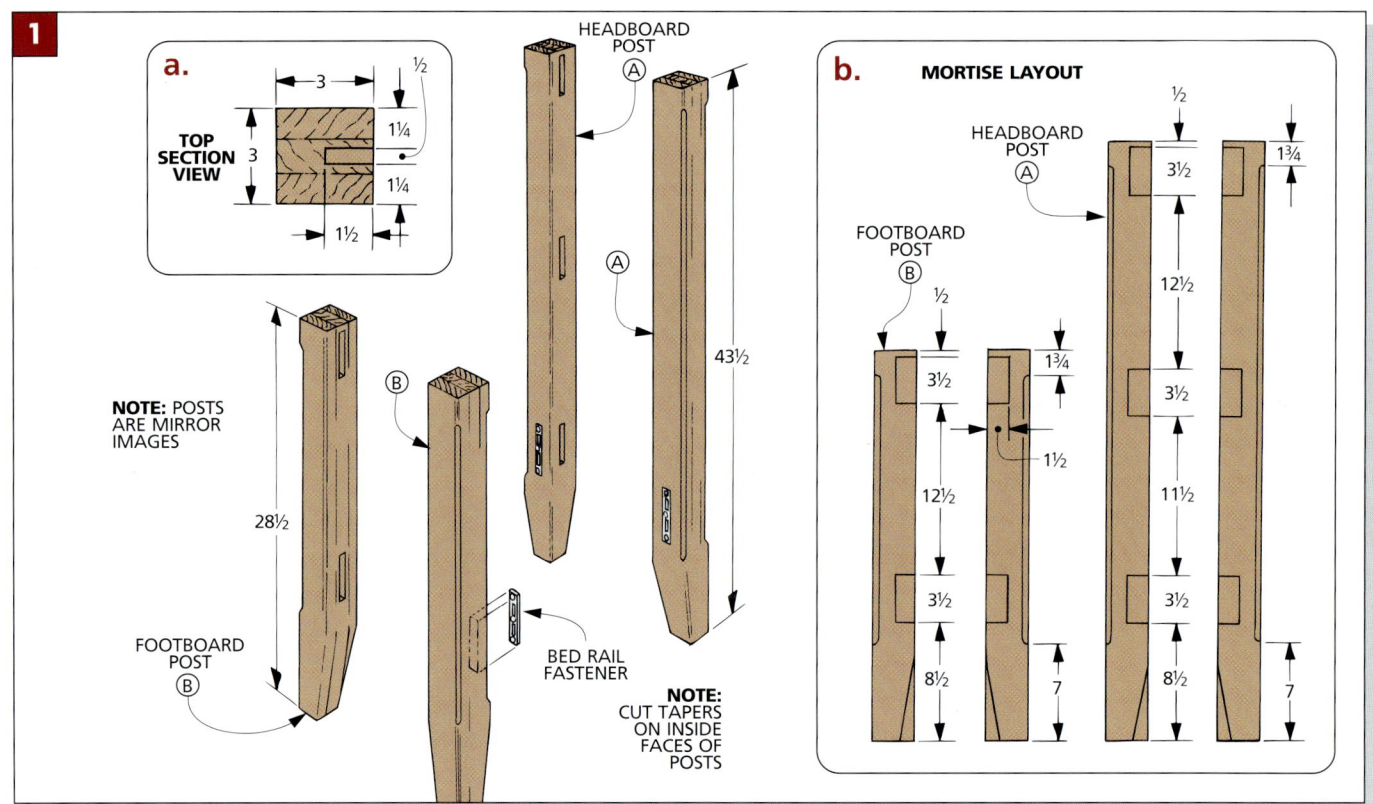

POSTS

Whenever I build a large project, I like to break the construction down into separate assemblies. In the case of the bed, I built the headboard and footboard first. Then I connected the headboard and footboard with side rails and added the mattress slats between them.

POSTS. The first step in making the bed is to make the headboard posts (A) and footboard posts (B) *(Fig. 1)*. Each post is made up of three 1"-thick pieces of stock laminated together *(Fig. 1a)*. But when cutting these pieces, I didn't cut them to exact width or length. Instead, I left them a little wider and longer than necessary. Then after gluing up the posts,

they can be squared up and trimmed down to finished size.

MORTISES. Once you have the posts cut to finished size, the next step is to make the mortises on each post for the footboard and headboard rails. The footboard posts each receive two mortises. One is for the upper rail and one for the lower rail *(Figs. 1a and 1b)*.

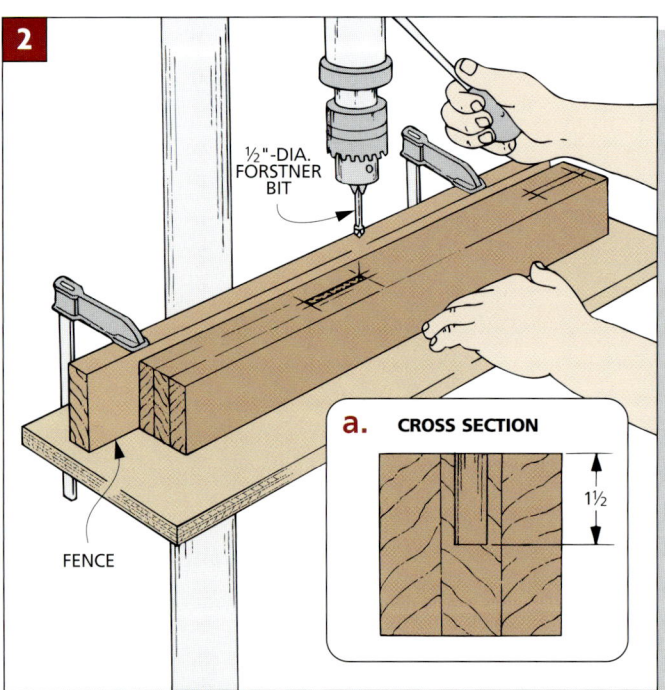

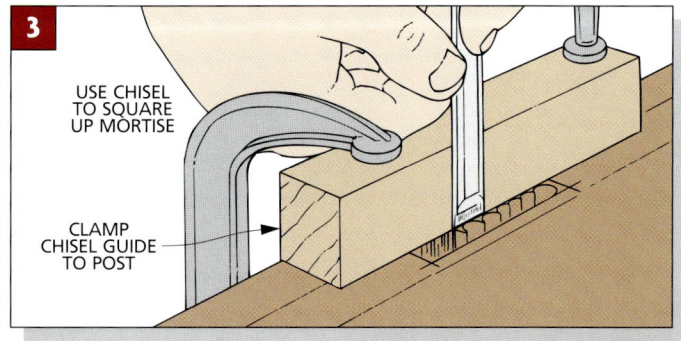

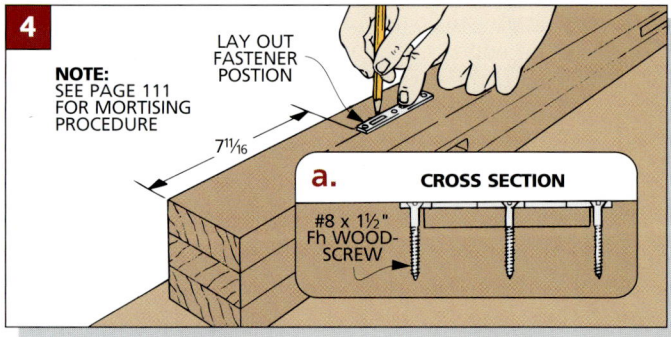

The headboard posts are also mortised for the upper and lower rails. However, because the headboard is so much taller than the footboard, it also has a stretcher closer to the bottom for added strength. So the headboard posts each receive an additional mortise for this stretcher *(Fig. 1b)*.

The mortises in the posts are fairly deep (1½"). So to remove most of the waste, I drilled a series of overlapping holes with a ½"-dia. Forstner bit in the drill press *(Fig. 2)*. Then I squared up the sides and corners with a paring chisel *(Fig. 3)*. I like to clamp a piece of scrap along the edge of the mortise to guide the chisel straight down along the side.

Once the mortises for the rails and stretcher were completed, I turned my attention to attaching the bed rail fasteners *(Fig. 4)*. The fasteners come in two pieces (see photo at right). One piece has a pair of slots and is mortised into the posts of the bed. The other piece gets attached later to the side rails of the bed and has a pair of hooks that fit and lock into the slots of the first piece.

To determine on which face of each post to mount the fastener, it helps to lay the posts out as they will be when the bed is assembled *(Fig. 1)*. (The details about making the mortises and installing the fasteners are covered in the Hardware article on page 111.)

TAPERS. After inserting the fasteners in the mortises and screwing them in place, I tapered the bottom of each post. But notice that only the two inside faces of each post are tapered — not all four faces *(Figs. 5 and 5a)*.

Because the posts are so thick, I used a band saw instead of a table saw to cut the tapers. The easiest way to do this is to lay out the tapers on each post and cut to the waste side of the line. Then smooth out the taper by using a sanding block to sand right up to the pencil line.

ROUND OVER EDGES. The next step is to soften the look of the posts by rounding over the edges. I used a ¼" roundover bit in the router table to do this *(Fig. 6)*. But not all of the edges are rounded over. The top edges of the posts are left square. (A cap will be added later that covers these.) And because the inside and bottom edges of the tapered section won't sit flat on the router table, I didn't rout these edges either. Instead, give them a light sanding — just enough to round over the sharp corners and blend them in with the long edges *(Fig. 6b)*.

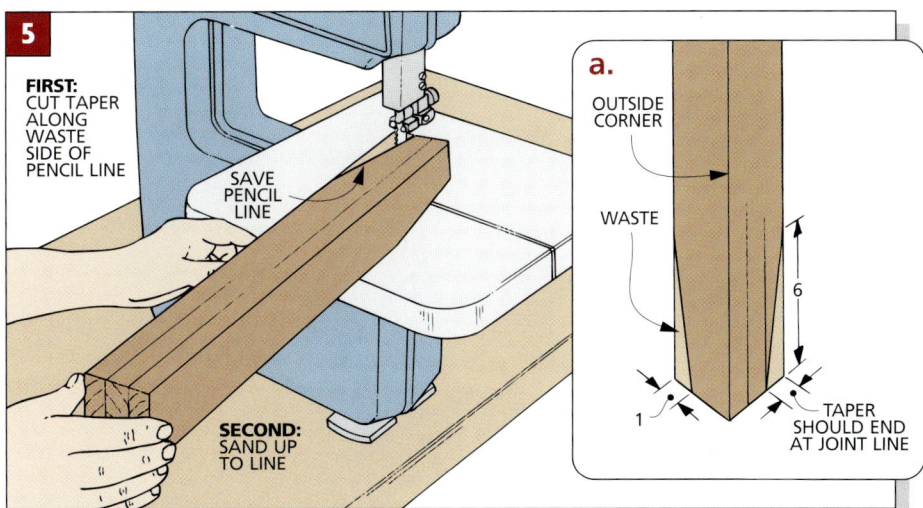

STOPPED CHAMFERS. There's one more detail to add to the posts to finish them off. The two outside edges of each post have ⅜" stopped chamfers (similar to those on the cabinets in the set) *(Fig. 1)*.

Laying out a stopped chamfer isn't difficult — just mark a couple of stop lines on the edges of the posts to indicate the ends of the chamfers. The chamfers start 7" from the bottom of each post and end 1¾" from the top *(Fig. 7)*. To rout the chamfers, start near one end and carefully backrout up to the stop line. Then rout forward to the opposite stop line. Take light cuts to avoid chipout.

The chamfer bit will leave the ends of the chamfers a little rough and uneven. So I smoothed them out by hand. To do this, just wrap some sandpaper around a

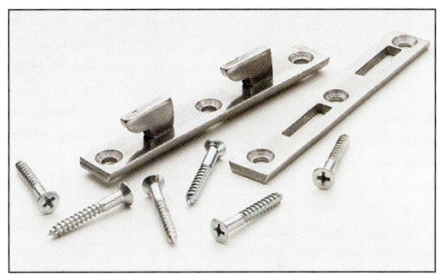

Bed rail fasteners are a type of knock-down fastener that provide a secure way to fasten the rails to the posts. Installation is covered on page 111.

dowel and lightly sand the ends of each chamfer *(Fig. 7b and the Shop Tip on page 117)*. This is also a good way to remove any burn marks that may have been left behind by the router bit.

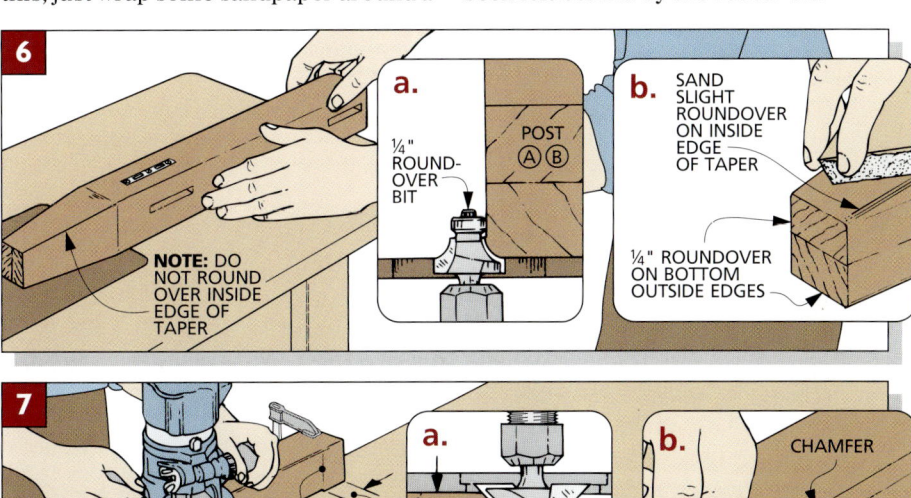

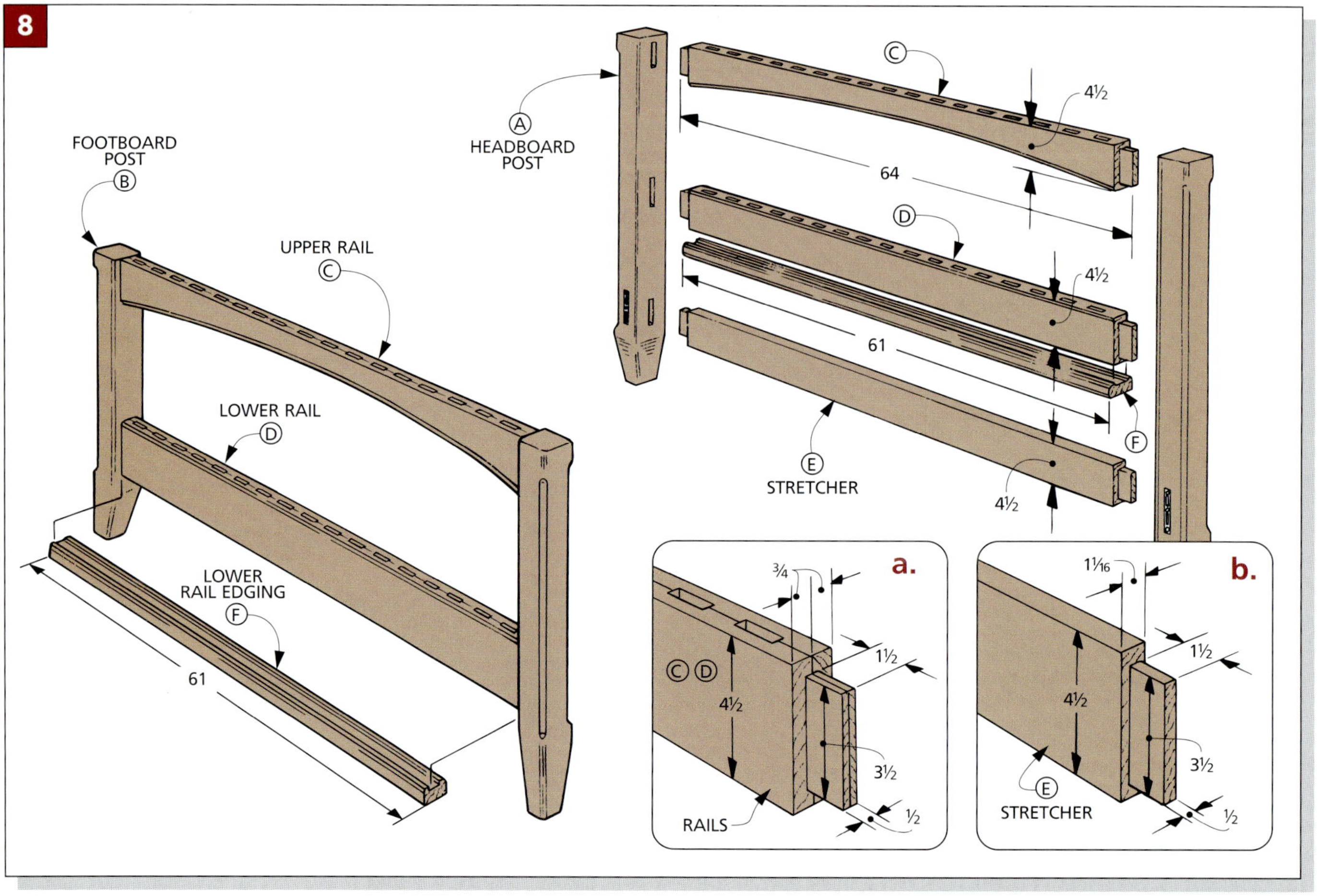

8

FOOTBOARD POST Ⓑ

HEADBOARD POST Ⓐ

UPPER RAIL Ⓒ

LOWER RAIL Ⓓ

LOWER RAIL EDGING Ⓕ

61

Ⓒ
4½
64
4½

Ⓓ
61
Ⓕ

Ⓔ STRETCHER
4½

a.
¾
1½
4½
3½
½
Ⓒ Ⓓ
RAILS

b.
1 1/16
1½
4½
3½
½
Ⓔ STRETCHER

RAILS

With the posts completed, I began working on the rails that connect them *(Fig. 8)*. Each set of posts is joined by an upper and lower rail. Mortises in these rails hold a row of vertical slats.

RAILS. The upper rails (C) and lower rails (D) each start off as two 5" x 64" pieces of ³/₄"-thick stock. This allows you to rout a series of shallow (¹/₄") dadoes in

each half *(Fig. 9)*. Then when the two pieces are glued together, you end up with a row of mortises *(Fig. 10)*. (For details about this, see the Shop Jig and Technique articles on pages 105 and 106.)

After the mortises are cut and the rails are glued up, they can be trimmed to their final width (4¹/₂").

The next step is to cut tenons on the ends of each rail *(Fig. 8a)*. But trying to cut tenons on pieces this long is tricky. So

to help support the rails, I used an "out-rigger" alongside my table saw and a hold-down clamped to my miter gauge fence. (See the Technique on page 104.)

I like to cut tenons with a dado blade, using my rip fence as a stop to control the length of the tenon. The only problem I have found with this method is that sometimes the four shoulders of the tenon wind up "stepped" or uneven. To prevent this, I intentionally cut stepped

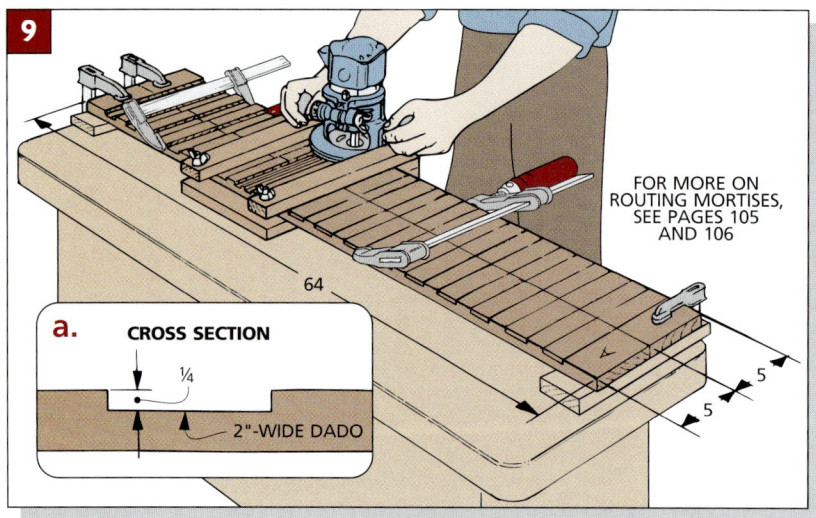

9

FOR MORE ON ROUTING MORTISES, SEE PAGES 105 AND 106

64

5
5

a. CROSS SECTION
¼
2"-WIDE DADO

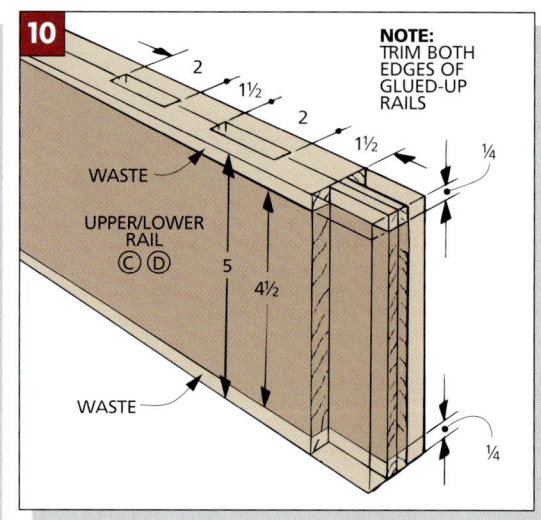

10

NOTE: TRIM BOTH EDGES OF GLUED-UP RAILS

2
1½
2
1½
¼

WASTE

UPPER/LOWER RAIL Ⓒ Ⓓ
5
4½

WASTE

¼

To get even shoulders all the way around the wide tenons of the bed, I intentionally left a "step" on the top and bottom. Then you can trim the shoulder perfectly flush with a chisel.

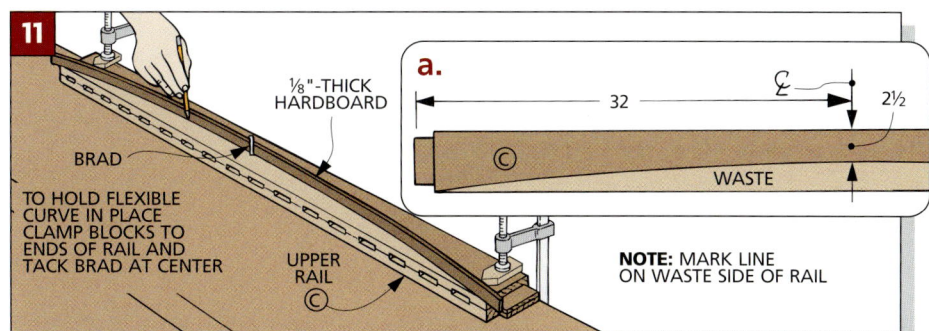

shoulders by sliding the workpiece about $\frac{1}{16}$" away from the rip fence when cutting the top and bottom shoulders of the tenon. Then later I came back with a chisel and trimmed these shoulders so they were flush (see the photo above).

ARCS. Once the tenons were cut, I laid out the arcs on the upper rails *(Fig. 11)*. I used a piece of $\frac{1}{8}$"-thick hardboard as a flexible curve. To hold the hardboard in place, tack a small brad in the center of the rail on the waste side of the curve and clamp a couple of wood blocks at each end of the rail.

I cut the arc on a band saw, making sure to cut on the waste side of the layout

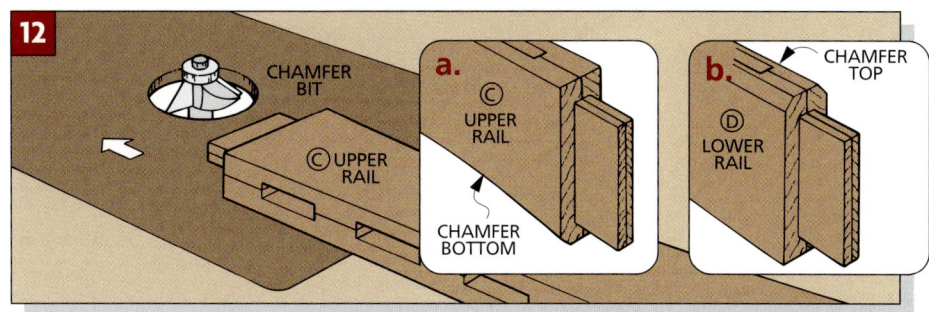

line. And a well-sharpened spokeshave made quick work of removing the saw marks left behind by the band saw (see the Shop Info box below).

CHAMFERS. To add a finishing touch to the arcs, rout a $\frac{1}{4}$" chamfer on each edge *(Fig. 12a)*. Then chamfer the top edges of the lower rails to match *(Fig. 12b)*.

SHOP INFO .... *Spokeshaves*

While many hand tools have been replaced with modern versions that plug in, there's still no better way to smooth a long, curved, or irregular edge than with a spokeshave.

There's not really much to a spokeshave *(Fig. 1)*. It's just a blade fitted into a small body with a couple of handles.

The key to the spokeshave is its bottom, or sole. The sole is much smaller than that typically found on most hand planes. This allows it to ride smoothly over the surface of a curved workpiece.

The shape of the sole also has a lot to do with a spokeshave's ability to handle curves. For smoothing convex curves, a

flat-soled shave works best. But for the concave arc on the bed rails, I used a spokeshave with a curved sole *(Fig. 1)*.

SHAVINGS. As the name implies, spokeshaves are designed to lightly shave the wood, not hog off large pieces.

Using the adjusting screws, move the blade forward until it just barely peeks out from the throat opening. (I find it easier to do this by carefully feeling the blade rather than looking at it.)

Then, before you start using the spokeshave, make sure that your workpiece is firmly clamped to your bench or in a vise. This allows you to concentrate on the tool, not on trying to hold the workpiece.

USING A SPOKESHAVE. A spokeshave can be used with either a push or pull stroke. I find that I have better control when pushing the tool. But whether you push or pull, it's important to work in the direction of the grain to avoid tearout.

The secret to using a spokeshave is to hold it at the proper angle to produce a nice, clean cut. With a hand plane, the angle of the blade is fixed. But with a spokeshave, you control the angle by tilting the tool forward or backward.

Experiment to find the right angle. As you push the spokeshave forward, try pivoting your wrists until the blade starts to take a crisp shaving off the wood.

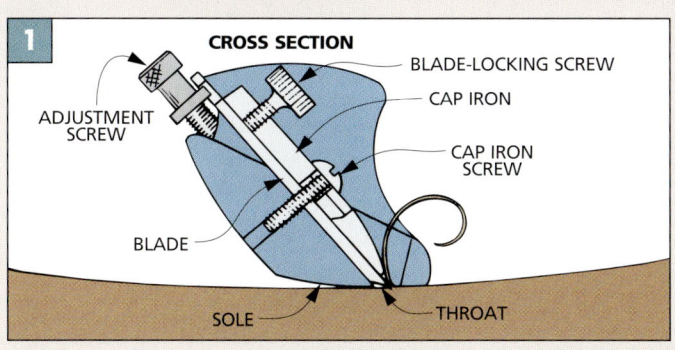

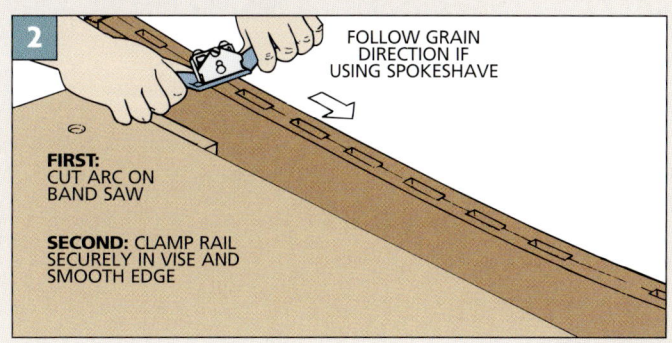

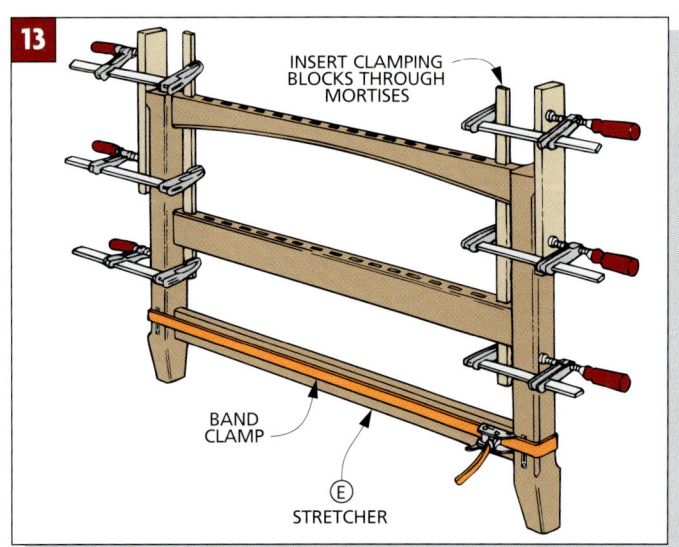

13
INSERT CLAMPING BLOCKS THROUGH MORTISES

BAND CLAMP

E
STRETCHER

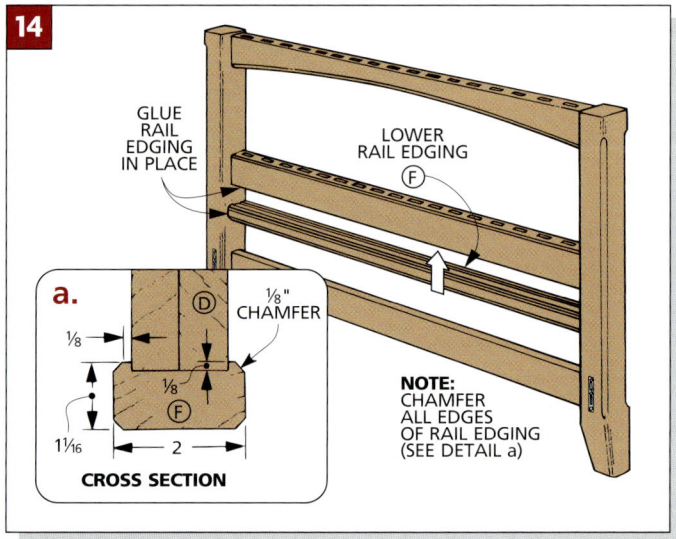

14
GLUE RAIL EDGING IN PLACE

LOWER RAIL EDGING
F

NOTE: CHAMFER ALL EDGES OF RAIL EDGING (SEE DETAIL a)

a.
D
$\frac{1}{8}$
$\frac{1}{8}$" CHAMFER
$\frac{1}{8}$
F
$1\frac{1}{16}$
2
CROSS SECTION

STRETCHER. Before assembling the rails and posts, there's one more part to make. To give the headboard a little more stability, a stretcher (E) is added below the rails (refer to *Fig. 8* on page 102).

Because the stretcher will be concealed by the mattress and box spring, I didn't worry about making it the same thickness as the rails. I used a piece of $1\frac{1}{16}$"-thick stock, but you could glue up two pieces of $\frac{3}{4}$"-thick stock if that's what you have available.

As with the upper and lower rails, the stretcher needs $1\frac{1}{2}$"-long tenons cut on each end (refer to *Fig. 8b* on page 102).

ASSEMBLY. After cutting tenons on the ends of the stretcher, I was ready to start assembling all the pieces. But I ran into a slight problem as I dry-assembled things. I discovered that I didn't have clamps long enough to span the width of the headboard and footboard.

So I improvised. I used a band clamp around the stretcher, and half a dozen smaller clamps, some clamping boards, and a couple of scrap blocks cut to fit down through the rail mortises *(Fig. 13)*.

EDGING. After gluing up the headboard and footboard, the next step is to add edging (F) to the bottom of the lower rails *(Fig. 14* above and *Fig. 8* on page 102). This edging serves two purposes. First, it covers the exposed ends of the mortises. And by doing that, it prevents the slats from sliding down all the way through the mortises.

The edging is just a piece of $1\frac{1}{16}$"-thick stock, cut 2" wide and long enough to fit between the posts of the headboard and footboard *(Fig. 14)*. A groove cut along the length of the edging allows it to fit snug over the lower rails *(Fig. 14a)*.

Before attaching the edging, I routed $\frac{1}{8}$" chamfers on all four edges. Then glue and clamp the edging to the bottom rails.

TECHNIQUE . . . . *Tenons on Long Rails*

The length of the upper and lower rails and the stretcher made them a challenge to work with, especially when it was time to cut their tenons. I had a tough time trying to keep the workpiece moving straight across the table saw while still supporting the outside edge.

To help steady the workpieces, I created an "outrigger" to support the ends during a cut (see drawing). I clamped a long board to a sawhorse so it matched the height of my saw's table. Make sure the outrigger is positioned so that it supports the piece before the blade and through the cut.

Then, to help steady the piece even more, I screwed an auxiliary fence to my miter gauge. And I clamped a hold-down to the auxiliary fence (detail 'a'). The hold-down is positioned to keep the workpiece from tipping up.

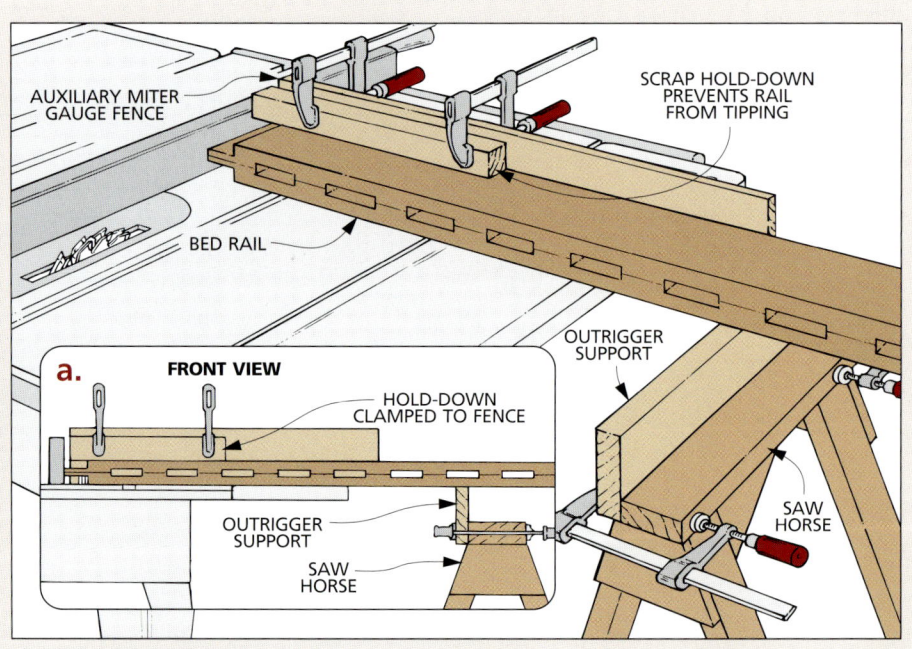

AUXILIARY MITER GAUGE FENCE

SCRAP HOLD-DOWN PREVENTS RAIL FROM TIPPING

BED RAIL

OUTRIGGER SUPPORT

a. **FRONT VIEW**
HOLD-DOWN CLAMPED TO FENCE

OUTRIGGER SUPPORT

SAW HORSE

SAW HORSE

SHOP JIG .... Dado Routing Guide

Mortises don't have to be cut with a chisel or drilled at the drill press. By using this jig to rout matching dadoes in two pieces, then laminating the pieces, you can create through mortises.

This jig starts with a base made out of 3/4"-thick MDF *(Fig. 1)*. To square the jig with the edge of the workpiece, an edge guide is glued to one end.

Note: This guide should be exactly the same thickness as your rail pieces.

Next, cut a couple of 2"-wide strips for the fences to guide the router. The important thing is to attach the first fence at a perfect right angle to the edge guide. To do this, I used a square to position the fence as I glued and screwed it in place.

The second fence must also be square to the edge guide, but this time I used a different approach. To make sure the fences were parallel, I used a spacer to position the second fence *(Fig. 2)*. But since the width of the dadoes will be determined by the distance between the fences, the width of the spacer is critical.

To find the spacer's width, simply subtract the diameter of your router bit (I used a 3/4" straight bit) from the diameter of your router base (6" in my case). Then add 2" for the width of the dado. (I ended up needing a 7 1/4"-wide spacer.)

After positioning the second fence, I added carriage bolts and wing nuts at the end of each fence *(Fig. 2)*. These allow the fences to be tightened down over the rail pieces. (You'll need to drill a hole and counterbore for each bolt.)

ROUT NOTCH. Finally, clamp a piece of scrap in the jig and rout a notch in the edge guide *(Fig. 3)*. This notch is used as a reference to line up the jig with the layout lines. (See the next page.)

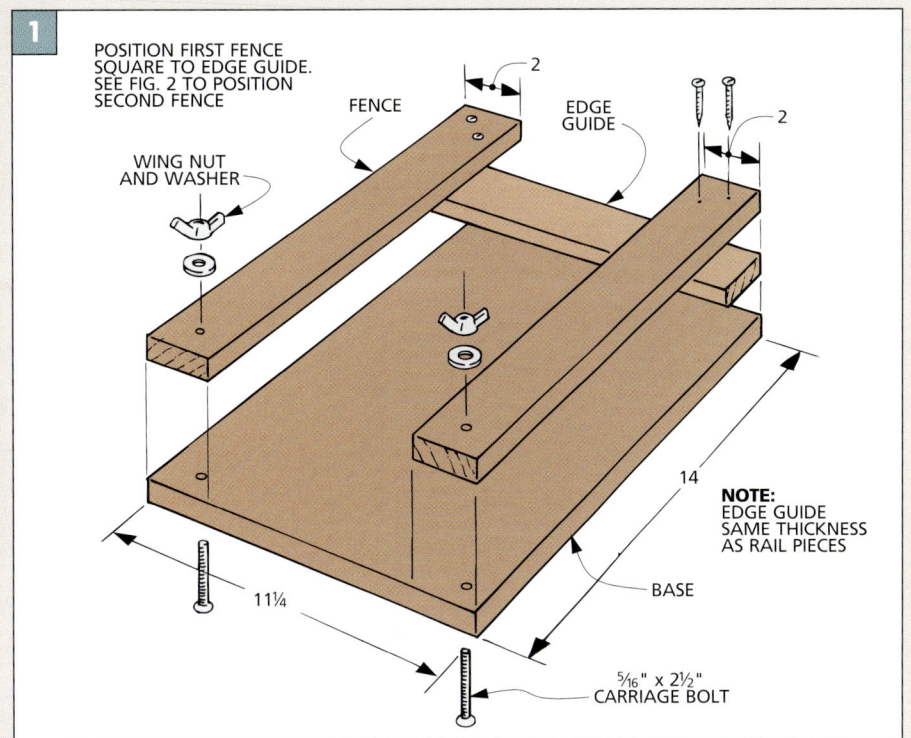

1 POSITION FIRST FENCE SQUARE TO EDGE GUIDE. SEE FIG. 2 TO POSITION SECOND FENCE

FENCE
EDGE GUIDE
WING NUT AND WASHER
2
2
14
NOTE: EDGE GUIDE SAME THICKNESS AS RAIL PIECES
11 1/4
BASE
5/16 " x 2 1/2 " CARRIAGE BOLT

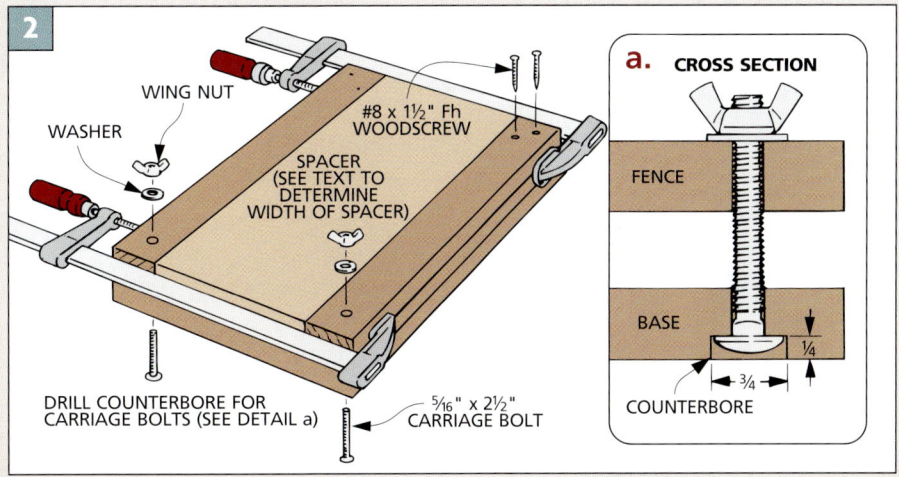

2
WING NUT
WASHER
#8 x 1 1/2" Fh WOODSCREW
SPACER (SEE TEXT TO DETERMINE WIDTH OF SPACER)
DRILL COUNTERBORE FOR CARRIAGE BOLTS (SEE DETAIL a)
5/16 " x 2 1/2 " CARRIAGE BOLT

a. CROSS SECTION
FENCE
BASE
COUNTERBORE
1/4
3/4

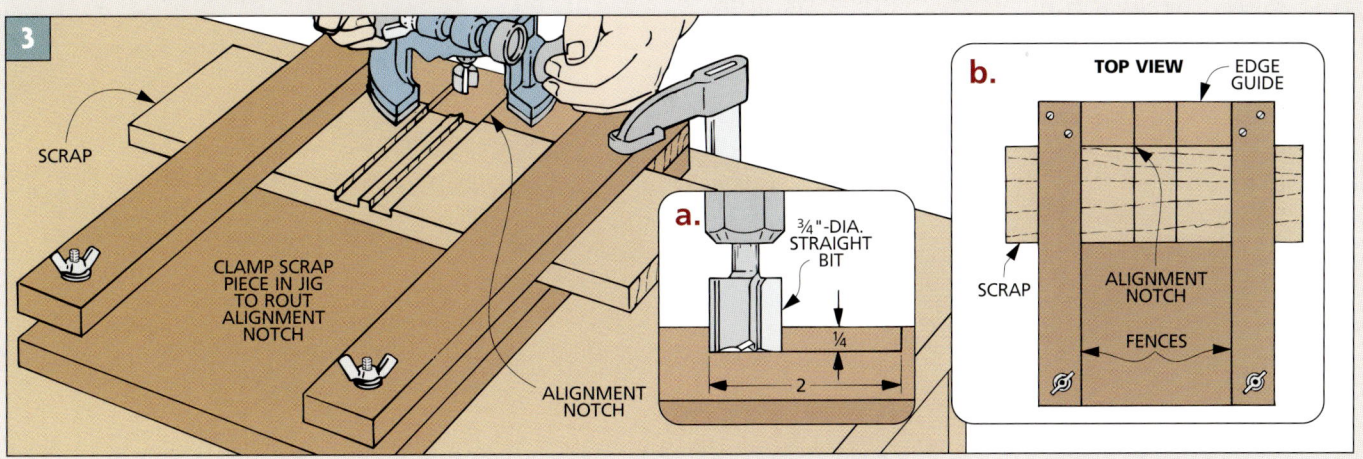

3
SCRAP
CLAMP SCRAP PIECE IN JIG TO ROUT ALIGNMENT NOTCH
ALIGNMENT NOTCH

a. 3/4"-DIA. STRAIGHT BIT
1/4
2

b. TOP VIEW
EDGE GUIDE
SCRAP
ALIGNMENT NOTCH
FENCES

When I first saw the design for the cherry bed, I really liked it. It's a great-looking piece. Then I began to think about how much time it would take to make all those mortises for the slats in the headboard and footboard.

But after some more thought, I came up with an unusual technique that really speeds up the process for making all these mortises. Instead of cutting traditional mortises in a solid rail, I used a special jig to rout a series of shallow dadoes in a pair of boards (see photo). Then the boards are glued together so the dadoes face each other. What you end up with is a rail with a completed row of through mortises. (Instructions for building the jig are on page 105.)

LAYOUT

There are eight rail pieces in the bed (two for each rail). But I started by laying out the dadoes on just one board. To do this, clamp a tape measure to the board. Then starting 3" from either end, mark out 2"-wide dadoes spaced 1½" apart (*Figs. 1 and 2a*). (The 3" at each end allows for a tenon plus the space between the slats and the bed post.) Then make an "X" in the waste areas.

To keep the dado spacing identical in all the rails, I used this piece as a guide or "story stick" for laying out the dadoes on the other boards. But since the dadoes are cut in pairs, you only need to draw layout lines on one board from each pair. So just transfer the lines from the first board to three others (*Fig. 2*).

SETUP. Before you start routing the dadoes, there are a couple of things to do to make the job even easier. The first is to label each pair of rail pieces so you can keep them together when it comes time for assembly (*Fig. 3*).

Second, find a couple of scrap pieces to place under the rails so they won't rock when they're placed in the jig (*Fig. 3*).

ROUTING

With all of the dadoes laid out, the next step is to rout them. The trick here is to keep the router inside the layout lines. That's where the jig comes in. A notch in

1

RAIL PIECE

STARTING 3" FROM END OF RAIL, LAY OUT 2"-WIDE MORTISES, 1½" APART

TAPE MEASURE

SPRING CLAMP

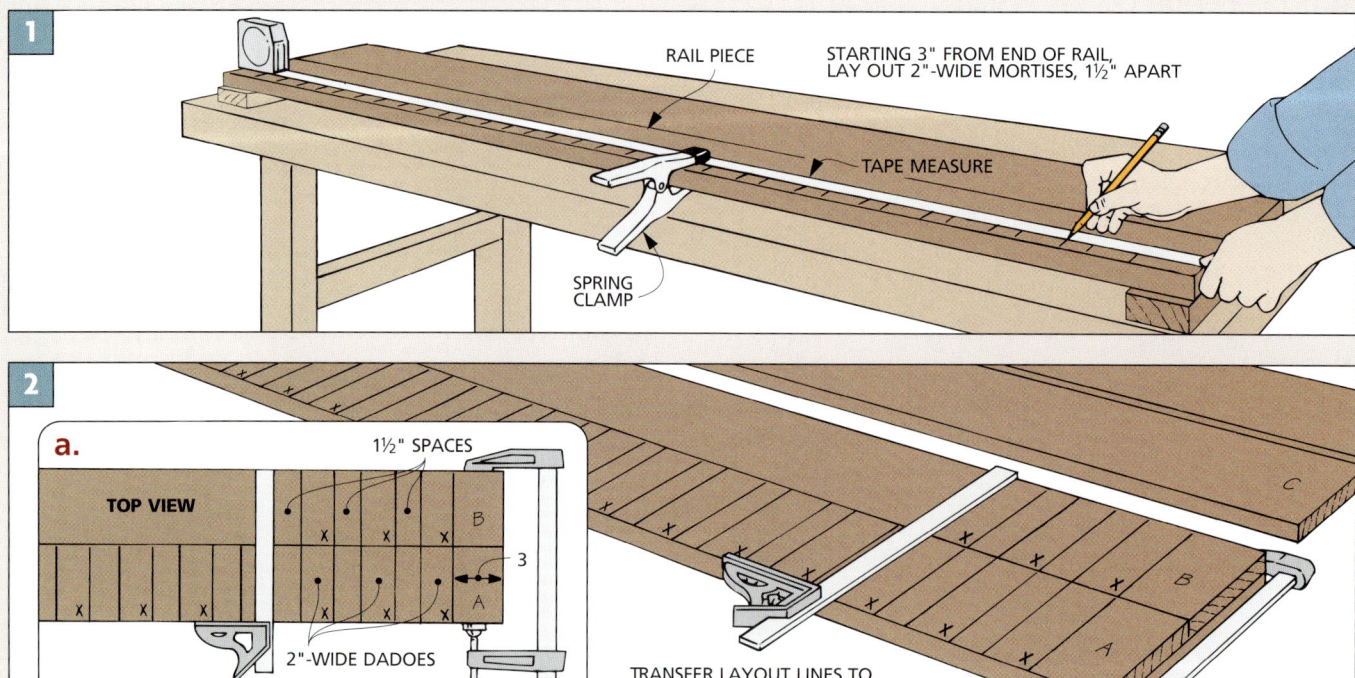

2

a.

TOP VIEW

1½" SPACES

B

3

A

2"-WIDE DADOES

MARK DADO AREAS WITH "X"

TRANSFER LAYOUT LINES TO THREE OTHER RAIL BOARDS

the base aligns with the layout marks. Then the fences that straddle the work-pieces guide the router.

Simply slide the jig over the first pair of rails and clamp the rails together and then down to your workbench.

To rout the first pair of dadoes, align the notch in the base of the jig with the first set of layout lines and tighten down the wing nuts. Since the bit I used was only 3/4" wide, I routed each dado in three passes (*Fig. 3*). And because the bit is not always perfectly centered in the base of the router, make sure to hold the router in the same relative position for each pass. (In other words, don't rotate the router between passes.)

After you rout the first dado, just loosen the wing nuts, move the jig down to the next set of layout lines, and repeat the process. When you've routed all the dadoes in one rail, do the same with the other three rail pairs.

GLUE-UP

The last of the process is gluing the rail halves together (*Fig. 4*). There's just a couple of points to keep in mind.

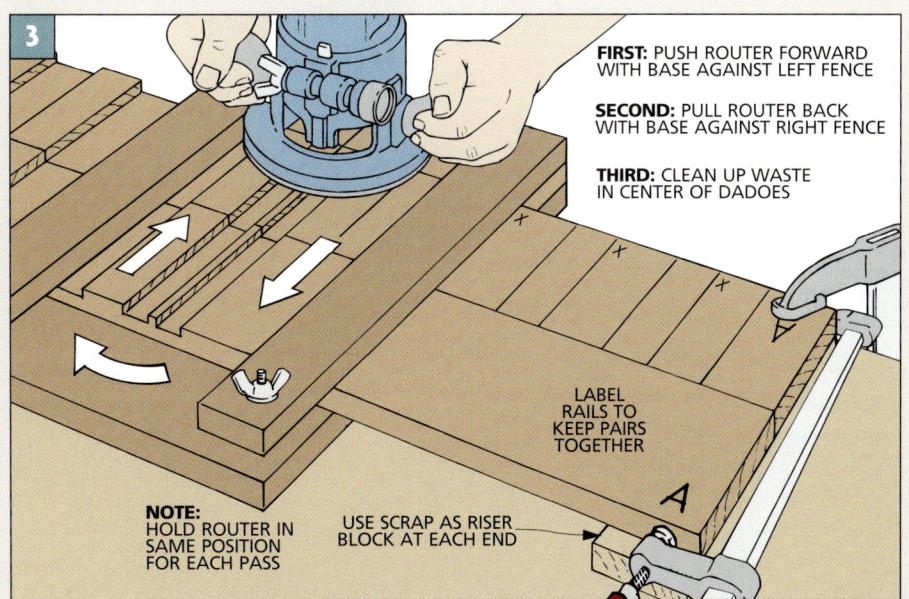

FIRST: PUSH ROUTER FORWARD WITH BASE AGAINST LEFT FENCE

SECOND: PULL ROUTER BACK WITH BASE AGAINST RIGHT FENCE

THIRD: CLEAN UP WASTE IN CENTER OF DADOES

LABEL RAILS TO KEEP PAIRS TOGETHER

NOTE: HOLD ROUTER IN SAME POSITION FOR EACH PASS

USE SCRAP AS RISER BLOCK AT EACH END

First, I wanted to avoid having to clean up a lot of glue squeeze-out inside the mortises. So I applied the glue sparingly, spread it with a brush, and I kept it away from the edges of the dadoes.

Second, I wanted to make sure the dadoes remained lined up while clamping the pieces together. So I made a couple

of spacer blocks to fit in the mortises (*Fig. 5*). Then, after clamping up a rail, I ran a thin piece of wood through each mortise to remove any glue (*Fig. 5a*).

Finally, after the glue was dry, I removed the clamps and cut about 1/4" off each edge of the rails to trim them to finished width (4 1/2").

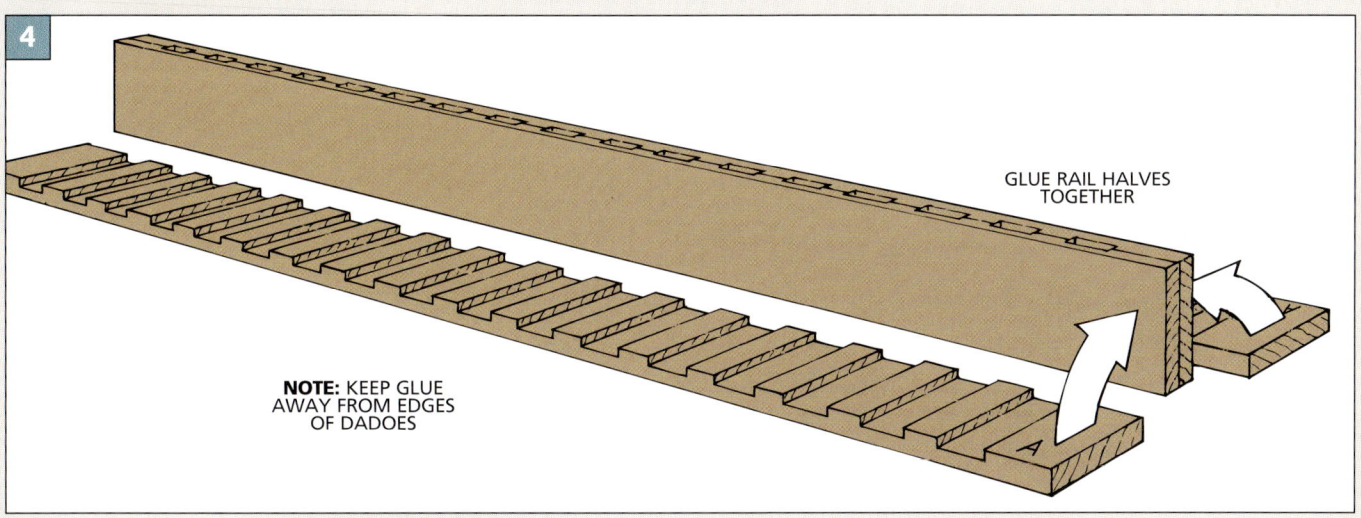

GLUE RAIL HALVES TOGETHER

NOTE: KEEP GLUE AWAY FROM EDGES OF DADOES

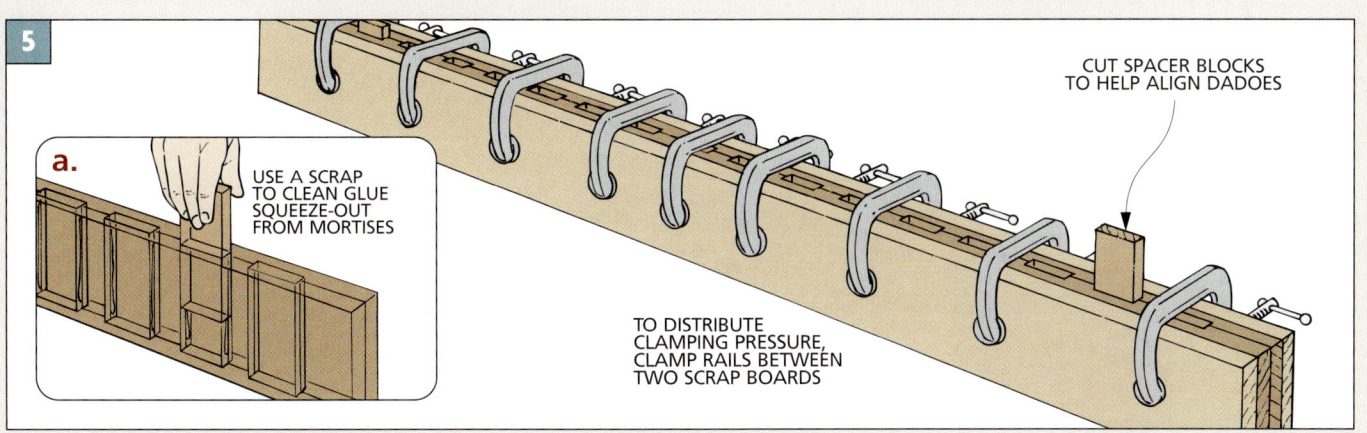

CUT SPACER BLOCKS TO HELP ALIGN DADOES

a. USE A SCRAP TO CLEAN GLUE SQUEEZE-OUT FROM MORTISES

TO DISTRIBUTE CLAMPING PRESSURE, CLAMP RAILS BETWEEN TWO SCRAP BOARDS

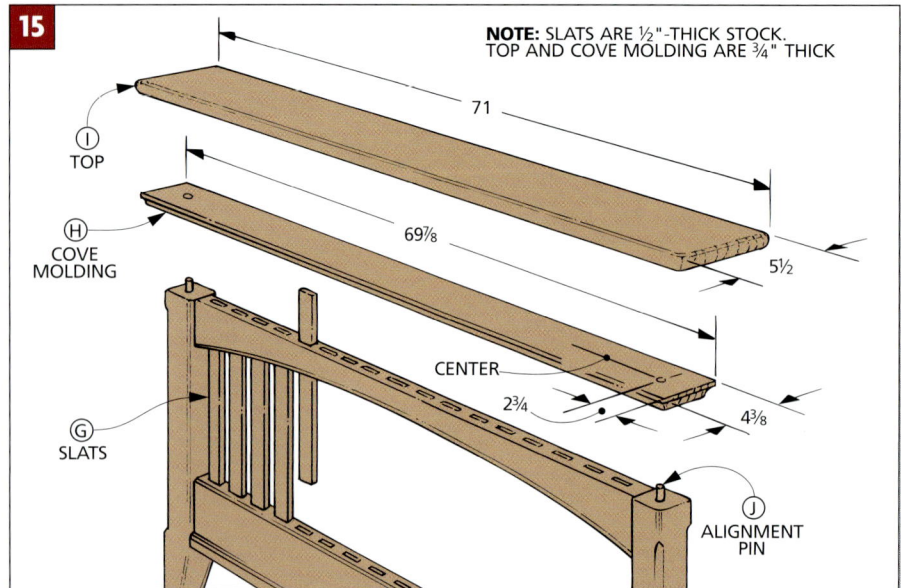

15

NOTE: SLATS ARE ½"-THICK STOCK.
TOP AND COVE MOLDING ARE ¾" THICK

71

I
TOP

H
COVE
MOLDING

69⅞

5½

CENTER

G
SLATS

2¾

4⅜

J
ALIGNMENT
PIN

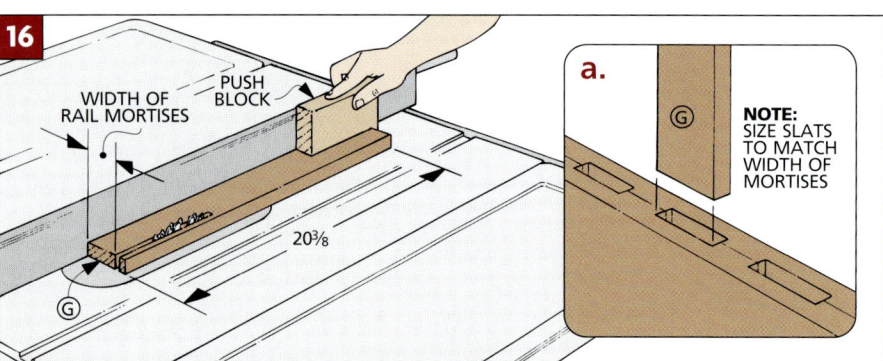

16

WIDTH OF
RAIL MORTISES

PUSH
BLOCK

20⅜

G

a.

G

NOTE:
SIZE SLATS
TO MATCH
WIDTH OF
MORTISES

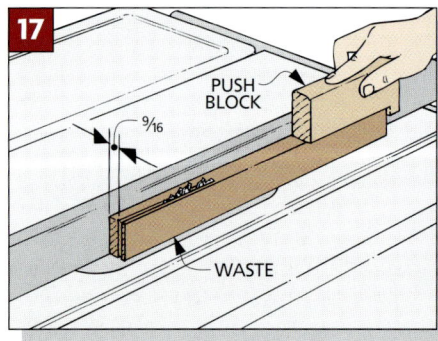

17

PUSH
BLOCK

⁹⁄₁₆

WASTE

18

SCRAP

USE MALLET
TO GENTLY
TAP SLATS
IN PLACE

SLATS

With the posts and rails glued up, the next step is to add the slats (G) *(Fig. 15)*. Since the slats don't require tenons on the ends, it's simply a matter of cutting them to fit in the mortises in the rails.

CUT TO LENGTH. The first step in making the slats is to cut them to length. The slats fit all the way through the mortises in the rails and are cut to fit ⅛" below the top of the upper rail.

To determine the length of the slats, I slipped a thin, narrow piece of scrap down through the mortises and measured the distance to the top of the rail. Then I cut all the slats ⅛" shorter than this measurement out of ¾"-thick stock. (Mine were 20⅜" long.)

The next step is to rip all of the slats to finished width *(Fig. 16)*. This should match the width of the mortises in the rails (2" in my case).

Safety Note: Since the slats are so narrow, I used a push block to safely feed them past the saw blade *(Fig. 16)*.

THICKNESS. Now all that's left is to reduce the slats to the proper thickness to fit in the mortises. (My slats ended up ½" thick.) To do this, I started by resawing all the slats so that they were slightly thicker than the mortises (⁹⁄₁₆") *(Fig. 17)*. Again, I used a push block to keep my hands away from the blade.

When all the slats were resawn, I was able to sneak up on the final thickness for a perfect fit in the mortises. A thickness planer is the easiest way to do this. But if you don't have one of these tools, another way is to use a drill press set up with a fence and a large drum sander. (See the Technique box below.)

INSERTING THE SLATS. Once you've finished sanding all the slats, they can be inserted in the headboard and footboard.

TECHNIQUE .... *Drum Sander Thicknessing*

All you need to reduce the thickness of the bed slats is a drill press and a drum sander. (Since the slats are 2" wide, the drum sander should be at least 2½" tall.)

FENCE. Just clamp a fence to your drill press table near the drum sander. Then feed the slats through the sander one at a time, pushing them along the fence (see drawing).

Make sure to feed the slats against the rotation of the drum (detail 'a').

Also, you'll get better results if you don't try to sand the slats down to finished thickness in a single pass. Instead, make a number of passes, removing less than ¹⁄₃₂" each time. Move the fence a little closer to the drum between passes so you can "sneak up" on the final thickness.

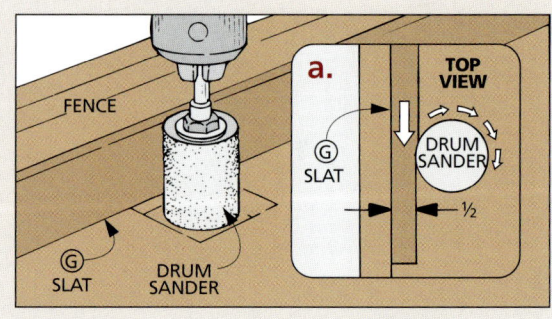

FENCE

a.

G
SLAT

DRUM
SANDER

G
SLAT

TOP
VIEW

DRUM
SANDER

½

I didn't use any glue on the slats — they'll be held in place between the lower rail edging and the cap that's added later. Most of the slats slipped right into place without any trouble. But for a few of the more stubborn slats, I used a mallet and a thin piece of scrap wood to gently tap the slats home *(Fig. 18)*.

CAP

All that remains to complete the headboard and footboard is to add a two-piece cap to them *(Fig. 15)*. The cap consists of a cove molding and a top piece with a bullnose edge profile.

COVE MOLDING. The two cove moldings (H) are pieces of $\frac{3}{4}$"-thick stock that are cut to finished size. I made my cove molding pieces $4\frac{3}{8}$" wide and $69\frac{7}{8}$" long. Then I routed a $\frac{1}{2}$" cove around all four bottom edges of each piece *(Fig. 19)*.

To complete the cove molding, all that's left is to drill a couple of $\frac{1}{2}$"-dia. holes that accept a pair of alignment pins *(Fig. 20)*. To drill these holes, I centered the cove moldings on the length and width of the headboard and footboard and clamped them in place. Then I drilled holes through the molding pieces and $\frac{1}{2}$" deep into the posts.

TOP. The two tops (I) are also pieces of $\frac{3}{4}$"-thick stock ($5\frac{1}{2}$" x 71"). Both the top and bottom edges of the top are rounded over to create a bullnose profile. First I rounded over the bottom edges with a $\frac{1}{2}$" roundover bit *(Fig. 21)*. Then for the top edges, I used a $\frac{1}{4}$" roundover bit, but I set it only $\frac{3}{16}$" above the surface of the router table *(Figs. 22 and 22a)*.

Like the cove molding, the top also has holes for the alignment pins, but the procedure for drilling them is a bit different. Start by laying the top face down on your workbench. Then center the cove molding on top of the top piece, also top

face down *(Fig. 23)*. Now clamp the two pieces down and use the holes in the cove molding as guides for drilling two $\frac{1}{2}$"-deep holes in the top piece *(Fig. 23a)*.

ASSEMBLY. Before assembling the cove molding and top to the bed, I cut four $1\frac{11}{16}$"-long alignment pins (J) from a

piece of $\frac{1}{2}$"-dia. dowel. Then I glued them into the holes in the posts. The pins keep the cap pieces aligned during the glue-up.

To attach the caps, glue and clamp the cove moldings to the head and footboard. Finally, glue the tops down to the cove moldings *(Figs. 24 and 24a)*.

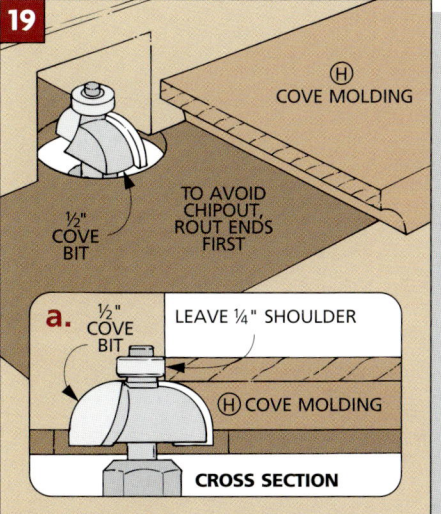

19
COVE MOLDING
$\frac{1}{2}$" COVE BIT
TO AVOID CHIPOUT, ROUT ENDS FIRST
a. $\frac{1}{2}$" COVE BIT — LEAVE $\frac{1}{4}$" SHOULDER
(H) COVE MOLDING
CROSS SECTION

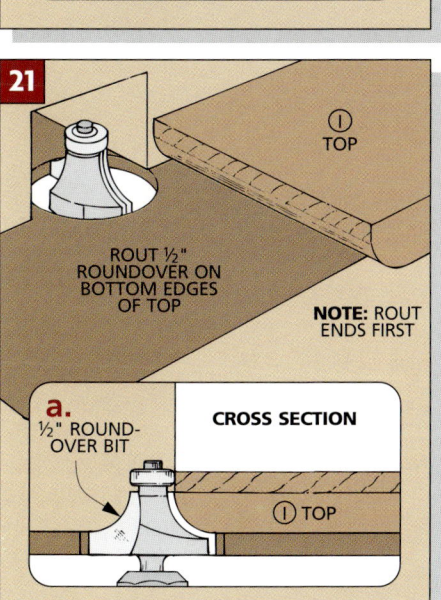

21
(I) TOP
ROUT $\frac{1}{2}$" ROUNDOVER ON BOTTOM EDGES OF TOP
NOTE: ROUT ENDS FIRST
a. $\frac{1}{2}$" ROUND-OVER BIT
CROSS SECTION
(I) TOP

20
TAPE STOP
(H) COVE MOLDING
$2\frac{3}{4}$
$\frac{1}{2}$"-DIA. FORSTNER BIT
NOTE: CLAMP COVE MOLDING TO TOP OF HEADBOARD/FOOTBOARD
a. (H)
CROSS SECTION
POST (A)(B)
$\frac{1}{2}$

22
(I) TOP
ROUT $\frac{1}{4}$" ROUNDOVER $\frac{3}{16}$" DEEP ON TOP EDGES
NOTE: ROUT ENDS FIRST
a. $\frac{1}{4}$" ROUND-OVER BIT SET $\frac{3}{16}$" DEEP
CROSS SECTION
(I) TOP

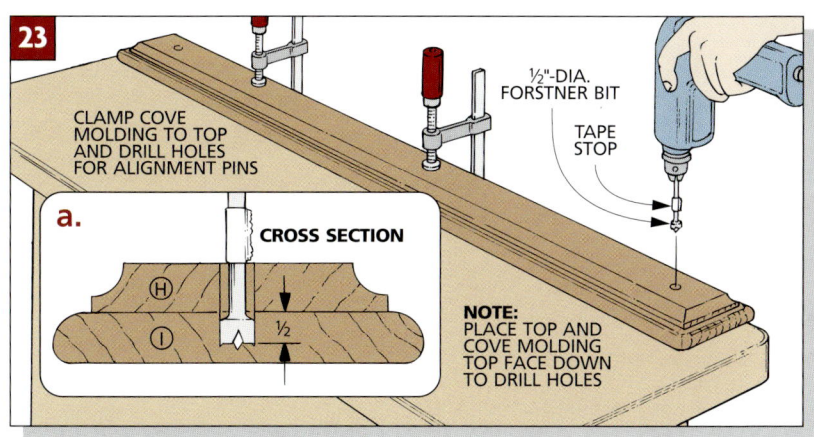

23
CLAMP COVE MOLDING TO TOP AND DRILL HOLES FOR ALIGNMENT PINS
$\frac{1}{2}$"-DIA. FORSTNER BIT
TAPE STOP
a. (H) (I) $\frac{1}{2}$
CROSS SECTION
NOTE: PLACE TOP AND COVE MOLDING TOP FACE DOWN TO DRILL HOLES

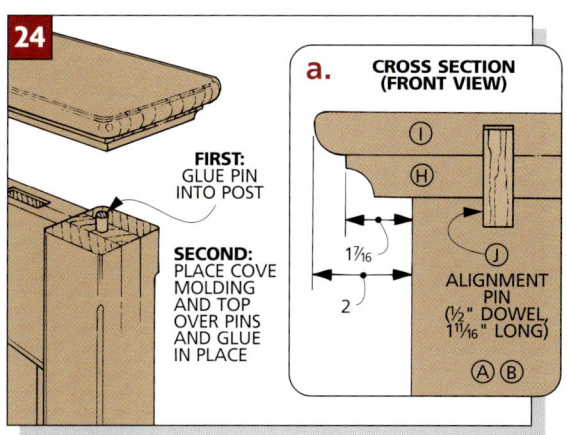

24
FIRST: GLUE PIN INTO POST
SECOND: PLACE COVE MOLDING AND TOP OVER PINS AND GLUE IN PLACE
a. **CROSS SECTION (FRONT VIEW)**
(I) (H)
$1\frac{7}{16}$
2
ALIGNMENT PIN ($\frac{1}{2}$" DOWEL, $1\frac{11}{16}$" LONG)
(J)
(A)(B)

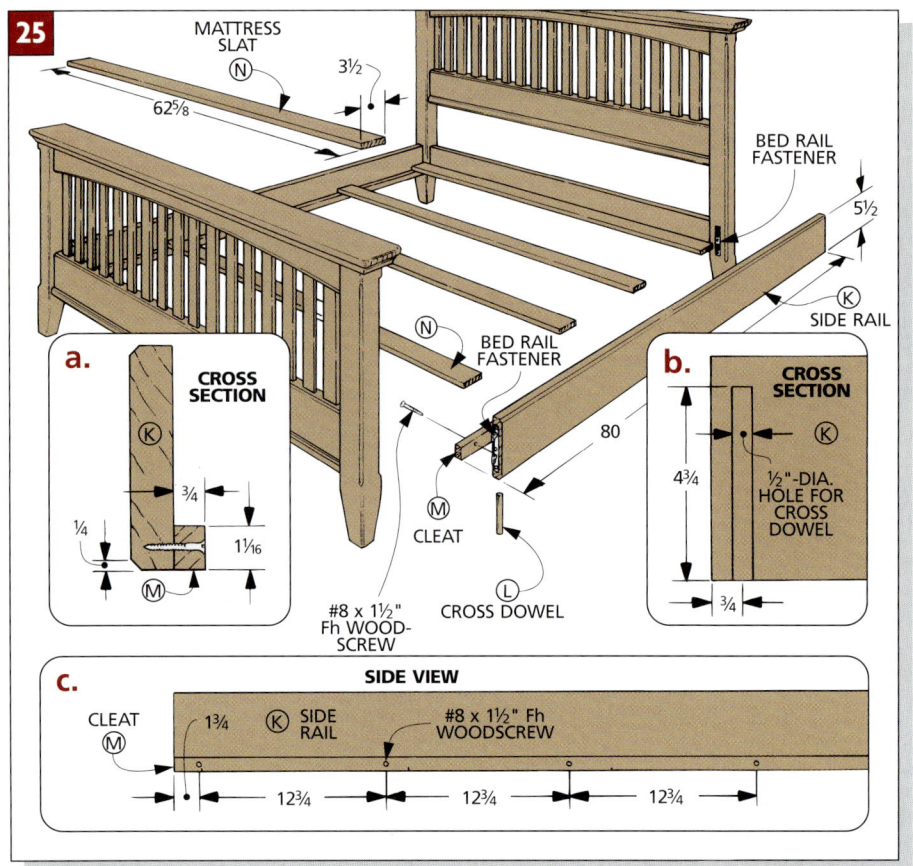

25

MATTRESS SLAT (N)

62⅝ 3½

BED RAIL FASTENER

5½

SIDE RAIL (K)

(N) BED RAIL FASTENER

a. CROSS SECTION

(K)

¾ ¼ 1¹⁄₁₆

(M)

(M) CLEAT

#8 x 1½" Fh WOOD-SCREW

CROSS DOWEL

(L)

(M) CLEAT

b. CROSS SECTION

80

(K)

4¾

½"-DIA. HOLE FOR CROSS DOWEL

¾

c. SIDE VIEW

CLEAT (M)

1¾ (K) SIDE RAIL

#8 x 1½" Fh WOODSCREW

12¾ 12¾ 12¾

SIDE RAILS

Once the headboard and footboard are complete, all that's left is to connect them with a pair of side rails (K). These are just a couple of boards cut to size from 1¹⁄₁₆"-thick stock (*Fig. 25*). Chamfers are routed on the outside edges (*Fig. 25a*).

The side rails are attached to the bed posts with bed rail fasteners. Earlier, a "mortise" plate was attached to each post. Now the "tenon" plate that hooks into the mortise plate is attached to each end of the rails. The plate sits in a shallow mortise. (See *Steps 6 and 7* in the Hardware article on the facing page.)

Once the fasteners are fitted into the mortises, they're held in place with 1½" woodscrews. But I was worried about the screws holding, since they're driven into end grain. So I gave the screws something more solid to "bite" into. All I did was drill a hole in the bottom edge of each side rail and insert a ½"-dia. cross dowel (L) (*Fig. 25b* and *Steps 8 and 9* on the opposite page).

CLEATS. Before attaching the side rails to the bed, I added a cleat (M) to each one. These cleats provide a support for the mattress slats that are added next. The cleats are just a couple of pieces of hardwood that are glued and screwed to the side rails (*Figs. 25a and 25c*).

MATTRESS SLATS. The side rails and cleats support the mattress and box spring of the bed. But for additional strength, I added five mattress slats (N) (*Fig. 25*). I used cherry for the mattress slats, but since they'll be concealed by the box spring, any hardwood will work. The slats aren't fastened to the bed — they just sit on top of the cleats.

FINISH. Finally, to finish the bed I wiped on three coats of an oil finish, sanding lightly between coats. ∎

DESIGNER'S NOTEBOOK

It's easy to adjust the size of the headboard and footboard to hold a different size mattress.

TWIN & FULL-SIZE

■ Twin-size and full-size mattresses are shorter, so cut the side rails (K) and cleats (M) only 74" long.

■ A twin-size bed only needs 22 slats (on left drawing). Also, remember to allow for the tenons on the rails and stretcher.

■ A full-size bed needs 30 slats (on right in drawing). The space between the side rails and box spring will be about 2".

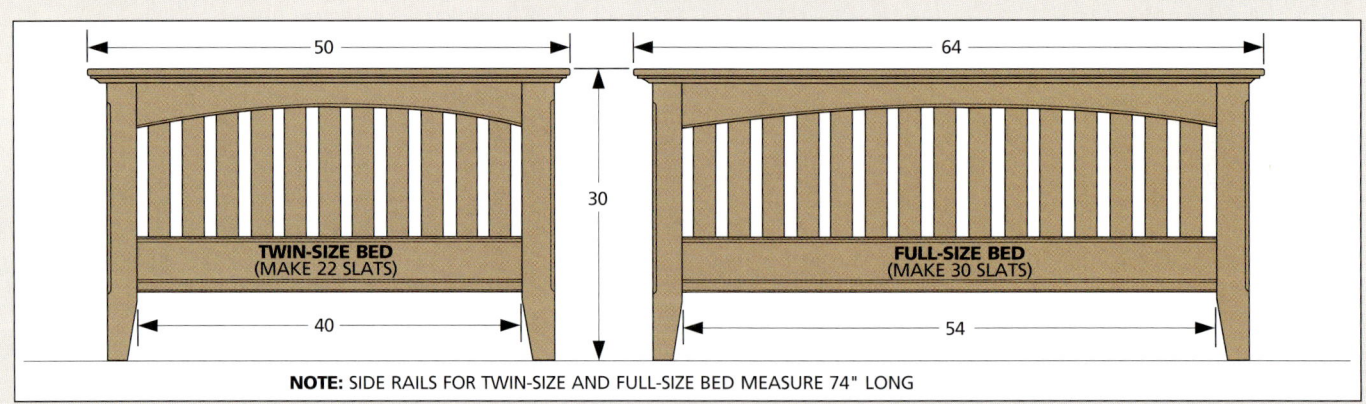

50 64

30

TWIN-SIZE BED (MAKE 22 SLATS) FULL-SIZE BED (MAKE 30 SLATS)

40 54

NOTE: SIDE RAILS FOR TWIN-SIZE AND FULL-SIZE BED MEASURE 74" LONG

HARDWARE .... *Bed Rail Fasteners*

Bed rail fasteners are a strong way to join the bed rails to the posts. The fasteners consist of two steel plates that fit together somewhat like a locking mortise and tenon joint. The "tenon" plate has two tapered hooks that fit in the "mortise" plate and draw the two together.

MORTISE PLATE. After laying out the location of the mortise plate *(Step 1)*, a two-tiered mortise is drilled. The deeper mortise provides clearance for the hooks on the tenon plate *(Step 2)*.

The second set of holes creates a shallow mortise that puts the plate flush with the face of the post *(Steps 3, 4, 5)*.

TENON PLATES. The tenon plates have small "nubs" on their back faces. So after laying out the position of the plate on the

end of the rail (K) (it's centered), I drilled two shallow clearance holes *(Step 6)*.

Next, the plate needs to be mortised into the ends of the side rails. I used a hand-held router *(Step 7)* and a chisel.

CROSS DOWEL. Finally, to give the screw threads some long grain to "bite" into, I added a 1/2"-dia. cross dowel (L) near the end of each rail *(Step 8)*.

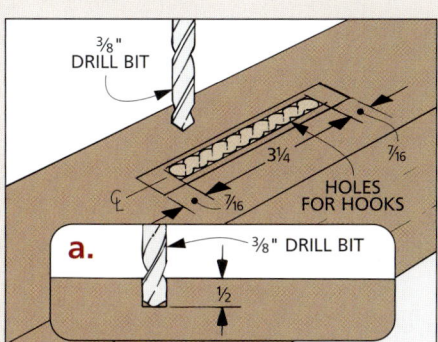

1 To begin, position the mortise plate on the post. For a clean mortise, carefully scribe around the plate with a razor knife.

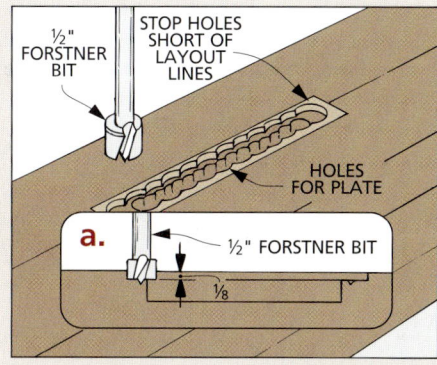

2 Next, drill overlapping 3/8"-dia. holes that will provide clearance for the hooks on the tenon plate. Leave the holes rough.

3 To set the mortise plate flush with the post's surface, use a 1/2" Forstner bit to drill another set of overlapping holes.

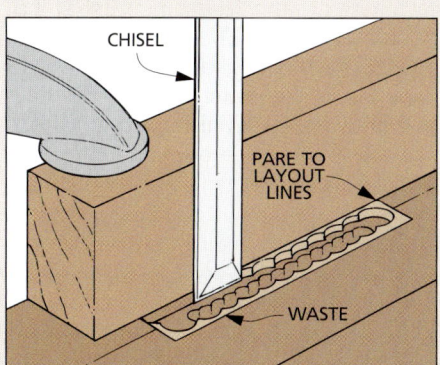

4 Now clean up the second set of holes with a chisel, using a scrap piece as a straightedge to guide the chisel.

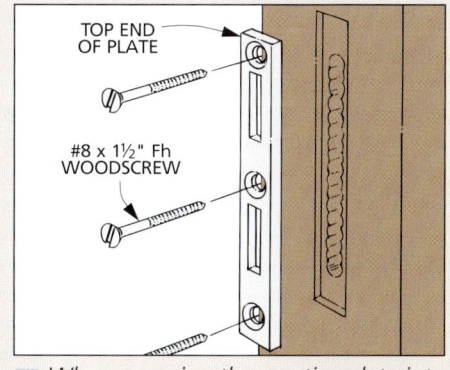

5 When screwing the mortise plate into the post, be sure the mortises are oriented nearest the top of the post.

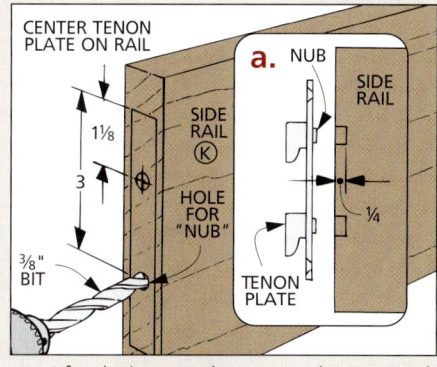

6 After laying out the tenon plate on each end of the rail, drill two holes for the nubs on the back face of the plate.

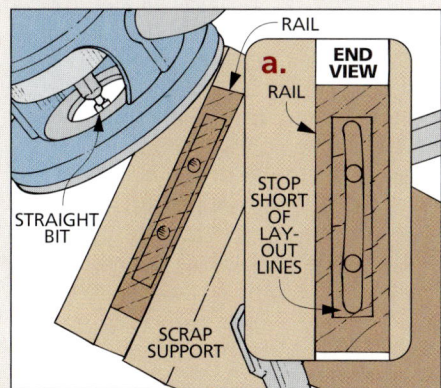

7 Next, rough out the mortise for the plate with a router and a straight bit. Then clean up the sides as in Step 4.

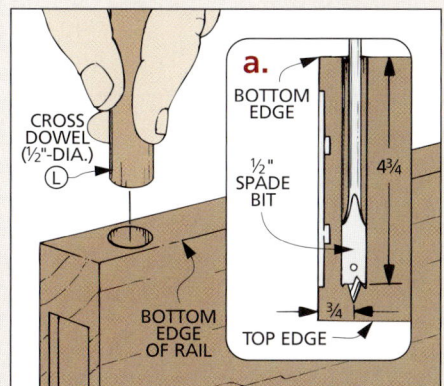

8 To strengthen the holding power of the screws, I drilled a 1/2"-dia. hole under the rail and glued in a cross dowel.

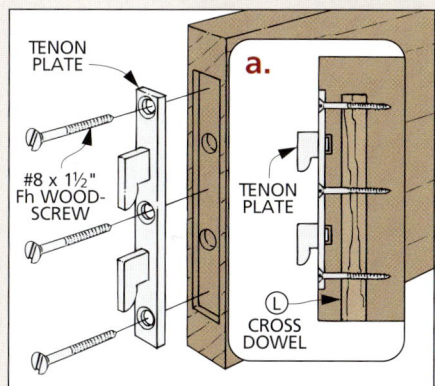

9 With the dowel in place, the tenon can be screwed to the rail. Then the side rail can be hooked onto the post.

Chest-on-Chest

This dresser will be an elegant focal point in any bedroom. It's the largest cabinet in the cherry set and also the most versatile. It can be built as one large unit or the upper and lower chests can stand alone.

Though this Chest-on-Chest is tall, don't let its imposing size and classic details fool you. Like the other cabinets in the Classic Cherry Set, the joinery and construction aren't complicated. The cases are made up of frame and panel assemblies built with tongue and groove joinery. And the machine-cut, half-blind dovetails make quick work of assembling all seven of the drawers. Even the bevels on the drawer fronts are easier than they look. (They're simply cut on the table saw or the router table.)

ONE CHEST OR TWO. To further simplify the building process, the upper and lower chests are built separately. (You'll especially appreciate this if you're working in a small shop.) Then the two cabinets are fastened together with some machine bolts that tighten into threaded inserts. And because the Chest-on-Chest is two separate cabinets, it's also the most easily customized piece of the set.

If you're building an entire set of bedroom furniture, this dresser offers several options. First you can build it as you see in the photo. Or with a few minor modifications, you can turn the upper and lower chests into two separate pieces of furniture. All you need to do is add a solid-wood top to the lower chest and a kickboard base to the upper chest. So you could build just the upper or lower chest. None of these changes are difficult and they're detailed in the Designer's Notebooks on pages 120 and 125.

And for yet another option, you can dress up the kickboard with a cutout pattern. This is shown in the Designer's Notebook on page 90.

HARDWARE. There isn't much hardware needed to build this dresser. The most noticeable is the pulls on the drawers. These are available from several sources (see page 126). And to see how the drawers look with a different style of pull, check out some of the ideas in the Designer's Notebook on page 94.

EXPLODED VIEW

OVERALL DIMENSIONS:
38¾"W x 20⅜"D x 26¼"H
(LOWER CHEST)
(COMBINED HEIGHT OF
BOTH CHESTS IS 60⅜")

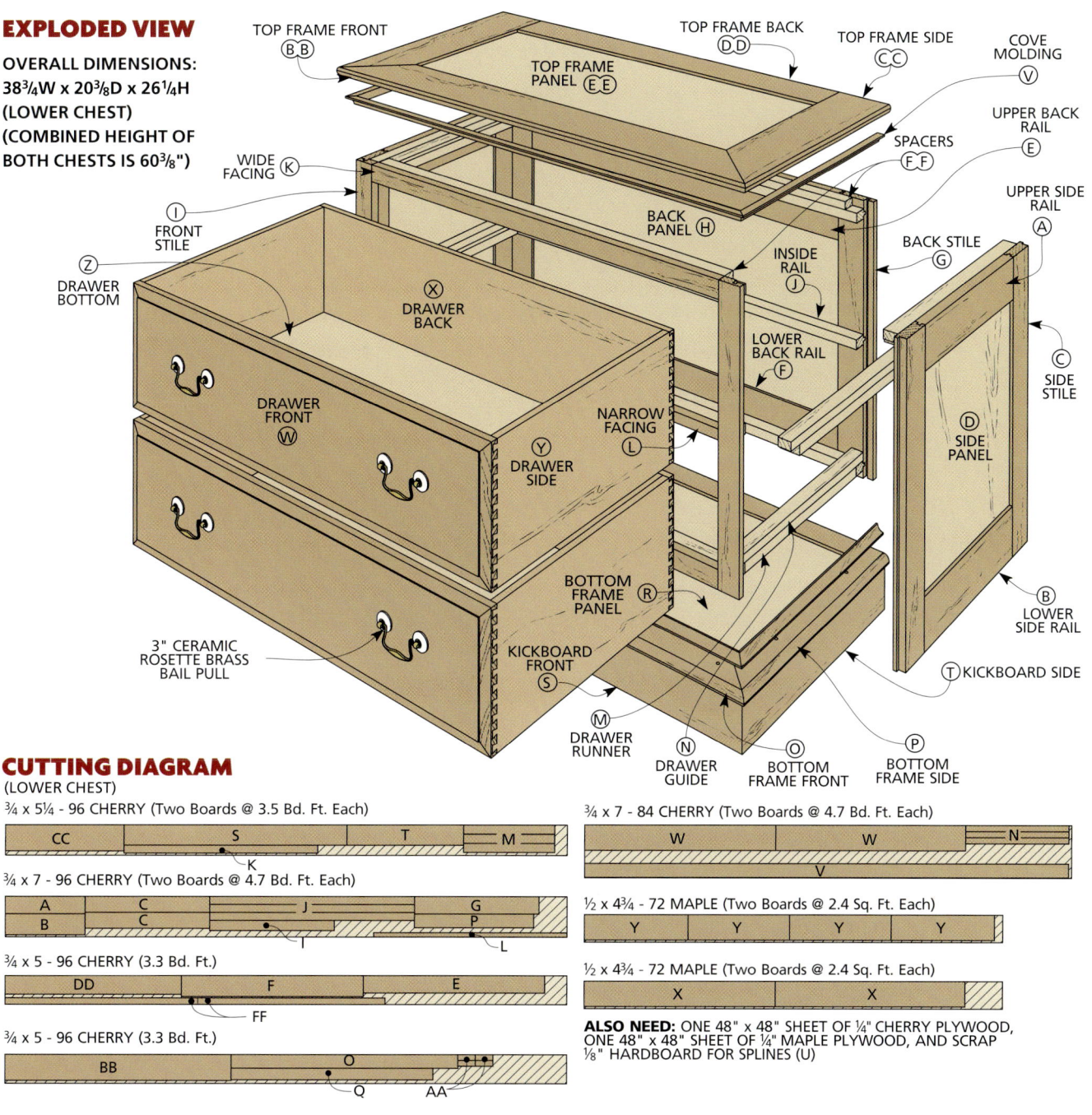

CUTTING DIAGRAM
(LOWER CHEST)

¾ x 5¼ - 96 CHERRY (Two Boards @ 3.5 Bd. Ft. Each)

CC · S · T · M · K

¾ x 7 - 96 CHERRY (Two Boards @ 4.7 Bd. Ft. Each)

A · C · J · G · B · C · I · P · L

¾ x 5 - 96 CHERRY (3.3 Bd. Ft.)

DD · F · E · FF

¾ x 5 - 96 CHERRY (3.3 Bd. Ft.)

BB · O · Q · AA

¾ x 7 - 84 CHERRY (Two Boards @ 4.7 Bd. Ft. Each)

W · W · N · V

½ x 4¾ - 72 MAPLE (Two Boards @ 2.4 Sq. Ft. Each)

Y · Y · Y · Y

½ x 4¾ - 72 MAPLE (Two Boards @ 2.4 Sq. Ft. Each)

X · X

ALSO NEED: ONE 48" x 48" SHEET OF ¼" CHERRY PLYWOOD, ONE 48" x 48" SHEET OF ¼" MAPLE PLYWOOD, AND SCRAP ⅛" HARDBOARD FOR SPLINES (U)

MATERIALS LIST

WOOD (For Lower Chest)

A	Upper Side Rails (2)	¾ x 3 - 13¾
B	Lower Side Rails (2)	¾ x 3⅝ - 13¾
C	Side Stiles (4)	¾ x 2¾ - 21¼
D	Side Panels (2)	¼ ply - 13¾ x 15⅛
E	Upper Back Rail (1)	¾ x 3 - 31
F	Lower Back Rail (1)	¾ x 3⅝ - 31
G	Back Stiles (2)	¾ x 3 - 21¼
H	Back Panel (1)	¼ ply - 31 x 15⅛
I	Front Stiles (2)	¾ x 1¾ - 21¼
J	Inside Rails (6)	¾ x 1⅜ - 35
K	Wide Facings (2)	¾ x 1⅜ - 33
L	Narrow Facing (1)	¾ x ¾ - 33
M	Drawer Runners (6)	¾ x 1⁹⁄₁₆ - 15½

N	Drawer Guides (6)	⅝ x 1¹⁄₃₂ - 17¾
O	Btm. Frame Front (1)	¾ x 2⅜ - 38¾
P	Btm. Frame Sides (2)	¾ x 2⅜ - 20⅜
Q	Btm. Frame Back (1)	¾ x 2 - 34½
R	Btm. Frame Panel (1)	¼ ply - 16½ x 34½
S	Kickboard Fr./Bk. (2)	¾ x 3½ - 38
T	Kickboard Sides (2)	¾ x 3½ - 20
U	Splines (4)	⅛ hdbd. - 3½ x ¹¹⁄₁₆
V	Cove Molding	⅝ x ⅝ - 160 ln. in.
W	Drawer Fronts (2)	¾ x 8¾ - 32⅞
X	Drawer Backs (2)	½ x 8¾ - 32⅞
Y	Drawer Sides (4)	½ x 8¾ - 17¾
Z	Drawer Bottoms (2)	¼ ply - 17⅝ x 32⅜
AA	Drawer Stops (4)	¼ x 1 - 3

BB	Top Frame Front (1)	¾ x 4½ - 38¾
CC	Top Frame Sides (2)	¾ x 4½ - 20⅜
DD	Top Frame Back (1)	¾ x 3¼ - 30¼
EE	Top Frame Panel (1)	¼ ply - 13⅛ x 30¼
FF	Spacers (2)	⅝ x 1⅛ - 32⅞

HARDWARE SUPPLIES
(8) No. 8 x 1¾" Fh woodscrews
(8) No. 8 x 1¼" Fh woodscrews
(20) ⅝" x 19 gauge wire brads
(4) 3" ceramic rosette brass bail pulls
(6') Nylon glide strip
(2) Plastic turnbuttons w/ screws

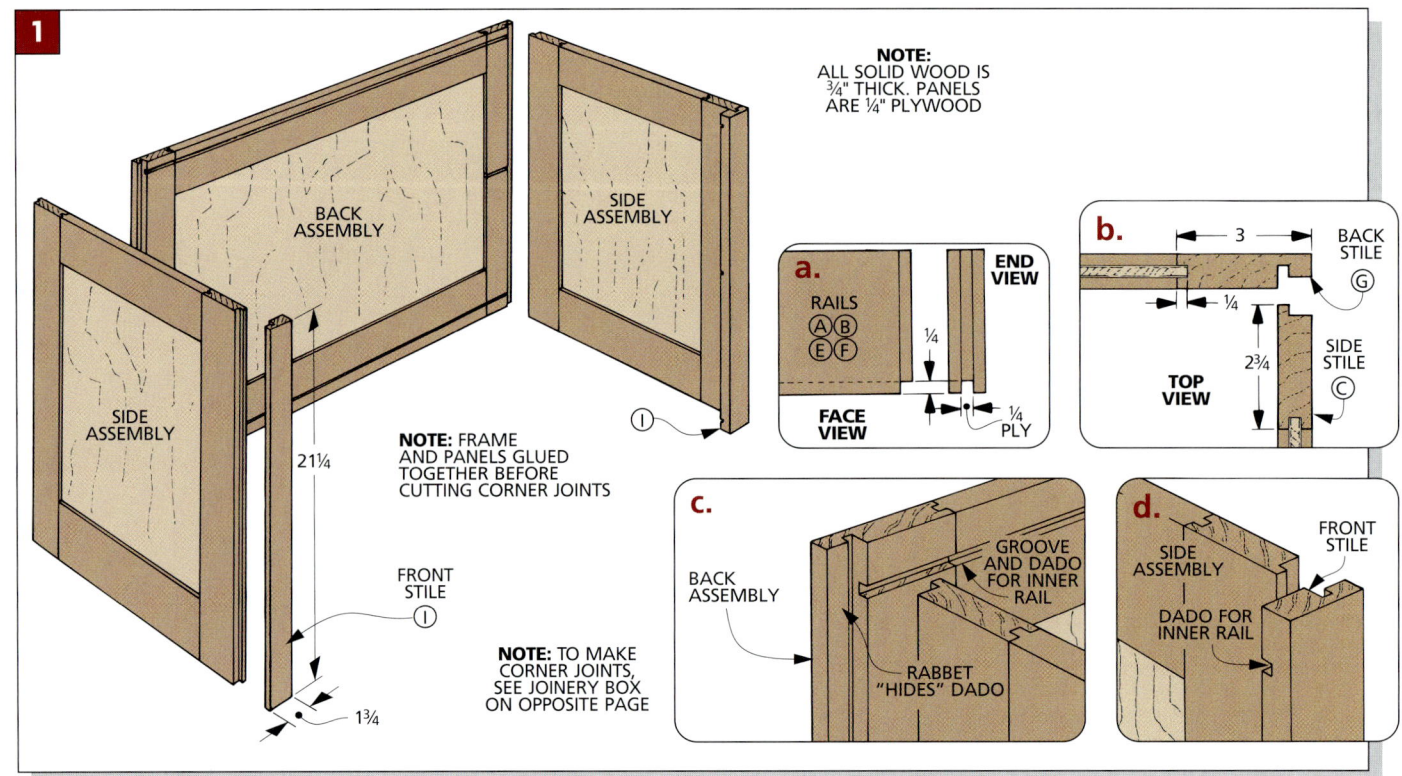

1

NOTE:
ALL SOLID WOOD IS
¾" THICK. PANELS
ARE ¼" PLYWOOD

BACK
ASSEMBLY

SIDE
ASSEMBLY

SIDE
ASSEMBLY

21¼

1¾

FRONT
STILE
(I)

NOTE: FRAME
AND PANELS GLUED
TOGETHER BEFORE
CUTTING CORNER JOINTS

NOTE: TO MAKE
CORNER JOINTS,
SEE JOINERY BOX
ON OPPOSITE PAGE

a.
RAILS
(A)(B)
(E)(F)
FACE
VIEW
END
VIEW
¼
¼
PLY

b.
3
BACK
STILE
(G)
¼
2¾
SIDE
STILE
(C)
TOP
VIEW

c.
BACK
ASSEMBLY
GROOVE
AND DADO
FOR INNER
RAIL
RABBET
"HIDES" DADO

d.
SIDE
ASSEMBLY
FRONT
STILE
DADO FOR
INNER RAIL

---

2   **SIDE ASSEMBLY (MAKE TWO)**

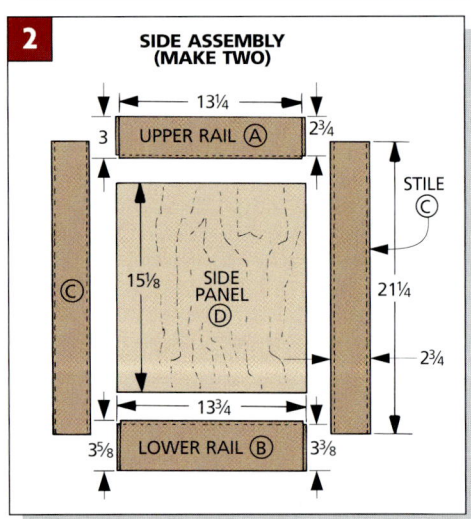

13¼

UPPER RAIL (A)   2¾

3

STILE
(C)

(C)

15⅛   SIDE
PANEL
(D)

21¼

2¾

13¾

3⅝   LOWER RAIL (B)   3⅜

---

3   **BACK ASSEMBLY**

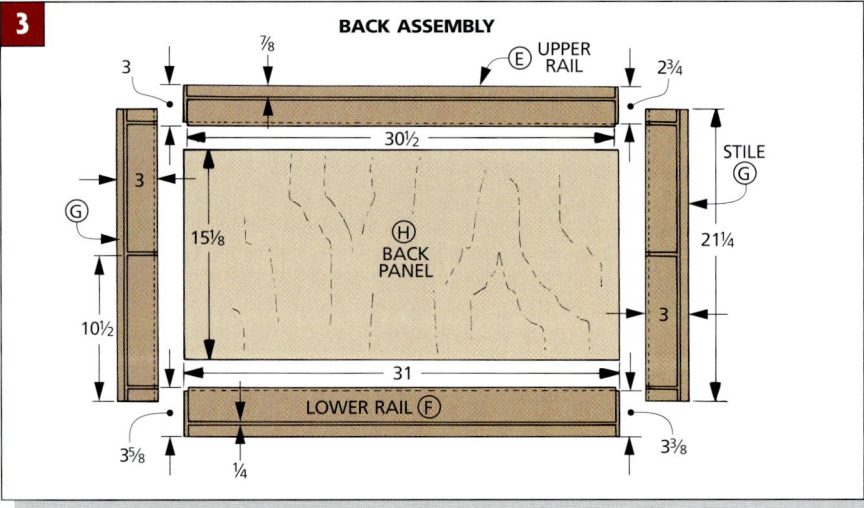

⅞

3

(E) UPPER
RAIL   2¾

30½

3

(G)

15⅛   (H)
BACK
PANEL   STILE
(G)

21¼

10½

31   3

3⅝   LOWER RAIL (F)   3⅜

¼

LOWER CHEST CASE

The upper and lower chests are nearly identical, so you can start with either piece. Since I tend to work from the ground up, I began by building the case of the lower chest.

FRAMES AND PANELS. The case is made up of three frame and panel assemblies glued into a U-shape with two stile pieces added to the front *(Fig. 1)*. For now, I began work on the frame pieces.

The back frame is longer, but otherwise the three frames are quite similar. Both sides and the back have a lower rail, upper rail, and two stiles. The upper rails (A, E) are all the same width (3"), as are the lower rails (B, F) (3⅝"). However, the side stiles (C) are slightly narrower (2¾") than the back stiles (G) *(Figs. 2 and 3)*. That's because the side assemblies fit between the back and the front stiles. So these pieces make the side stiles look wider *(Fig. 6)*. And to make sure all these frame pieces didn't get mixed up, I labeled them carefully.

Once all the frame pieces were cut to size, I mounted a rip blade in the table saw. (My rip blade cuts a flat-bottomed groove.) Then I cut centered grooves ¼" deep on all the pieces to hold the plywood panels *(Fig. 1a)*.

To complete the frames, I cut a stub tenon on each end of all the rails, centered on their thickness, sizing the tenons to fit into the grooves *(Fig. 1a)*.

Already, you're at the point where you can dry-assemble the frames and cut the side panels (D) and back panel (H) to fit in the grooves. Just keep a close eye on the direction of the grain when cutting the back panel — it should run vertically like it does on the sides.

FRONT STILES. After the frame and panel assemblies have been glued together, the two front stiles (I) can be cut to size *(Fig. 1)*. Once that's done, you're ready to cut the corner joints for the case.

CORNER JOINTS. The corners of the case are held together with tongue and groove joints. But there's something a little out of the ordinary about this joint. After cutting the groove in both the front stiles and the stiles on the back assembly, you'll need to cut an extra rabbet on the stiles (see the Joinery box below).

At this point, it's hard to see the purpose for these rabbets. But when some dadoes are cut in the back assembly and front stiles later, these rabbets will prevent the dadoes from being visible on the outside of the case (*Figs. 1c and 1d*).

Note: When cutting the corner joints, make sure that the good face of the plywood will end up on the outside of the case when it's assembled.

RAIL DADOES. After the mating tongues are cut on the side assemblies (*Step 3* in box below), the dadoes I just mentioned can be cut. These dadoes will hold rails that create the drawer openings. Their positions on the front stile and back assembly are the same, so cut them at the same time (*Figs. 4 and 5*). But there are a couple of things I should mention.

First, since the rails create the drawer openings, the center dado on each piece should be positioned carefully so the openings end up the same height. Second, the dadoes are cut $\frac{1}{4}$" deep, but they should be just a smidgen less than the rabbet cut earlier (*Figs. 1c and 1d*). The dadoes shouldn't cut across the shoulder of the rabbet, or you'll see them after the case is assembled.

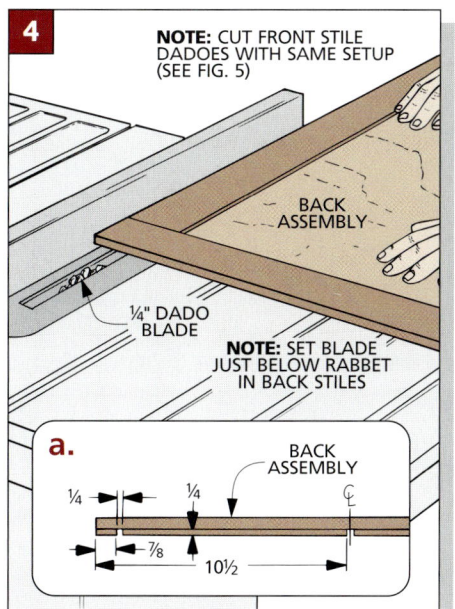

4 NOTE: CUT FRONT STILE DADOES WITH SAME SETUP (SEE FIG. 5)

BACK ASSEMBLY

$\frac{1}{4}$" DADO BLADE

NOTE: SET BLADE JUST BELOW RABBET IN BACK STILES

a. BACK ASSEMBLY

$\frac{1}{4}$ $\frac{1}{4}$ $\frac{7}{8}$ $10\frac{1}{2}$

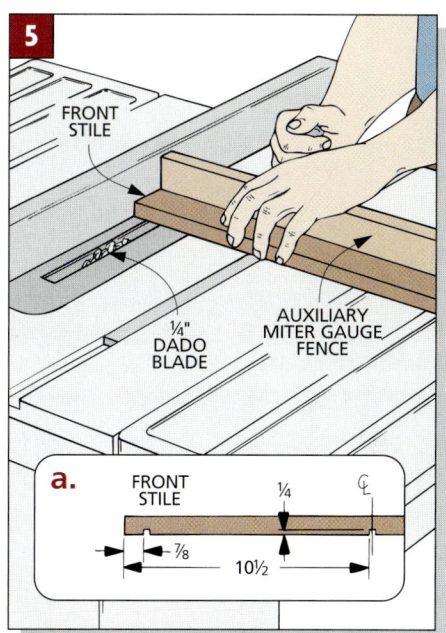

5 FRONT STILE

$\frac{1}{4}$" DADO BLADE

AUXILIARY MITER GAUGE FENCE

a. FRONT STILE

$\frac{1}{4}$ $\frac{7}{8}$ $10\frac{1}{2}$

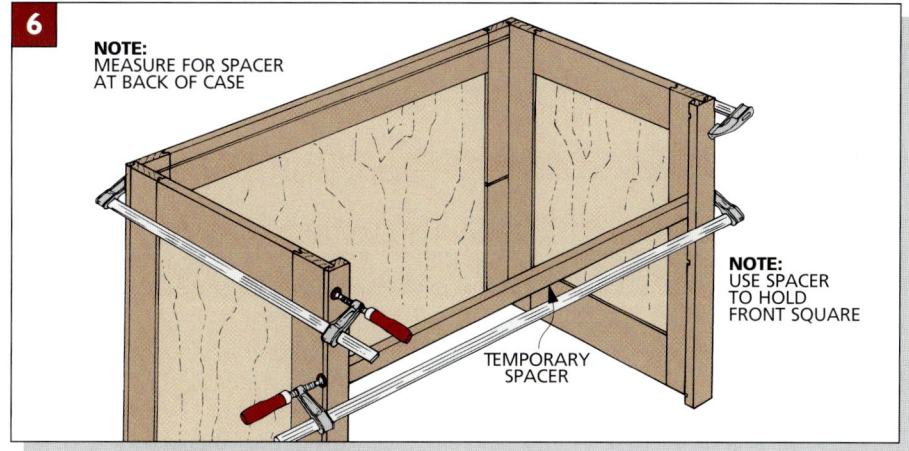

6 NOTE: MEASURE FOR SPACER AT BACK OF CASE

NOTE: USE SPACER TO HOLD FRONT SQUARE

TEMPORARY SPACER

JOINERY . . . . *Rabbetted Tongue & Groove*

Each corner of the case is held together with an ordinary tongue and groove joint. What's out of the ordinary is the "extra" rabbet cut on the grooved pieces (the front and back stiles).

The purpose of this rabbet is to hide some dadoes that are cut later so you won't be able to see them on the outside of the case.

I started by cutting the groove on the inside face of the front and back stiles (*Step 1*).

Then I added some chippers to my dado set, and attached a plywood auxiliary fence to the rip fence (*Step 2*). With the blade partially buried in the auxiliary

fence, the rabbet is cut along the edge of the stiles.

Note that the position of the blade isn't really critical

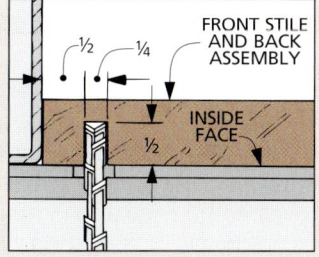

1 First, using a $\frac{1}{4}$"-wide dado blade, cut a groove $\frac{1}{2}$" deep along the back assembly stiles and two front stiles.

FRONT STILE AND BACK ASSEMBLY

$\frac{1}{2}$ $\frac{1}{4}$

INSIDE FACE

$\frac{1}{2}$

(although the height is). You just need to remove material between the groove and the edge of the stile.

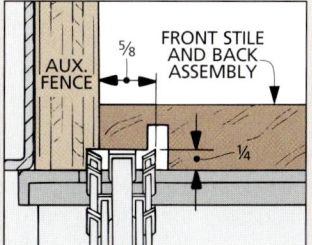

2 Now on the same edges as the grooves, cut a $\frac{1}{4}$"-deep rabbet with a dado blade buried in an auxiliary fence.

AUX. FENCE

$\frac{5}{8}$

FRONT STILE AND BACK ASSEMBLY

$\frac{1}{4}$

And finally, bury the dado blade deeper in the fence and sneak up on the tongues on the side assemblies (*Step 3*).

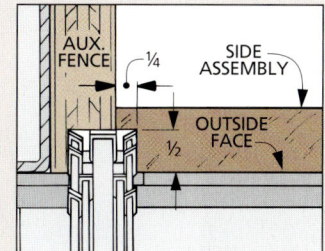

3 Finally, tongues can be cut on the side assemblies to fit into the $\frac{1}{4}$"-wide grooves in the back and front stiles.

AUX. FENCE

$\frac{1}{4}$

SIDE ASSEMBLY

OUTSIDE FACE

$\frac{1}{2}$

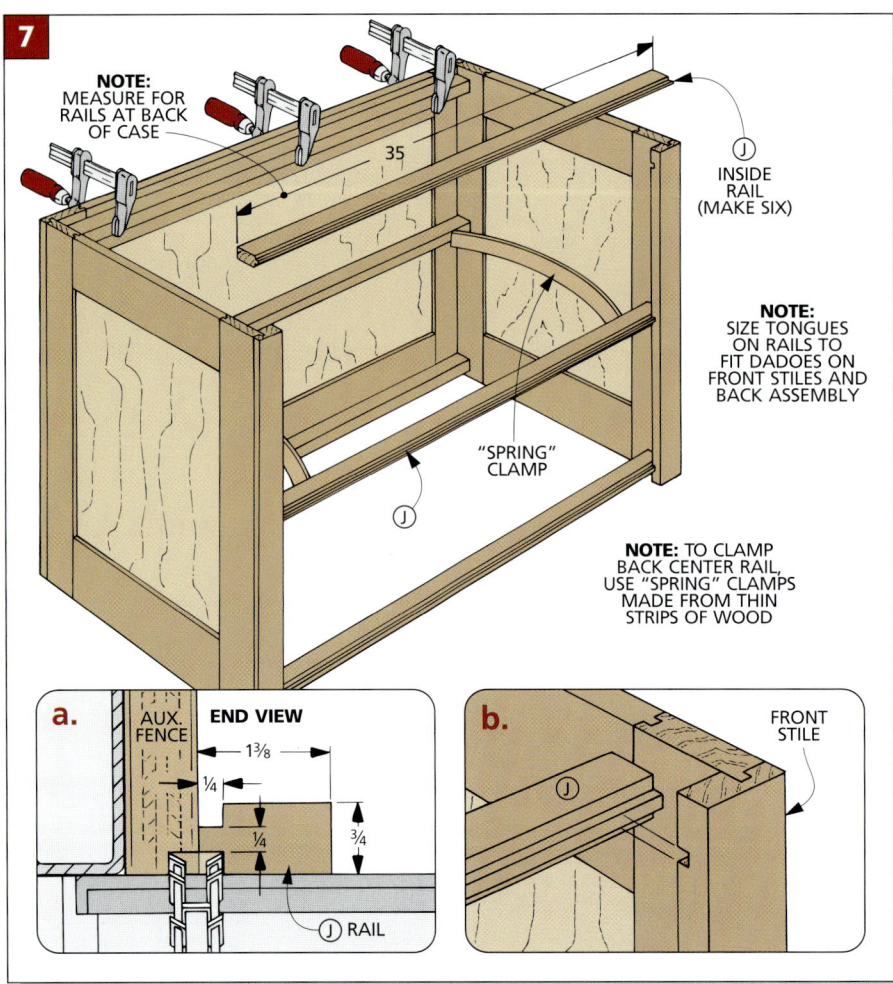

7

NOTE: MEASURE FOR RAILS AT BACK OF CASE

35

J
INSIDE RAIL
(MAKE SIX)

NOTE: SIZE TONGUES ON RAILS TO FIT DADOES ON FRONT STILES AND BACK ASSEMBLY

"SPRING" CLAMP

J

NOTE: TO CLAMP BACK CENTER RAIL, USE "SPRING" CLAMPS MADE FROM THIN STRIPS OF WOOD

a. AUX. FENCE | END VIEW

$1\frac{3}{8}$

$\frac{1}{4}$

$\frac{1}{4}$

$\frac{3}{4}$

J RAIL

b. FRONT STILE

J

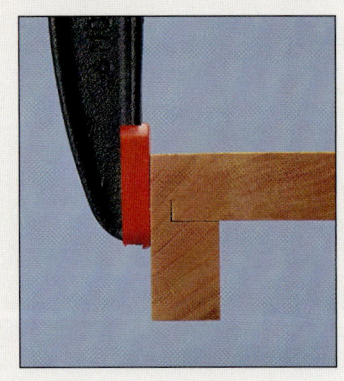
ASSEMBLY

At this point, the case is ready to be glued together (refer to *Fig. 6* on page 115). Though there are front stiles, you're basically dealing with a three-sided assembly, and keeping the corners square can be a trick. My solution was to add a "fourth" side to the assembly by clamping a piece of scrap as a temporary spacer between the sides. To determine the length of the spacer, measure between the grooves in the back assembly.

Even with the spacer, you'll still want to position your clamps carefully (see the Shop Tip at left). And once the clamps are applied, check the diagonal measurements. If they are identical, the cabinet is clamped up square.

INSIDE RAILS. After the glue has dried, six rails can be added to the case *(Fig. 7)*. These strengthen the front of the case and create the drawer openings, and they slide into the dadoes already cut in the case. So after cutting the inside rails (J) to fit snug between the sides (take the

measurement at the back of the case), a tongue can be cut along one edge of each rail *(Fig. 7a)*. The tongue is centered on the thickness of the workpiece.

Gluing the inside rails is pretty straightforward — just clamp them in place. However, you won't be able to get clamps on the middle rail in back. But a couple of thin scraps will work as "spring" clamps. These are wedged between the front and back rails *(Fig. 7)*.

TRIM

With the rails glued inside the case, there are a few steps left to complete the case. First, the front rails need some trim pieces. Then drawer runners and guides need to be added to the case. Finally, I routed some decorative chamfers.

RAIL TRIM. At this point, the inside rails aren't flush with the front of the case. And the tongue on each one is exposed. So I added facing pieces cut to fit between the front stiles *(Fig. 8)*. The wide facing (K) covers the rails and the openings above the top rail and below the bottom rail *(Fig. 8a)*. The narrow facing (L) simply covers the middle rail, just like edging on a piece of plywood.

To attach the facing pieces, just cut grooves to fit over the tongues on the rails *(Fig. 8a)*. Then glue them in place. Note that the groove is cut in the wide facing so the facing is flush with the inside faces of the rails *(Fig. 8a)*.

DRAWER RUNNERS & GUIDES

Now the case is really starting to take shape. For the next step, I added runners and guides for the drawers that "bridge" the rails inside the case *(Figs. 9 and 9b)*. These two-piece assemblies will support the sides of the drawers and guide them in and out of the case.

First, I cut six runners (M) to fit between the rails *(Figs. 9 and 9b)*. Their thickness matches that of the rails.

Then the guides (N) can be planed or resawn $\frac{5}{8}$" thick. (This way, the ones on top will be flush with the top of the case.) The guides are ripped to width so they stick out from behind the front stiles $\frac{1}{32}$" *(Fig. 9c)*. This way, the drawers rub against the guides, and not the stiles, as they are opened and closed.

With the pieces cut to size, each guide is glued to a runner with their outside edges flush and the runner centered on the length of the guide *(Fig. 9a)*. Then

Sanding Chamfers

Because of the angle on the cutting edge of the bit, the end of a routed chamfer isn't symmetrical. The cut on one face extends a little farther than the cut on the adjacent face.

The solution is simple. Just wrap a dowel with some sandpaper. Sand with the grain to even things up.

this assembly is glued and clamped to the rails inside the case.

CHAMFERS. The last thing to do is rout some chamfers. The ones on the outside corners are no big deal. I clamped stop blocks to the case to set the start and stop points (*Fig. 10* and the Shop Tip on page 91). Then I cleaned up the ends (see the Shop Tip above).

There are also stopped chamfers on the insides of the frames, and these require a different approach (*Fig. 11*). Since the plywood panels get in the way of the bearing on a chamfer bit, I used a quick, shop-made edge guide and a 45° V-groove bit. (Refer to the Technique box on page 80 for more about this.)

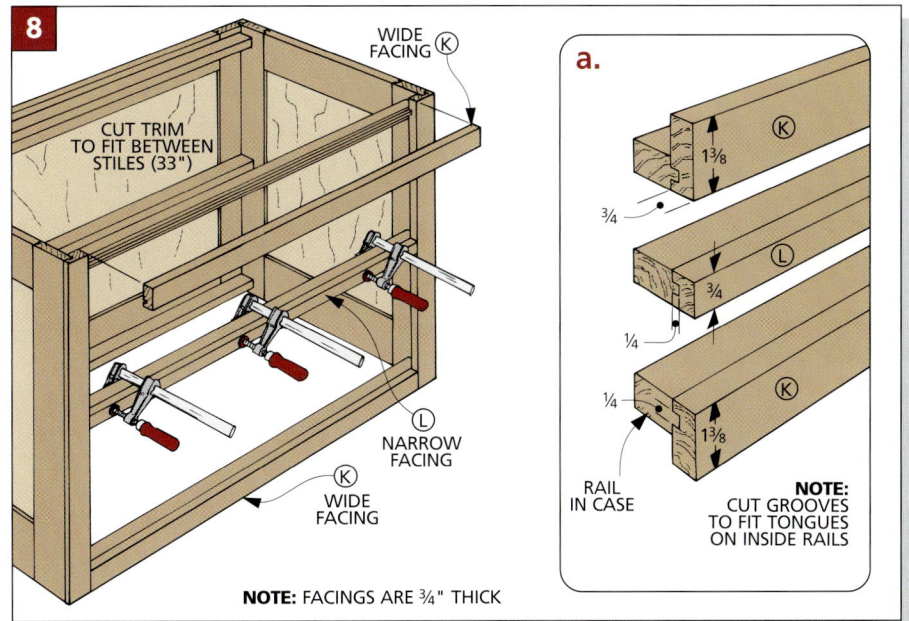

8

CUT TRIM TO FIT BETWEEN STILES (33")

WIDE FACING Ⓚ

NARROW FACING Ⓛ

Ⓚ WIDE FACING

NOTE: FACINGS ARE ¾" THICK

a.

Ⓚ 1⅜

¾

Ⓛ ¾

¼

¼ 1⅜ Ⓚ

RAIL IN CASE

NOTE: CUT GROOVES TO FIT TONGUES ON INSIDE RAILS

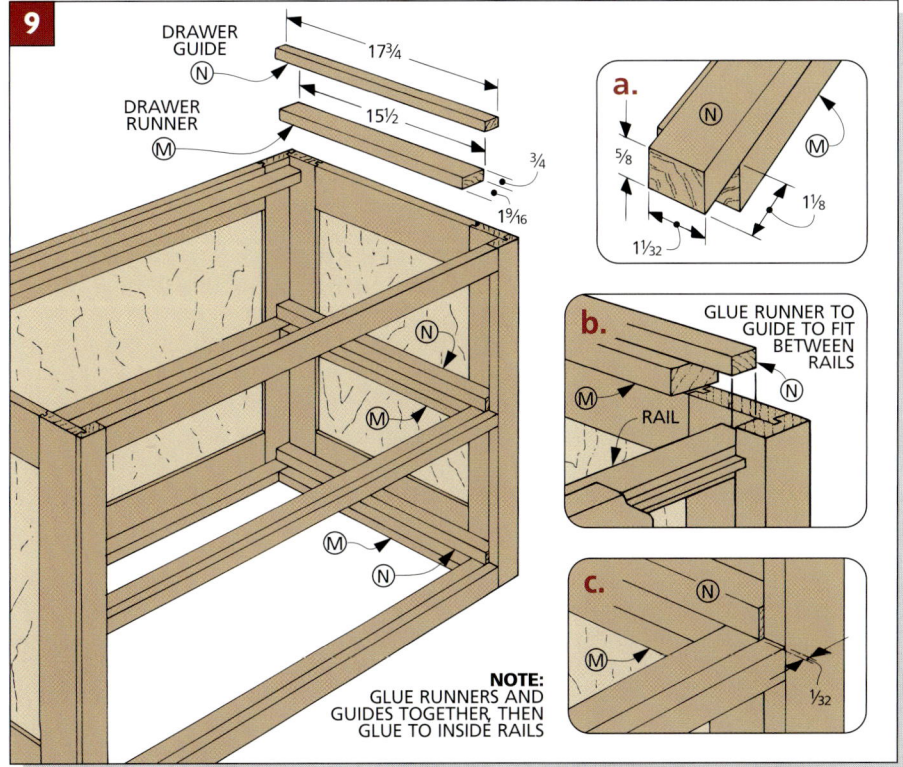

9

DRAWER GUIDE Ⓝ 17¾

DRAWER RUNNER Ⓜ 15½

¾ 1⁹⁄₁₆

Ⓝ Ⓜ Ⓝ Ⓜ Ⓜ Ⓝ

a. Ⓝ Ⓜ 5/8 1⅛ 1½₂

b. GLUE RUNNER TO GUIDE TO FIT BETWEEN RAILS

Ⓜ RAIL Ⓝ

c. Ⓝ Ⓜ ¹⁄₃₂

NOTE: GLUE RUNNERS AND GUIDES TOGETHER, THEN GLUE TO INSIDE RAILS

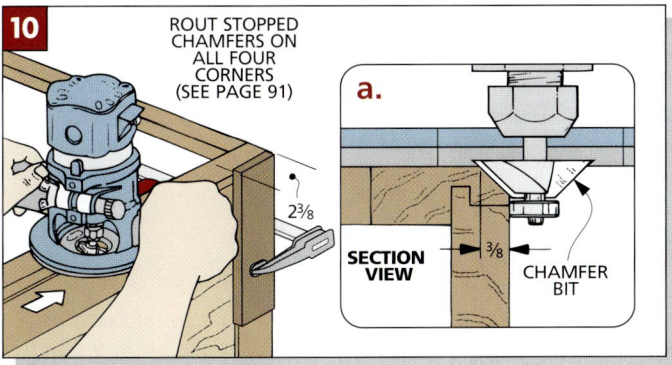

10 ROUT STOPPED CHAMFERS ON ALL FOUR CORNERS (SEE PAGE 91)

2⅜

a.

SECTION VIEW ⅜ CHAMFER BIT

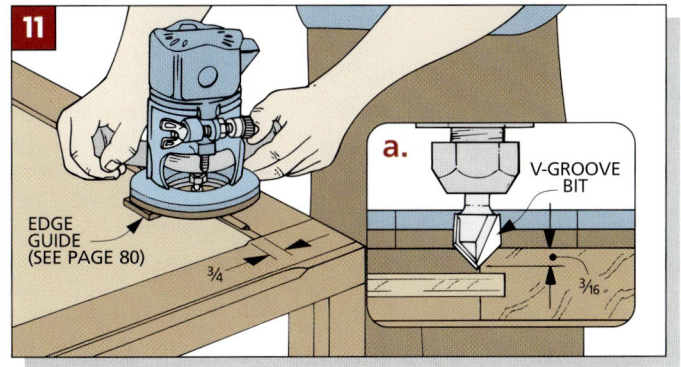

11

EDGE GUIDE (SEE PAGE 80) ¾

a. V-GROOVE BIT ³⁄₁₆

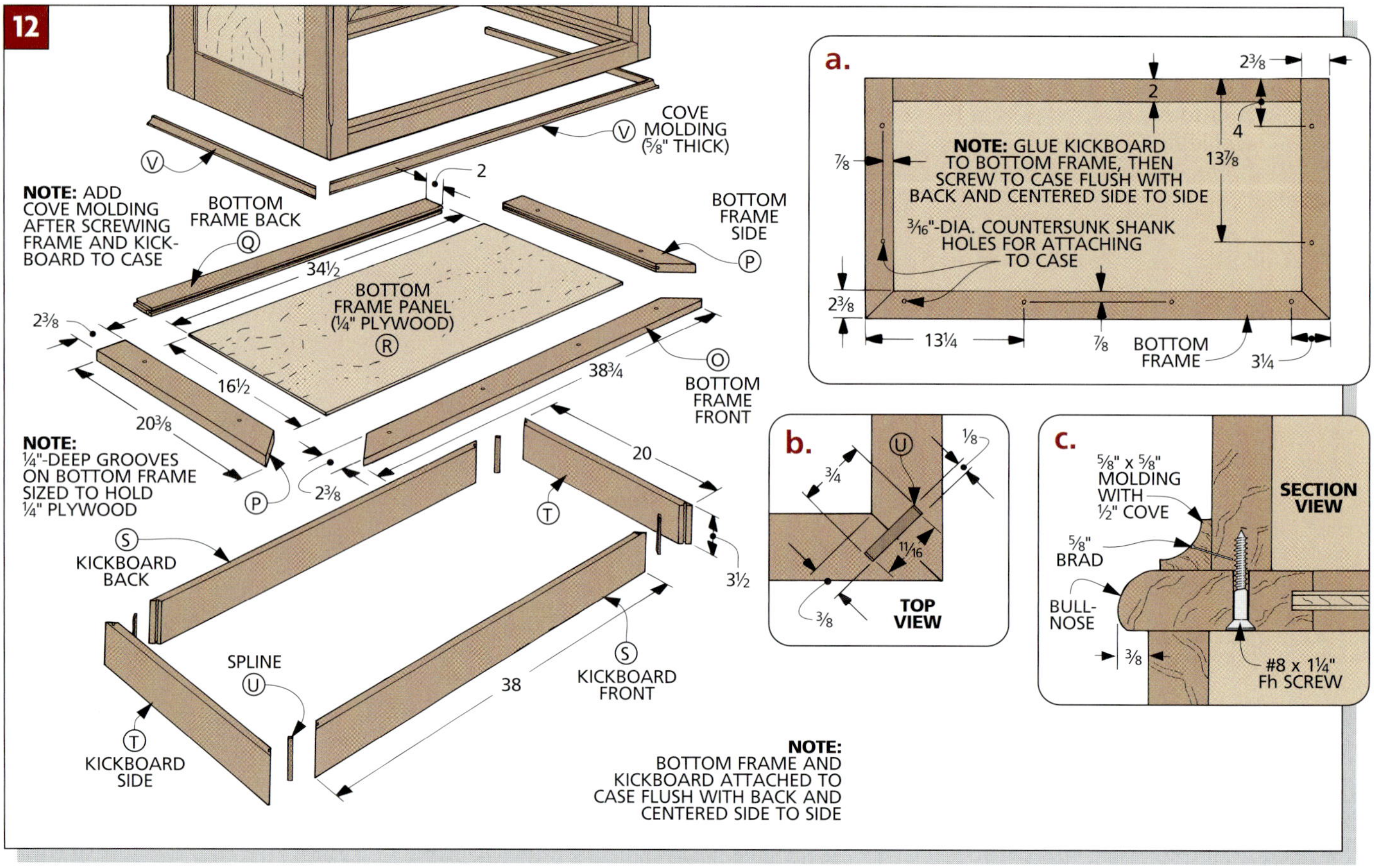

a.

NOTE: ADD COVE MOLDING AFTER SCREWING FRAME AND KICKBOARD TO CASE

COVE MOLDING (⅝" THICK) ⓥ

ⓥ

BOTTOM FRAME BACK ⓠ

2

34½

BOTTOM FRAME PANEL (¼" PLYWOOD) ⓡ

2⅜

16½

20⅜

BOTTOM FRAME SIDE ⓟ

38¾

BOTTOM FRAME FRONT ⓞ

ⓟ 2⅜

NOTE: ¼"-DEEP GROOVES ON BOTTOM FRAME SIZED TO HOLD ¼" PLYWOOD

ⓢ KICKBOARD BACK

20

ⓣ

3½

ⓣ

SPLINE ⓤ

ⓢ KICKBOARD FRONT

38

ⓣ KICKBOARD SIDE

NOTE: BOTTOM FRAME AND KICKBOARD ATTACHED TO CASE FLUSH WITH BACK AND CENTERED SIDE TO SIDE

NOTE: GLUE KICKBOARD TO BOTTOM FRAME, THEN SCREW TO CASE FLUSH WITH BACK AND CENTERED SIDE TO SIDE

2⅜ 2 4 13⅞ ⅞ 2⅜ 13¼ ⅞ BOTTOM FRAME 3¼

3/16"-DIA. COUNTERSUNK SHANK HOLES FOR ATTACHING TO CASE

b. ⓤ ⅛ ¾ 11/16 ⅜ ⅜ TOP VIEW

c. ⅝" x ⅝" MOLDING WITH ½" COVE SECTION VIEW ⅝" BRAD BULL-NOSE ⅜ #8 x 1¼" Fh SCREW

LOWER BASE

With the case complete, I began work on the two-part base it sits on *(Fig. 12)*. The first part is just a frame with a bull-nose profile that surrounds a plywood panel. This assembly sits on a kickboard that is mitered at the corners.

BOTTOM FRAME. To make the bottom frame and panel, cut the frame front (O),

The cove molding and a combination of roundovers on the base provide an easy visual transition from the case to the kickboard base of the cabinet.

sides (P), and back (Q) to finished width but rough length. Then to hold the ¼" plywood panel, a centered groove is cut on each piece. The front corners are mitered so the completed frame will overhang the case 1⅛" at the front and sides. (It's flush with the back.) The back piece is cut to fit between the sides, but remember to allow for the stub tenons that are cut to fit in the grooves *(Fig. 12)*.

After the frame pieces are cut to size, they can be dry-assembled so you can measure for the frame panel (R). Once the panel is cut to size, the frame can be glued up around it.

To complete the bottom frame, I routed a bullnose profile around the sides and front *(Fig. 12c)*. This is done in two steps with two different-sized roundover bits *(Steps 1 and 2 in Fig. 13)*. Note that the ½" roundover is on the top face.

KICKBOARD. Next, I worked on a kickboard assembly that consists of a front (S), back (S), and sides (T) *(Fig. 12)*. These pieces are mitered on both ends. The frame will overhang the kickboard ⅜" on the front and sides *(Fig. 12c)*.

With any frame that has beveled miters, I like to add splines to the corners *(Fig. 12b)*. This both strengthens the frame and makes it easier to assemble.

The kerfs for the splines are cut ⅜" deep into each piece. I cut the splines (U) 11/16" long so they don't prevent the miters from closing tightly *(Fig. 12b)*.

When the kickboard is assembled, you can glue and clamp it to the bottom of the bullnose frame (the face with the ¼" radius) *(Fig. 12c)*.

ASSEMBLY AND COVE MOLDING. Now the frame and kickboard assembly can be screwed to the case, flush with the back and centered from side to side *(Figs. 12a and 12c)*. Then I created the cove

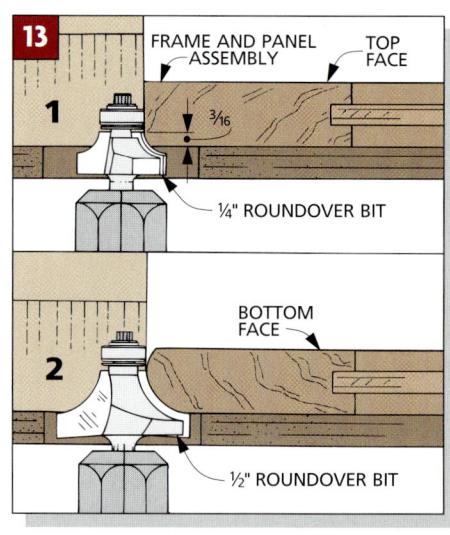

13

FRAME AND PANEL ASSEMBLY TOP FACE

1 3/16 ¼" ROUNDOVER BIT

BOTTOM FACE

2 ½" ROUNDOVER BIT

molding (V) with a $1/2$" cove bit. Start with a $5/8$"-thick blank that's extra wide. Rout the profile, then rip the molding $5/8$" wide. (Refer to *Figs. 15 and 16* on page 93.) This molding is mitered to fit around the front and sides of the case and is glued and nailed in place *(Fig. 12c)*.

DRAWERS

With the base of the lower chest complete, I began work on the two large drawers *(Fig. 14)*. These feature raised panel fronts and half-blind dovetails at the corners. I routed these with a common router jig (see page 56).

Note: Due to the larger size of these drawers, I chose maple for the backs and sides instead of poplar.

CUT TO SIZE. The first thing to do is cut the drawer fronts (W) to size from $3/4$"-thick stock and the backs (X) to the same size from $1/2$" maple *(Fig. 14)*. These pieces are sized so that when the assembled drawers are placed into the case, there will be a $1/16$" gap at the top and bottom and on each side. Then the sides (Y) can be cut from $1/2$" maple.

After routing the half-blind dovetails on each piece, I cut a groove in each to hold a bottom (Z). Don't worry too much about the exact dimensions here. The important thing with this groove is that it's sized to hold $1/4$" plywood and is centered on the bottom tail on the side pieces.

RAISED PANELS. Before assembling the drawers, there's still a couple of things to do. First, I cut the raised panels on all the fronts. This can be done on the table saw, with the blade tilted 12° and an auxiliary fence added to support the fronts *(Fig. 14b)*. Or you can cut them with a straight bit in the router table. (See the Technique article on page 96 for more.)

Second, two notches are cut in each back piece so they will fit over the drawer stops that will be added later.

PULLS. After assembling the drawers, I added the bail-style pulls *(Fig. 14a)*. My first inclination was to center the mounting holes top to bottom. But looks are deceiving here. The drawer front looks better if the holes are drilled above center *(Fig. 14)*. Plus, since the pulls are mounted with a threaded post and a nut, I drilled a counterbore inside the drawer to hide the nut and post. (I also trimmed the length of the post slightly.)

GLIDE STRIPS. Now all that's left are some little details to add to the case that will make the drawer easier to open and

close. First, I added a nylon glide strip to each runner *(Fig. 15)*. This makes the drawer slide more smoothly, but it also "lifts" the drawer off the rail and facing, eliminating wear.

Next, I added two $1/4$"-thick stops (AA) to the rails below the drawers *(Fig. 15)*. They stop the drawers flush with the front of the case. And since there will be

twelve stops (including the upper chest), I made a rabbeted spacer to position them. The shoulder of the spacer rests on top of the rail and matches the thickness at the edge of the drawer front *(Fig. 15a)*.

Finally, I screwed a turnbutton to the rails that are above the drawers so you can't accidentally pull the drawers all the way out (refer to *Fig. 22b* on page 125).

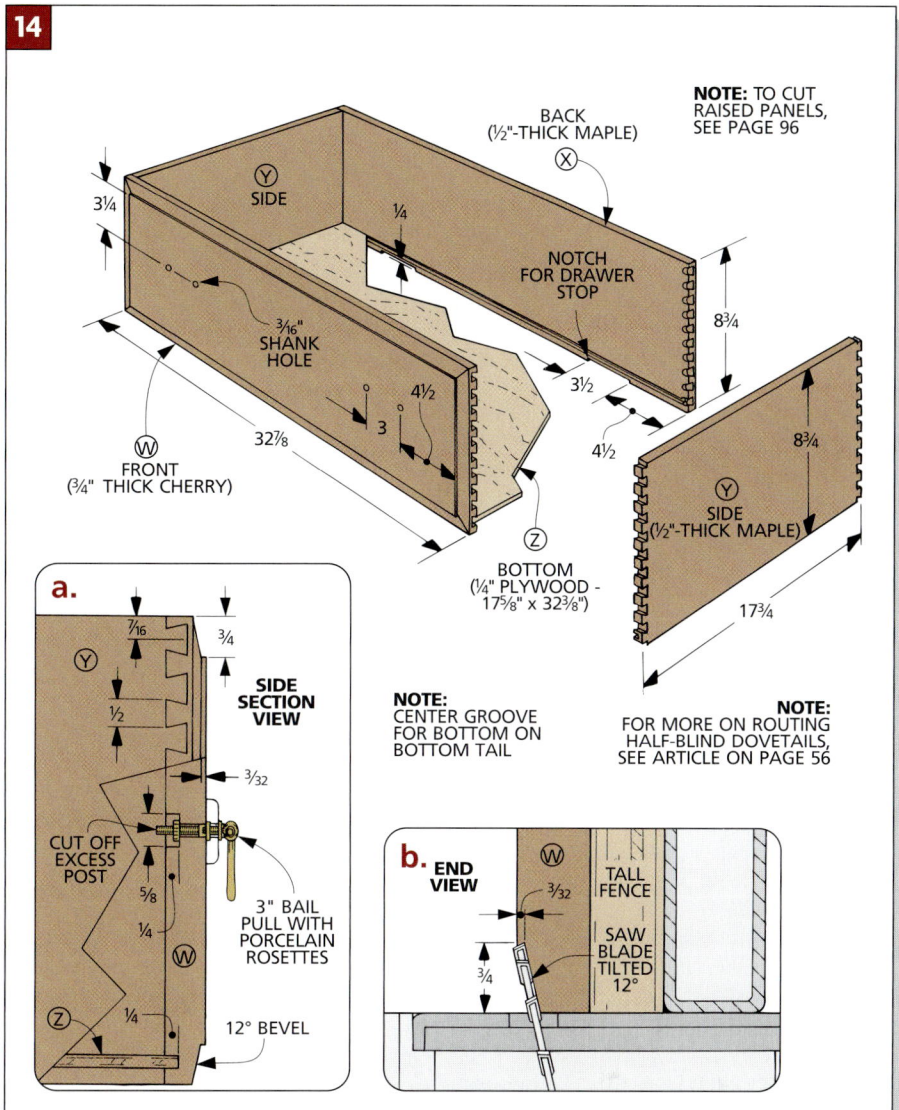

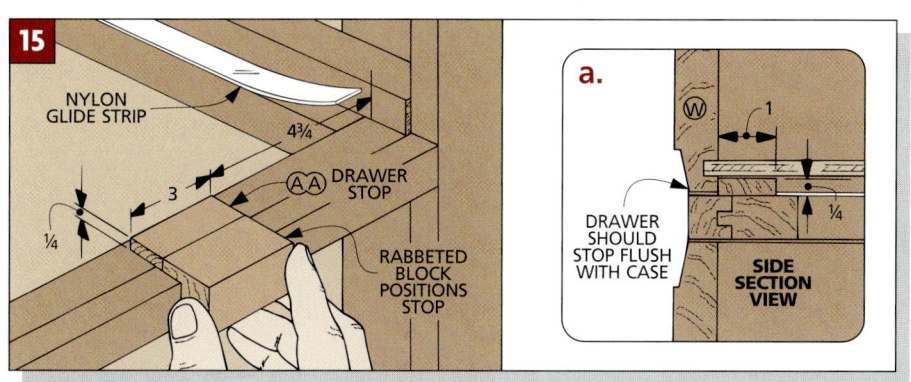

DESIGNER'S NOTEBOOK

Turn the lower cabinet into a separate piece of furniture. All you need to do is add a solid-wood top.

CONSTRUCTION NOTES:

■ To add a solid-wood top to the cabinet, just glue up a $3/4$"-thick panel and cut it to the same dimensions as the frame and panel top would have been ($20^3/8$" x $38^3/4$") (see *Fig. 16* below).

■ Then rout the bullnose profile on the front and sides of the panel. (The $1/2$" roundover is on the bottom.) Do the ends first so that any chipout at the corners can be cleaned up when the front is routed.

■ Before screwing the panel in place, drill oversize shank holes in the spacers to allow the panel to expand and contract.

SOLID-WOOD TOP

MATERIALS LIST

NEW PART

GG Top Panel (1) $3/4$ x $20^3/8$ - $38^3/4$

TOP FRAME

All that's left is to add the top to the case *(Fig. 16)*. This frame and panel assembly is nearly identical to the bottom one you built earlier. But this time, the pieces are wider so you can attach the upper and lower chests with threaded inserts and machine screws later. And the profile on the edge is oriented differently — here the $1/2$" roundover will end up on the bottom of the frame.

After the top frame front (BB), sides (CC), back (DD), and panel (EE) have been glued together, it can be screwed to the top of the case, and the cove molding can be added. But first, to fill in the gaps at the front and back, I added a couple of $5/8$"-thick spacers (FF) *(Fig. 16b)*.

OPTIONAL TOP. If you're just building the lower chest, you'll want to make a solid-wood top instead of the frame and panel assembly. See the Designer's Notebook above.

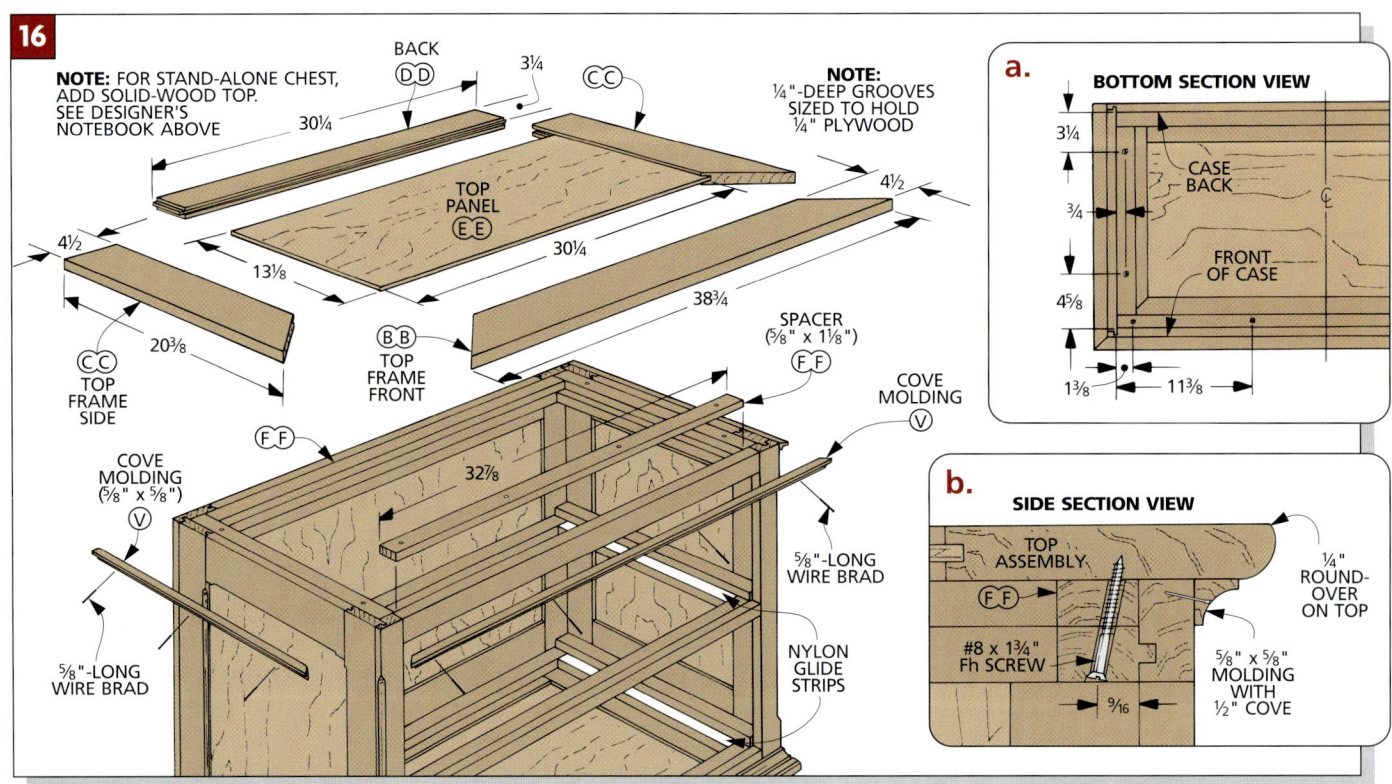

UPPER CHEST

It doesn't take long to see that the upper unit is nearly identical to the lower one (see photo). The case construction is the same, and the drawers are too. There are a few notable differences, though.

The uppermost opening is divided to make room for two narrow drawers; there's no kickboard (unless you're building just this unit, see the Designer's Notebook on page 125); and the top is a solid-wood panel.

EXPLODED VIEW

OVERALL DIMENSIONS:
36½W x 19¼D x 34⅛H
(UPPER CHEST ONLY)

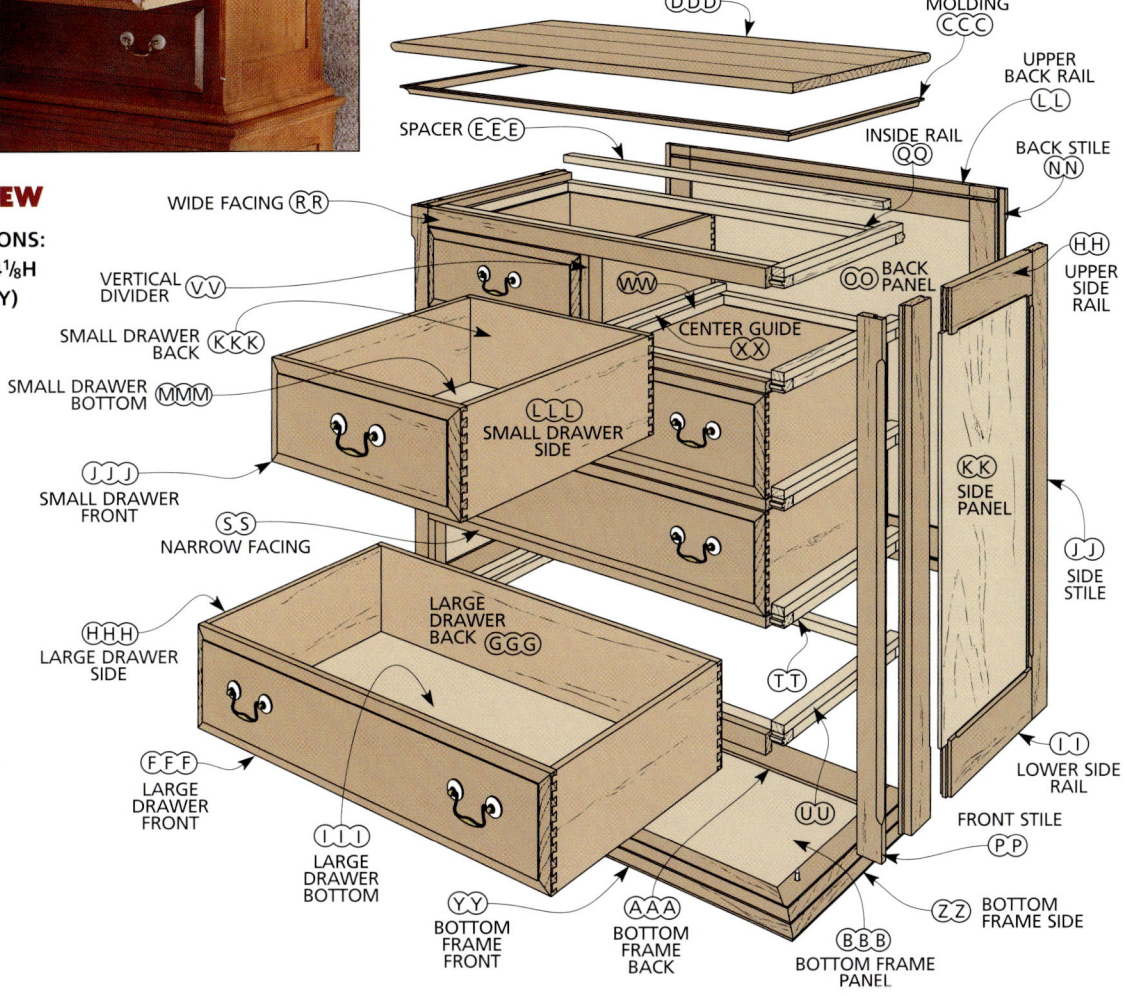

TOP PANEL DDD
COVE MOLDING CCC
SPACER EEE
UPPER BACK RAIL LL
INSIDE RAIL QQ
BACK STILE NN
WIDE FACING RR
HH UPPER SIDE RAIL
VERTICAL DIVIDER VV
WWW
BACK PANEL OO
SMALL DRAWER BACK KKK
CENTER GUIDE XX
SMALL DRAWER BOTTOM MMM
LLL SMALL DRAWER SIDE
KK SIDE PANEL
JJJ
SMALL DRAWER FRONT
JJ SIDE STILE
SS
NARROW FACING
HHH
LARGE DRAWER SIDE
LARGE DRAWER BACK GGG
TT
FFF
LARGE DRAWER FRONT
III LARGE DRAWER BOTTOM
UU
LOWER SIDE RAIL II
FRONT STILE PP
ZZ BOTTOM FRAME SIDE
YY BOTTOM FRAME FRONT
AAA BOTTOM FRAME BACK
BBB BOTTOM FRAME PANEL

MATERIALS LIST

	WOOD (For Upper Chest)							
HH	Upr. Side Rails (2)	¾ x 3 - 12⅝	**VV**	Vertical Divider (1)	¾ x 1½ - 6¼	**KKK**	Sm. Dwr. Backs (2)	½ x 6⅛ - 14⅞
II	Lwr. Side Rails (2)	¾ x 3⅝ - 12⅝	**WW**	Ctr. Dwr. Runner (1)	¾ x 1⅞ - 14⅜	**LLL**	Sm. Dwr. Sides (4)	½ x 6⅛ - 16¾
JJ	Side Stiles (4)	¾ x 2¾ - 32⅝	**XX**	Ctr. Dwr. Guide (1)	¾ x 1³⁄₁₆ - 15⅞	**MMM**	Sm. Dwr. Btms. (2)	¼ ply - 16⅝ x 14⅜
KK	Side Panels (2)	¼ ply - 12⅝ x 26½	**YY**	Btm. Frame Fr. (1)	¾ x 3⅜ - 36½			
LL	Upr. Back Rail (1)	¾ x 3 - 28¾	**ZZ**	Btm. Frame Sds. (2)	¾ x 3⅜ - 19¼	**NNN**	Drawer Stops (8)	¼ x 1 - 3
MM	Lwr. Back Rail (1)	¾ x 3⅝ - 28¾	**AAA**	Btm. Frame Bk. (1)	¾ x 3⅜ - 30¼			
NN	Back Stiles (2)	¾ x 3 - 32⅝	**BBB**	Btm. Frame Pnl. (1)	¼ ply - 13 x 30¼	**HARDWARE SUPPLIES**		
OO	Back Panel (1)	¼ ply - 28¾ x 26½	**CCC**	Cove Molding	⅝ x ⅝ - 150 ln. in.	(8) No. 8 x 1¾" Fh woodscrews		
PP	Front Stiles (2)	¾ x 1¾ - 32⅝	**DDD**	Top Panel (1)	¾ x 19¼ - 36½	(8) No. 8 x 1¼" Fh woodscrews		
QQ	Inside Rails (10)	¾ x 1⅜ - 32¾	**EEE**	Spacers (2)	⅝ x 1⅛ - 30⅝	(20) ⅝" x 19 gauge wire brads		
RR	Wide Facings (2)	¾ x 1⅜ - 30¾	**FFF**	Lg. Dwr. Fronts (3)	¾ x 7 - 30⅝	(8) 3" ceramic rosette brass bail pulls		
SS	Narrow Facings (3)	¾ x ¾ - 30¾	**GGG**	Lg. Dwr. Backs (3)	½ x 7 - 30⅝	(5) Plastic turnbuttons w/ screws		
TT	Dwr. Runners (10)	¾ x 1⁹⁄₁₆ - 14⅜	**HHH**	Lg. Dwr. Sides (6)	½ x 7 - 16¾	(15 feet) Nylon glide strip		
UU	Dwr. Guides (10)	⅝ x 1¹¹⁄₃₂ - 16⅝	**III**	Lg. Dwr. Btms. (3)	¼ ply - 16⅝ x 30⅛	(4) ¼"-20 x 1¼" Rh machine screws		
			JJJ	Sm. Dwr. Fronts (2)	¾ x 6⅛ - 14⅞	(4) ¼"-20 brass threaded inserts		

Once you've got the lower chest completed, construction of the upper chest will seem familiar.

SIDE AND BACK PANELS. As with the lower unit, I began by building the side and back panels *(Fig. 17)*. After cutting the side and back rails (HH, II, LL, MM) and stiles (JJ, NN) to size, I cut the grooves and stub tenons that would hold the side and back panels (KK, OO). Then the three frame and panel assemblies can be glued together.

At this point, the front stiles (PP) can be cut to size, and the tongue and groove joints (with the extra rabbet on the front stile and back assembly) can be cut for the corners of the case *(Fig. 17b* and the Joinery box on page 115).

Now before you can glue up the case, there are a few dadoes to cut. These will hold the inner rails, so you'll need to cut five dadoes in the front stiles and back assembly *(Figs. 17 and 17a)*. Again, position the dadoes carefully. The bottom three drawer openings should end up the same — you don't want to have to custom-fit each drawer.

When you've got all the dadoes cut, the case can be assembled. This chest is slightly taller than the lower unit, but the assembly is exactly the same. The number of pieces is the same, and I used a temporary spacer at the front to hold the

case square just like I did before (refer to *Fig. 6* on page 115).

INNER RAILS AND FACING. After the glue is dry, cut ten inside rails (QQ) to fit between the sides of the case *(Fig. 18)*. Tongues are cut on these rails to fit into

the dadoes in the front and back of the case, and then the rails can be glued in place. Here again, you'll need to use "spring" clamps (thin strips of wood) to hold the middle back rails in place (refer to *Fig. 7* on page 116).

CUTTING DIAGRAM
(UPPER CHEST)

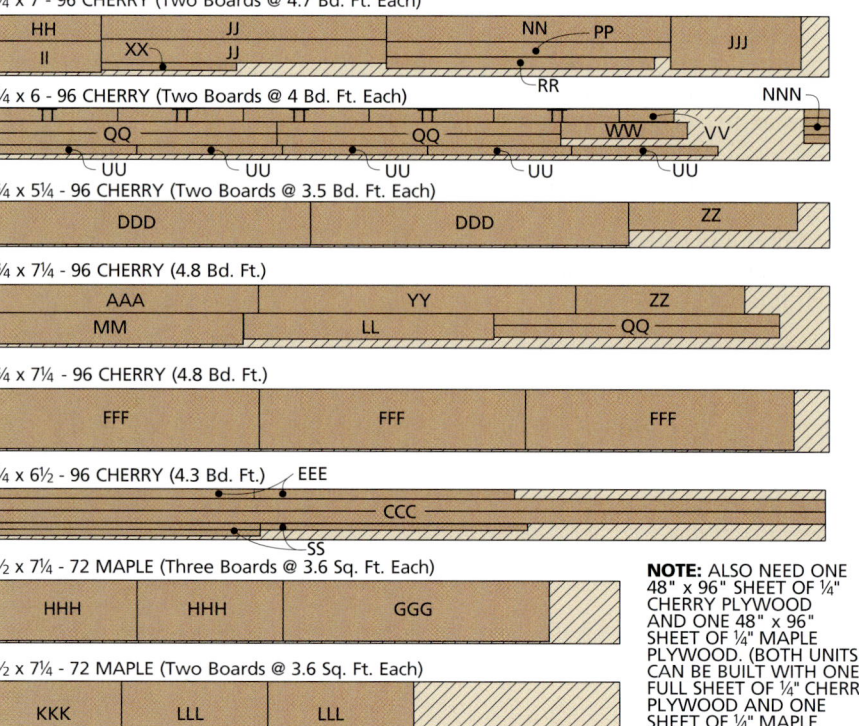

NOTE: ALSO NEED ONE 48" x 96" SHEET OF ¼" CHERRY PLYWOOD AND ONE 48" x 96" SHEET OF ¼" MAPLE PLYWOOD. (BOTH UNITS CAN BE BUILT WITH ONE FULL SHEET OF ¼" CHERRY PLYWOOD AND ONE SHEET OF ¼" MAPLE PLYWOOD)

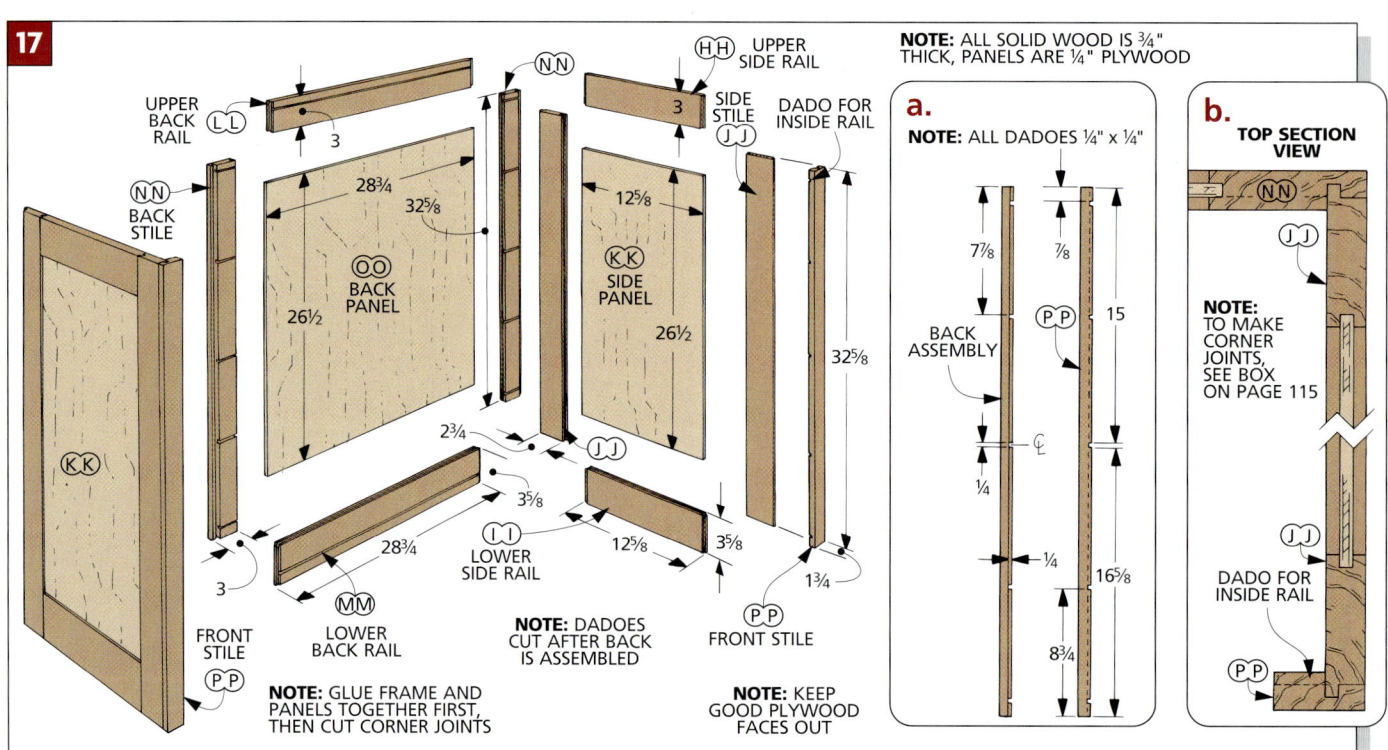

Next, the wide facing (RR) and narrow facing (SS) can be cut to size. Then you can cut the grooves that fit over the tongues on the rails *(Figs. 18 and 18a)*.

After the facing has been glued in place, the chamfers on the inside and outside of the case can be routed. These are identical to those on the lower case, and I used the same jig for routing around the insides of the frames (see page 80).

With the chamfers routed, it's time to work on the pieces inside the case that support and guide the drawers. As on the lower chest, the ten drawer runners (TT) and drawer guides (UU) will end up glued together as a single assembly, with the runners fitting between the rails and the guides resting on top of the rails *(Figs. 18b and 18c)*. But remember — the important thing is that when these assemblies are added to the case, the guides need to stick out past the front stiles $1/32$" so the drawers don't rub against the stiles *(Figs. 18c and 18d)*.

DRAWER DIVIDER. At this point, there are a couple of "new" pieces to add to the case. To divide the top opening in half for the two narrow drawers, a vertical divider along with an additional drawer guide and runner assembly need to be added to the case *(Figs. 19 and 20)*.

The vertical divider (VV) is simply a $3/4$"-thick piece of stock that's cut to fit between the upper two rails and facing pieces *(Fig. 19)*. As I was measuring for the divider, I noticed a slight bow in one of the rails. This isn't uncommon since the case is fairly wide. And the solution is simple. Measure the height between the rails at the side of the case, where there is no chance of bowing. Then after cutting the divider to this length, screw it in place, centered side to side and flush with the front edge *(Fig. 19a)*. This eliminates the bow in the rail.

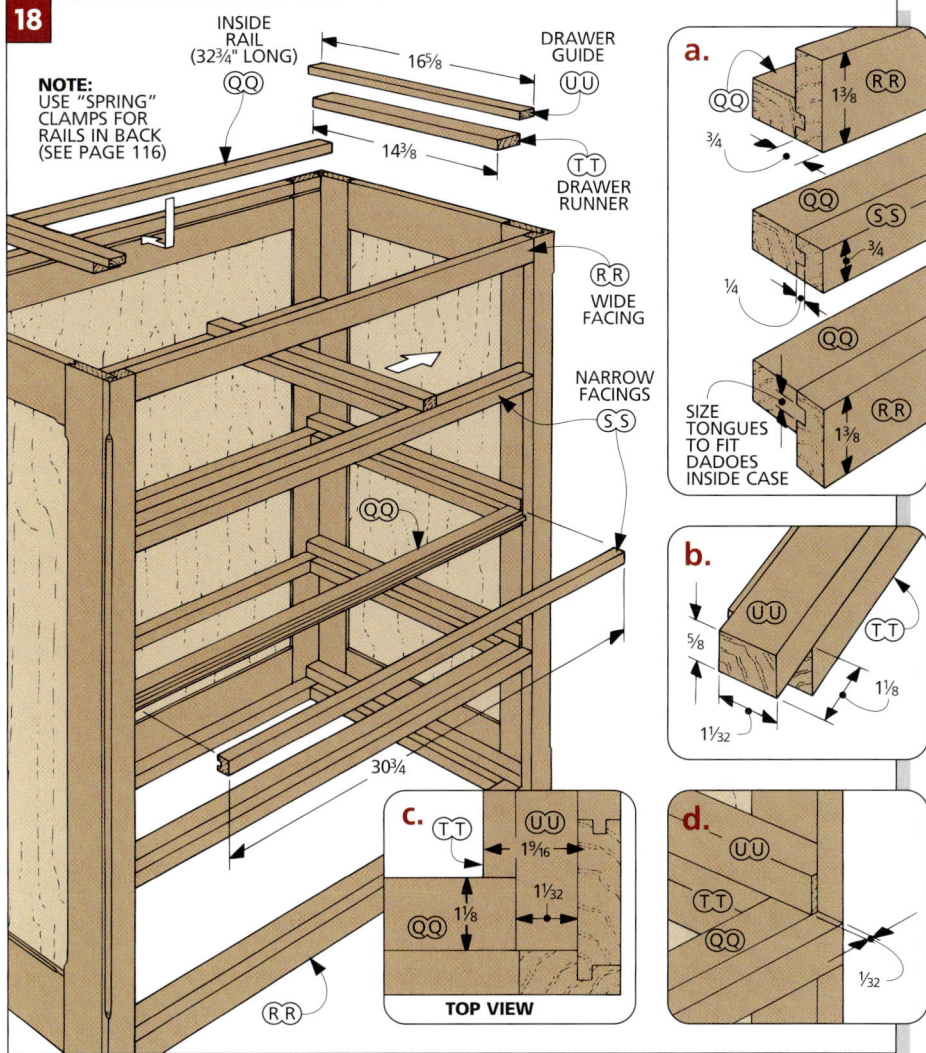

CENTER RUNNER AND GUIDE. With the divider in place, the last pieces to add are the center drawer runner (WW) and center drawer guide (XX) *(Fig. 20)*. These do the same thing as the other runner and guide assemblies. But here, the pieces extend past the center divider on both sides, so one runner and guide will work to support the inside edge of both drawers *(Fig. 20a)*. (When glued in place, the guide should stand proud of the divider $1/32$" on each side.) Also, so that the assembly will fit behind the drawer divider, the runner sets back from the end of the guide only $3/8$" in the front *(Figs. 19a and 20)*.

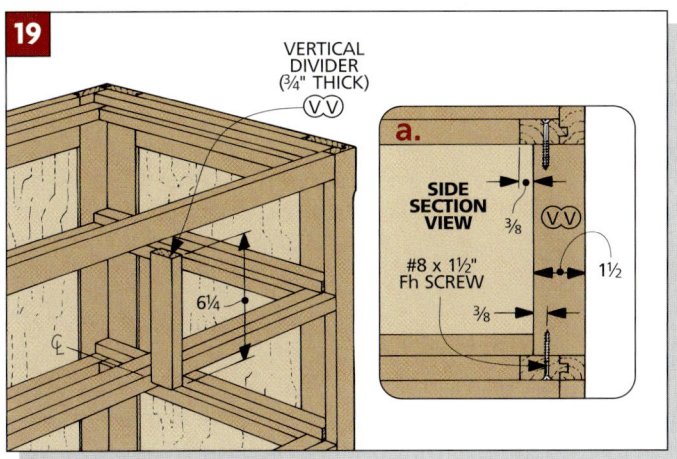

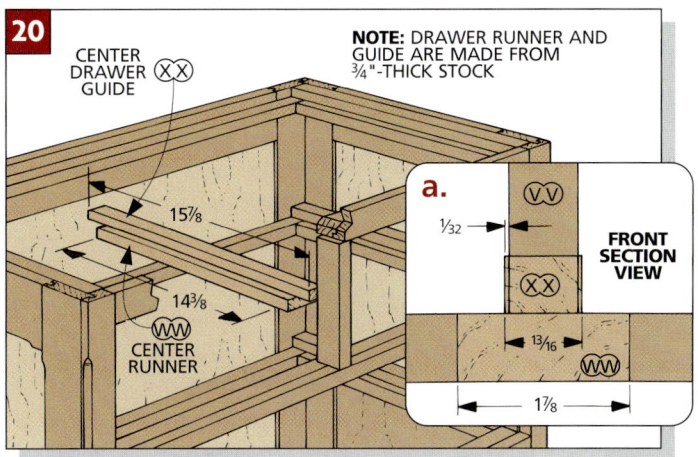

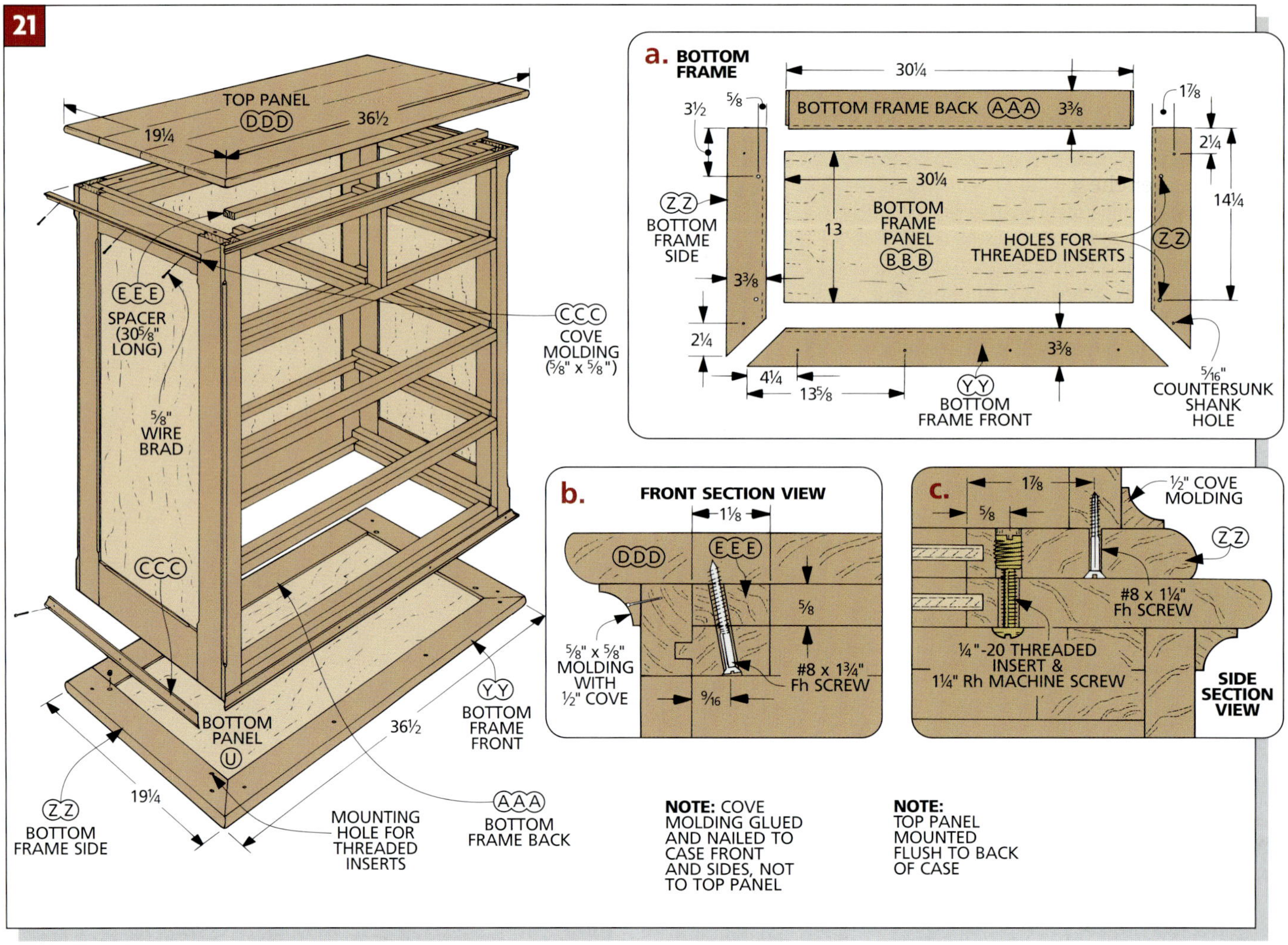

21
TOP PANEL
DDD
19¼
36½
EEE
SPACER
(30⅝" LONG)
⅝" WIRE BRAD
CCC
COVE MOLDING
(⅝" x ⅝")
BOTTOM PANEL
U
YY
BOTTOM FRAME FRONT
36½
19¼
ZZ
BOTTOM FRAME SIDE
MOUNTING HOLE FOR THREADED INSERTS
AAA
BOTTOM FRAME BACK
a. BOTTOM FRAME
30¼
BOTTOM FRAME BACK AAA
3⅜
3½
⅝
1⅞
2¼
14¼
ZZ
BOTTOM FRAME SIDE
30¼
13
BOTTOM FRAME PANEL
BBB
HOLES FOR THREADED INSERTS
ZZ
3⅜
2¼
3⅜
4¼
13⅝
YY
BOTTOM FRAME FRONT
5⁄16" COUNTERSUNK SHANK HOLE
b. FRONT SECTION VIEW
1⅛
DDD
EEE
⅝
⅝" x ⅝" MOLDING WITH ½" COVE
#8 x 1¾" Fh SCREW
9⁄16
c.
1⅞
⅝
½" COVE MOLDING
ZZ
#8 x 1¼" Fh SCREW
¼"-20 THREADED INSERT & 1¼" Rh MACHINE SCREW
SIDE SECTION VIEW
NOTE: COVE MOLDING GLUED AND NAILED TO CASE FRONT AND SIDES, NOT TO TOP PANEL
NOTE: TOP PANEL MOUNTED FLUSH TO BACK OF CASE

TECHNIQUE . . . . *Installing Inserts*

When it was time to fasten together the upper and lower units of the Chest-on-Chest, I had a few threaded inserts to install. I made a threaded insert tool to help with this (see drawing).

The tool is just a block of hardwood with a notch cut in one corner (see drawing). A counterbored hole is drilled through the notch to hold a hex-head bolt and a 1"-long nylon bushing. The through hole is sized to hold the bolt. The counterbore is drilled 1¼" deep to accept the bushing that holds the bolt straight while you tighten it down.

Finally, I added a spring between the bushing and the nut and washer that are tightened against the insert. It provides just enough downward pressure to help the threads on the outside of the insert to begin cutting into the wood.

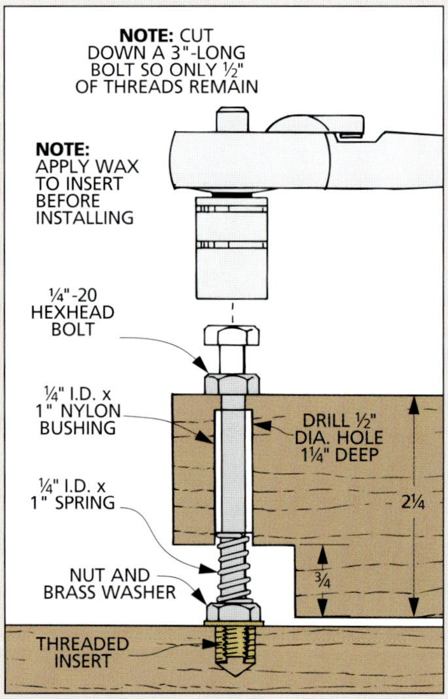

NOTE: CUT DOWN A 3"-LONG BOLT SO ONLY ½" OF THREADS REMAIN
NOTE: APPLY WAX TO INSERT BEFORE INSTALLING
¼"-20 HEXHEAD BOLT
¼" I.D. x 1" NYLON BUSHING
DRILL ½" DIA. HOLE 1¼" DEEP
¼" I.D. x 1" SPRING
2¼
¾
NUT AND BRASS WASHER
THREADED INSERT

BASE & TOP

You're on the home stretch now. To complete the upper chest, all that's left is to add a base frame, a solid-wood top panel, and some drawers.

BOTTOM FRAME. Like the lower chest, I worked on the base first. But where the lower base has a frame and panel *and* a kickboard, the base here is just a frame with a front (YY), sides (ZZ), back (AAA), and panel (BBB) *(Figs. 21 and 21a)*. The front corners are mitered, the back has stub tenons that fit the grooves for the panel, and the bullnose profile is routed on both the front and sides. (The ½" roundover is on top.) And after screwing the frame to the case, some ⅝"-thick cove molding (CCC) can be glued and nailed to the case *(Fig. 21c)*.

Note: If you're building the upper chest by itself, you'll need to build a kickboard for it. (See the Designer's Notebook on the next page.)

TOP. The top of this chest is solid wood. So rather than make a frame and panel, I glued up a ¾"-thick top panel (DDD) and cut it to finished size *(Fig. 21)*.

DESIGNER'S NOTEBOOK

With a kickboard base, the upper chest stands on its own.

CONSTRUCTION NOTES:

■ The upper chest can also be built as a stand-alone piece of furniture. (It'll end up $37\frac{5}{8}$" tall.) All you need to do is build a kickboard like the one for the lower chest. The only difference is that this kickboard is sized so the bottom frame overhangs it $1\frac{1}{2}$" on the front and sides (see drawing and detail 'a'). The kickboard is flush with the back of the bottom frame.

■ Adding splines to the corners will make the assembly easier and stronger (refer to *Fig. 12b* on page 118).
■ To attach the kickboard, first glue it to the bottom frame and then screw and glue the assembly to the case (detail 'a').

KICKBOARD BASE

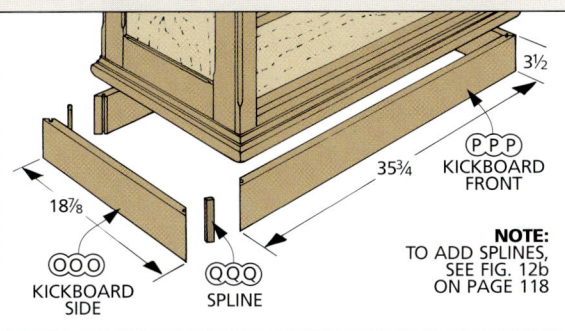

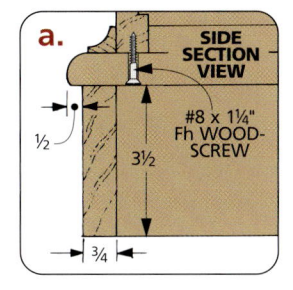

NOTE: TO ADD SPLINES, SEE FIG. 12b ON PAGE 118

MATERIALS LIST		
NEW PARTS		
OOO Kickbd. Sides (2)	$\frac{3}{4}$ x $3\frac{1}{2}$ - $18\frac{7}{8}$	
PPP Kickbd. Fr./Bk. (2)	$\frac{3}{4}$ x $3\frac{1}{2}$ - $35\frac{3}{4}$	
QQQ Splines (4)	$\frac{1}{8}$ hdbd. - $\frac{1}{2}$ x $3\frac{1}{2}$	

Like the top on the lower chest, this panel still gets the bullnose roundover (with the $\frac{1}{2}$" roundover on the bottom this time). And when attaching it to the case, it requires the same spacers (EEE). But this time, the shank holes should be oversized so the panel can expand and contract *(Fig. 21b)*. This expansion and contraction also means you don't want to glue or nail the cove molding to the top panel — only to the sides of the case.

DRAWERS

Finally, there are a few drawers to build *(Fig. 22)*. You'll need three large and two narrow drawers. The large and small drawer fronts (FFF, JJJ) are $\frac{3}{4}$" thick. The backs (GGG, KKK) and sides (HHH, LLL) are $\frac{1}{2}$"-thick maple, and the bottoms (III, MMM) are $\frac{1}{4}$" plywood.

As before, I joined the drawers with half-blind dovetails routed with a dovetail jig (see page 56) and cut the raised panels on the table saw (see page 96). And inside the case, I added a nylon glide strip, $\frac{1}{4}$"-thick drawer stops (NNN), and plastic turnbuttons *(Figs. 22a and 22b)*. But note that on the small drawers, there's only one stop centered in the opening and one notch cut on the drawer back.

ATTACH UPPER AND LOWER CHESTS. Finally, you can attach the upper and lower chests. To secure them, I mounted

four threaded inserts into the bottom of the upper chest *(Figs. 21a and 21c)*.

To get a threaded insert in straight can be a real trick, and I typically use a nut and a section of a bolt chucked into a drill press, turning the chuck by hand. But here, instead of balancing the frame on the drill press, I used a shop-made hand tool to get the insert in straight (see page 124). Then I drilled the mounting holes in the lower chest and attached the two with machine screws *(Fig. 21c)*. ■

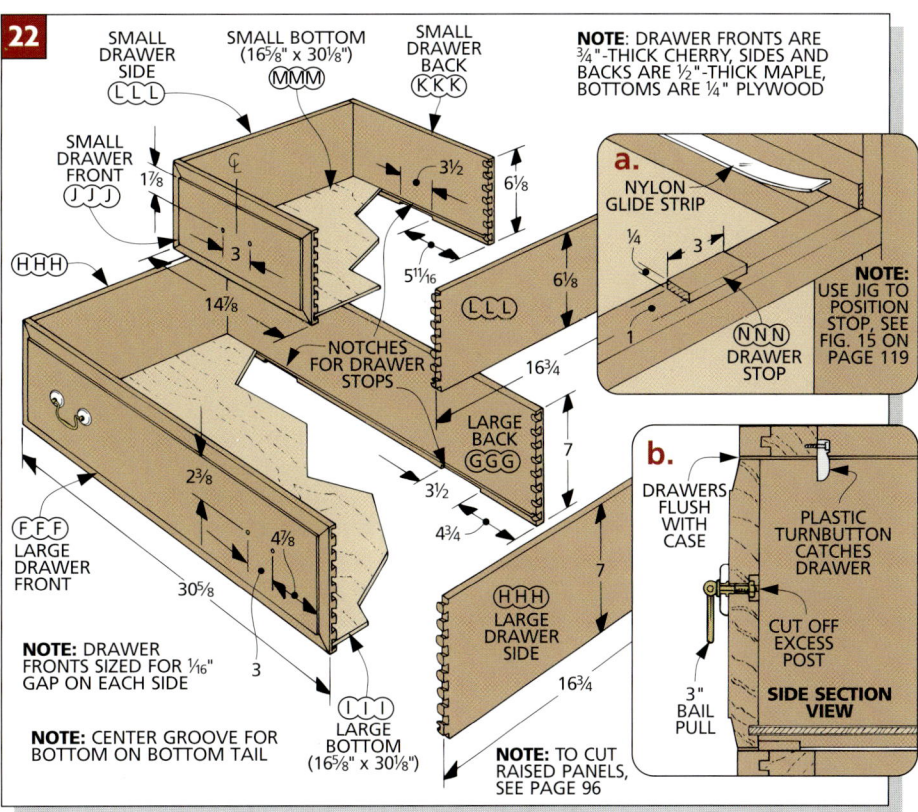

SOURCES

Something we take into consideration when designing projects at *Woodsmith* is the hardware. Does it complement the project and is the style appropriate? And equally as important, is the hardware affordable and readily available?

You should be able to find most of the hardware and supplies for the projects in this book at local hardware stores or home centers. For some of the less common items, you may have to order the hardware through the mail. If that's the case, we've tried to find reputable sources with toll-free phone numbers and web sites (see the Mail Order Sources box at right).

MAIL ORDER SOURCES

Some of the most important "tools" you can have in your shop are mail order catalogs. The ones listed below are filled with special hardware, tools, finishes, lumber, and supplies that can't be found at local hardware stores or home centers. You should be able to find many of the supplies for the projects in this book in these catalogs.

It's amazing what you can learn about woodworking by looking through these catalogs. If they're not currently in your shop, you should have them sent to you. Most are also on the web and offer online ordering.

Note: The information below was current when this book was printed. August Home Publishing does not guarantee these products will be available nor endorse any specific mail order company, catalog, or product.

THE WOODSMITH STORE

10320 Hickman Road
Clive, IA 50325
800-835-5084
www.woodsmithstore.com
Our own retail store with all kinds of hardware including pulls for the cabinets in the Classic Cherry Set, hand and carving tools, router bits, dovetail jigs, and finishing supplies. We don't have a catalog, but we do send out items mail order.

ROCKLER WOODWORKING & HARDWARE

4365 Willow Drive
Medina, MN 55340
800-279-4451
www.rockler.com
A very good hardware catalog with a full line of hardware supplies including knobs, inserts, glides retainer strips, locks, hinges, nylon glide tape, bedbox rollers, and a nice variety of finishing supplies. They also sell dovetail jigs and router bits.

WOODCRAFT

560 Airport Industrial Park
Parkersburg, WV 26102-1686
800-225-1153
www.woodcraft.com
Just about everything for the woodworker, including all knds of knobs, threaded inserts, swivel casters, hinges, bed hardware, drawer pulls, dovetail jigs and router bits.

VAN DYKE'S RESTORERS

39771 S.D. Hwy. 34
P.O. Box 278
Woonsocket, SD 57385
800-558-1234
www.vandykes.com
This is a great catalog full of hard-to-find period hardware and supplies. They have a good selection of hinges, pulls, knobs and wood plugs, as well as inlay strips, marquetry inlays, and finishing supplies.

LEE VALLEY TOOLS

P.O. Box 1780
Ogdensburg, NY 13669-6780
800-871-8158
www.leevalley.com
Several catalogs with hardware, tools, and finishes. A good source of hinges, half-mortise locks, knobs pulls, and nylon glides. You'll also find blind nailers, dovetail jigs, attachments, and a full line of dovetail bits.

CONSTANTINES

1040 E. Oakland Park Blvd.
Ft. Lauderdale, FL 33334
800-443-9667
www.constantines.com
One of the original woodworking mail order catalogs. A specialty is inlays and veneers. They also carry an extensive line of hardware including knobs, hinges, locks, pulls, and threaded inserts, plus dovetail jigs, router bits, and blind nailers.

INDEX

A B C

Apron Cutout, 90
Banding strip, 66
Beds
    Classic Cherry, 98-111
        Twin and Full-Size, 110
        Frame and Panel Headboard, 8-13
            Alternative sizes, 9
            Traditional, 13
Blind nailing, 93
Building drawers, 28-29
Carving
    Incise, 40
Chest of Drawers, 20-29
    Traditional, 27
Chest-on-Chest, 112-125
    Apron Cutout, 90
    Kickboard Base, 125
    Pulls, 94
    Solid-Wood Top, 120
Cheval Mirror, 41-49
Classic Cherry Bed, 98-111
    Twin and Full-Size, 110
Coves, 62

D E F G

Drawers, 19, 26, 27, 28-29, 84, 94, 119,
    125
    Double-Deep, 95
    Guides, 26, 80, 90-91, 117, 123
Dressers
    Chest of Drawers, 20-29
    Chest-on-Chest, 112-125
    Lingerie, 86-97
Drum sander
    Fence, 39
    Thicknessing, 108
Edge jointing basics, 82-83
Finishing
    Brushing lacquer, 71
Frame and Panel Headboard, 8-13
    Alternative sizes, 9
    Traditional, 13

H I J K

Half-mortise lock, 64-65
Hardware
    Bed box wheels, 52, 55
    Bed rail fasteners, 101, 111
    Butt hinge, 67, 85
    Button plug, 67
    Ceramic rosette pulls, 84, 95, 119,
        125
    Half-mortise lock, 64-65
    Knobs, 18, 27, 85, 94
    Nylon glide strip, 84, 94, 120, 125
    Nylon glides, 19, 25
    Piano hinge, 55

Plastic turnbuttons, 84, 95, 125
Pulls, 84, 94, 119, 125
Swivel mirror screw, 49
Threaded inserts, 47, 124
Headboards
    Frame and Panel, 8-13
    Traditional, 13
Incise carving, 40
Installing threaded inserts, 124
Jewelry Box, 70
Jewelry Case, 60-73
Jigs
    Dado routing guide, 105
    Slotting jig, 46
Joinery
    Blind nailing, 93
    Cross dowels, 110
    Half-blind dovetails, 19, 26, 27, 28-
        29, 53, 56-59, 84, 94, 119, 125
    Machine-cut dovetails, 56-59
    Mortise and tenon, 10, 38-39, 100,
        104
        Loose tenons, 48
        Tenons on long rails, 104
    Rabbeted tongue and groove, 55,
        115
    Rabbets, 52, 68
    Splined miters, 43, 62-63, 81, 92,
        118, 125
    Stub tenon and groove, 54
    Through mortises, 106-107

L M N O

Lingerie Dresser, 86-97
    Apron Cutout, 90
    Double-Deep Drawers, 95
    Pulls, 94
Marquetry, 66
Marquetry Top, 72-73
Mirrors
    Cheval, 41-49
    Traditional, 33
    Wall, 30-33
Night Stands
    Classic Cherry, 76-85
        Apron Cutout, 90
        Door, 85
        Pulls, 94
    Contemporary, 14-19
    Traditional, 18

P Q R

Patterns, 38, 40, 48
Quilt Rack, 36-40
Raised panels, 96-97
Routing
    Backrouting, rabbets, 32
    Bullnose, 67, 81, 92, 109, 118

Cove molding, 81, 93
Dadoes, 23, 105
Dovetails, 28-29, 53, 56-59
Hinge mortise, 54
Inlay recess, 73
Inside chamfers, 80
Jointing, 83
Molded edges, 45, 67
Mortises, 38, 111
    Stepped, 64
Rabbets, 32, 53, 67, 68
Raised panels, 96-97
Shadow lines, 16
Slots, 45
    Jig for, 46
Stopped chamfers, 91, 117
Stopped roundovers, 47
Through mortises, 102, 106-107
Tongues, 16, 23

S T U V

Shop Tips
    $22^1/_2°$ miters, 43
    Clamp position, 116
    Cove sanding block, 63
    Cutting splines, 44
    Drum sander fence, 39
    Long piece clamps, 12
    Non-slip clamping bar, 58
    Sanding chamfers, 117
    Trimming half-frames, 44
Small Storage Box, 55
Spokeshaves, 103
Storage Boxes
    Small, 55
    Under-Bed, 50-59
Templates, 45, 48, 62
Tenons on long rails, 104
Traditional Chest of Drawers, 27
Traditional Headboard, 13
Traditional Mirror, 33
Traditional Night Stand, 18
Under-Bed Storage Box, 50-59
    Small Storage Box, 55

W X Y Z

Wall Mirror, 30-33
    Traditional, 33
Web frames, 17, 24-25

AUGUST HOME
PUBLISHING COMPANY

President & Publisher: Donald B. Peschke
Executive Editor: Douglas L. Hicks
Project Manager/Senior Editor: Craig L. Ruegsegger
Creative Director: Ted Kralicek
Art Director: Doug Flint
Senior Graphic Designers: Robin Friend, Chris Glowacki
Assistant Editor: Joel Hess
Editorial Intern: Cindy Thurmond
Graphic Designers: Jonathan Eike, Vu Nguyen

Designer's Notebook Illustrator: Chris Glowacki
Photographer: Crayola England
Electronic Production: Douglas M. Lidster
Production: Troy Clark, Minniette Johnson
Project Designers: Chris Fitch, Ryan Mimick, Ken Munkel, Kent Welsh
Project Builders: Steve Curtis, Steve Johnson
Magazine Editors: Terry Strohman, Tim Robertson
Contributing Editors: Vincent S. Ancona, Jon Garbison, Phil Huber,
Brian McCallum, Bryan Nelson, Ted Raife
Magazine Art Directors: Todd Lambirth, Cary Christensen
Contributing Illustrators: Harlan Clark, Mark Higdon, David Kreyling,
Erich Lage, Roger Reiland, Kurt Schultz, Cinda Shambaugh, Dirk Ver Steeg

Corporate V.P., Finance: Mary Scheve
Controller: Robin Hutchinson
Production Director: George Chmielarz
Project Supplies: Bob Baker
New Media Manager: Gordon Gaippe

For subscription information about
Woodsmith and *ShopNotes* magazines, please write:
August Home Publishing Co.
2200 Grand Ave.
Des Moines, IA 50312
800-333-5075
www.augusthome.com/customwoodworking

Woodsmith® and *ShopNotes*® are registered trademarks of August Home
Publishing Co.

Oxmoor House®

Oxmoor House, Inc.
Book Division of Southern Progress Corporation
P.O. Box 2463, Birmingham, Alabama 35201

ISBN: 0-8487-2692-8
Printed in the United States of America

To order additional publications, call 1-205-445-6560.
For more books to enrich your life, visit **oxmoorhouse.com**